The Rise
of
Sinclair Lewis
1920–1930

THE
PENN
STATE
SERIES
IN THE
HISTORY
OF THE
BOOK

James L. W. West III, General Editor

The series publishes books that employ a mixture of approaches: historical, archival, biographical, critical, sociological, and economic. Projected topics include professional authorship and the literary marketplace, the history of reading and book distribution, book-trade studies and publishing-house histories, and examinations of copyright and literary property.

Peter Burke, The Fortunes of the *Courtier*: The European Reception of Castiglione's *Cortegiano*

James M. Hutchisson, The Rise of Sinclair Lewis, 1920–1930

James M. Hutchisson

The Rise
of
Sinclair Lewis
1920–1930

The Pennsylvania State University Press
University Park, Pennsylvania

Library of Congress Cataloging-in-Publication Data

Hutchisson, James M.
    The rise of Sinclair Lewis, 1920–1930 / James M. Hutchisson.
        p.   cm. — (Penn State series in the history of the book)
    Includes bibliographical references and index.
    ISBN 0-271-01503-9 (alk. paper)
    1. Lewis, Sinclair, 1885–1951. 2. Novelists, American—20th
century—Biography. I. Title. II. Series.
PS3523.Z94Z58 1996
813'.52—dc20
    [B]   95-15482
                                                                    CIP

It is the policy of The Pennsylvania State University Press to use acid-free paper
for the first printing of all clothbound books. Publications on uncoated stock satisfy the minimum requirements of American National Standard for Information
Sciences—Permanence of Paper for Printed Library Materials, ANSI Z39.48–1992.

For My Parents

Contents

List of Illustrations

Acknowledgments

Portions of chapters 2, 3, and 6 appeared in a different form in *Journal of Modern Literature*, *Studies in the Novel*, and *South Dakota Review*. I am grateful to the editors of these periodicals for allowing me to reprint parts of those articles here.

The copyright to all unpublished material by Lewis is held by the Estate of Sinclair Lewis. I am grateful to the estate and to Paul Gitlin, Esq., its executor, for granting me permission to use these documents. I also wish to acknowledge the permissions granted by the following libraries, where various of Lewis's papers are housed: the Beinecke Rare Book and Manuscript Library, Yale University (Lewis Collection); the Harry Ransom Humanities Research Center, University of Texas at Austin (Grace Hegger Lewis Collection); the George Arents Research Library, Syracuse University (Dorothy Thompson Papers); the Baker Memorial Library, Dartmouth College (Ramon Guthrie Papers); the Lilly Library, Indiana University (Upton Sinclair Papers); and the Library of Congress, Manuscripts Division (Hersholt Collection). Thanks are also due to the staffs of the Library of the American Academy and Institute of Arts and Letters, the New York Academy of Medicine, and Macalester College. Sharon Schmitt, corporate librarian for Harcourt, Brace, Jovanovich, kindly helped me locate information on the printing histories of Lewis's Harcourt titles. Betsey Carter and Debbe Causey, of the Daniel Library at The Citadel, were invaluable in tracking down interlibrary loan materials.

A travel grant from the National Endowment for the Humanities made possible trips to New Haven and Austin in the summer of 1990. The bulk of this work was funded by grants from the Citadel Development Foundation, which has supported my research in every conceivable way. Dean Roger C. Poole also provided funding at a crucial stage.

James L. W. West III read an early draft of this book and made numerous useful suggestions. Other colleagues were generous in answering queries or critiquing my work-in-progress, among them Daniel D. Chabris, Lee Ann Draud, Robert E. Fleming, Philip L. Gerber, Robert L. McLaughlin, and Sally E. Parry. Past and present English department heads at The Citadel—Edward F. J. Tucker and Robert A. White, respectively—have been instrumental in providing a congenial scholarly atmosphere in which to work. Giselle Cheeseman assisted me with typing and with library legwork. Allison Butler verified citations, helped with the proofing and indexing, and performed innumerable other chores cheerfully and efficiently.

Lastly, I wish to acknowledge the wholehearted support given me by my wife, Rachel, during the writing of this book. She has been my best critic and my best friend.

Introduction

This book is a study of the literary career of Sinclair Lewis during the period of his greatest achievement, the 1920s. In that decade, Lewis wrote a series of best-selling satiric novels that debunked several of the most cherished American myths. He began with *Main Street* (1920), which criticized the hypocrisy of small towns. He moved on to "standardized" American business in *Babbitt* (1922), the medical profession in *Arrowsmith* (1925), and evangelical Christianity in *Elmer Gantry* (1927), ending with a treatment of the American in search of culture abroad in *Dodsworth* (1929). He also published two novels of lesser quality, *Mantrap* (1926) and *The Man Who Knew Coolidge* (1928). Together, these works placed Lewis in the ranks of Theodore Dreiser, Sherwood Anderson, H. L. Mencken, and other iconoclastic spokesmen for the literary movement Carl Van Doren later termed "The Revolt from the Village."

During the 1920s Lewis's literary stock seemed to rise almost daily, and he became an important public figure. Everywhere Lewis went, his presence was front-page news (even in Europe), and the press routinely sought his comments on matters of national importance. Before 1920 Lewis had been known only as a reasonably talented hack writer, author of five novels—*Our Mr. Wrenn* (1914), *The Trail of the Hawk* (1915), *The Job* (1917), *The Innocents* (1917), and *Free Air* (1919)—and several dozen short stories for mass-circulation magazines. After *Main Street* was published, Lewis suddenly found himself not only an overnight celebrity but also a national spokesman for a disillusioned postwar world. His dramatic rise was highlighted by his winning (and then refusing) the Pulitzer Prize for *Arrowsmith* in 1926, and in 1930 he became the first American to be awarded the Nobel Prize for Literature. Then came a precipitate decline. For the remaining twenty-one years of his life, Lewis published ten more novels and numerous stories, articles, and book reviews, but they are quite uneven in quality. Some of them are downright bad; yet as Alfred Kazin said recently, they are not so much inferior to his 1920s novels as they are pointless. Lewis simply lost touch with the times. He was a satirist with nothing left to satirize.[1]

At the peak of his career, however, Lewis's examination of American life was so incisive that he gave the words "Babbitt" and "Main Street" special meanings that these terms still possess. His novels taught Americans new ways of looking at themselves in the aftermath of World War I. Lewis was remarkably perceptive about the national character, and some of his writings could almost be termed prophetic. His analyses of the American middle class later found confirmation in such sociological studies as *The Lonely Crowd* and such novels as *The Man in the Gray Flannel Suit*. *Babbitt*'s Good Citizens' League is today's Moral Majority. Television evangelists such as Jimmy Swaggart seem to be latter-day Elmer Gantrys. And the most influential president of recent times, as David D. Anderson has noted, was a former actor whose favorite predecessor was Calvin Coolidge.[2] Lewis's novels also confirmed the worst prejudices of Europeans about the United States and gave them a new set of stereotypes for Americans.

Despite the continuing relevance of his work, scholarship on Lewis has been scant over the last thirty years.[3] Much of the interest that once existed in Lewis was curtailed by the publication in 1961 of Mark Schorer's lengthy biography, *Sinclair Lewis: An American Life*. The sheer mass of data that Schorer recorded in his 867-page book seems to have led many people to believe that there was nothing left to say about Lewis, or if there was, that it wasn't worth saying. Schorer did not conceal his dislike of his subject: in the biography he came not to praise Lewis but to bury him, either by belittling his achievements or by damning with faint praise.

Schorer concluded his biography with this backhanded compliment: "He was one of the worst writers in modern American literature, but without his writing one cannot imagine modern American literature."[4]

If what Martin Bucco called Schorer's "Flaubertian detachment" were to be explained, it might be said that Schorer was ill-equipped to deal with a writer like Lewis, largely because Schorer was a disciple of the New Criticism. In fact, during the 1940s and 1950s he became one of its leading exponents, writing two of the most influential essays on formalist methods, "Fiction and the 'Matrix of Analogy'" and "Technique as Discovery." Finding Lewis's novels lacking both structure and deliberate ambiguity, Schorer simply wrote Lewis off. Nevertheless, he generated a great amount of writing about Lewis: in addition to the biography, Schorer wrote ten essays on Lewis, a pamphlet for the University of Minnesota American Writers series, an article on *Main Street* for *American Heritage,* and a preface to a biography of Lewis for teenage readers. Schorer also edited a collection of reviews and criticism of Lewis's work. He effectively had the market on Lewis cornered from approximately 1951, when he began work on the biography (with exclusive access to Lewis's papers), to 1972, when the last of a series of eight paperback editions of Lewis's novels appeared with Schorer's "Afterword."[5] It is correct to say that Schorer defined Lewis's modern academic reputation.

This is not the place to analyze Schorer's legacy in detail; however, it is important at least to understand his influence on Lewis scholarship. Many critics have accepted Schorer's judgments as definitive. Even those who admire Lewis have felt compelled to apologize for his weaknesses each time they point out his strengths, as if in deference to Schorer's decrees. Most important, many critics have dwelled disproportionately on Lewis's failure to develop after 1930, instead of concentrating on his achievements in the preceding decade. As Malcolm Cowley observed,

> I think we have been placing too much emphasis on the slow decline that followed [the Nobel Prize]. The truth is that most writers decline at some time or another. Writing is normally a hazardous profession and those who retain the power of growth from year to year are the fortunate exceptions. The real task of critics is not to explain the decline in each case, but rather to explain the height and nature of the achievement from which it started. In the case of Sinclair Lewis they still have a great deal to explain.[6]

Cowley wrote those words in 1951, the year of Lewis's death. More than forty years later, there is still much to explain about the "height and nature" of Lewis's achievement.

As the title of this book indicates, I attempt to do just that: explain Sinclair Lewis's phenomenal rise to literary and cultural prominence during the 1920s. If Lewis was an inelegant stylist and a shallow thinker, then how was he able to attract and hold millions of readers, create archetypes and new words for generations of Americans, and win both the Pulitzer and Nobel prizes in the space of ten years? For all of Schorer's labors, he ultimately evaded this basic question. I believe that Lewis was a shrewd and unusually industrious writer who planned carefully and labored diligently to reach the heights that he did. He was primarily a satirist who mastered that form of writing and who knew the ingredients for fiction that appealed to audiences in the 1920s. He was perfectly attuned to the important developments and issues in American life during that time. A topical novelist who chose his subjects carefully, he reached the widest possible audience by speaking to a controversy in which there were two clear constituencies, both of which wanted to read what Lewis wrote. In addition, he was an active self-promoter with a keen eye for the demands of the literary marketplace and a good manager of his products, manipulating them for maximum publicity and financial gain.

My method is to examine the making of each major novel—its sources, composition, publication, and subsequent critical reception. Lewis planned his novels carefully and revised them methodically. Most of his notes, outlines, and drafts still exist, primarily in the Beinecke Rare Book and Manuscript Library at Yale University and the Humanities Research Center at the University of Texas at Austin. Although these materials offer fascinating documentary evidence of a writer at work, Schorer virtually ignored them and thereby passed over a gold mine of revealing evidence. These papers show how Lewis selected usable materials and shaped them, through his unique vision, into novels that reached and remained part of the American imagination.

Beginning with *Babbitt,* Lewis went through a slow, systematic process in creating each novel. He made copious notes on the subject or "field" of the novel. He wrote lengthy biographies of the chief characters and developed demographic data for his locales, sometimes inventing for them a complete history from their founding to the present day. Next he drew up an outline or plan that described the action scene by scene. Sometimes, too, he drew intricately detailed maps of the interior and exterior settings of the novel—all of this before writing a word of the first draft. Then came two complete typescripts, which Lewis laboriously revised, even using different colored pencils to distinguish between changes in style and content. These documents help show why his novels turned out as they did—for better or for worse—and how each in turn helped shape his career.

The story I tell in the following pages is therefore about not just the creation of each novel, but also the phenomenon of Lewis's career as it developed during this time and how its course affected both the genesis and the reception of each novel in its turn. Chapter 1 shows how in planning and writing *Main Street,* Lewis crafted his material and his narrative stance so that readers would be receptive to his satire of the small town. A crucial ingredient in the success of *Main Street* was Lewis's discovery of his mimetic talent. Lewis had a well-tuned ear that enabled him to reproduce the cadences and idiom of American speech with almost phonographic exactness. By extension, he was able to "absorb" other elements of people—their thinking, behavior, and general manner—and then transform these elements into fiction with great accuracy. He did this by immersing himself in the world about which he intended to write, mingling with the types of people that the novel would concern and registering their behavior and their attitudes—rather as Zola did on his documenting expeditions to the tenements, government offices, and outdoor markets of Paris. As Lewis planned *Main Street,* he studied his wife, Grace Hegger, and her reactions to the small town that he grew up in (Sauk Centre, Minnesota) during a summer that they spent there in 1916. He also drew on boyhood memories of Sauk Centre in creating the fictional Gopher Prairie. In so doing, Lewis created a sympathetic protagonist in Carol Kennicott, and hundreds of readers saw themselves in Carol, just as dozens of small towns in the Midwest saw themselves in his depiction of Gopher Prairie.

Lewis then applied this same technique on a larger scale for his next novel, *Babbitt,* the subject of chapter 2. Lewis created the fictional city of Zenith by immersing himself in the life of various cities in the Midwest. Lewis also struggled with the problems of typicality and individualization as he created his eponymous protagonist. Most of the reviewers of *Main Street* had praised Lewis's achievement on social rather than literary grounds, so in *Babbitt* Lewis sought to satisfy those critics by attempting to reveal something of the inner life of George F. Babbitt as opposed to merely his surface characteristics. However, Lewis was only partly successful. After the publication of *Babbitt,* he came to feel that it was incumbent on him to write a nonsatiric novel in which his own standards for the American—what he actually believed in—would be sufficiently clear. In his next novel, *Arrowsmith,* which is covered in chapter 3, Lewis successfully answered his critics by creating a hero of whom he approved. Lewis did this by applying his mimetic skills to their fullest extent: he modeled his protagonist on a young research scientist named Paul De Kruif, whom Lewis kept in residence with him and "absorbed" as he planned the narrative and developed the central character.

Lewis took this method a step further in the creation of *Elmer Gantry,* the subject of chapter 4. On a research trip to Kansas City in the spring of 1927, Lewis learned what the ministry was like by literally acting out the role of a preacher, even to the point of speaking in several pulpits. This novel is Lewis's most broadly satiric (and pessimistic) work of the 1920s, primarily because the ministers he surrounded himself with in Kansas City were themselves much like Elmer Gantry: shallow men of limited integrity. The unusually harsh satire in this novel and the grotesqueness of its protagonist can also be attributed to the turmoil in Lewis's personal life at this time. He was beginning to battle alcoholism, he was not coping well with fame, and his marriage, which had been unstable from the start, was collapsing.

As one might expect, Lewis's labors—in particular his research trips and his compilation of copious notes, outlines, and maps for each novel— eventually took a heavy toll on him. After finishing *Elmer Gantry,* Lewis was on the verge of complete mental collapse. When he wrote *Dodsworth,* his last novel of this period, he therefore abandoned his practiced methods of research and planning and looked inward. Instead of investigating a segment of American society for this novel, Lewis wrote a largely non-satiric narrative about a failed marriage, drawing on his own experiences with his wife for material. Although *Dodsworth* contains some effective nonsatiric passages, Lewis was not a particularly good analyst of the subjective life. Chapter 5 reveals how his mimetic method enabled him to observe other people and record external details of their world with great accuracy, but not to depict himself and his own world. Lewis was instinctively a satirist, and when he tried to be touching or profound, as he did in *Dodsworth,* his writing was somewhat flat and artificial. By the end of the 1920s the vein of material that Lewis had mined had run out, and although he went on to write ten more novels and numerous other works, including plays, he had lost his taste for lengthy, repeated immersions into particular spheres of society. Still, between 1920 and 1930 Lewis had a remarkable ten-year run that few of his peers could match in terms of critical regard, wealth, and fame as a public figure.

Throughout these chapters I have interwoven the story—one might even say saga—of Lewis's on-again, off-again work on a novel about the American labor movement, a novel he planned several times and talked about frequently but never wrote. Lewis's greatest literary aspirations rode on the labor novel, because throughout his career he wanted to be recognized not just as a satirist or a social critic but as an artist. The project would have united his talent as a satirist with his ambition to be a true novelist. Chapter 6 discusses his last, most concerted efforts to write the labor novel in the 1920s and early 1930s and speculates about why he could not do so.

Lewis's story from 1920 to 1930 is also the story of American publishing during that time. In the 1910s Lewis had worked as a book reviewer, press agent, and manuscript reader, and he naturally put those skills to use in orchestrating his own career. He was assisted at virtually every step by Alfred Harcourt, who published all of Lewis's novels of the 1920s under the imprint of the house he had begun in 1919: Harcourt, Brace, and Company. Harcourt worked hard on Lewis's behalf and was an important factor in Lewis's tremendous success. Although Harcourt functioned only occasionally as a true editor for Lewis—that is, actually vetting his manuscripts—he helped him tremendously in other ways. It was Harcourt, in fact, who encouraged Lewis to write *Main Street* and who pushed him into doing so by promising to publish it and promote it heavily. Lewis and Harcourt broke off their business relationship in 1931, after Lewis was awarded the Nobel Prize; Lewis moved on to Doubleday, Doran and later to Random House. He published several best-sellers with both of these houses, but his period of greatest sustained success in both artistic and commercial terms was exactly coequal with his association with Harcourt. This study is therefore a chapter in the professional life of Alfred Harcourt as well.

The appendixes at the end of this volume contain material that is discussed in the text and that either has not been published before or is not widely available. These are a chapter that Lewis deleted from the typescript of *Main Street,* possibly at Alfred Harcourt's suggestion; an article entitled "The Pioneer Myth" that Lewis published in the 5 February 1921 issue of the *New York Evening Post Literary Review;* a draft of an essay on that same topic, and on the idea of Babbittry, that Lewis considered printing as an introduction to *Babbitt;* Hugh Walpole's introduction to the British edition of *Babbitt;* and Lewis's two most famous public statements— his letter to the Pulitzer Prize committee rejecting that award for *Arrowsmith* on 6 May 1926 and his speech accepting the Nobel Prize for Literature on 12 December 1930.

The portrait of Lewis that emerges in this study is not that of an artist of the stature of Henry James or William Faulkner, but of a very good writer nonetheless—disciplined, influential, and alert both to the problems of his generation and to the demands of his craft. It is a remarkable success story.

1

Main Street

1905–1920

Sinclair Lewis's first great success was *Main Street,* published on 23 October 1920. In this novel, Lewis shattered one of the most sacred American myths, that of the friendly village. *Main Street* quickly became the center of a national debate: people argued either that Lewis had libeled the small town or that he had revealed the long-suspected but unspoken truth about it. In either case, readers bought the novel. Within six months of its publication more than 180,000 copies had been sold, and Lewis's publishers estimated that within two years *Main Street* had been read by more than two million people. The impact of the novel on the American public was so great that its title quickly became part of the language. In fact, Lewis gave the term "Main Street" special meanings that it still possesses today.

In *Main Street,* Lewis told the story of Carol Kennicott, a young woman who moves from St. Paul to the village of Gopher Prairie as the bride of Will Kennicott, a country doctor. Carol is an idealist who goes to Gopher

Prairie as much for the challenge of beautifying it and reforming its social and political views as for the love of her husband. But Carol is rebuffed by the townspeople when she tries to interest them in social reforms, and she finds that, for all their outward displays of friendliness, they are inwardly small-minded and hypocritical. Soon Carol realizes that even her husband has no real ambition or desire for change; he regards medicine merely as a job, and his interest in saving lives is no greater than his interest in working on motorcars. After several superficial rebellions, Carol finally separates from Kennicott and goes to live in Washington, D.C., expecting to find a liberal, cosmopolitan society there. Instead she discovers that Washingtonians are merely an accumulation of people from the thousands of Gopher Prairies throughout the country. She returns to her husband, having lost her war against the village but feeling satisfied that she has won some battles and remained true to her ideals.

Many American novels before *Main Street* were critical of the small town—Edward Eggleston's *Hoosier Schoolmaster,* Edgar Lee Masters's *Spoon River Anthology,* Sherwood Anderson's *Winesburg, Ohio*—but this negative view had made only a small impression on the popular consciousness, remaining primarily a literary idea. *Main Street* changed that. The novel permanently ended the tradition of depicting the small town as a place of pleasant piety, simply by the force of Lewis's closely packed documentation. Gopher Prairie sprang to life so vividly in the novel that many readers believed it to be modeled on their own villages. Unlike his predecessors, Lewis chose to write about his subject satirically instead of solemnly, so that even his most vicious characters were also comic, and readers could recognize people they knew (and perhaps also themselves) in the portraits of such types as the village atheist, Miles Bjornstam, or the local gossip, the Widow Bogart. Within the satiric superstructure of village life, Lewis also gave readers a likable protagonist with whom they could identify. Carol Kennicott represented the modern woman—independent-minded and headstrong, but realistic enough to be willing to compromise with convention. Carol's situation was one in which many of Lewis's readers, especially women, found themselves.

An account of the making of *Main Street* can be pieced together from Lewis's correspondence, from the published recollections of people who were close to him during this period, and from some notes for the novel and a partial typescript of it that are today preserved in the Lewis Collection at the Humanities Research Center of the University of Texas at Austin. These various documents reveal a classic tale of a writer discovering his material, finding his narrative voice, and developing his talents at invention and composition.

Lewis conceived of the novel as early as 1905, but with a very different protagonist in mind: a bitter, defeated figure based largely on himself. Lewis had grown up in Sauk Centre, Minnesota, a village much like the fictional Gopher Prairie. He carried with him many of his youthful resentments toward the town, and for a long time these feelings impeded his progress on the novel. Lewis changed his initial concept of the book in 1916 when he visited Sauk Centre with his new bride, Grace Hegger, a well-educated, progressive woman, and began to see the village from her perspective. At this time, Lewis also discovered his remarkable talent for observing people in particular milieus, taking in their personalities and actions, and then transforming them into fictional characters. Carol Kennicott was inspired by Grace.

As he pressed on with *Main Street* during the next four years, Lewis struggled to craft the novel so that it would appeal to a wide audience. Initially he had told Carol's story through the voice of an intrusive and cynical persona, but he dropped that voice, cutting much of it in the draft typescript and channeling his criticisms instead through the consciousness of Carol Kennicott herself. In this draft, Lewis's satire of the village was more shrill and destructive than in the published novel and Carol was a weaker and less appealing character—a quixotic dreamer who learns little from her failures. In revising Lewis blunted the force of some of his satire and adjusted the characterization of Carol so that she would eventually grow and achieve some sense of self-worth, putting away her illusions about the town and understanding "the nobility of good sense." He altered several episodes so that rather than simply despair over her attempts to reform the town, Carol would exercise critical intelligence and learn from her mistakes. Lewis thus made the novel both an attack on the American village and the story of Carol's education, a record of how she arrived at that blend of dream and reality that ultimately enables her to recognize her failures but not give up her aspirations.

The story of the creation of *Main Street* begins properly with Sinclair Lewis's youth in Sauk Centre, for it was there that his perceptions of village life were formed. He was born Harry Sinclair Lewis on 7 February 1885. His father, Edwin J. Lewis, was a physician; Lewis later said that he was a cold and unfeeling person who showed little affection for his son. His older brother, Claude, favored by his father, became a stolid, dependable man and followed Dr. Lewis in becoming a physician himself. (Parts of the personalities of both Claude and Dr. Lewis can be seen in the character of Dr. Will Kennicott in *Main Street*.) Six years after Lewis was born, his mother, Emma, died after a protracted illness. Not long thereafter, Dr.

Lewis married Isabel Warner, who had a strong influence on the young Lewis. He later described Isabel as "more mother than step-mother" and "psychically my own mother."[1] Lewis formed a strong bond with Isabel because, like him, she did not easily conform to village life. Just as Will Kennicott in *Main Street* takes Carol away from St. Paul, Dr. Lewis brought Isabel to Sauk Centre from Chicago. Like Carol in her experience of leaving the city and moving to a small town, Isabel too went through a difficult period of adjustment. Lewis witnessed this process and identified with his stepmother's feelings. In *Main Street*, Lewis based some of Carol's social agonies in Gopher Prairie on his stepmother's similar experiences in Sauk Centre, just as some of Carol's social triumphs in the town, especially her reforms, were drawn from Isabel's own victories as she eventually assimilated herself into the social fabric of Sauk Centre.

Lewis, however, was never able to do so himself. He was ill at ease among the other villagers. On top of his unorthodox ideas about foreign books and his desire to travel, Lewis had the additional handicaps of being physically weak and unattractive: these factors created in him a gritty dissatisfaction with life and a strong streak of self-dislike.

By the summer of 1905, when he was twenty years old, Lewis's sense of dislocation had evolved into a deep aversion for Sauk Centre and a feeling that the popular belief in the American village as a place of goodness and neighborliness was fraudulent. This feeling was at the root of his first conception of *Main Street*. As yet Lewis had only a vague idea of what he wanted to write about and, of course, no concrete sense of how to dramatize it. But that summer, while home on vacation from his second year at Yale, Lewis recognized fully for the first time the deleterious effects of what he later called the "ghetto-like confinement of the small town." What he was thinking about that summer is made clear in his preface to a special edition of *Main Street* published in 1937:

> Back in 1905, in America, it was almost universally known that though cities were evil and even in the farmland there were occasional men of wrath, our villages were approximately paradise. They were always made up of small white houses under large green trees; there was no poverty and no toil worth mentioning; every Sunday, sweet-tempered, silvery pastors poured forth comfort and learning; and while the banker might be a pretty doubtful dealer, he was inevitably worsted in the end by the honest yeomanry. But it was Neighborliness that was the glory of the small town. In the cities, nobody knew or cared; but back home, the Neighbors were one great big jolly family. . . . I was converted to the faith that a

good deal of this Neighborliness was a fake; that villages could be as inquisitorial as an army barracks.[2]

In this preface, Lewis recalled that he had begun writing *Main Street* that summer under the title "The Village Virus" (that phrase appears in Lewis's diary from this time). He completed twenty thousand words of a narrative but became frustrated and threw the manuscript away. Lewis further revealed that he envisioned the novel from the point of view of a newcomer to the town, a young lawyer who quickly succumbs to its stifling provincialism. This character seems to have been a composite of Lewis himself and a friend from that period whom Mark Schorer identified as Charles T. Dorion, a lawyer who had recently moved to Sauk Centre. Like Lewis, Dorion was an outsider in the village and the only person in Sauk Centre with whom Lewis could discuss "emancipated ideas." Dorion thus became Lewis's confidant and role model. In his diary Lewis described Dorion as "very well read particularly . . . in socialistic writers & up to date contemporaries—Jack London, Upton Sinclair, etc." They enjoyed talking of "music, socialism, Christian Science."[3]

Oddly, Lewis did not mention Dorion in the 1937 preface; he said that the character of the lawyer was to have been drawn "in the image" of himself, "Doc Lewis's youngest boy, Harry."[4] Lewis may simply have forgotten Dorion by 1937, as Mark Schorer suggests, or perhaps he was inventing a more interesting version of the origins of *Main Street*. What is clear is that Lewis's initial conception of the protagonist was a partly real and partly idealized image of himself. Had Lewis been able to bring his projected protagonist to life in 1905, the character would have been angry and resentful, as young Harry Lewis was at the time. It is worth noting that whenever Lewis tried to portray himself fictionally, as he would do most directly in *Dodsworth,* the result was not entirely successful. He was to discover that his talents lay in observing others and depicting them in fiction.

Lewis did not forget about this character, however; the young lawyer eventually evolved into Guy Pollock in the published text. Pollock is a bachelor attorney who is something of an aesthete; he reads modern poetry and professes socialism. Pollock is Carol's confidant. In their talks, he tells her that long ago he contracted "the village virus," which deadened his intellectual interests. He warns Carol to protect herself from the virus. Pollock himself is trapped in Gopher Prairie—a fact symbolically indicated, perhaps, by his initials, G. P.

That is about all that came of "The Village Virus" of 1905. The animus of the novel existed, but Lewis did not yet have a fully developed protagonist or a satisfactory form of expression. After graduating from Yale in June 1908 (he had dropped out for one year to travel), Lewis worked as a reporter and editor for various city newspapers. Then he moved to New York, where for the next five years he held positions with publishing houses, working as an editor, a publicity agent, and a manuscript reader. He learned much about the reading tastes of the public, as well as the editing and promotion of books.

During this time, Lewis began to compose his own short fiction and to try his hand at writing novels. He discovered the themes and character types that he would develop fully in his 1920s novels. In these early narratives, Lewis found his basic plot paradigm: youthful or middle-aged seekers rejecting convention in favor of adventure and escaping from a dull existence, then either retreating to the safety of routine, partly satisfied that they have found their true selves, or opting for an unconventional, peripatetic life. Lewis would employ this concept in one variation or another in six of the seven books he published in the 1920s, beginning with *Main Street,* as well as in most of the novels he wrote after 1930.[5] In writing *Main Street,* Lewis found he could place this basic plot within a satiric framework—as he would do again with *Babbitt* and *Elmer Gantry,* and to a lesser degree with *Arrowsmith* and *Dodsworth.* In the early novels, one can also see glimmers of satire as Lewis began to experiment with different character types—preachers, political activists, businessmen, and professors—that would reappear in more fully developed form in the 1920s novels.

Lewis's apprentice novels were moderately successful, and they led him to make a second attempt at "The Village Virus" in the summer of 1916. At this point he solved the problem that had marred his first conception of the book: he found a controlling intelligence for his story by observing Grace in Sauk Centre. Her presence there inspired him to envision the character of a well-educated city woman whose progressive ideas clashed with the narrow-mindedness of the villagers. Lewis thus moved the Dorion character (who became Guy Pollock) to a secondary position in the novel and decided to tell the story through the consciousness of a woman like Grace. This character became Carol Kennicott.

Because Grace would have a significant impact on her husband's writing during the 1920s, one should know something of her background. Lewis met her in September 1912, when he worked for the publishing house of Frederick A. Stokes. Grace was working in the same building as Lewis, several floors above him in the editorial offices of *Vogue* magazine. She wrote captions for the fashion advertisements in *Vogue* as well as items for its society pages. She seems to have had some literary ambitions; she wrote several freelance articles during the 1920s on travel and fashion and tried her hand at short fiction. After her divorce from Lewis in 1928, she published a roman à clef about their life together entitled *Half a Loaf* (1931), and after Lewis's death in 1951 she produced a memoir, *With Love from Gracie* (1955). Grace served Lewis as an editor and a sounding board. She read through the drafts of his work-in-progress and made suggestions for revision, which Lewis often adopted.

Grace's family background and her personality are also important, because Lewis based many of his female characters (besides Carol Kennicott) on her.[6] She came from a good family: her father, Frank Hegger, who died when she was fifteen, owned an art gallery in Manhattan. Both he and Grace's mother, Maud, were of indeterminate British ancestry; Grace, who was born in New York City and educated at a convent school there and a boarding school in Philadelphia, liked to think that she was descended from the aristocracy, and she could often be something of a snob. Her most noticeable trait, which nearly everyone who met her commented on, was her habit of affecting an indistinct British accent that seemed to come and go, depending on the occasion. She enjoyed being waited on and pampered. These characteristics seem unappealing, but to the awkward, country-bred Lewis, Grace seemed a true sophisticate with her knowledge of art and her "frequent Atlantic crossings."[7] To her credit, she supported her family with her job; like Carol Kennicott, she was independent—the very embodiment of the modern woman. Lewis wooed her persistently for a year and a half, and they were married on 15 April 1914.

Lewis and Grace were compatible in an odd way, and their relationship would provide Lewis with the material for some of his best satiric writing. She saw him as a rough-hewn but clever young man who with proper training could be made socially presentable. He was pleased that so beautiful a woman would be interested in him (especially considering his physical shortcomings), and he played to her pretensions, romancing her by taking the role of Lancelot to her Elaine in dozens of sentimental, quasi-medieval poems that he sent to her. This arrangement worked well for the first few years of their marriage, but once Lewis was a celebrity and once Grace had reached the social plateau to which she aspired, they were no longer useful to each other. Grace tried increasingly to control Lewis, and as her pretentiousness became more evident, Lewis came to think of her as a fraud. In response to her attempts to domesticate him, he sought refuge initially by traveling without her, then by drinking, and later by satirizing her in a series of progressively more uncomplimentary portraits of women in his novels—first in *Arrowsmith,* then in *Elmer Gantry,* and finally in

Dodsworth, where she appears as Fran, the pretentious and ultimately castrating wife of the protagonist, Sam, whom Lewis partly modeled after
himself.

At the beginning of their marriage, however, Grace helped Lewis. She
showed him how to dress more stylishly, for instance, and how to modify
his flat midwestern accent. His gratitude to Grace can be seen in the sympathy he shows toward Carol Kennicott in *Main Street.* (The qualities in
Carol that Lewis dislikes, especially her airs of superiority, can also be
attributed to Grace.) Grace encouraged Lewis to pursue fiction writing full
time. By the end of 1915 Lewis was having enough consistent success
placing short stories with mass-circulation magazines (including the prestigious *Saturday Evening Post*) that he decided to leave his job at Doran and
attempt to write his "village virus" novel. On 3 December Lewis and
Grace embarked on a cross-country automobile journey that brought them
to Sauk Centre in April 1916.

Until this point, Lewis had been able to envision his "village virus"
story only through the experience of his own unhappy childhood. Now,
however, Lewis saw the dramatic possibilities inherent in describing "the
friendly village" satirically, through the perceptions of someone like
Grace. He could make the villagers into character types like those in his
early novels, and he could portray Carol as a young seeker. Lewis did not
model Carol literally on Grace; rather, it was Grace's presence in Sauk
Centre that summer that enabled him to see the dramatic contrast between
someone like her and someone like his father or his brother Claude (who
frequently came to visit from nearby St. Cloud). Looking at them together, Lewis must have imagined the tension that would be created if two
such people were married.

Some parts of Lewis himself went into the characterization of Carol, but
Lewis realized that his criticisms of the village would probably be more
widely accepted if he presented them through the consciousness of a female protagonist. In choosing to write a novel about a woman, Lewis was
responding to a set of current issues in postwar American life: women's
attitudes were shifting during this period of political emancipation and
social change. Lewis also knew from his experience in publishing that the
majority of fiction readers were women. Most important, in Grace's presence he discovered that he had a talent for studying individuals, registering
their behavior, and then dramatizing them. Simply by being in someone's
presence for awhile, Lewis could absorb attitudes and emotions, making
that person the model for his character and thus presenting that type of
character with the accuracy of firsthand knowledge.

One event of that summer, recounted by Grace in her memoir, reveals how her presence in Sauk Centre stimulated Lewis. Grace remembered one morning when "the curse" was upon her and Lewis requested that a breakfast tray be brought to their bedroom. Grace recalled the reaction of Lewis's father to this request: "The Doctor complained about 'New York fol-de-rols' and making extra trouble for the girl, and said sharply: 'If Grace is well enough to eat breakfast she is well enough to come down and get it.'" When Lewis saw his family "through the eyes of New York and of marriage," he was appalled by "his father's overbearing rudeness, his senseless laying down of the law, and the docile acceptance by his stepmother."[8] Lewis and Grace also went calling about town, and Lewis saw how provincial the village seemed to her. Lewis took her to various social clubs, to the offices of the local newspaper, even to the corner drugstore. He was immersing himself in the town and observing Grace's reactions to this environment. Lewis was finding his way toward the mimetic method that would make him so successful in the 1920s.

Having found the central consciousness for his novel and settled on the basic plot, Lewis now set to work gathering material. For detail about his setting he had only to look around Sauk Centre. Rowe's Hardware Store became Sam Clarke's Hardware Store; the Bryant Library in Sauk Centre became the village library in Gopher Prairie; and the Parker House (where Lewis had worked as a desk clerk one summer) became the Minnimashie House of the novel. Various other places and people from the town likewise were put into *Main Street*. Grace said that during that summer Lewis recorded such details in two looseleaf notebooks, a black, pocket-sized one that he carried with him and a larger one covered in gray cloth, into which he apparently transferred and reordered the notes made in the small book.[9] These notebooks apparently do not survive, but the actual details do not matter so much as the fact that Lewis was learning to place his observations of a certain locale within a fictional matrix and to construct from it a composite setting. The Main Street of Gopher Prairie became, as Lewis tells us in the prologue to the novel, "the continuation of Main Streets everywhere." Similarly, in *Babbitt* Lewis would make the city of Zenith a microcosm of various cities he had visited in the Midwest. He seems to have had a pictorial imagination. He could call up from short-term memory such things as gestures, conversations, and settings. He seems to have planned a narrative in terms of episodes—brief scenes inspired by what he observed and jotted down in his notebook.

For material with which to embroider the narrative, Lewis drew on memories of his youth in Sauk Centre and of his stepmother, Isabel. Her self-improvement/discussion club, called the Gradatim, became the Thanatopsis in the novel (its members undertake to discuss all of English poetry in a single afternoon meeting); Carol Kennicott's vigorous involvements with social groups and betterment campaigns were drawn from Isabel's reforms—such as her establishing a hospitality room for the wives of the German and Swedish farmers who came to Sauk Centre to sell their produce. In addition, Lewis gave Carol some of his stepmother's other interests, such as her work on behalf of the local library and her participation in the Musical Club, the Congregational Church, and the Embroidery Club. The physical layout of his father's office, where Lewis had spent many afternoons as a boy, was the model for Kennicott's waiting room, with its "straight chairs, shaky pine table, and those coverless and unknown magazines which are found only in the offices of dentists and doctors" (181). Dr. Kennicott's performing an operation in a farmhouse kitchen—with Carol assisting him by giving the patient ether in the presence of an open flame—came from Lewis's similar experience with his father at age thirteen. Lewis recalled summers spent at cottages on nearby lakes, Chautauqua meetings, church socials, community theatrical performances, and other events, and he made them part of life in the fictional Gopher Prairie.

This period of thinking and observing may have produced a partial draft. According to Grace, Lewis made a start of between ten thousand and thirty thousand words on the novel that summer. Schorer doubted Grace's statement, saying that Lewis's time was instead spent writing *The Job*, which was published by Harpers in 1917. No draft of *Main Street* from the period survives, but it would not have been impossible for Lewis to write at least some of this novel while simultaneously writing *The Job*. By this point, Lewis had become an extraordinarily industrious writer who worked with impressive speed. Grace estimated that in writing *The Job*, Lewis turned out from three thousand to five thousand words a day.[10] It is therefore quite possible that Lewis wrote something of *Main Street* that summer—how much, we do not know. He certainly had the materials at hand. He had sketched the outlines of his protagonist and had developed a tentative plot.

In early August 1916 Lewis and Grace left Sauk Centre and continued their automobile journey, taking a circuitous route that brought them back to Minnesota in the fall of 1917. They settled temporarily in the Minneapolis suburb of Fergus Falls. While writing magazine fiction, Lewis continued to plan "The Village Virus," or *Main Street*, as he referred to the novel in a letter of 24 May 1918 to Joseph Hergesheimer.[11] Some results of this third phase of the gestation of the novel do survive. In the late spring of 1918 Grace took their newborn son Wells to Cape Cod for the summer, and Lewis went to New York City to work on *Main Street;* on the weekends, he visited his family at the Cape. Several years later, Grace came across five sheets of yellow paper that contain material pertaining to *Main Street*. She dated its origin to the summer of 1918 on Cape Cod. At the time she was trying to write a short story based on her recent pregnancy; some notes for it are inscribed on the rectos of these pages.

These holograph pages are preserved today in the Lewis Collection at Austin. Grace reprinted them in her memoir (pp. 118–21) but offered no commentary on them. They are of interest because they are the earliest surviving materials that show us how Lewis worked. They also reveal at least one crucial piece of information about the development of *Main Street*: at this point Lewis had not yet found an appropriate narrative voice, probably because his youthful resentments toward the village were still with him. Certainly they are much in evidence in this material.

The first page bears the heading, "The Thesis of Main St. / Use somewhere in Part II, / as beginning of a chapter / Chap—." Although the four sheets are paginated XZ-1, XZ-2, XZ-3, and XZ-9, they make sense when read in sequence:

[XZ-1] In even her vaguest gropings toward the ideal of perfection in the towns of the Northwest, Fern did rather inarticulately have a complete philosophy of the matter which may be stated here, humorlessly, ponderously, and at length.

She believed—or at least her historian insists that she must have believed, as her faith in her lucidity of mind, however little he may defend the ineffectuality of her *efforts*—that her desire for beauty in prairie [XZ-2] towns was but one tiny aspect of a world-wide demand [for] alteration of all our modes of being and doing business; that it was one with universal & growing diplomats, camouflaging lawyers, insincere writers and *all manner of* kings, noblemen, leaders of society, and their paid or unpaid valets. She believed that this ambition of hers was one with the world-wide inquiry into war, into that system of growing and distributing [XZ-3] force which, since it permits hunger at one end and surfeit at the other is palpably false. She most energetically & violently believed that the first duty of mankind is to hang, boil, quarter, & bury beside Hohenzollern & the 400, all brisk, spectacled, motor-driving business men who say "Hell bosh! I don't see any of this poverty you hear these agitators yammering so much about. I tell you I pay my employees only too well,["] and [XZ-9] casually he causes children to be born, & casually he dies & is praised by a casual preacher as a thoughtful & constructive pillar of society.

The philosophers of criticism today—philosophers which our av-

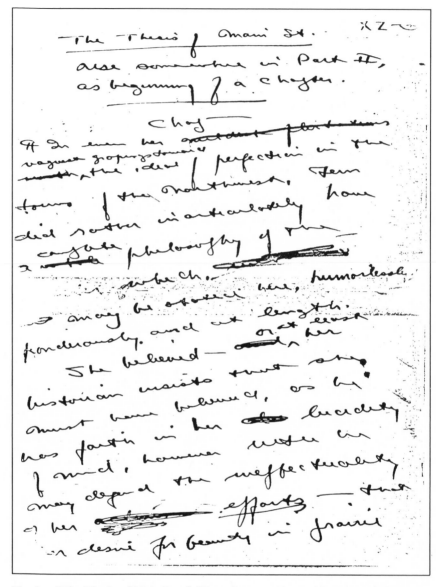

Fig. 1. "The Thesis of *Main Street*" (Harry Ransom Humanities Research Center, University of Texas at Austin)

erage casual man sniffs at & casually dismisses as being "destructive", whatever that casual word may mean—are highly diverse in
appearance; but from ultra Bolshevism to a business man's mildly
inquiring discontent with the filing of letters in his office

Lewis's reference here to "Fern" is apparently to an earlier name for Carol;
Lewis retained the name in the published text for another character, Fern
Mullins, who is much like Carol. She is accused of licentious behavior
with the young Cy Bogart and is forced to leave Gopher Prairie. Fern's
predicament foreshadows Carol's chaste affair with the young aesthete,
Erik Valborg, who is similarly driven from town by gossip.

This document shows us something of Lewis's working methods. After
he had gathered his material for a novel, he needed a rather long period of
time to plan the narrative. During this stage, he usually engaged in some
sort of preliminary writing exercise (sometimes there were several of
these) before he actually began to compose a draft. He almost always
needed to write out, in a formal manner, the themes and arguments of his
novel. These steps would become more elaborate (and more efficiently
carried out) when he wrote *Babbitt* and later books. He moved quickly
through the penultimate stage of his work on a novel, generating a draft;
later, he slowly revised what he had written. In this fragment, Lewis was
exploring the topics he would treat and searching for the best method for
expressing his criticisms. He was trying to create an appropriate voice and
settle on a narrative stance, a way of articulating these ideas that would be
forceful but not threatening. In the fragment, the authorial voice is
haughty and sarcastic. In the published text, Lewis's voice is considerably
less intrusive and polemical. He channels most of his criticisms of the village through the consciousness of Carol, or he allows the other characters
to reveal their shortcomings in dialogue. The fragment also previews
some of the directions in which Lewis's career would go. This statement is
not so much the thesis of *Main Street* as it is the thesis of all that Lewis
would write about in the 1920s—the businessman, the labor leader, the
preacher, the displaced intellectual.

The fifth sheet is a typescript page that bears the heading "MAIN STREET /
Chapter I." It reads as follows:

The platform of the Gopher Prairie station was hot to the touch,
and gave out a dry smell of resin, on this early September day.
Leisurely preparations were under way for the great event of the
day—the arrival of No. 5 from Minneapolis. The Minnimashie
House motor 'bus, Sim Duncan commanding, had bumped over

the tracks and drawn up with its back against the platform. Sim and the M'Gonegal boys sat inside it, now, with their boots in the air while they smoked Dandy Dick cigarettes and regarded the outgoing passengers with amused loftiness.

Except for the Minnimashie House, little of this material remained in the published text. The M'Gonegal boys were deleted; evidently, too, Lewis originally did not intend to begin the novel with Carol's college years, as he eventually did. This paragraph suggests that she would arrive in Gopher Prairie by train at the beginning of the book, but Lewis might also have had her married to Kennicott and living there when the novel opened.

These fragments indicate that Lewis had made some headway with *Main Street,* but they seem to have led him temporarily into another dead end. By late October 1918, when Lewis returned to Fergus Falls, he was hard at work not on *Main Street* but on a serial for the *Saturday Evening Post* entitled *Free Air.* (This story was based loosely on his automobile trip from Minneapolis to Seattle with Grace.) However, Lewis's resolve to write *Main Street* was still strong. In December he told Hergesheimer: "I by God *will* write Main Street. It's in my mind every day."[12] He continued to write short stories, and by the end of March 1919 he was working on a two-part continuation of *Free Air* for the *Post* entitled "Danger—Run Slow." He then intended to revise the two pieces for publication as a novel.

Toward that end, he had been in contact with Alfred Harcourt, an editor at Henry Holt and Company. The two men had been friends since 1914, when Lewis was working for Doran. By February 1919 Lewis had become dissatisfied with Harpers; that month, he went to New York for the opening of his play, *Hobohemia,* and while there he met with Harcourt. Lewis agreed to give Holt his next book (the expanded version of *Free Air*), as well as an option on the novel following that.[13]

Lewis's decision to leave Harpers was pivotal in his career, because Harcourt was primarily responsible for Lewis's writing *Main Street.* As H. L. Mencken recalled, Lewis "owed an immense debt to Harcourt," because Lewis talked to Harcourt a great deal about his ambition to write such a novel and Harcourt supported the idea at a time when "all the other New York publishers" whom Lewis had approached "laughed at his bombastic talk about it."[14] Perhaps part of the reason that Lewis had been floundering with *Main Street* was that he lacked a sounding board. Lewis always needed such a person; as we will see, he developed such relationships with a variety of people when he wrote later novels. Grace had helped him in the previous three years (and she would continue to do so), but Lewis needed to talk to someone with a more direct involvement in writing and publishing.

In the twelve to eighteen months before *Main Street* was published, Harcourt fulfilled this role. He and Lewis took to each other naturally because they had similar temperaments and backgrounds. Like Lewis, Harcourt had been born in a small town (New Paltz, New York), and he also held onto much of his animosity toward the narrow-mindedness of his hometown. In Harcourt's memoir, *Some Experiences* (1951), he recalled that he and Lewis would swap stories about their youth: "From those talks," Harcourt said, "I saw that he could write a first-rate novel about the small town, and I urged him to think about that."[15] In a way, Lewis's conversations with Harcourt are early examples of another process that Lewis apparently had to undergo before he could compose a draft: talking out incidents and inventing stories about characters, many of which would go into the novel he was writing.

Harcourt was an ideal sounding board because he was sympathetic to Lewis's views of American society. This also made Harcourt the ideal publisher for Lewis. Like Lewis, Harcourt was progressive minded; he despised old-guard conservatism and admired the new literature of the twentieth century. Harcourt also possessed an entrepreneurial personality similar to Lewis's: he enjoyed courting controversy and liked to take risks in publishing. In fact, these very qualities were what caused Harcourt to resign from Holt in the spring of 1919 shortly after he had met with Lewis, who had returned to Minnesota to complete *Free Air* as soon as he could and then begin work on *Main Street.*

Harcourt had been hired by Henry Holt directly upon his graduation from Columbia University in 1904 with a bachelor's degree in journalism. In 1910 Holt had gone into semiretirement, and Harcourt had been made director of the company's general literature department. Holt had been regarded as something of a radical publisher in the nineteenth century, but his ideas and methods of doing business had become conservative by twentieth-century standards—too conservative for Harcourt's taste. Over the past few years, Harcourt had developed into an aggressive business-man, bringing in books that were a bit unorthodox for Holt. He was the first American publisher to go to England after the end of World War I, for instance, leaving only three weeks after the signing of the armistice. One of the books he obtained there was Bertrand Russell's *Roads to Freedom,* a study of several revolutionary philosophers.

When he learned that Harcourt had made a contract with such a conspicuous radical as Russell, Holt canceled it by cable. When Harcourt returned to New York and discovered what Holt had done, he persuaded the publisher to honor the agreement, although Holt demanded that the title of the book be amended to the less controversial *Proposed Roads to Freedom*. After this incident, Holt began to ease Harcourt out of the firm and to install his son, Roland, in his place. Harcourt resigned from the firm shortly afterward. He recalled: "I saw I was not going to be able to publish books dealing with the new ideas with which the world was seething, and that Henry Holt would never feel safe with me again." Harcourt realized that "the old economic principles were ingrained in [Holt]: private property, ruling classes, the right of the individual to exploit others."[16] Those principles, among others, would be attacked by Lewis in his satiric novels of the 1920s.

After resigning from Holt, Harcourt considered offers from other houses—but then Lewis intervened. Just as Harcourt was instrumental in convincing Lewis to write *Main Street,* so too was Lewis instrumental in convincing Harcourt to start his own firm, an idea that Harcourt had been toying with but did not consider seriously until Lewis, in a characteristically dramatic way, pushed him to do it. In the spring of 1919, Harcourt wrote Lewis that he did not know whether to accept a position with another house or start his own firm. Lewis wired Harcourt to meet him the following Sunday morning at Grand Central Station. In his memoirs Harcourt remembered Lewis saying the following when he stepped off the train:

> Hell, Alf, I got your letter. I wrote you a letter, I wrote you a long night letter, and then I said to myself, "This is important." I drove 125 miles to Minneapolis, put my car in a garage, bought a railroad ticket and berth, and sent you a telegram to meet me here this morning. What I came on to say is, "Don't be such a damn fool as ever again to go to work for someone else. Start your own business." I'm going to write important books. You can publish these. I've got a little money saved up and you can have some of that. Now let's go out to your house and start making plans."[17]

Harcourt's recollections evoke the same pioneer imagery that Lewis used satirically in his novels. But Lewis was earnest in his promise to Harcourt and obviously thought highly of him. Lewis was taking an enormous risk that few other young writers would have contemplated, for it meant leaving an established house and signing on with a new firm that might or might not get off the ground. Lewis was gambling that a young and hun-

gry firm headed by such a person as Harcourt would give his books the
attention and enthusiasm that an older house would not. Lewis trusted
Harcourt to such an extent, in fact, that he invested two thousand dollars
of his own money (a considerable sum then) to help capitalize the firm.
His fortunes were thus linked with Harcourt's in more ways than one.
During the next ten years Lewis became an active business partner in the
firm, which was incorporated on 29 July 1919 as Harcourt, Brace, and
Howe.[18] Lewis scouted new talent, tried to lure established writers away
from other houses, and helped considerably with the advertising and the
production details of his own books.

For his part, Harcourt advanced Lewis's career in several important
ways. His approach to working on Lewis's novels was quite conservative.
He made only substantive suggestions after Lewis had completed a draft,
and only if he thought Lewis had genuinely departed from his main intentions in the novel or had made an obvious blunder. Harcourt's real contributions to Lewis's success were of a different sort. For one thing, he encouraged Lewis. Although the two men were approximately the same age,
Harcourt adopted a paternal attitude toward Lewis, looking after the author as he wrote *Main Street*. He advised Lewis to work on only that
particular project, and he encouraged him not to serialize the novel because that would have cut into sales of the first edition and furthered the
critics' impression of Lewis as a literary lightweight—a magazine writer.
Harcourt was also a shrewd manager of Lewis's literary property, acting
as his agent in negotiating contracts for subsidiary and foreign rights to his
novels. Harcourt was a good promoter and marketer of Lewis's public
image as well; often he gave Lewis wise counsel on such matters, and
Lewis followed his advice. As their relationship matured, Harcourt also
looked after Lewis's general well-being and helped him cope with a variety of problems that Lewis contracted when he became famous—in particular, alcoholism and an unstable marriage.

While Harcourt was setting up shop in New York that summer, Lewis
was immersing himself in the atmosphere of the Middle West. By the end
of July he had completed thirty thousand words of a new draft. Then,
according to Grace, Lewis grew tired of Minnesota and his "over-femi-
nized existence" there, surrounded by Grace and her mother, who was
taking care of Wells.[19] Lewis was a restless man who never stayed in any
one place for long. His creativity depended on contact with different people and places, and he forever feared being trapped in the type of conventional life that his characters lived.[20] At this time, he also seems to have
wanted to talk out his novel with an objective listener and to show that
person the new material he had generated. Harcourt could not give the

book his full attention at that point, with the demands of a new business pressing on him.

Lewis therefore sought out the novelist James Branch Cabell, with whom he had corresponded off and on since 1915 but had never met. On 24 July 1919 he wrote Cabell to ask if he and Grace might visit him at his home in Rockbridge Alum Springs, Virginia, and discuss *Main Street*. Cabell responded with an invitation to stay with him and his wife, Priscilla, and so on 31 July the Lewises left Grace's mother in charge of Wells and the Mankato house, and they traveled through Illinois, Indiana, Kentucky, and Tennessee. They arrived at Cabell's home on 13 August, and the two men spent several days sitting beneath gigantic maple trees discussing Lewis's thirty-thousand-word start on *Main Street*.

Unfortunately, it is not possible to determine exactly what Lewis had written in the draft to that point, because he later rewrote these first thirty thousand words and evidently destroyed the original version.[21] However, we have Cabell's recollections of their meeting in *Straws and Prayer-Books* (1924). Cabell remembered making four suggestions about the draft, three of which Lewis accepted. The first two concerned relatively minor changes in the plot. Cabell recommended that the schoolteacher Vida Sherwin be married to the shoe salesman Raymie Wutherspoon. He also persuaded Lewis to limit the role of Carol's housekeeper, Bea Sorenson. Lewis had intended to make her a major character to contrast with Carol, showing "how Bea's assets and humbler ambitions let her find happiness in Gopher Prairie."[22] In the published novel, the contrast is implicit; Cabell's suggestion got rid of some of Lewis's tendencies toward triteness and sentimentality.

The other two suggestions bore more directly on the artistic form of the novel. Cabell recalled that Lewis's draft contained a good deal of constructive suggestion—passages in which Lewis, through a character who served as his mouthpiece for reform, suggested various remedies for curing the social ills of Gopher Prairie. (This figure might have been the Dorion/Pollock character.) Cabell thought that this material should be deleted, as it would have "blunted the book's edge." Lewis took Cabell's advice and made the cuts. Most important, Cabell wanted Lewis to have Carol consummate her relationship with Erik Valborg. Lewis rejected this idea, probably for several reasons. He might have worried that anything sexually adventurous in the novel would alienate readers. Or perhaps, because Carol was modeled on Grace, he could not bring himself to have her commit adultery, even with a character based in part on himself. In Lewis's imagination, it might also have seemed genuinely out of character for Carol to have a fling. When Cabell wrote Lewis after the publication of *Main Street*, praising the novel as a whole but still regretting that Lewis did not allow Carol to succumb to Erik's advances, Lewis replied: "I, too, wanted Erik to seduce Carol, but she would [have] none of it—for all her aspirations to rebellion she was timorous; she was bound; she would never have endured it."[23] Lewis's response was probably sincere.

In revising the draft typescript, Lewis purged the novel of any hints of sexual impropriety on Carol's part. In fact, he deleted an entire chapter that contained sexually suggestive overtones. Carol is an effective character because she reflects the middle-class attitudes of Lewis's contemporary audience. She only thinks she is a radical; in truth, she is really quite prosaic. Her rebellion is against not sexual prudishness but chauvinistic nationalism—against the doctrine that, as Carl Van Doren said in speaking of the novel, "to be a good American one must agree with every prevailing orthodoxy."[24] Carol also matures in the novel: at the end, she begins to direct her scattershot idealism at things she is actually capable of accomplishing and accepts the reality of her life in Gopher Prairie. An adulterous affair would have impeded Carol's education. Her limited victory at the close of the novel is perhaps the only kind that Lewis thought would be possible for an ordinary·woman in Carol's position.

Lewis often used sexual liaisons as measures of a character's growth. All but one of the protagonists of his later novels (each is a man) has a fling. Babbitt's affair is relatively harmless, and he tries to atone for it, but he does not possess the self-awareness to learn from the experience and fulfill his potential as a human being. Elmer Gantry has no self-knowledge at all; he is an opportunist whose philandering enables him to manipulate his environment for power and financial gain. Sam Dodsworth's affair with Edith Cortright is condoned by Lewis, but only because of Fran Dodsworth's own sexual adventurism and her cruelty toward him. Sam grows more than Babbitt does, but he also does not seem to fulfill the potential that Lewis envisions for him at the beginning of the novel. The only exceptions to this pattern are Martin Arrowsmith, who is Lewis's only fully drawn idealist, and Carol, who does not achieve the heroic stature that Arrowsmith does but who is at least partly successful in transcending her environment.

Cabell's advice helped Lewis overall, but he seems to have wanted yet another opinion. On 29 August 1919, after leaving the Cabells, Lewis and Grace arrived in West Chester, Pennsylvania, where they stayed near Joseph Hergesheimer and his wife for about three weeks. There is no record of what took place during this visit, but Lewis most likely showed Hergesheimer his draft of *Main Street* and solicited his advice about it. *Main Street* was dedicated to both Hergesheimer and Cabell, presumably in gratitude for their help.

After leaving West Chester, Lewis and Grace settled in Washington,

D.C., and at this point Lewis was finally ready to compose a complete draft. Here, from the end of September 1919 to approximately the end of July 1920, Lewis rewrote the thirty thousand words he had shown to Cabell (and presumably to Hergesheimer), pushed through with the rest of the draft, and then revised it.

In Washington, the Lewises rented a house at 1814 16th Street. Lewis rarely did his writing in domestic surroundings, however; this time he leased a spartan office near the Mayflower Hotel, furnished only with a desk, a reading lamp, and some chairs. He kept regular hours in his "office," typing the draft of *Main Street* on a portable Smith-Corona machine. Lewis seldom wrote prose in longhand; usually he even typed his notes— typing was his "natural thinking medium," Grace said.[25] In composing a first draft of a novel, speed was more important to him than finding the precise form of expression. He always wrote the initial draft quickly, then went back and slowly revised it by hand. Many of his revisions were minute alterations in phrasing that he then changed again, sometimes three or four times. It was as if he thought that the material he had carried around in his mind for so long would vanish if he did not quickly put it down on paper. There was a kind of atmospheric tension about Lewis: just as he would come to a snap decision to go somewhere or do something, so too he would start writing and at once set an astonishingly rapid pace, as if he were beset by the furies. Grace said that words flowed from him in an "avalanche," and that he had once remarked to her, "Perhaps if I wrote in long hand instead of typing my writing would be more leisurely, better conceived." But when he tried this, Grace reported, "his thoughts came so fast that his . . . fingers would tire of holding the pen or pencil and he would throw the . . . manuscript into the basket with a 'to hell with it!' and return to the typewriter."[26]

His work was always ordered. Dorothy Thompson, his second wife, remembered that "with the tools of his work he was as scrupulous as his father was with his surgical instruments. . . . Sharpened pencils, notebooks, paper, carbon were always in the same place. His writing table was never littered, and what he had written was neatly stacked each day."[27] In this manner, Lewis worked ten to twelve hours a day on *Main Street* through the fall and winter of 1919–20. Grace assisted him in different ways. She recalled:

> *Main Street* was with us day and night. We talked about it constantly when we were alone (though never with guests unless they had some specific information Hal needed); he often phoned me from his workroom to tell me some adroit situation which had just

come to him or to discuss the right word to use when the *Thesaurus* failed him. He brought home a dozen pages at a time for me to read, never taking his eyes off me as I went through them, and demanding to know what in the pages had caused each change in my expression as I read, what had brought a smile or a laugh, what had made me cry. I was his barometer, but I was more than that, for after I had finished reading we would go over the pages line by line, Hal defending his points of view, his over-fondness for certain words, his too-elaborate avoidance of cliche, but giving in quickly on some things.[28]

What specific comments Grace might have made concerning the draft we do not know. There are some faint pencil markings on it that are no longer legible; these may have been made by her.[29] Lewis obviously tested his material on her, gauging her reactions to certain scenes. Lewis also asked Grace to supply him with various details about what Carol would wear, what types of household chores she would assign to the maid, or "what kind of pictures . . . there [would] be on the wall when Carol does over the living room."[30] We also know that Lewis needed to have Grace near him as he worked on the novel. He needed to be around the person or persons on whom he was drawing in depicting a character in order to absorb their personalities and behavior and then reproduce these features in the novel.

Lewis's confidence in what he was writing was high, because he was working at a furious pace. "I'll NEVER do a novel more carefully planned and thought out and more eagerly written than *Main Street*," he told Harcourt.[31] Lewis was a disciplined writer: he devised a schedule for completing the draft and was able to produce 100,000 words by 15 December. He then wrote an additional 50,000 words by 20 January 1920 (to page 301 of the typescript) and finished the draft on 27 February. Grace stated that the complete document totaled "738 pages of 300 words to a page," or more than 221,000 words.[32] Thus, between 20 January and 27 February, a period of about five weeks, Lewis wrote the final 430-odd pages—well over half of the novel. This was writing at an astonishing rate. Once Lewis had completed his planning for a novel, he could write a draft with incredible speed. He was a prodigious worker, and in fact he seems rarely to have been afflicted by writer's block. On the contrary, he seems to have needed to write: the act itself may well have provided an outlet for his nervous energy and frequent restlessness.

During the next five months, Lewis revised his draft of *Main Street*. Presumably he had a clean copy of it typed before submitting it to Harcourt on 17 July 1920; Lewis changed something in nearly every sentence, and it is unlikely that he would have given Harcourt a messy manuscript.[33] The clean copy, from which type was set, apparently does not survive. Approximately one-third of the revised draft, however, is today preserved in the Lewis Collection at Austin. The extant portion of the draft totals 271 pages, including numerous rewritten pages and additions. The last page of the draft is numbered 755; therefore, as many as 500 pages could be missing from it. Mostly the omissions are of a page or two, here and there. Only in a few places are any lengthy sections of the typescript missing.[34] Lewis may have judged these pages to be sufficiently legible, with their changes, to go into the copy he submitted to Harcourt, thus saving him the cost of retyping. Harcourt accepted the manuscript for publication in late July, and proofs were generated quickly—by mid-August. The proofs are not extant, but collation of the surviving portion of the draft typescript with the published text indicates that Lewis made the majority of his changes on the draft.

The typescript shows how meticulously Lewis revised his drafts. He seems to have worked through this document several times: most pages bear markings in several different colors of ink or pencil lead—red, blue, black, and green. He concerned himself with both small- and large-scale details. Nearly every sentence contains some type of local revision, and many show how particular Lewis was in choosing the mot juste. Grace speculated that this was a holdover from his days of writing advertising copy for publishers. She also noted that Lewis worked as a "skilful editor" and not as a "self-conscious stylist."[35] He often circled words that he thought he was overusing or that were not precise. In some instances he would list alternate choices in the margins and then evidently cross off those he rejected and circle his final choice. He also read his sentences aloud or had Grace read them to him, "to get the ring of them."

Although the typescript is not complete, one can still see some of Lewis's aesthetic strategies in the revisions he made. The cuts and changes show his concern with making *Main Street* appeal to a clearly defined audience of mostly middle-class readers, many of them women. It appears that he did this in at least two ways. First, instead of writing pervasively in an intrusive and moralistic authorial voice—like that of the prologue, for example, and that of the "thesis" fragment from 1918—Lewis kept this voice mostly in the background of the narrative. On the typescript, he cut a large number of generalized polemics, satiric sections that bore no direct relevance to his analysis of the small town. For instance, in chapter 22 we find a series of minisermons on the YMCA, "the art of advertising," and several subjects that Lewis would take up in later novels—"the optimistic

MAIN STREET

CHAPTER I

On a ~~xxxxxxxxxx~~ hill by the Mississippi River, ~~x xxxx~~ from which
~~xxxx~~ seventy years ago, the signal fires of the Sioux Indians smoked men-
acingly, stood a girl in relief against the cornflower blue of a northern
sky. She saw no Indians ~~xx~~ she saw the mills and ~~glittering-windowed~~
skyscrapers ~~xxx xx xxxx xxxxx xxxxxx xx~~ two ~~great~~ cities, Minneapolis
and St. Paul. Nor was she thinking of squaws and hungry portages and
the pioneers whose shadows were all about her. She was, ~~in prosaic~~
~~Irony considering~~ walnut fudge, the plays of Brieux, child welfare,
~~xxx xxx mystic reason why runs start so quickly in their stockings.~~
A breeze lifting straight from Lake Superior, from ~~the ugly inland~~
~~sea and desolate~~ shores of thick pines ~~above~~ painted cliffs, ~~shxxxxxxxxx~~
bellied her skirt in a line so graceful, so full of animation and ~~xxxxxx~~
beauty, that the ~~brooding~~ heart of ~~the~~ watcher below the hill ~~was lost~~
~~in his perception of~~
~~xxxx~~ her quality of suspended freedom, ~~as he saw her in silhouette x~~
~~slxx xxxx,~~ young, credulous, ~~xxxxxxxxxxxxxxxxxxxx~~ drinking the air as
she longed to drink life. She lifted both her arms, ~~her hair touched her~~
~~cheek,~~ she ~~xxxx~~ leaned back against the breeze, her skirt fluttered, ~~again~~
~~xx xxxxx~~ on a hilltop, ~~a figure immortal,~~ the eternal aching comedy of
expectant youth.

It ~~was~~ Carol Milford, fleeing a moment from the ~~amiable-briskness of~~
~~her-xxxxxxxxx college to the solitary hill which she loved.~~

prose-poems on business efficiency syndicated in the newspapers, the music of jazz orchestras, Christian Science . . . and other forms of mothball-scented metaphysics, the mumbo-jumbo of 'lodges,' the influence of business men upon the press, [and] the importance of illiterate evangelists" (TS 446–47). In chapter 12 there are similar disquisitions on the Republican party, the Baptist church, the higher criticism, and the novels of Harold Bell Wright (TS 269–70). Elsewhere, Lewis cut longish passages that satirized New Thought, spiritualism, and other phenomena of popular culture. He seems to have been exploring elements of American life that he could satirize (business, religion), as he had done in the 1918 fragment.

Lewis also cut a large number of passages that satirized village life, and he redirected most of these criticisms of Gopher Prairie through the mediating perspective of Carol Kennicott. For example, at several places in the draft Lewis deleted long set speeches satirizing the American myth of pioneering. This type of cut occurs, for instance, in chapter 22, just after the well-known passage in which Carol thinks about the two false images of village life—that of "whiskered rusticity" and that of "friendship, honesty, and clean sweet marriageable girls" (first edition, 265; 264). In the typescript, Lewis had followed this passage with a lecture, written in the authorial voice, in which he blamed the pioneer myth for the lack of material progress in small towns:

> Our mediocrity we cannot excuse by our pioneering. . . . Pioneers must beyond all things help one another. . . . Peculiarities of thought, eccentricities of manner, must be discouraged, because they render a member of a pioneering community less dependable as hewer and carrier and hunter. This leveling produces an authentic democracy, with the poet, the oaf, and the potential financier yoked in service. But it also produces that democracy of the spirit which is called mediocrity. The physical democracy has disappeared. The millionaire and the yokel and the artist no longer work together. But the spiritual mediocrity persists, as the symbol and result of a condition now dead. (TS 446–47)

In this additional material, Carol's awareness of the difference between the myth of village life and its reality is disrupted by the voice of an alien cynic who intrudes to moralize about the deterioration of democracy in America. In the draft, these types of passages are scattered throughout the narrative in an almost random fashion. Lewis cut a large number of them, and those he retained for the published text are more logically placed in the narrative. They are clustered in chapters of satire or attack that counterpoint other chapters describing some development in Carol's private war with the town. In other words, the satire of the village subserves Lewis's presentation of Carol's disillusionment and rebellion. The satire in *Main Street* is effective because most of the time Lewis shows rather than tells, letting the difference between expectation and reality manifest itself without authorial commentary—often by letting the villagers reveal their startling banality through dialogue.

The second variety of change in the typescript is more interesting: Lewis adjusted his depiction of Carol, softening some of the abrasive elements of her personality. In many passages Carol was smug and self-righteous; in the published novel, Lewis pokes fun at Carol's self-importance, but in general he sympathizes with her. In chapter 29, for instance, when Carol goes to Mrs. Swiftwaite's dress shop, she acts condescendingly toward that woman, whose shop seems "rustic" to her compared with city stores. In this scene in the published text, Mrs. Swiftwaite tells Carol, "I know my New York styles. I lived in New York for years, besides almost a year in Akron!" Carol then wonders to herself "whether her own airs were as laughable as Mrs. Swiftwaite's" (354). In the typescript, however, Lewis had been much more judgmental of Carol. He had written:

> The superior Carol who yet had never been East of Chicago looked unhappily at this being who had actually lived in the great city. It made her own prized slight exoticism seem cheap. Two years in New York, and yet here she was, cheaply enameled, a village vampire. Carol wondered miserably if her own hauteur and exoticism was as ridiculous to others as Mrs. Swiftwaite's was to her. (TS 589)

Lewis made several changes of this sort in chapters 7 and 11, at the meetings of the Jolly Seventeen and the Thanatopsis. In the typescript, Carol overreacts to the women's coldness toward her; her thoughts are nearly as mean-minded as those of the villagers. In revising, Lewis softened Carol's reactions and had her see the benevolent elements of their characters: he added Carol's sympathizing with Mrs. Hicks, who is awed by the group, her applauding Mrs. Perry's efforts to lead the Thanatopsis discussion of art, and her recognizing her own patronizing attitude: "She wanted to be one of them. They were so loyal and kind. It was they who would carry out her aspiration" (128). However dreamy Carol's thoughts may sound, here she makes her first sincere effort to assimilate herself into the community. These types of revisions enabled Lewis to have Carol

years -- besides almost a year in Akron!"

"Really?" ~~The superior Carol who yet had never been East of Chi-~~
~~cago looked unhappily at this being who had~~ actually lived in
~~the great city. It make her own prized slight exoticism seem~~
~~cheap. Two years in New York, and yet here she was, cheaply enameled,~~
a village vampire. Carol wondered ~~miserably~~ if her own hauteur
~~seemed~~ as ridiculous to others as Mrs. Swiftwaite's ~~seemed~~ to her.
She was polite, and ~~she~~ went home unhappily.

~~[heavily struck-through lines]~~

in a mood of self-depreciation, ~~almost of self-hatred.~~
or not, this was the picture she saw in the mirror:

neat rimless eyeglasses. Black hair,
clumsily tucked in below ~~[blacked out]~~ mauve straw hat that would
have suited a spinster. Cheeks clear, almost ~~translucent, anemically~~
~~lacking in riotous blood.~~ gentle mouth and chin. A modest muslin
blouse with ~~polite~~ edging of lace at the neck. A virginal ~~[blacked out]~~
~~[blacked out]~~ sweetness and timorousness -- ~~[blacked out]~~ flare of ~~[blacked out]~~ gaiety, ~~with~~
~~which she had come to Gopher Prairie, with which~~ brazenly stirred
~~the town in her Chinese party; not one distinctive~~ suggestion of
cities, music, ~~sophisticated people~~ quick laughters ⟶

Fig. 3. Detail from *Main Street* typescript (Harry Ransom Humanities Research
Center, University of Texas at Austin)

achieve some measure of intellectual and emotional growth. Carol's recognizing her high-mindedness is an important phase of her education.

In revising the typescript Lewis also made Carol less bitter and pessimistic about the possibilities for reforming the town. In the published version of her trip with Kennicott from Gopher Prairie to the neighboring village of Joralemon, Carol realizes that "in adventuring from Main Street, Gopher Prairie, to Main Street, Joralemon, she had not stirred" (305). In the typescript, however, Carol's comments on Joralemon were much harsher. "She abandoned effort," Lewis had written, "to try to find gaiety in this baking, rusty, shrieking, pounding, mirthless festival." She sees "the permanent reality of the town, behind the booths and the Beavers unhappily strolling . . . in tight, stinging new shoes" and is repulsed by it (TS 515).

Another example of this type of change may be found at the end of chapter 37 (typescript chapter 38), where Carol realizes that in fleeing Gopher Prairie and moving to Washington, D.C., she has not removed the source of her unhappiness: "She defined 'dullness' as inability to recognize signs of change, whether in social systems or in social desires, combined with rich ability to ridicule the possibility of change as the contempt of privilege, economic, spiritual, artistic privilege, for the suggestion that such privilege is not sacred and eternal" (TS 714). In this passage, which Lewis cut, Carol seems too coldly analytical and despairing—not at all the idealist of the published text. Lewis replaced this paragraph with a less high-minded and more commonsensical statement that indicates Carol's growth: "Not individuals but institutions are the enemies, and they . . . insinuate their tyranny under a hundred guises and pompous names, such as Polite Society, the Family, the Church . . . and the only defense against them, Carol beheld, is unembittered laughter" (430).

In another passage that Lewis also deleted, this one concerning Carol's pregnancy, she lashes out at the "murky superstition and tittering and advice with which the village matrons turned the normal process of childbirth into a tinsel miracle." During her pregnancy, Lewis tells us, she "doubted or scoffed at all the fond traditions she had ever heard about mother-love, mother-devotion, mother-instinct" (TS 406–7; cf. first edition, 240–41). He must have recognized that in such passages Carol was not presented sympathetically enough for readers to identify with her. Lewis carefully revised these chapters, which form the emotional and structural centerpiece of the novel, so that Carol would find semisatisfaction in being a mother. Up to this point she has tried out different roles, none of which she is suited for: happy young bride, helpmate for her spouse, charity worker, aesthete, intellectual. She achieves satisfaction only with motherhood—the most conventional of these roles.[36] These chapters signal her eventual coming to terms with her life in the village. And it is motherhood—her concern for Hugh's welfare and a second pregnancy—that at the end of the novel compels her to return to Gopher Prairie.

In these revisions, Lewis softened some of the harsher and unappealing elements of Carol's character, making it possible for her to learn and grow. He also separated his presentation of her from his analysis of Gopher Prairie. In later novels, such as *Babbitt*, Lewis's characters cannot break free from their environment. One reason that Babbitt is less appealing than Carol is that Babbitt is in and of Zenith, the character and his milieu virtually one and the same. But in *Main Street*, as Edith Wharton told Lewis, he produced "a sense of unity & of depth by reflecting Main Street in the consciousness of a woman who suffered from it because she had points of comparison, & was detached enough to situate it in the universe."[37]

Lewis made the most important alteration of this type in the latter fourth of *Main Street*—from the time of Carol's liaison with Erik Valborg through her exile in Washington and subsequent return to Gopher Prairie. He cut an entire chapter, numbered 36 in the typescript. Had Lewis retained this chapter, and a short section later in the draft that was also cut, the novel would have been significantly darker and Carol would have been more fully defeated by her environment.

In these thirteen heavily revised typescript pages (included in appendix 1), Carol encounters Guy Pollock one afternoon and has a long talk with him, a conversation that Carol feels establishes "a close, dear friendship" between them. She thinks of Guy as being "halfway between Erik and Will": he combines "Erik's fineness" with "Will's solidity." Carol thinks that Guy is the "solution" to her problem of how to exist peacefully in Gopher Prairie (TS 686). Carol also has fleeting thoughts of Guy as a lover. Sometime later, in another conversation, Guy announces to Carol that he has found a way "to beat the Village Virus"—by writing "a book about the town" (TS 687). However, Guy does not follow through on his idea; instead he marries a vapid young girl named Elizabeth whom he has met on a business trip to Wakamin. Guy then changes dramatically. He is embarrassed by how he had earlier bared his soul to Carol, and he tries to transform himself from an aesthete into a "he-man." He unknowingly becomes a monstrous parody of the professional booster Jim Blausser, though ultimately he cannot play this role convincingly. Carol is devastated by the change in Guy's personality, and she descends into a deep depression:

Guys   689   [to ample?]

~~The~~ legal affairs took him ~~away~~ for a week, ~~and only to the county~~
~~seat but to Minneapolis from~~ ^and he^ he sent her a card ~~showing the~~
~~lakes lovely with summer, with its legend,~~ ^with the message,^ "Like ~~the~~ idea of the book;
you'll see some manuscript before long."

Three days ~~after he returned~~ ^later, when^ the afternoon train ^had come in,^ she answered ~~the~~
~~bell,~~ and he bounced into the hall chuckling, "Carol! I've brought you
the beginning of the book!"

But he had no manuscript ~~papers nor anything at all in~~ his hand. ~~She~~
~~looked at him, said in a wondering way,~~ ^¶^ "Where is it, Guy?"

"Left it out on the porch -- to ~~make~~ surprise you. You're to be
the first in town to see it." ~~Chuckling again he~~ ^He^ opened the door, ^and^
shouted, "Come on, she doesn't suspect a thing!" ^A girl appeared, in^
~~the door,~~ a slight inconspicuous girl of twenty. Guy said ~~then~~ with
elaborate intonation, "Mrs. Carol, allow me to present my wife! "

~~Was it aloud or only in her heart that Carol said "My God!" She~~
^¶ Carol^ could not speak. There was nothing in this girl to which to speak. ~~She~~ ^The child^
was anemic, meekly sulky; there was no light in her face, no distinc-
tion in her ~~new~~ ^raw^ new frock with its fussiness of ribbons and ~~buttons~~
buttons and braid and beads; she was the small-town backfisch in ^clumsy^
~~nature~~ perfection. ~~She was a healthy~~ ^she had the prettiness of ~~home~~ youth of a.^ ^calf x^ ^healthy^

"I said I'd ~~take her for a trip~~ bring her to you first of all. I'm
going to ~~surprise the town.~~ ^bowl the town over!^ Nobody ever thought the old bach would
marry," said Guy -- no, not the ~~same~~ ^familiar^ Guy, but a fatuous bridegroom.

Carol was kissing ~~her and~~ ^her^ as ardently as she could ~~stopping her~~ ^and^
~~brain from insanely repeating, "but why did he have to marry her,"~~
crooning, "You must be so tired, ~~darling~~ dear, after your ~~long~~ trip."

~~For an instant the child~~ ^¶^ The child submitted stupidly to the caress,
and ~~spoke for the first time.~~ ^mumbled,^ "Yes. It was hot. I liked Minneapolis.
We had a room with a bath.. ~~ness~~ "^))^

"And I showed her the flour-mills. But it made the little head
ache, didn't it, chickabiddy!" gloated Guy.

"Why — why — why?" How could Guy marry her? Why couldn't
he be decent and manly enough to realize what he really wanted?
Why couldn't he run off with her, and desert her, leave her to the
freedom of suicide, instead of betraying her into marriage, into
years of being puzzled and hurt by his whimsicality? . . . "I had
nothing, a few weeks ago, a decent bare nothing. Now I have less
than nothing. It's not death and hunger that are tragic—it's standing before the world a presumptuous fool." (TS 691–92)

Carol is filled with "cynical bitterness." Of Elizabeth, she says: "She'll
have five children and misrear three of them and let the other two die, so
this admirable human race will be carried on to produce other Elizabeths
who will produce other Elizabeths designed to produce other Elizabeths"
(TS 692). Carol is angry because Elizabeth is "welcomed by the town as
she herself never had been." The scene ends there, but Lewis picked up
this narrative thread in the next chapter: in a deleted passage on typescript
page 725, Lewis describes a letter from Kennicott that Carol receives while
she is in Washington. From the letter she learns that Pollock has died. Two
months after that, Lewis tells us, Elizabeth Pollock marries another man
and moves away with him.

Lewis's original motive in writing this scene seems to have been to
counterpoint Guy's marriage to Elizabeth with Carol's separation from
Kennicott. The scene would also have come at the midpoint between
Carol's affair with Erik Valborg (chapters 31 and 32) and her going to a
movie in Washington and seeing Valborg on screen; he has become an
actor named "Erik Valour" (chapter 38). Lewis often used such structural
irony: he employs it earlier in the novel when Carol's unpleasant tour of
Main Street is contrasted with Bea Sorenson's favorable impressions as she
looks at the same scene. Similarly, in chapter 15 of *Babbitt* Lewis juxta-
poses the disastrous dinner party the Babbitts give for the upper-class
McKelveys with the equally disastrous one that the down-on-their-luck
Overbrooks give for the Babbitts. Had Lewis used the deleted scene,
Carol might have become involved in another love affair, to judge from
Carol's feelings of betrayal when Guy marries Elizabeth.

The chapter seems to have been deleted because it was too dark for
Lewis's purposes in *Main Street*. For one thing, Carol is quite unappealing
in this section; but more important, had Lewis used the scene, it would
have made her exile in Washington destructive rather than therapeutic. In
the published text, she is able to return to Gopher Prairie with the sense
that she can cope with life there. This scene would have made it difficult,
if not impossible, for Lewis to return Carol to Gopher Prairie, because the

village and marriage would have killed Guy Pollock. The scene runs counter to Lewis's relatively optimistic view of human character in the novel.

It is also interesting to view this material in a biographical context. In this scene, Lewis seems to return to his initial conception of the novel, giving Guy Pollock a prominent role and basing the character to a large degree on himself. Pollock is an *auteur manqué;* Carol tells him to make the book he is writing about the town "an honest one." She urges him to "be fair to the generous people, but don't lie—don't assert that whatever is ours must therefore be perfect" (TS 687). Such sentiments are probably expressive of Lewis's state of mind as he worked on *Main Street,* drawing on his memories of growing up in Sauk Centre.

One particular passage is quite revealing. In the scene in typescript chapter 39 (TS 725) when Carol learns of Guy Pollock's death, we see an exceptionally dark description of Carol's emotional state. She thinks of Guy just as she thinks of her little boy, Hugh, and this reverie leads her to remember the tragic death of Miles and Bea Bjornstam's son, Olaf: "There was so much of the wistful small boy in Guy: he would go down the dark way like Olaf Bjornstam, alone and hurt and not quite understanding. Thinking of him Carol held Hugh tight, and somehow identified Her boy Hugh with Her unhappy child Hugh & Her unhappy child Guy." Here, Lewis seems to be associating a youthful version of himself with Guy Pollock and with Hugh—both of them "children" who are trapped in Gopher Prairie and thus never able to lead a fulfilling life.

All of these typescript changes show how Lewis made *Main Street* appeal to a wide audience: by creating a realistic, sympathetic protagonist; by tempering some of his satire so that it was not overly destructive of character and ideals; and ultimately by counterpointing the emotional and intellectual sterility of the villagers (especially the women) with Carol's vitality and the beginnings of her growth as an individual. When she returns to Gopher Prairie she is as rebellious as ever, but she is willing to accept life there on the terms that the villagers have always offered to her. She continues to think of herself as independent in spirit and remains liberated, at least in her mind, from the confines of the prairie village. As we will see, these were the elements of the novel that appealed to Lewis's readers and that called forth from them so much sympathetic identification with the heroine.

Lewis delivered the manuscript to Harcourt in his New York office on the morning of Saturday, 17 July 1920. Harcourt felt that he needed "twenty-four quiet hours" to read the novel before he talked to Lewis about it, so he left the city and went to his home in Mount Vernon, New York. He finished reading the manuscript on Sunday night and was virtually over-whelmed by it: "It was the truest book I ever read," Harcourt said. The next morning, a jubilant Lewis went to Harcourt's home, and they dis-cussed the novel. The only thing about Main Street that displeased Har-court was its length. He commented that "toward the end" of the type-script Lewis gave him, there was a twenty-thousand-word episode that he thought "belabored the plot, although it was amusing in itself." He urged Lewis to delete it, but Lewis would not give in. Harcourt bet Lewis that if taking out the scene required no more than ten changes elsewhere in the manuscript, then it could not be "deep in the fiber of the book." Lewis finally removed the episode and later admitted to Harcourt that in doing so he had to make only seven changes—all but two of them occurring after the cut passage. Harcourt recalled: "I was so relieved that I tore up the manuscript of that part and threw it into the wastebasket without a thought of its possible value as a literary curiosity."[38]

This incident is something of a mystery. Harcourt did not say specifi-cally what the "episode" in the manuscript concerned, and his memoir is the only source for this anecdote. Grace offered no additional information on it in her memoir; she simply quoted these lines from Harcourt's book. Lewis did not mention the incident to Harcourt or anyone else in his sub-sequent published correspondence. And oddly, Harrison Smith, in his edi-tion of Lewis's letters, recorded that Lewis made "only minor alterations" in the manuscript when he discussed it with Harcourt.[39] The deletion of a twenty-thousand-word passage (approximately sixty-five pages) could hardly be called a "minor" change, and the original passage should be in the draft typescript at Austin, but it is not.

It is possible that Lewis added this episode after revising the extant type-script—while the clean copy was being typed for submission to Har-court—but this is highly unlikely. Lewis was aware that at more than 225,000 words, the draft of the novel was significantly longer than the 176,000 words he had estimated. It would therefore have been illogical for him to add another twenty thousand words to the draft after cutting so much of it already. It is also possible that these twenty thousand words were part of an eighty-page gap between chapters 10 and 13 in the extant typescript; but that would not be "near the end of the book," and the number of typescript pages missing there corresponds roughly to the number of printed pages that that section occupies in the first edition.

Two conclusions that one can draw are that Harcourt's memory was faulty and there never was such an episode, or that Harcourt did prevail on Lewis to cut a scene but not one of that length. The episode to which Harcourt referred in his memoir might have been the deleted chapter 36; it is not canceled in the draft typescript, so it was likely part of the final draft that Lewis submitted to Harcourt. Although it is not "amusing," parts of it might be construed as such, and it does "belabor the plot." It also occurs near the end of the book. Harcourt's statement in his memoir that the episode was "twenty thousand words" long may simply have been an error for "two thousand words"—the approximate length of the scene.

If this is the case, then Harcourt should be credited with convincing Lewis to make a crucial adjustment in the book, one that made the characterization of Carol consistent with the foregoing parts of the manuscript and that accorded with Lewis's general intentions in the novel. Judging from Harcourt's methods in reading and commenting on the manuscripts of Lewis's later novels, this was the way Harcourt worked. He would offer only minor advice to Lewis while the first draft was being written. Then, after Lewis had revised it to his own satisfaction, Harcourt would make his suggestions.

While Lewis was putting the final touches on his manuscript, Harcourt was helping him in other ways. Lewis was a highly enthusiastic person who thought that every idea he had about writing and publishing was a good one. For example, Lewis was concerned about how *Main Street* would be received by the critics, who knew him only as the author of innocuous romances. As early as December 1919 Lewis had suggested to Harcourt that he send a "prospectus" of the novel to reviewers: "I've thought (and rather worried) a lot," he told Harcourt, "about the problem of the *real* critics assuming that *Main Street* is another *Free Air* and not really reading it, or giving it to assistants." He wanted to send letters to H. L. Mencken, Heywood Broun of the *New York Tribune,* Francis Hackett of *The New Republic,* and many other critics, including Walter Lippman, Van Wyck Brooks, Floyd Dell, Franklin P. Adams, and Stuart Pratt Sherman, as a way of "counteracting the danger of [*Main Street*] being neglected as another magaziney tale."[40] Harcourt thought this idea presumptuous, and he adroitly deflected Lewis's attention away from this matter, reacting instead to "the good news" that Lewis was "really at work on *Main Street.*" When Lewis pressed Harcourt again in August to do this, Harcourt diplomatically told him that he could do so, but that he had already "made a point of running into a number of [such critics], and doing part of it by word of mouth."[41] Lewis also often sent Harcourt "publicity notes" for *Main Street.* Although many of Lewis's ideas were useful, many others were merely hucksterism, and these Harcourt quietly ignored. For example, to Lewis's suggestion that Harcourt hire someone full time for the task of "occasionally Planting A Story" about him in the press, Harcourt tactfully replied: "We do have some trained people to do special publicity. You know I don't believe much in the John-Hobank-has-stubbed-his-third-toe-and-so-can't-finish-his-new-novel-until-Thursday sort of publicity, and thank heaven you don't either."[42]

Lewis was confident that *Main Street* would be a best-seller and that it would establish his reputation. Several times during the spring and summer of 1920 he optimistically referred to *Main Street* as the "real beginning" of his career.[43] He spoke to Harcourt of *Main Street* being the firm's "big book" for the fall 1920 list, as well as "a big seller for some seasons after."[44]

All of Lewis's instincts about himself and about *Main Street* proved to be accurate. The novel was published on 23 October 1920, and from the start sales were strong, helped initially by a glowing prepublication review by Heywood Broun in the 22 October issue of the *New York Tribune*. *Main Street* sold steadily through the end of the year. Approximately forty-seven thousand copies had been sold by Christmas 1920; about forty thousand of these were purchased in or near New York City. Then the Christmas trade boosted sales considerably as word of *Main Street* spread from New York to other parts of the country. Is it possible that copies of the novel were given as Christmas presents from persons living in New York (where there was "the greatest aggregation of those who come from 'Main Street,'" as Harcourt said) to their friends and relatives in the provinces? During January 1921 sales more than doubled, reaching 105,000. One morning, calls came in to the Harcourt offices for more than 9,800 copies.[45]

The evidence suggests that the high sales of *Main Street* were mostly due to word-of-mouth publicity—there was very little print advertising. People who read the novel saw themselves in Carol; or they recognized friends and neighbors in the satiric portraits of the villagers; or they thought of their own small-town origins when they read the descriptions of Gopher Prairie. By April 1921 *Main Street* was the number-one seller in bookstores across the country as well as the most frequently requested title in public libraries. At this point, sales had reached 180,000 copies, and Harcourt began to order larger printings of approximately ten thousand copies each. Sales of the novel then took off so dramatically that at one point Harcourt had "the equivalent of three freight-car loads" of books available for distribution.[46] Harcourt recalled that "it was a mad scramble all that spring to keep the stores supplied. . . . If the book had suddenly stopped selling the consequences would have been very serious for so young a firm as ours. But it didn't stop. . . . we were never out of stock for more than a few hours." By October 1921, one year after its publication, *Main Street* had sold well over 295,000 copies. It was the number-one selling novel not only for the year 1921, but also for the entire period from 1900 to 1925.[47]

With the success of *Main Street,* Sinclair Lewis suddenly became a best-selling author. He was inundated with letters from other writers, who congratulated him enthusiastically on his achievement; among them were Sherwood Anderson, F. Scott Fitzgerald, Rupert Hughes, Hamlin Garland, Vachel Lindsay, Compton MacKenzie, Hugh Walpole, May Sinclair, H. G. Wells, Rebecca West, Granville Barker, Zona Gale, John Galsworthy, and Waldo Frank.[48] (Some of these letters resulted from Alfred Harcourt's promotional efforts, but many came independently, and all of them conveyed genuine enthusiasm.) *Main Street* made news in many major papers in the country and sparked a debate in the editorial pages about whether Lewis's depiction of the small town was distorted. The term "Main Street" quickly entered the vernacular. A popular song entitled "Main Street" came out in 1921, and several parodies of Lewis's story appeared during that year. (The most amusing of these was Carolyn Wells's *Ptomaine Street: The Tale of Warble Petticoat,* in which a shallow-minded waitress from Pittsburgh moves to a small town whose residents are zealously interested in architecture, poetry, and democratic reforms.) According to Schorer, "the name of the old home town itself, Sauk Centre, became archetypal in jokes about small towns told across the country."[49] As the publishers of *Main Street,* the firm of Harcourt, Brace also became quite well known. The success of the novel gave Alfred Harcourt the capital and the influence with which to expand his publishing enterprise.

Main Street found such a large audience because Lewis had chosen to write about the small town at a propitious historical moment. By the end of World War I the village was no longer an important element in a capitalist economy, and the social and moral attitudes that it represented were regarded as outdated. Lewis also profited from the general mood of self-reflection in postwar America. Lewis saw that most Americans—especially those who lived in small towns—were at least partially aware of the stultifying conventionality of their lives. Then and now, many people believe that there is a secret self beneath the day-to-day exterior they show the world, and that this person is really much more unconventional and rebellious than the self that other people see. Like Carol Kennicott (and George F. Babbitt), they long to indulge the rebellious sides of their personalities. Lewis sensed this frustration among women in particular. In chapter 16 of the novel, Carol tells Guy Pollock:

> I want you to help me find out what has made the darkness of the women. Gray darkness and shadowy trees. We're all in it, ten million women, young married women with good prosperous husbands, and business women in linen collars, and grandmothers that gad out to teas, and wives of underpaid miners, and farmwives

who really like to make butter and go to church. What is it we want—and need? . . . I think perhaps we want a more conscious life. We're tired of drudging and sleeping and dying. We're tired of seeing just a few people able to be individualists. (201)

As Edward A. Martin has recently concluded, Lewis sympathized with the need of women to create lives for themselves "free of the ordinary domestic values of traditional middle-class American life." Carol, subjected to this conflict, "struggles for self-definition."[50]

When *Main Street* was published, hundreds of women saw themselves in Carol Kennicott. Among Lewis's papers in the Beinecke Library at Yale University is a sheaf of letters written to him by female readers who felt that in the novel Lewis was speaking directly to them. One woman wrote him to say, "I lived every page of *Main Street* for fifteen years." Another correspondent told him, "you have done the biggest thing yet for women"; still another sent him a poem she had written, entitled "Carol," in which she identified with "the aesthetic Carol hemmed in by unconquerable environment." Some readers, after expressing their gratitude to Lewis for making public their plight, asked, "What should I do now?" A letter from a woman in San Antonio is representative:

> I have been an actress, a Little Theatrite, so to speak. Three years ago I left dear New York, and Washington Square, to marry a salesman, and came here to Main Street. . . . Will you please tell me what people are doing and saying in New York? Every day I repeat: "I must go on." I have sat on the slippery edge of a bath tub and privately wept, many and many a time. Dear tender treasured longings which cause us who hunger to weep!

Other readers praised Lewis's diagnosis of "the village virus." One person wrote to say that the novel was "the truest picture of American small town life that I have ever read, and I know a little something about it."[51] Many thought that in *Main Street* Lewis was satirizing not them and their village but those other people living in less enlightened towns:

> I appreciate your great work: you know the small town. Just now, a few of us are raising by popular subscription $6000 to beautify the grounds around our new $200,000 school house. There is a park of maples in front of it. We hired landscape architects, and are doing the work right. . . . But are our folks as provincial as "Main Street's"? No, because over 50 per cent of them have traveled ex-

PHONE 197

E. F. BEACH & SON

"Insurance of Every Description"

{ CATTARAUGUS, N. Y. } 11.17.1920
P op. — 1300

Sinclair Lewis, Esq.,
    Gopher Prairie, U.S.

Dear Mr. Lewis-

          I am writing to ask if you will autograph my first edition of "Main Street" ? I have many autographed books, and a few first editions. I have practically all of Christopher Morley's books inscribed - all except a first of "Shandygaff", and I'm searching for that.

by popular subscription

          I appreciate your great work: you know the small town. Just now, a few of us are raising $6000 to beautify the grounds around our new $200,000 school house. There is a park of maples in front of it. We hired landscape architects, and are doing the work right. We had to cut down several maples; and the small-town villagers hollered - bellered. They will be the first ones to admit the beauty when the job is completed. Our tax rate is probably higher than any village in the state - and that is as it should be, for we are getting value received for our money. But are our folks as provincial as "Main Street's "? No, because over 50 per cent of them have traveled extensively. I was Elbert Hubbard's secretary for two years, and traveled these states with him. And I know there isn't a more beautiful village, naturally, anywhere. It is among the soft, low hills— the foothills of the Alleghenies.

        More power to y' !

          Yours sincerely,

Fig. 5. Letter from a reader of *Main Street* (Yale Collection of American Literature, Beinecke Rare Book and Manuscript Library, Yale University)

tensively. . . . And I know there isn't a more beautiful village, naturally, anywhere. It is in among the soft, low hills—the foothills of the Alleghenies. More power to y'![52]

These types of letters show how well received *Main Street* was by readers. Lewis's reception from the critical establishment, however, was not so overwhelmingly favorable. This is not to say that *Main Street* did not get good reviews; in fact, nearly all of the reviews were favorable. Still, most reviewers tended to praise the book on social rather than literary grounds. Although nearly all critics agreed that *Main Street* was undoubtedly one of the most important books of its age, they faulted Lewis for a lack of depth in his characterizations. In employing his gifts for satire and verisimilitude, Lewis had not concerned himself with the inner lives of his characters. Instead, he presented them as types and defined them in terms of their surroundings and their possessions—"cheap motorcars, telephones, ready-made clothes, silos, alfalfa, kodaks, phonographs [and] unread sets of Mark Twain" (264). Reviewers criticized Lewis for this superficiality. Ludwig Lewisohn, for example, in an otherwise favorable review of *Main Street* in the *Nation,* said that the novel lacked "spiritual significance." Similarly, in the *New Republic* Francis Hackett wished that Lewis· had more fully explored the psychology of Carol Kennicott and probed deeper than the "exterior vision" present in the novel.[53]

Lewis paid close attention to these negative comments, and he kept them in mind as he planned his next novel, *Babbitt*. When he began work on that book, Lewis set out to win critical approval not just as a satirist or social critic, but as an artist. He would continue to write in a comic-satiric vein, but he would also attempt to explore George F. Babbitt more deeply and meaningfully than he had Carol Kennicott.

2

Babbitt

1920–1922

Lewis began planning *Babbitt,* his "next great realistic novel," before he finished correcting proofs of *Main Street* in the late summer of 1920. Having explored the world of the prairie village in *Main Street,* he next addressed himself to the world of the medium-sized, midwestern city. The ideas for a character such as Babbitt seem to have been gestating with Lewis during the composition of *Main Street.* One can see glimpses of this figure in such characters as Perce Bresnahan, who is proud to be a "red-blooded Regular Fellow," or in "Honest" Jim Blausser, who starts Gopher Prairie on a campaign of boosterism. In George F. Babbitt, Lewis created an archetype—the total conformist—that has remained in America's cultural consciousness. In writing the novel, Lewis also coined another term—Babbittry—that is still part of the vernacular today.

In *Babbitt,* Lewis once again dramatized his familiar subject of the person who longs for self-fulfillment but whose environment enslaves him and prevents him from finding freedom. Compared to Carol Kennicott, however, Babbitt is a much more frustrated individual, and the moderate optimism Lewis reveals at the end of *Main Street* is not much in evidence at the end of *Babbitt*. To Lewis, Babbitt is doomed: he is both the product and the victim of a culture of conspicuous consumption and boosterism. He is a forty-six-year-old realtor who leads a standardized and utterly conventional life; he is aware of the spiritual emptiness of his existence and desires a more meaningful one but does not know how to achieve it. Lewis establishes the hollowness of Babbitt's life on the first page of the novel: as the story opens, Babbitt is awaking from a dream about a fairy-girl, who beckons to him. We then follow him, for the first six chapters, through a typical day in his life, until he goes to bed and dreams again of the fairy-girl. In scene after scene, Lewis shows us that although Babbitt owns an expensive car, lives in an ultramodern house, belongs to the right club, attends an impressive church, and succeeds as a businessman and social climber, he is not satisfied. Yet he continues to act the way his acquaintances expect him to act.

Babbitt's complacency is shattered when his best friend Paul Riesling becomes so enraged at the pointlessness of his own existence that he has a nervous breakdown and attempts to murder his wife. Babbitt then rebels against his own life, first by having an affair with a quasi-bohemian woman named Tanis Judique who, like the social set she belongs to, "the Bunch," has no spiritual substance and thus no power to tap into Babbitt's human potential and help him grow. Unsettled and still searching for a means of fulfillment, Babbitt next shifts his political sympathies from right to left and aligns himself with the prolabor views of an old college friend, Seneca Doane, a radical lawyer. In the end, however, the lure of Babbitt's old friends and old ways of living overpowers his desire for change. He returns to the fold, as conventional as always. He can only hope that the next generation, embodied in his son, Theodore Roosevelt Babbitt, does not make the same mistakes he has.

In *Babbitt*, Lewis attempted to build on his achievement in *Main Street* in two ways: he heightened and broadened the scope of the comic-satiric element in his writing, and he tried to delve more deeply into Babbitt's psychology than he had into Carol Kennicott's. Lewis was trying to be two different types of writer at the same time. On the one hand, he was expanding the satiric vision he had shown in *Main Street*: Babbitt is a symbolic prototype—the booster—and Lewis satirizes his business life, family life, and leisure activities. Lewis was strongly influenced by H. L. Mencken, whose *boobus Americanus* is a precursor to Babbitt. Mencken had praised *Main Street,* and he and Lewis began their long friendship during

1920 and 1921. On the other hand, Lewis also tried to incorporate into *Babbitt* a novelistic vision—in the full sense of that word—and to explore the psychological motivations and inner life of his protagonist. In this regard, Lewis was responding to his critics. He told Alfred Harcourt that in *Babbitt* he wanted to overcome those limitations that reviewers had spotted in *Main Street,* namely, superficiality and lack of character analysis.[1] Lewis's attempts to weave both of these elements—which are essentially contradictory—into the fabric of his narrative created a dual focus. This helps to explain a persisting criticism of the novel: that *Babbitt* is a combination of two types of literary exposition. There is a limited presentation of a sensitive, humane Babbitt whose validity is undercut (or even canceled) by the parody Babbitt, whom Lewis was unable to humanize.

The prepublication materials for *Babbitt,* today preserved in the Lewis Collection at the Beinecke Library, contain evidence of these various intentions. These documents provide fascinating illustrations of Lewis's working methods, which he had experimented with in *Main Street* and now put into regular practice.

First, there is a 168-page looseleaf notebook in which Lewis recorded his observations of middle-class life in the 1920s—an expansion of the mimetic procedure he had used in *Main Street.* Some of the material in this notebook indicates that Lewis intended *Babbitt* to inaugurate a series of interrelated novels set in and around the fictional locale of Zenith, a city in the Midwest. He visited cities he considered possible models for Zenith, and he compiled intricately detailed "biographies" of the leading characters. He even drew maps of the interior and exterior settings in the novel, literally immersing himself in a fictive world.

There is also a fragment of a rejected outline for an early chapter of the novel and a completed draft typescript. Both of these documents contain notes and revisions that point up the basic contradiction in the characterization of Babbitt. In some places Lewis tempered his exaggerated portrait, making Babbitt less of a satiric type. But elsewhere (primarily in the typescript) Lewis cut a good deal of material in which he had tried to emphasize the "human" qualities of Babbitt's character and therefore make him less of a type and more of an individual.

Throughout the composition of the novel, Lewis struggled with the problems of typicality and individualization in drawing his protagonist. He wanted to define Babbitt in a way that would make him, as he told Alfred Harcourt, the "typical T. B. M. [tired businessman]" but also a human figure who would represent "all of us Americans at 46, prosperous but worried, wanting—passionately—to seize something more than motor cars and a house *before it's too late.*"[2]

After vacationing during August and September 1920 at Lake Kennebago, a resort in Maine, the Lewises spent a month in Manhattan, then returned to Washington, D.C., on 17 October 1920 and took a house in the northwest section of the city, near where they had lived earlier in the year. Lewis again rented an office in the building where he had written *Main Street*, and there he started work on his new novel. He was a creature of habit—he seems to have needed the comfort of familiar surroundings when he wrote—yet his constant restlessness also led him to search for new places in which to write. From Washington he went to the Midwest to do research; he then went to England, where he wrote approximately half of the first draft. He finished the draft in Italy, went back to England to revise what he had written, and finally returned to the United States for the publication of the novel, awaiting the reviews and simultaneously beginning his research and planning for the next book.

Lewis began work on *Babbitt* by considering the name of his central character and the title of the book, which he decided should be the same—a pattern he would follow in most of his subsequent novels. He was helped in this process by Harcourt, who patiently debated the merits of some two dozen names with Lewis by mail and continued to encourage the novelist in the same strong way that he had during the composition of *Main Street*. The first name that Lewis chose was "G. T. Pumphrey" of "Monarch City." That name, however, was discarded by Lewis because he thought that it was "too English and mite be thought humorous." Next, Lewis suggested to Harcourt the name "Burgess," which Harcourt said he liked; but when Lewis decided that he didn't like it himself, Harcourt wrote back to say that Burgess was actually "too freakish."

Harcourt was letting Lewis's imagination run freely and not making substantive critiques of his ideas. Between the fall of 1920 and early 1921, Lewis sometimes wrote Harcourt as many as three letters in one day with progress reports on his new novel. Harcourt did not reply to each letter; typically, he would write back after a week or so and respond favorably to Lewis's news. Harcourt probably realized that these letters were a way for Lewis to keep focused—to think through, or "talk out," his ideas. Lewis ultimately decided that the "title name" should not be "too common—like Jones, Smith, Robertson, Thompson, Brown, Johnson—for the reason that then people will associate the name not with the novel but with their numerous acquaintances who have that common name." Lewis explained to Harcourt that "titles that are names are rather successful in sticking in mind," and he cited a long list of "pretty good precedents," such as Arnold Bennett's *Clayhanger,* George Eliot's *Adam Bede,* Flaubert's *Madame Bovary,* and a number of Dickens titles. By the end of November, Lewis had settled on something entirely different—"Fitch."[3]

Lewis stuck with the name Fitch through the middle of December as he began the slow and accretive process of inventing material. In *Babbitt,* Lewis moved beyond the world that he knew—that of Sauk Centre as it appears in the guise of Gopher Prairie in *Main Street*—and began to explore another, much different world. In writing *Main Street,* Lewis had discovered his talent for rendering a certain environment realistically. Lewis now took that mimetic ability and applied it on a larger scale to create the city of Zenith, a composite setting drawn from various cities in Ohio, Illinois, and Michigan. He would soon visit these cities, absorb what he saw there, and then record his observations, constructing from them an ordered fictive world—a kind of Balzacian or Faulknerian landscape—filling in the supporting details, and documenting it all on paper. These details are set down in the 168-page notebook at the Beinecke, which contains abundant documentary evidence of a writer at work— gathering material, filtering it through his imagination, then transforming it into fiction.[4]

The precision of these notes is remarkable. There are entries for "City Institutions," "Largest Industrial Corporations," businesses located "On the Ground Floors of Office Buildings," "Lines of Industry," "City Song," "City [political] Organization," "Kinds of Houses in Floral Heights," "Department Stores," and "Movie Palaces." For the characters, Lewis wrote biographical sketches varying in length from one paragraph to three pages. This, for example, is part of his biography for the poet Chum Frink:

T. CHOLMONDELEY FRINK ("Chum")
Zenith's Great Author. Syndicates Versermons and Poemulations, really famous and rich, lectures, gets out bks of his "poems", writes short stories and Zip Tips and Boostographies. Terrifyingly a Good Fellow; fond father of seven kids, good husband, kind neighbor, hates (he says) New York and literary society there, except for one or two editors like Andy Anson whom he brings out and introduces; loves Zenith (and what he gets out of it), enthusiastic member of Boosters and chairman of Publicity Committee of Chamber of Commerce, silver-tongued after-dinner speaker, ex-messenger- boy and ex-cigar-store-clerk (and fond of referring to it), ex-reporter, president of Chum Frink Promotion and Advertising Corporation and right on the job (writes Poemulations on typewriter at eleven every morning), enthusiastic member Chatham Road Presbyterian Church and its Men's Club, teaches Sunday school, likes a drink, does publicity for Floral Heights Improvement Association and owns several houses there.

(T. CHUMLEY FRINK, originally spelled
T. CHOLMONDELEY FRINK   ("Chum").   *Versermons +*
Zenith's Great Author.   Syndicates Poemulations,
really .famous and rich, lectures, gets out bks
of his "poems", writes short stories and Zip
Tips and Boooomgnanhthaam Boostographies.   Terrifyingly a Good Fellow; fond father of seven kids,
good husband, kind neighbor, hates (he says)
New York and literary society there, except for
one or two editors like Andy Anson whom he brings
out and introduces; loves Zenith (and what he
gets out of it), enhtusiastic member of Boosters
and chairman of Publicity Committee of Chamber
of Commerce, silver-tongued after-dinner speaker,
ex-messenger-boy and ex-cigar-store-clerk (and
fond of feferring to it), ex-reporter, president
of Chum Frink Promition and Advertising Corporation and right on the job (writes Poemulations
on typewriter at eleven every morning), enhtusiastic member Chatham Road Presbyterian IIIIIMIIIM
Church and its Men's Club, teaches Sunday school,
likes a drink, does publicity for Floral Heights
Improvement Association and owns seven houses
there which are rented by Babbitt, (Bab's chief
famooser pride is in knowing him and he refers
to Frink always on Pullmans etc.)
Fond of explaining why changed
spelling of name????

Combine:
Sid
Eddie Guest
Walt Mason
Frank Crane
Bruce Barton
Herb Kaufman

"He found virtue so much
more profitable"

See Omnon 2

Asso. m. him in firm

Fig. 6.   Chum Frink "biography" (Yale Collection of American Literature,
Beinecke Rare Book and Manuscript Library, Yale University)

Lewis drew Frink as a composite portrait of several actual poets of this type. There is a note in the lower right-hand corner of this notebook page that reads: "Combine: Sid, Eddie [Edgar A.] Guest, Walt Mason, Frank Crane, Bruce Barton, Herb Kaufman."

In creating Babbitt, Lewis constructed a genealogy of his family, listed what courses he would have taken in college (by reading the 1888–89 University of Michigan catalog), described how he met his wife Myra, determined when they were married, and so on—a complete past, which Lewis ultimately did not elect to use in the novel, but which is relevant to changes he made later in his characterization. The notebook also contains biographical data on characters who do not appear in the novel at all, but whom Lewis created as citizens of his mythic city. These included "Members of [the] Boosters Club," "Members of the Union Club," "Staff of Babbitt-Thompson Realty Co.," and "Neighbors of Babbitt who are not Close Friends." There is even an entry for "Babbitt's Competitors—Realtors and His Allies," whose specialties are identified by abbreviations such as "BU" for business properties and "RM" for farm land.

The copious detail in the notebook suggests that in planning *Babbitt,* Lewis was planning future novels as well. He seems to have been envisioning a series of interrelated novels, perhaps inspired by Balzac's *Comédie humaine.*[5] There is specific evidence that he was thinking ahead to *Dodsworth* (1929), for he included a page listing "Important Early Families with Descendants in Zenith Today"; at the top of this chart is the name "Dodsworth." Although no information is given about the family, there are other references to the Dodsworths in the notebook: the Dodsworth Theatre is listed under "City Institutions," and under "Largest Industrial Corps. in Zenith" appears the "McKelvey and Dodsworth Construction Company," with one Putnam Dodsworth as "third v.p." On two other pages, Lewis worked out a separate genealogy for characters he called "Great Souls," where we again see the name Dodsworth and also that of Lucile McKelvey, a character who appears in *Babbitt* and who is mentioned in *Dodsworth.*

Lewis was therefore planning at least one other novel, which would concern the anti-Babbitts, or "great souls."[6] This was most likely a novel about the labor movement in America, a project that Lewis worked at sporadically throughout his career but never completed. The earliest version, which I discuss in the next chapter, was to have featured Seneca Doane, the radical labor lawyer who instigates Babbitt's brief fling with nonconformity. There are many other characters in the notebook who did not survive the planning stages, although Lewis used some of them in later novels. For example, Benoni Carr, whom Lewis intended to be the New

CHARACTERS -- 1

GEORGE F. BABBITT
(Hidden middle name, Follansbee)
Central character. The Babbitt-Thompson Realty Co.
Born ~~1000~~. *1874. Grad. U, 1896. met myra
*1895. married ~~1897~~ " make # " *1908 ±
~~S~~
~~H~~ *46 in 1920*

MYRA THOMPSON BABBITT, his wife.
Born ~~1870~~, married ~~1895~~. *45 in 1920*
1875
1897

Their children: *1895*
VERONA, born ~~1895~~ ~~1899~~ — *22 in 1920 (Rone)*
~~ALEXANDER~~
~~born 1903~~
KATHERINE, Tinka, born ~~1910~~. *1910 — 10 in 1920*
THEODORE ROOSEVELT — Ted — b. 1903 — 17 in '20

HENRY T. (Terry) THOMPSON, Babbitt's father in law,
manufacturer of kitchen cabinets, partner with
Jake Offutt in manufacture of trolley car bodies,
and sleeping partner with Babbitt. None of these
interests large, tho (very small share with Offutt)
and not rich, only "comfortably well off." *B. 1848 —*
began in civil war — 72 in 1920
SENECA ~~DOANE~~, the successful rebel: lawyer, mayor,
outcast. Classmate of Babbitt. *DOANE*

MAX KRUGER, jester in college where knew Babbitt;
banker, dandy, gambler, harassed ennuye.

IRVING TATE, Babbitt's classmate; college grind,
manufacturer and public utility investor,
secretary then successor to ~~offutt~~ tight,
concentrated, humorless millionaire. *Lincoln*
KELVEY *Goodhue in R.C. Tool Co*
CHARLEY MC ~~KELVEY~~, suave, big, becomes fixer and
engineer-builder. *(speculation builder — ...*
deal, ~~his~~ $100,000 operation on ... each
building from civil engineer.)

Fig. 7. "Characters" page from the *Babbitt* notebook (Yale Collection of American Literature, Beinecke Rare Book and Manuscript Library, Yale University)

BABBITT'S COMPETITORS --- "Realtors" ← 1
and his ALLIES
**Residential N.E. ** (These are Bab's especial
rivals, dealing in houses from Bellevue and
East Heights to Tonawanda and Dorchester)
SW - brokers for So.W. residential property.
GEN - General residential properties
BU - business properties; stores, offices.
FL - flat properties; brokers and managers.
XXXXXX
RM - farm lands. broker
FAC - broker in factory and stable property
ALL - broker in all kinds of real estate
INS - Insurance broker as well as real estate
LOAN - Loans as well as real estate.

"Pussy Foot"

CHANDLER MOTT ------ *(Bus w glasses)*
~~EVART C. AVERY~~ GEN, FL, INS, LOAN. Has bldg. in
XXXXXXXXXXXXXXXXXXXXXXXXXXXXXXXXXXX same block as Bab,
on opposite side. Old, genteel -- a la F.A.S.,
and properly crooked. Lately concentrates on
Linton, East Heights, Floral, Dorchester, so becomes **. Prest R.Es. Bd. one year. Bab loves him
publicly and hates him privately. He is a didactic
appraiser and speaker. *manages Wildwood
Cemetery. NOT "in" socially - but very respectable*

EAST SIDE HOMES AND DEVELOPMENT CO. **, BU in NE,
INS, FL......President, ARNOLD LOUGEE. Bab's
particular rival. Office on Smith St. Bab regards Lougee as Avery and Rountree regard Bab -
as insignificantly low-class.

DORCHESTER REAL ESTATE COMPANY, run by XX
AARON PRITCHARD. In Dorchester. **.

MARTIN LUMSEN AND SONS, who own and operate, without broker, Avonlea, development on edge of Silver Grove, so, in opposition to Glen Oriole, **.

THAYER AND GRANT, *(Winthrop)* ALL, **, LOAN, INS. (Alvin
Thayer, ~~Harry~~ Grant). Largest firm in town. 35
salesmen, eight stenogs and clerks, phone central,
two office boys, etc. Auctioneers also. XXXXX
XXXXXXXXXXXX They cut into Bab's business in all
sorts of ways, especially huge Dorchester development CAPRI, but they're so big he can't hate 'em;
always trying, sometimes succeeding, get scraps
from them.

Fig. 8.   List of Babbitt's competitors (Yale Collection of American Literature,
Beinecke Rare Book and Manuscript Library, Yale University)

Thought preacher in *Babbitt*, was reincarnated as the sham medical professor in *Arrowsmith*.

Throughout the fall of 1920 Lewis invented the demographics of Zenith and kept adding material to his notebook. As sales of *Main Street* climbed higher and higher, he grew more confident of his talent and remained in high spirits. Lewis began to write fewer short stories for magazines, and he channeled most of his creative energy into planning *Babbitt*. Earning money, which at this point in his career was not a serious problem, became even less of a concern now: sales of *Main Street* were so strong that Lewis agreed to a "joint gamble" with Harcourt whereby one-third of his 15 percent royalty on all copies of *Main Street* sold would be used to advertise the novel. Apparently, Lewis and Harcourt had the same arrangement for all of Lewis's novels during the 1920s. Redistributing part of the profits from his novels to advertising kept Lewis's name almost constantly in the public eye. By the following summer, Lewis's total royalties on *Main Street* (excluding his share of advertising costs) would amount to fifty-two thousand dollars—an enormous sum for the time.[7]

By 17 December Lewis had finished his preliminary research for the new book and had settled on a new name for the title character: "Babbitt." He told Harcourt prophetically that "two years from now we'll have them talking of Babbittry."[8]

Lewis's thinking about and planning of *Babbitt* manifested itself in ways besides the material in the notebook. Sometime during the late summer or early fall of 1920 he wrote a sixteen-page introduction to the novel that was never published in his lifetime. (This document is reprinted in appendix 3.) This introduction can be compared with the thesis fragment that Lewis wrote for *Main Street* in 1918: both documents served as formal, preparatory writing exercises, ways of finding out how he wanted to treat his material. Lewis saved this introduction and placed it in the back of the "Babbitt Notebook," a fact that led Lewis's literary executor, Melville Cane, to conclude that it "was written toward the end of the period of gathering material for the book"[9]—that is, April or May 1921. I believe that the introduction was written much earlier, possibly as early as August 1920, when Lewis was first thinking about *Babbitt* while correcting the proofs of *Main Street*. The central character is referred to as "Pumphrey," the name that Lewis was using for him then. The basic description of the central character, "the Tired Business Man," is rendered in much the same language that Lewis used in letters to Harcourt at that time. Also, Lewis filed his notebook material by topic or theme, not according to when he wrote a particular note. The notebook, which is a ring binder, was probably reorganized several times as Lewis discarded or expanded various notes. It would have been natural for him to relegate this unused introduction to the rear of the notebook.

Dating the introduction from the late summer or early fall of 1920 instead of the late spring of 1921 is important because it shows how *Main Street* contributed to one of Lewis's aesthetic problems in *Babbitt*. In the earliest stages of planning the novel, Lewis was headed in two different directions at the same time. One took him into an anthropological analysis of the midwestern city, a natural progression from his analysis in *Main Street* of the small town. The other direction led him into a study of an American type such as Babbitt.

After the heading "Intro / 1," Lewis wrote: "(I.E. Basic theme—which may or may not appear specifically in book, as intro or otherwise; which may be merely implied & expressed)." The first topic that Lewis addresses is Babbittry itself, at this point identified as "Pumphreysie" (a coinage that sounds much like Mencken's "Booboisie"). The character of Pumphrey is not fleshed out much beyond the descriptions that Lewis had earlier given Harcourt: "This is the story of the ruler of America. The story of the Tired Business Man, the man with toothbrush mustache and harsh voice who talks about motors and prohibition in the smoking compartment of the Pullman car, the man who plays third-rate golf and first-rate poker at a second-rate country club near an energetic American city." The introduction also reveals Lewis's desire to draw the character in a realistic, multidimensional way. Here we see the first indications of Lewis's contradictory conception of Babbitt: "Distinctly, however, Pumphrey is not a satiric figure, nor a Type. He is too tragic a tyrant for the puerilities of deliberate satire. And he is an individual, very eager and well-intentioned, credulous of pioneering myths, doubtful in his secret hours, affectionate toward his rebellious daughter and those lunch-mates who pass for friends—a god self-slain on his modern improved altar."

The second topic treated in this introduction is "the complex phenomena" of "American cities of from 80,000 to 1,000,000." This part of the document represents Lewis's earliest ideas about *Babbitt:* that it would be a novel as much about the phenomenon of the American city as about "the Tired Business Man." Lewis considered printing this part of the introduction as an appendix to the novel, under the title "Main Street vs. the Boulevard vs. Fifth Ave." Lewis discusses various aspects of medium-sized cities: their industrial magnificence, their centers of commerce, and the faith in standardization that their citizens profess. He describes such cities as "transitional metropolises" or "overgrown towns." In so doing, Lewis was trying to establish continuity between *Main Street* and *Babbitt,* again possibly thinking of a series of novels.

The basic argument of this introduction is developed in another document from this period, a short article that Lewis wrote called "The Pioneer Myth," which appeared in the "Literary Review" section of the *New York Evening Post* on 5 February 1921. (The article is reprinted in appendix 2.) In the article, Lewis again sets up a straw man, this time the character Sam Clarke from *Main Street*. Clarke rails at his college-aged son, Orrin, for wanting to be a highbrow writer for such magazines as the *Atlantic* or the *Century* instead of the author of what his father prefers, "a good snappy love story" for "one of the popular magazines." In the essay, Lewis argues that the pioneer myth, embodied by hardware dealers like Sam who think of themselves as forest-clearers and Indian-fighters, enables Americans to justify their unwillingness "to ponder anything but bookkeeping and amours" and to claim that they have no time for "economics or belles-lettres." This philosophy, of course, is echoed by George F. Babbitt. The article therefore provides another glimpse into the gestation of this character in Lewis's mind as a satiric type. Although "The Pioneer Myth" evidently did not attract much notice, Lewis seems to have meant it also to be a public gesture to distinguish himself from the magazine fiction writers and especially the "pioneer writers" who portray "all decent American males . . . as inhabiting ranches, lumber camps, mining camps, or New York cabarets of a sort more brutal and incomparably more naive than any ranch." In the months following the publication of *Main Street,* Lewis did all he could to help shape the critics' and the public's perception of him as a serious writer, an effort that paid off in numerous ways throughout the 1920s. One might say that as Lewis was planning *Babbitt,* he was also planning his career.

Lewis was alert to critics' comments on his work. The opinion of one person in particular seems to have influenced him as he struggled to make Babbitt both a satiric type and a fully developed character. This person was H. L. Mencken, who reviewed *Main Street* enthusiastically in the January 1921 issue of the *Smart Set,* the periodical that he coedited with George Jean Nathan. Lewis's association with Mencken would be the most influential literary relationship he would have in the 1920s. Mencken had begun his long journalistic career in 1899 as a reporter for the *Baltimore Morning Herald.* He rose to prominence in the 1910s as coeditor of the *Smart Set,* a witty literary journal, and later as sole editor of a rather more weighty periodical, the *American Mercury.* Through the columns and book reviews that Mencken published in these magazines, and through the essays collected in his volumes of *Prejudices,* he became the central figure in the "debunking" or demythologizing of various American institutions— such things as political moralism, religious evangelism, boosterism, and commercialism in all its forms (particularly as it was practiced in small towns and middle-sized cities). Eventually these philosophies coalesced into a figure that Mencken routinely used to illustrate his criticisms, the *boobus Americanus* or "the Booboisie." Mencken advocated a primarily satiric, irreverent prose literature that would depict this figure and other national types and that would capture the fantastic surfaces of American life in all its vulgarity and variousness. Lewis's novels of the 1920s possess these same characteristics, and Babbitt closely resembles Mencken's "Booboisie." Like Lewis, Mencken also understood a thing or two about self-promotion.

The two men met just before the publication of *Main Street,* in late September 1920. In his memoirs, George Jean Nathan recalled the scene. One evening, Mencken and Nathan had gone to the apartment of T. R. Smith, the managing editor of *Century* magazine, and there they were introduced to "a tall, skinny, paprika-headed stranger":

> Barely had we taken off our hats and coats . . . when [Lewis] simultaneously coiled one long arm around Mencken's neck and the other around mine, well nigh strangling us and putting resistance out of the question, and—yelling at the top of his lungs—began: "So you guys are critics, are you? Well, let me tell you something. I'm the best writer in this here gottdamn country and if you, Georgie, and you, Hank, don't know it now, you'll know it gottdamn soon. Say, I've just finished a book . . . and it's the gottdamn best book of its kind."

When they left, Mencken reportedly told Nathan, "Of all the idiots I've ever laid eyes on, that fellow is the worst!" But three days later, Nathan received a note from Mencken telling him to "prepare for a terrible shock! I've just read the advance sheets of the book of that *Lump* we met . . . and, by God, he has done the job! It's a genuinely excellent piece of work. . . . I begin to believe that perhaps there isn't a God after all. There is no justice in the world. Yours in Xt., M."[10]

Mencken reviewed *Main Street* in the next issue of the *Smart Set* that was still open—January 1921—and he not only gave Lewis his coveted stamp of approval, but also depicted him as virtually a latter-day Walt Whitman, emerging from the ranks of the unknown to lead a decade of literary change:

> There is yet hope. . . . Authors with their pockets full of best-seller money are bitten by high ambition, and strive heroically to scramble out of the literary *Cloaca Maxima*. Now and then one of them

succeeds, bursting suddenly into the light of the good red sun with the foul liquors of the depths still streaming from him, like a prisoner loosed from some obscene dungeon. . . . Now comes another fugitive, his face blanched by years in the hulks, but his eyes alight with high purpose. His name is Sinclair Lewis, and the work he offers is a novel called *Main Street*.[11]

From this point on, Mencken and Lewis remained in close contact, and their friendship had a significant effect on Lewis's writing. Mencken's review of *Main Street* appeared as Lewis was planning *Babbitt* in early 1921. It affected Lewis's conception of that novel—specifically, that of the central character. In early 1922 Lewis wrote Mencken a letter in which he acknowledged his indebtedness, saying that *Babbitt* was "curiously associated with yourself." Lewis said that Mencken's review of *Main Street,* in which he suggested that "what ought to be taken up now is the American city—not NY or Chi but the cities of 200,000 to 500,000—the Baltimores and Omahas and Buffaloes and Birminghams," had helped Lewis "to decide on this particular [topic] as against one or two others, which, at the time, I also wanted to do."[12] In the review, Mencken also noted approvingly that Lewis did not "attempt . . . to solve the American cultural problem, but simply to depict with great care a group of typical Americans. . . . The figures often remain in the flat [and] . . . in their externals, at all events, they are done with uncommon skill." Lewis was probably also pleased that Mencken approved of his concern with surface details and his unwillingness to explore his characters' inner lives.

These comments, coming as they did from a source of critical authority that Lewis much respected, must partly account for Lewis's tendency to treat Babbitt as a satiric type and not draw him as a multidimensional character. Mencken's biographers have been a bit overzealous in saying that Lewis wrote *Babbitt* at Mencken's instigation; but it can be said that Lewis was following Mencken's lead in depicting certain national types, and that Lewis also clearly wanted to please Mencken.[13] He recognized the value of being in Mencken's good critical graces. Lewis wrote, "I think you'll like it—I hope to Christ you do," and, "Of this I'm sure—if you don't like the book, nobody in the entire *Vereinigen* will."[14] Such comments suggest that Lewis looked to Mencken for critical approval—and he got it. Mencken's 6 February reply was encouraging:

> Your plan looks to me to be excellent. The big city right-thinker seems to me to be even more typical of the Republic than the Main Street right-thinker. He is more influential. What he says and does

today is imitated in the grass towns tomorrow. I have known and revered many such operators, and stood enchanted before their doings during the war, particularly in the matter of the Liberty Loan drives. In my old days here in Baltimore I invented the name of Honorary Pallbearers for them, and it still sticks, but only here. Did you ever notice that half of their time is given to acting as honorary pallbearers for one another?[15]

When *Babbitt* was published, Mencken praised it enthusiastically—not as a novel but as "a social document of a high order." He saw George Babbitt as a type—"an almost perfect specimen—a genuine museum piece."

Mencken always brought out the satiric tendencies in Lewis, and he usually discouraged (at least indirectly) any expression of Lewis's latent idealism or sympathetic identification with his characters.[16] In other words, Mencken found Lewis's writing to be brilliant when Lewis was being a mocking satirist—and rather uninteresting when he was trying to be a straightforward novelist. As we will see, Mencken would often suggest topics for Lewis to treat in his novels, and the most thoroughly satiric of Lewis's writings during the 1920s—*Babbitt, Elmer Gantry,* and *The Man Who Knew Coolidge*—either had their roots in Mencken's writings or were written at Mencken's urging.[17]

Instead of attempting to draw his characters as fully developed human figures, Lewis used his extraordinary skills of observation and his mimetic talent to highlight their surface characteristics and then present them as types, figures who embody the major traits of their class. During February, March, and half of April 1921 Lewis went to the Midwest on a research trip, visiting several cities in Illinois, Wisconsin, Michigan, and Ohio to immerse himself in these environments and gather material on his subject. Lewis spent the majority of his time in Cincinnati, where he established a pied-à-terre at the Queen City Club. (Grace did not accompany Lewis; she had grown annoyed with their peripatetic existence and wanted a permanent home. This would contribute to the eventual collapse of their marriage.) From Cincinnati, Lewis wrote to Harcourt: "Bully time, met lots of people, really getting the feeling of life here. Fine for *Babbitt*."[18] Like Zola on his documenting expeditions to the tenements, food markets, and newspaper offices of Paris, Lewis went about his research almost in the manner of an anthropologist, mingling with the sorts of people the novel would depict and writing down what he observed.

One thing that he carefully recorded in the notebook and consciously worked into *Babbitt* was idiom and slang. Lewis had been tuning his ear and practicing his technique in the novels he wrote during the 1910s, and he had experimented with it in *Main Street.* His mimicry is most clearly in evidence in *Babbitt,* where it sounds effortless. In one section of the notebook entitled "Locutions," Lewis listed whole catalogs of expressions and variations on them: "How's the old Bolsheviki / anarchist / grouch today?" Or, "If (——) happens, my name is pants / I'm a gone goose / my goose is cooked." Some notes are less precise, but no less methodical—such as "*at least* as a connective." Lewis marked various entries as "used" after he had incorporated them into *Babbitt,* such as Babbitt's parting comment to Paul Riesling at the end of chapter 5: "don't take any wooden money" (67), or the Reverend John Jennison Drew's description of the church choir as providing "mountains of melody, mountains of mirth" (206), phrases that Lewis jotted down on a bulletin from the First Congregational Church of Oak Park, Illinois.

Lewis's ear for the language was only one part of his mimetic gift. As he sat in Pullman cars on train trips, took his meals in the dining rooms of athletic clubs, and in general insinuated himself into the world of the middle-class businessman, he was able to "absorb" or "memorize" people to such an astonishing degree that, like Dickens, to whom he has often been compared, he could virtually become them—speak as they spoke, walk the way they walked, anticipate their responses to certain statements, and render with eerie accuracy their facial expressions, hand gestures, even eye movements.[19] The novelist John Hersey, who was Lewis's secretary during the summer of 1937, recalled that when Lewis launched into one of the impromptu satiric monologues that he became famous for at social gatherings, "one forgot his cadaverous face and *saw* John L. Lewis, F.D.R., Huey Long, Father Coughlin."[20] Another of Lewis's secretaries recalled that on automobile trips Lewis was fond of playing a game in which he and his traveling companion pretended to be salesmen for competing products. They would enter a restaurant arguing, each one vehemently defending the superiority of his wares. Their loud squabble would continue throughout their meal; then they would depart, leaving behind an astonished audience of customers and waitresses.[21] On another occasion, after Lewis had completed his research on the ministry for *Elmer Gantry,* he was able to write a prayer for a cleric who found it so good that he used it the following morning in his sermon.[22] These incidents not only explain why a character such as Babbitt seems lifelike—they also suggest how completely Lewis immersed himself in the world about which he was writing and how deeply his art depended on his mimetic abilities.

Clippings from Cincinnati newspapers provided some of the material in *Babbitt.* Beside one article in the notebook listing city districts that would be affected by road construction, among them "Dorchester" and "Silver Grove," the names of two districts in which Babbitt holds rental properties (37), Lewis wrote: "models for names of city suburbs, streets, etc." Once he obtained the raw data, Lewis embellished it and wrote a note outlining how he would use the material in the novel. In this case, Lewis wanted to give a "Picture of, and [do] justice to, *all* the city" as "a cosmos," mentioning the "excellence of [the] suburbs in which U.S. equals the world," but also showing how businessmen do not appreciate the "fine park system" or the "good symphony orchestra." Lewis also clipped a number of society columns from local newspapers, then replicated their syntax and language in such places in *Babbitt* as chapter 2, where Babbitt reads in the *Zenith Advocate-Times* about a dinner given by the McKelveys (21–22). Underneath one such clipping Lewis wrote "By Elnora Pearl Bates," whom he identified in the "CHARACTERS" section of the notebook as the society reporter for the Zenith paper and who appears as such in *Babbitt*.

Objects of satire in the novel came from various quarters. The idea for Babbitt's being forced by his wife to attend a meeting of the "League of the Higher Illumination," for instance, derived from a brochure describing the International New Thought Alliance. The similarity between the information in the notebook and the details in the novel is close. In the novel, the speaker is Mrs. Opal Emerson Mudge, a field lecturer who talks on "Cultivating the Sun Spirit" (355), but she might just as well be the speaker noted on the bulletin, "Miss Harriet Hale Rix," whose subject is "The Truth Shall Set You Free."

The most detailed—and certainly the most technical—material in the notebook concerns real estate. As Harcourt recalled, Lewis put "as much study into the subject matter as a graduate student preparing a Ph.D. thesis."[23] Various entries list such things as the cost of an apartment house in 1920, "with 32 apartments, four stories high." On the back of one page are handwritten calculations that estimate the operating expenses for a firm such as Babbitt's. There is also a description of a real estate company Lewis visited in Wilmette, Illinois, which he seems to have used as the model for Babbitt's office. It is located on the "Ground floor of bldg containing on same hall a florist and W[estern]. U[nion]. office," and has a "Platform at window" with "pictures of houses, ad of smart cemetery" (cf. 32–34). Stanley Graff's telephone conversation with a prospective client in that same chapter is, but for a word or two, a verbatim transcription of Lewis's note, "Heard over phone here, 'I think I've got just the house that would suit you. Oh, you've seen it. Well, how'd it strike you? Oh, I see" (cf. 33).

ALEXANDRIA, VA.	ANNOUNCEMENT

ALEXANDRIA, VA.

Unity Study Class.
615 Prince Street.
Tuesdays, 8 p. m., Study of "Lessons in Truth."
Garnett January, Teacher.

These are all associated with

THE INTERNATIONAL NEW THOUGHT ALLIANCE.

Article II of the Constitution of the Alliance reads:

The purposes of this organization are to teach the Infinitude of the Supreme One; the Divinity of Man and his Infinite Possibilities through the creative power of constructive thinking, and obedience to the voice of the Indwelling Presence, which is our source of Inspiration, Power, Health and Prosperity.

General Headquarters,
Rooms 311-313 Ouray Building,
805 G St. N. W.
Washington, D. C.

Mr. James A. Edgerton, President.
Mrs. Melva J. Merrill,
Executive Secretary.

ANNOUNCEMENT

OF NEW THOUGHT MEETINGS AND TEACHERS

IN

WASHINGTON, D. C.
ALEXANDRIA, VA. *and*
BALTIMORE, MD.

The New Thought Association

UNION MEETINGS

at

Rauscher's Hall
Connecticut Ave. and L St.
Sunday, December 5, 1920, 11 A. M.
(Note Change of Hour)

Speaker, Miss Harriet Hale Rix,
of Los Angeles, Calif.,
Field Lecturer for the I. N. T. A.

Subject:
"The Truth Shall Set You Free."

Sunday, Dec. 12, 1920, 4 p. m.
Speaker, Melva J. Merril,
Executive Secretary of the I. N. T. A.

Subject:
"Divine Attainment."

Fig. 9.   New Thought Alliance brochure (Yale Collection of American Literature, Beinecke Rare Book and Manuscript Library, Yale University)

In sum, the notebook reveals Lewis's extremely strong concern with verisimilitude in *Babbitt*. It also suggests that he was interested as much in the sociohistorical detail of his subject matter as in the psychological complexities of his characters. Mark Schorer commented that "in some ways *Babbitt* is hardly a novel at all," but rather "a highly conscious, indeed systematic series of set pieces, each with its own topic."[24] The documentation in the notebook may suggest that Lewis was something of a slave to his research and was therefore unable to let the characters, plot, and themes of the novel evolve freely. This fact may also account in part for the episodic nature and relative thinness of the plot, as compared with the more unified and substantive narratives in *Main Street* and *Arrowsmith*. Most important, the notebook may explain the lack of development in Babbitt's inner character in the published novel. Indeed, evidence in both the fragmentary outline for the book and the draft typescript indicates that Lewis had trouble keeping his focus on the central character and not letting his analysis of Zenith (or his descriptions of other "types") dominate the novel.

In late April 1921 Lewis returned to New York and reported to Harcourt on the success of his research trip to the Midwest; then he sailed for England with Grace in early May. When the Lewises arrived there later that month, they rented a country house in "the tiny old village of Bearsted, near Maidstone, in the heart of Kent farming country," and soon Lewis began "to feel that itch which means that I want to get back to writing."[25] On 12 July he enthusiastically announced to Harcourt that "He's started—*Babbitt*—and I think he's going to be a corker." In the same letter he told Harcourt that Kent was "a fine place for work": "I have a room to myself; I get on the job immejit after breakfast: work thru to tea time, then go for a walk or a swim or both, and read or talk in the evenings."

Although Lewis had been "writing a little," his work to this point had consisted mostly of "turning notes into a final plan."[26] This outline, a fragment of which is now among Lewis's papers at the Beinecke and is entitled "Babbitt Plan," was written with reference to material in the notebook. With *Babbitt,* it became Lewis's habit to write such an outline before he wrote the first draft. These outlines resemble the storyboards that film directors use to frame sequences of camera shots: like a director, Lewis blocked each step of the action in his plot, scene by scene. The outline was yet another stage in Lewis's slow and deliberative process of accumulating, mastering, and then shaping his material before writing a draft. It was as if he viewed these preliminary stages of research, note-taking, and planning as a kind of artistic workshop in which he constructed a frame or template for his book. Once he had done the exhausting work of assembling his characters, plot, and settings and deciding on his theme and tone, he joined these elements together, planed off the rough edges, and—with the frame in place—was able to write a draft very quickly. The portion of the "Babbitt Plan" that is extant is of great interest, because it differs significantly from the corresponding sections of the published text. This document reveals, among other things, that Lewis restructured at least part of the novel, removing much material that pertained to the city of Zenith. More important, the fragment indicates that Lewis altered the characterization of Babbitt.[27]

According to the draft typescript, Lewis intended chapter 1 to be Babbitt's speech before the Zenith Real Estate Board, the famous panegyric to "Our Ideal Citizen." At the suggestion of Alfred Harcourt, Lewis revised that chapter (which he initially called the "introduction"—not to be confused with the unpublished introduction in the notebook) and relocated it as part of chapter 14 before the novel was published. Harcourt wanted Lewis to cut the speech altogether: he worried that it gave away too much of Lewis's point of view, "rather than having it grow out of the development of the characters as the reader goes along." Lewis, however, did not want to delete the section because he felt that the speech "so completely sums up certain things in all contemporary Babbitts." This was evidently the only time during the composition of *Babbitt* that Harcourt made such a specific suggestion. It was unusual for Harcourt to do so while Lewis was still writing a draft. But Harcourt, like Mencken, thought that Lewis's talents lay in satire and parody, and he seems not to have wanted Lewis to spoil those elements for the reader by beginning the novel with a too-exaggerated presentation of the central character.[28]

The published novel therefore begins with Babbitt's dream of the fairy-girl. The four extant pages of the plan headed "CHAPTER II" show that Babbitt's dream was originally intended as the second chapter; it was to "end with him dreaming again." In Babbitt's dream Lewis planned to give a kaleidoscopic picture of the past—describing the founding of Zenith, tracing changes in the appearance of the city by 1885, quoting from Mrs. Trollope's account of travel in the United States in the late 1820s for a description of "Zenith in her day," and borrowing from other sources, such as the commentary about America found in the letters of the English historian James Bryce. Most of the details for this outline Lewis drew from his notebook. Two pages on the "History of Zenith" contain a strikingly detailed account, from the earliest exploration of the region through the founding of the town in 1792, when the city fathers "agreed to and signed a Solemn Covenant." The city was to have been named "Covenant," but in 1808, one Peter Dodsworth "had [the] name changed to Zenith, as better for business, i.e. for righteousness." Thus the founding fathers' visions of a "city of beauty and justice" (dubious even then, for Lewis noted parenthetically that these visions were "dimly . . . defined" and were "to be aristocratically controlled") quickly became the monument to materialism and rule by wealth that is the Zenith of the novel (plan, p. 12).

In creating Zenith, Lewis invented for it an entire history that would explain its character in modern times. Yet he elected not to use most of this information and in the typescript made cuts that similarly removed "historical" matter.[29] This material, together with the abundant sociological data in the notebook, suggests that at this point Lewis planned to feature Zenith in the novel more prominently than he ultimately did. Lewis's intentions in this regard must have shifted, because he made other changes in the typescript to focus the novel on Babbitt instead of on Zenith.[30]

First explorer was Pere Emile Fauthoux, who explored Chaloosa River in 1740-41, and is supposed
to have camped at the junction of the Chaloosa
and Appleseed during worst of winter. *this half-
breed guide Hilaire Bonneau died + buried here*

In 1767, Amasa Rudd started a trading station
with Indians at the junction of the Chaloosa and
Kennepoose Rivers. His clerk was John Dawes
White of Massachusetts. This trading station was
abandoned in 1777, during the Revolutionary War.
White had meantime returned to Mass., inherited
ships from uncle, and done well financially --
in the Revolutionary War he was a colonel.

In 1788, White and Caspar Schnell purchased from *congress*
700,000 acres in the Chaloosa Valley. Sold some
of it.

In 1792 White and others arrived to start a settlement. Influenced by the eloquent Rev.
Saltonstall Bennerm,   John Dawes White, Benner,
Caspar Schnell, William Eathorne, and Rufus
Chubbuck met on a bluff over the river (at or
near the present foot of filmum Coventant Street)
in a Conclave and agreed to and signed a Solemn
Covenant -- "who vow and bind their descendants
in the flesh or the emulating spirit to erect
a city comely, generous, righteous, and free;
devoid of the subtile snares of Mammon and of
strife betwixt brother and brother." *after 1st*
And they called the city Covenant. *lively ex-*
alteration.
But John Dawes White did not like it, and with
Peter Dodsworth and Hmumhm Epenetus Goodhue, *X*
who came 12 years afterward and soon were prominent, he had name changed to Zenith, as better
for business, i.e. for righteousness. But also
changed name of Hog Market Street to Coventant
Street (now runs thru Arbor with boarding houses, petty mfrs., lunch rooms, whore houses,
wholesaling). *in 1808*

*X - Rev.-
1st pres't,
U of Winnemac*

Fig. 10. History of Zenith (Yale Collection of American Literature, Beinecke
Rare Book and Manuscript Library, Yale University)

Scene of Babbitt teaching Sunday Sch?

But, home, a little doubtful, for first
time, re Pickergill, Smeeth -- a little
too much of them at once.

Jan 1921

KENNICOTTS come -- Dr. Will second cousin
of Babbitt. (Carol returned GP in June
1920; baby August 20. Will and she now
on dash to -- Florida?)

Babbitt feels great and urbane while entertaining them. Shows them the city.

Ken's boasts re G.P. Contrasts Bab and
Ken. Bab doesnt like Carol.

Beautiful scene of ordering dinner (they
take Kens to Thornleigh for dinner,-then
to theater. Lost. Asks waiter of each:
"The Long Island duckling good today?"
and to each waiter "Very good, sir."
Negatives: "You dont want any soup, do
you?" then, when all agree -- sadly --
all over again: "But would you like some
soup?" When all ordered, feeling ought to
to be something more, "And we better have
an order of French fried potatoes." Many
confidences to bored waiter. Kens smile
patiently and wait, suffering, and
look about. Comments on other diners afterward and laborious converse thru dinner, incl roast of an S.L.

When Myra goes theater, wears long white
gloves and carries (in blue velvet case)
gold-plate and mother of pearl lorgnon
(lorgnette?) with Zeiss lenses (given to
her years ago) tho not need nor use them

Fig. 11. Page of *Babbitt* plan (Yale Collection of American Literature, Beinecke
Rare Book and Manuscript Library, Yale University)

The plan shows that Lewis thought his way through Babbitt's past quite carefully. Originally Lewis intended to show that in his youth Babbitt had been an idealistic dreamer, and he meant to explore how he had changed. The next part of Babbitt's dream in the rejected plan for chapter 2 shows him as a college student with several characters who later become his friends: Paul Riesling, Irving Tate, Max Kruger, Charley McKelvey, and Seneca Doane. Page 12, entitled "IDYLLIC 1890," describes a planned scene "Before D[oane]'s graduation," in which Tate would make an "earnest prophecy" that "Bab [would] become [a] great reform mayor"; "Riesling [a] great composer"; "McKelvey [a] millionaire banker"; and Tate a "poor G[ree]k prof." Lewis then wrote a parallel list, showing how these characters had actually turned out twenty years later: "Became—Bab as we see [him]"; "Riesling in roofing occas. playing cello"; "McKelvey did become millionaire, as contracting builder AND Tate also (see note book)." The rest of the plan follows Babbitt at different points in his life. At age twenty he is in college, making his own prophecy:

> I tell you, a fellow hadn't ought to just loaf through life. He ought to have some ideals—like Prof. Udell says. He ought to support good honest political candidates and keep up good reading. He ought—I tell you a fellow ought to take part in all these movements, and make the world better. He hadn't ought to be a hog and just live for himself. (plan, p. 13)

In the novel, of course, Babbitt's idea of a "good honest political candidate" is Lucas Prout, the "mattress-manufacturer with a perfect record for sanity" (176), and his idea of "good reading" is not Conrad or Hergesheimer, but something that "enable[s] a fellow to forget his troubles" (271). On a later page of the plan, a young Paul Riesling suggests that Babbitt "take a whirl at politics," an idea that Babbitt ironically rejects out of hand: "Hunka! I've seen enough of politics to know they're dirty, and I want to keep out of them" (plan, p. 15). Other material describes Babbitt's "first big ambitions . . . nev[er] realized" and his desire to "pull off something—anything—*before it's too late*" (plan, p. 13). Lewis also outlined several scenes concerning Babbitt's interest in law school and his early disdain for real estate, then paralleled them with Paul Riesling's similarly lofty and unfulfilled ambitions (plan, pp. 13–14).

Throughout this plan, we see the irony of Babbitt's transformation from someone who dreamed of idylls in his youth to someone enamored of electric cigar-lighters and gleaming porcelain bathrooms in middle age. This is precisely the type of character analysis that Lewis largely sacrificed to broad satire and surface description in the published novel. There Lewis mentions, for example, that in college Babbitt was a liberal, but we do not see how he changed. As Sheldon Grebstein has noted, "Surely it is hard for us to believe he could ever have been a wild and dangerous dreamer."[31] In the plan we also see Babbitt in a more sympathetic light, the light in which his creator seems originally to have portrayed him. Babbitt's "human" qualities were somewhat reduced by Lewis's rejection of this part of the plan, and as he revised the typescript, Lewis continued to streamline the novel in ways that made it primarily satiric—ways that Mencken, for one, applauded when he reviewed *Babbitt*: "no plot whatever, and very little of the hocus-pocus commonly called development of character."[32]

Through July and early August 1921 Lewis was "Babbitt-ing away furiously." Writing the novel, however, was not his only occupation at this time. He had invested a substantial sum in his friend Alfred Harcourt's publishing business, so he was naturally concerned about its success, and he informally acted on behalf of the firm in various ways. As the celebrity author of *Main Street*, Lewis used his expanding contacts with the literary establishment to bring in new authors for Harcourt. For example, he told Harcourt about Evelyn Scott, whose novel *The Narrow House* Harcourt, Brace would bring out later in 1921.[33] At about the same time Lewis recommended publishing some work by Edith Summers Kelley, former secretary to Upton Sinclair and the first wife of Allan Updegraff. Lewis knew her from his days at Upton Sinclair's Utopian colony, Helicon Hall (she and Lewis had supposedly been engaged at one time). He wrote Harcourt:

> It sounds to me as tho she had a novel here, as tho she had grown from the poetic yearnings she had fifteen years ago when I knew her best to real stuff for a good American novel. She knows the Kentucky background of which she speaks; her husband and she farmed there for several years. Why don't you write her expressing willingness to see some ms?[34]

This novel about a family of tenant farmers Harcourt eventually published in 1923 as *Weeds*, a tough-minded, realistic narrative that has enjoyed a modest comeback in recent years. Later that fall in Rome, Lewis tried to persuade Edna St. Vincent Millay to sign a contract with Harcourt, Brace for a future novel, but he later decided that this would be a bad business move, because "she quite definitely plans to make this a novel that would be sure to be suppressed—and she wants enough advance to live on for four months while writing it!"[35] The following year he would enthusiastically endorse the Iowa-born Ruth Suckow, whom Mencken had praised; she later signed with Knopf.[36]

While living in Kent, the Lewises went up to London frequently, and they easily gained entrance to British literary society through Jonathan Cape, who was soon to become Lewis's British publisher. (The firm of Hodder and Stoughton had published the British edition of *Main Street* and had evidently bungled the marketing and promotion of it.) Earlier in his career, Lewis seems to have been wholly enthusiastic about many British authors. During the 1910s he spoke admiringly of Compton Mackenzie, Hugh Walpole, and Arnold Bennett, and his favorite authors had always been Britons. Lewis was welcomed by the British literati in London in 1921—but for reasons that he found patronizing and offensive. His natural garrulity may have made him a curiosity to his hosts instead of a literary equal. Rebecca West, for example, recalled that "his talk was wonderful, but . . . I could think of him only as a great natural force, like the aurora borealis."[37] In *One American,* Lewis's friend Frazier Hunt, a foreign correspondent for the Hearst syndicate (and Lewis's inspiration for the character of Ross Ireland in *Dodsworth*), explained why British writers were so eager to meet Lewis:

> He painted just the sort of picture of the American scene and its crude intolerances that the average Britisher wanted to read. They welcomed him as one of their own kind—superior, a bit snooty, and extremely critical of inferior breeds. But Red fooled them. He saw through their own sham and hypocrisy as easily as he could see through a freshly polished pane of glass. When great and near-great tried to patronize his own American self-criticism they were met by a stinging rebuff. Certainly he was not showing up the weakness and intolerance of his own land for the benefit of Englishmen.[38]

Lewis was unable to secure any authors for Harcourt in London; he wrote Mencken that "meeting the million Bright Young Authors . . . in England has comforted me about the artistic future of America."[39] Ironically, though, it may have been this same hypercritical opinion of America held by Europeans that helped Lewis win the Nobel Prize.

When he wasn't scouting new talent that summer, Lewis was finishing his plans for *Babbitt* and supplementing them with still more research. His eye for detail was sharp. He had Grace ask Harcourt to send him books on house plans, "big and little . . . Georgian, Dutch Colonial, and other suburban kinds," which Lewis needed for the "real estate developments" in the novel, and especially for the many "technical terms" that Babbitt

Figs. 12–13. Map of Zenith's business center with legend (George Arents Research Library, Syracuse University)

KEY TO
ZENITH CENTER
ZEN. BUSINESS CENT
BLOCKS MOST FAMIL-
IAR TO BAB -- 1
Maps.

1- Union Club
2- University Club
3 - Zenith Athletic Club
4- Chamber of Commerce
5- City Auditorium
6- National Guard Armory
7- The Arbor (worst & one of
   oldest pts of city; blind
   pigs /formerly saloons/
   cheap bd houses, houses
   of prostitution, small
   loft & shack factories,
   poor shops, etc.)
8- Newspapers
9-Hotel Thornleigh
10- O'Hearn House
11- Marquise Court
12- Hotel Hatton
13- Leroy Hotel
14- Grand Hotel
15- Smart specialty shops
16- Benson, Hanley & Koch's
    dept store -- the best
17- Parcher & Stein's -- ,
    largest dept store but
    cheapish
18- The Bee Hive, smaller &
    very cheap
19- Movies
20- Dodsworth Theater
21- Cheap lunch rooms and
    cafeterias
22- Babbitt's office
23- The N Nebraska Lunch -
    his fav. cheap restau.
24- The Elks' Clubhouse
25- Office buildings
26- Banks
    26A - First National
    26B - Miners and Drovers
27- California Building
28- Coates Building
29- Plymouth Building
30 - Phys. and Surg. Bldg.
31- Vanderbilt Bldg
32- Whitby Bldg.
33- Reeves (Bldg. — Occidental
34- City Hospital

35- Public Library
36- Art Institute
37- Masonic Temple
38- I.O.O.F. Building
39- Vecchia's - Caterer
40- Gunch's
41- Morecio's
42- London Stationery
43- Drum and Balmer
44- Oscar Ling
45- Teegarten
46- Titus Optical
47- Wengert
48- Yeager, florist
49- City Hall
50 - Central Market
51 - Cent. High School
52 - Stratford Row
(Half timber + plaster, 2 story)
Incl: Hafiz Book Shop
(Lloyd Mallam)
→Interior Decorator
Flotsam Shop
Cherry Bros. Oriental Shop

53 -

Zenith Genl (Hosp
14th to 15th SE
+ Elm to Spruce

AUTOMOBILE ROW is Wash'n Avenue South, 5th to 15th, and
adjoining side streets.

Movement of retail stores is out Conklin Ave.
+ to the East on 1st, + 2nd, 3d 4th S.E. etc.
Gt. residential movement (Bab lucky) to East + N.
- e.g. Crocus Hill, Silver Grove, Dorchester, Tonawanda.
(Dev. wds. exception)

Fig. 13

would use. Lewis also read "pompous pamphlets . . . which big N.Y. advertising agencies get out telling in phrases of pseudo psychology about their magnificent service," mining them for their "high-falutin 'psychology'"—and probably also for their idiom, which he reproduced so accurately in the novel. In addition he consulted realtors' publications, searching out "not only records of mortgages etc. but also real estate gossip and tips."[40] While in England, Lewis customarily worked "all morning and an hour or so in the afternoon," then went for a "walk or drive or swim" with Grace, "all the time talking *Babbitt*." Lewis also drew what Grace called "the most astonishingly complete series of maps of Zenith"—so that the city and its suburbs would all be clear in his mind when he wrote the draft.[41] The maps were discovered in 1961 in the study at Twin Farms, the house where Lewis lived with his second wife, Dorothy Thompson, in Barnard, Vermont. They are now kept among Thompson's papers at the George Arents Research Library of Syracuse University.[42]

These eighteen drawings show the precision with which Lewis imagined his setting, and they indicate how much he enjoyed immersing himself in his fictive worlds. The maps also provide further evidence that *Babbitt* was to be one in a series of related novels. For instance, one map depicts "The State in Which is Zenith," which went unnamed until *Arrowsmith*, where Lewis identified it as Winnemac. This imaginary state borders Illinois, Indiana, Michigan, and Ohio. Winnemac is the setting for most of *Babbitt* and for portions of *Arrowsmith*, *Elmer Gantry*, *Dodsworth*, and *The Man Who Knew Coolidge*. This last book, published in 1928, is a series of monologues delivered by a character named Lowell Schmaltz. Of the detailed drawings of downtown Zenith, one called "Vicinity of Babbitt's Office" shows a shop with the caption, "Lowell Schmaltz Suc[cessor] to Simplex Office Furniture and Rebuilt Typewriter Mart"; Lewis had therefore already projected this character into his imaginary society. A street diagram, "Zenith—Most Important Part," notes where the Babbitts (apparently denoting a class or level of society) live and also shows the site of the Kennepoose Canoe Club, which figures in *Dodsworth*. There are also intricately drawn maps of Floral Heights (the suburb Babbitt lives in) as well as highly detailed floor plans—complete with the placement of furnishings—of Babbitt's house and office.

After this lengthy planning process, Lewis finally began to write "a little of the actual text" of the novel during the first week of August 1921, and he thought it "corking."[43] He worked steadily—and again with astonishing speed—on his draft typescript through the early fall of 1921, then in October left England for Pallanza, Italy. Between leaving England and settling down in Italy he took a two-and-a-half-week "lay-off," which he later thought had been good for his work "not only because of the change but also because I've thought out some good things about it during the period—made those valuable readjustments in the general plan which one doesn't always make if he keeps too close to it for too long."[44] (These "readjustments" included the restructuring of chapter 2.) Lewis had completed seventy thousand words of the typescript and had read over it "minutely" by the time he settled in Pallanza. On 26 October he wrote Harcourt, "It strikes me as the real thing, with a good thick texture."[45] By 5 November Lewis had written an additional twenty-five thousand words "besides . . . doing a little revision on, and making a lot of later-to-be-taken-up suggestions on, the first 70,000 words."[46] Then in January 1922 he left Grace and Wells in Italy and returned to England, this time moving into rooms at an establishment called the Georgian House, in the St. James district of London. Here he worked, alone, and finished the draft by the end of February. Lewis evidently revised the typescript several times during March and April, then typed a clean copy of the revised draft (it totaled approximately 140,000 words) before sailing back to New York with his family on 13 May, completed manuscript in hand.

The "clean" typescript, which was most likely used as setting copy, apparently does not survive. But collation of the draft typescript (at the Beinecke) and the first edition shows that Lewis did most of his revising on the draft, just as he had for *Main Street*. There are only a few sentences that Lewis did *not* revise. Many of the changes, like those on the *Main Street* typescript, are stylistic; with his characteristic meticulousness, Lewis tightened sentences, cut out prolixity, and paid great attention to diction, once again writing lists of three or four words and then circling his final choice.

Most of the major revisions, however, involved the characterization of Babbitt. On one level, Lewis eliminated altogether or reduced the roles of several characters, evidently aiming to focus the novel almost exclusively on Babbitt. For example, in chapter 6 Babbitt was to have had a lengthy conversation with his father-in-law, Henry Thompson, as they drive to see Noel Ryland at the Zeeco Motor Car Company; Thompson tells Babbitt a Horatio Alger version of his own life, which Babbitt listens to with rapt attention (TS 97–98). Babbitt's mother (called "Madame Babbitt") originally attended Babbitt's dinner party in chapter 9.[47] Larger roles were also planned for Howard Littlefield and Sam Dopplebrau, Babbitt's next-door neighbors. Several scenes canceled in the typescript suggest that Lewis intended to use them as counterweights to Babbitt, placing the main character more obviously between the extreme conservatism of Littlefield and the extreme liberalism of Doppelbrau. Most interesting are the cuts

-51-

at two thousand on the ~~mmmmmmmmm~~ assessments. Period. New paragraph.

"You know I never annoy you with crank demands, and of course
I realize you aren't in business for your health -- no, I used that;
just ~~mmmmmmm stick in~~ something like that, Miss McGoun. But feel
I have gone into this matter thoroughly and hope you will trust my
judgment and deal will go through flying. And so on."

~~Then~~ he read and signed ~~that letter, in the afternoon,~~ Babbitt
reflected, "Now that's a good strong ~~live~~ letter, and clear 's a bell.
~~I never told~~ McGoun to ~~put~~ there! Wish ~~she'd~~
~~quit~~ trying to improve on my dictation! But what I can't understand
is: why can't ~~Graves get~~ Stan Graff or Chet Laylock ~~do~~ write a letter
like that? With punch! With a kick!"

~~The last letter Babbitt dictated was the most important. It was~~
the weekly form-letter ~~sent out,~~ mimeographed, to a thousand "pros-
~~xxxhxxxhxxhxhxhxxhxxxfxpxxmxmxxxxhxxhxxxtxxh~~ pects," a message of power
~~and import, a veritable "business-getter" epistle, in the cost style~~
~~of the magazine advertisements of tobacco and of books on the devel-~~
~~opment of the will-power.~~ ~~Babbitt~~ had written out ~~the~~ first draft, and
~~painfully, his coat off, his elbows agitated, his brow sweating, and~~
~~hxxxgxxxhxxxffxxxhxhxxhxhxxxhxxxhxxfxhxxhxxxhxxxhxxxhxxxhxxxhxxy~~ holding out the agitated sheet of yellow backing-paper containing his notes, he intoned
it like ~~an Irish poet~~:
        Say, old man! ~~Pardon my getting fresh but~~ I want to
    know can I do you a favor? Honest! No kidding!
    I know you're interested in getting a house, ~~and~~
    ~~not just~~ a place where you hang up the old bon-
    net but a love-nest for the wife and kiddies --
    and maybe for the flivver, out beyant the spud
    garden! Say, ~~jever~~ think that we're here to save
    you trouble? That's how we make a living -- you
    didn't spose folks paid us just for our manly
    beauty! ~~did juh?~~ Now take a look:

    Sit right down at the handsome carved mahogany
    escritoire ~~like you and I always use~~ and shoot
    us in a line telling us just what you want, and

involving the evangelist Mike Monday (an allusion to Billy Sunday), who appears briefly in chapter 7 (98–100). At this point in the typescript Lewis wrote an additional nine pages on Monday, whom he called "the world's greatest salesman of salvation," a man who has "by efficient organization . . . kept the overhead of spiritual regeneration down to an unprecedented rock-bottom basis" and converted "over two hundred thousand lost and priceless souls at an average cost of less than ten dollars a head" (TS 138). Possibly, Lewis eliminated the Monday passages in anticipation of some-day doing a preacher novel—*Elmer Gantry*—which he had considered be-fore writing *Babbitt*. But it seems clear that in reducing the roles of these and other characters in the typescript, Lewis wanted to focus on Babbitt rather than on a certain set of people within or outside Babbitt's class.

Accordingly, Lewis made many revisions in the depiction of his central character. Herein lies the most interesting shift in his intentions. These changes, like the other evidence that Lewis left behind, show him strug-gling to make Babbitt both a type and a multidimensional character. In a few places he softened the characterization of Babbitt, much as he had done with Carol Kennicott in the draft typescript of *Main Street*. In these revisions, Lewis restrained his tendencies toward harsh criticism of his protagonist. He thus made Babbitt less exaggerated, less of a caricature. But in a far greater number of places, mostly near the end of the typescript draft, Lewis deleted passages (often running to a half-dozen pages or more) in which Babbitt is more of a multidimensional character than he is in the published text. In these excised scenes, he is more realistic, more "human," and Lewis is without question in sympathy with Babbitt.

Evidence of Lewis's softening of Babbitt appears mainly in the early chapters—particularly in the original version of Babbitt's speech to the real estate board, which is harsher in typescript than it is in the published text. In his remarks about the "Ideal Citizen" as a churchgoer, for exam-ple, Babbitt was originally downright contemptuous of men who were not "modest, loyal Christians"; they did not "appreciate the fact that . . . this country [is] a good place to live in and do business in—a land equally free of the insane hell-raising communistic maniacs and of the rotten irre-ligious voluptuaries that burden other lands" (TS p. F). Elsewhere in the speech Babbitt was equally vituperative about the things that threaten America. In having Babbitt discuss literature, for example, Lewis indulged in various private jokes such as this one, in which Babbitt reacts against

> these hopeless literary groupies, these twenty-year-old know-it-alls, that go for one million dull sloppy pages describing every fly in the grocery stores on Main Street, or write about the love-affairs

and maybe ~~kind of cusses~~ cusses out the carburetor, ~~a little~~, and shoots out
home. ~~Then~~ He mows the lawn, or sneaks in ~~a little~~ some practise putting,
and ~~is~~ then he's ready for dinner. After dinner he tells the kiddies a story,
or takes the family to the movies, or plays a few fists of bridge,
or reads the evening paper, and ~~even~~ a chapter or two of some good
lively ~~detective or~~ Western ~~mmmmm~~ novel, if he has a taste for literature, and ~~mmmmmmmmm~~ maybe the folks next door drop in, and they
chin for ~~an hour or two~~ about ~~good old~~ their friends and the happy years
~~of boyhood.~~ — topics of the day. Then he goes happily to bed, his conscience clear, having contributed his honest mite to the prospperity of the city and to ~~the~~
his own bank-account.

"In politics, this Regular Guy is the canniest man on earth. He
stands neither for dukes and kinks ~~nnn~~ nor for a lot of ~~communism and~~
wild theories ~~mmmmmmmmmmmmmmmmmmmmmmmmmmmmmmm~~ and Bolshevism and the closed shop. He believes
in a business administration of the Government that will give a fellow
a chance to pile up a little money and yet not be a hog.

"In religion, even if he doesn't always go to church but maybe
once in a while on a fine Sunday, ~~he~~ does kind of slip off for a little drive,
~~or a little golf, just the same he is a plain,~~ still you can bet he's a modest, loyal Christian, ~~and~~ who supports the church generously, and appreciates the fact that
there's no body of men who are doing more than the preachers to keep
this country a good place to live in and ~~to~~ do business in. ~~— a land~~
~~equally free of the insane hell-raising communistic maniacs and of~~
~~the rotten irreligious voluptuaries that burden other lands.~~

"In the arts, this Sane Citizen, while he is not a highbrow and
he's ~~is~~ too everlastingly clear-headed to fall for pictures that are nothing but a crazy smear of paint, or for a ~~lot of~~ these ~~stories and~~
novels and books that ~~either~~ get in a lot of dirty immorality under
the pretense of beauty, or ~~else have such a grouch on the world~~ that just present the depressing
~~they present the familiar scenes of even our beloved country as noth-~~ side of life, that

of a young socialistic pup, or the sad sorrows of kitchen mechanics, or about a place called "Winesburg" but it ought to be called "Coca-Cola Center"! (TS p. J)

Similarly, Babbitt's dire prophecies about "irresponsible teachers and professors, long-haired pups who work under cover" and concoct "nefarious plots to wreck the Constitution," present him almost as a neurotic crank (TS p. N—A).

But by far the most revisions in the typescript worked in the opposite direction: Lewis deleted much material that made Babbitt a less clownish and a more fully rounded character. These revisions occur mostly in the last third of the novel, when Babbitt rebels. Very few of these passages are stylistically elegant or psychologically precise enough for Lewis to have kept them in the published text. It is clear why he deleted them: he recognized that he was not an acute enough analyst of Babbitt's psychology to make the passages sound convincing. But the passages are significant nonetheless in that they show Lewis trying to invest Babbitt with more self-knowledge than he ultimately has in the finished novel. Just as there is little sense in the published text of what drives Babbitt to rebel, there is equally little sense of how he feels about himself as he does so—or at least there is less sense of this in the published text than there is in the typescript. In many deleted typescript passages, Lewis tried to show Babbitt's thinking as he questioned his identity. In chapter 29, for instance, during the party held by "the Bunch" at Tanis Judique's apartment, Babbitt originally experienced this shock of vision: "To Babbitt came that ancient sorrow of the man who discovers, as man forever is discovering, that in gilded and celebrated vice . . . there is less joy than he had expected. . . . He crept off to the bathroom and drank much too much, and worried about his drinking while he did so, and hated himself rather spiritedly" (TS 277-C [477-C, misnumbered]). In the published text, Babbitt's feelings are not described; he simply goes home, "fully a member of the Bunch" (329). Similarly, Lewis removed two awkwardly written paragraphs from the end of chapter 23 that showed Babbitt alone in his house during his family's absence, "formlessly lonely as he lay on his cot on the sleeping porch, that night, his arms behind his head, the pillow poked and wadded, and he was naively young with the desire to be young" (TS 386).

Frequently Lewis deleted codas at the ends of chapters that he thought were clumsy. At the end of typescript chapter 25, for example, the conclusion of Babbitt's Maine holiday without Paul Riesling, he vows to return to Zenith a new man, "at forty-seven . . . a frontiersman, renowned for his cynical humor, his original philosophy, and his quiet intimidating courage." This is an ideal vision of himself, but as it turns out all Babbitt can think of after he returns is the "scandal and loud murmur in Zenith" over his innocent flirtation with Ida Putiak, the manicurist. This scandal haunts only Babbitt, for it exists exclusively "in the annals of the Babbitt family—for the sole absurd reason that they never happened except in Babbitt's dream that was so much more real [than] drudging reality" (TS 418). Lewis cut this paragraph; it is awkward, to be sure, but it is also more ironic and less hackneyed than its replacement: "Thus it came to him that merely to run away was folly, because he could never run away from himself" (300).

Elsewhere in the typescript Lewis depicted Babbitt as more obviously trying to understand why his "standardized" life no longer satisfies him. At the end of typescript chapter 21, when Babbitt learns that Paul Riesling has shot his wife, Zilla, Lewis appended this sentence, which does not appear in the first edition: "He sat mechanically holding the telephone receiver but hearing nothing; and he who had lived on the surface of life, a thing of shadow victories, purposeless hustlings, and thin desires, began to live below the surface, in a world turbulent, dark, and in its passion beautiful" (TS 359). This sentence foreshadows Babbitt's entry into a subterranean life of halfhearted "bohemianism" and shows us some of the emotions that compel him to do so. It is one of several attempts at a psychological probing of Babbitt's character that Lewis, it seems, could not execute well enough to use in the published text. Some cuts, like this one, were suggested by Grace, who read and commented on the manuscript as Lewis worked on it in Italy. Along the bottom right-hand edge of this page, Grace wrote, "Troppo forte! Molto diminuendo!" and drew a sketch of a figure that is unmistakably Lewis with a pained expression on his face and his fingers pinching his nose. Lewis evidently agreed that the passage was too strong, or "loud," for he canceled it in the typescript.

Some deleted passages seem to have been holdovers from the "plan"; these descriptions of Babbitt growing restless with his life and wanting to escape it are more detailed than those in the published text. In chapter 27, Lewis originally had Babbitt confide his doubts about himself to Myra, in a conversation occasioned by the ongoing labor unrest in Zenith:

> Ever since Paul—since that happened—I've felt a fellow oughtn't to jump at conclusions, and so on—see how I mean?—too soon. I don't—Oh, God, I don't know! I don't feel so cocksure about things as I used to. . . . Maybe I'm getting old. . . . But—Things don't seem as plain as they used to. All kind of black and white, that's how I used to see them. Even morals and that stuff. (TS 445)

~~and the distinguished visitors ------"~~

"George! Paul Riesling ------"

"Yes, sure, I'll phone Paul ~~about it~~ right away."

"Georgie! Listen! Paul is in jail. He shot his wife, he shot Zilla, this noon. She may not live."

~~line blank~~

~~He~~
~~NKWERXMXMM sat, mouth open, mechanically holding the telephone~~
~~and~~
~~receiver but hearing nothing; ~~he who had ~~MXXMXM~~ lived on the surface~~
~~of life, a thing of vague ambitions and purposeless hustlings, of shadow~~
~~victories and thin desires, began to live below the surface in a realm~~
~~turbulent, blind, and~~

~~line blank~~

He sat mechanically holding the telephone receiver but hearing nothing; and he who had lived on the surface of life, a thing of shadow victories, purposeless hustlings, and thin desires, began to live below ~~the surface, in a realm turbulent, dark, and in its passion beautiful.~~

Fig. 16. Detail from *Babbitt* typescript (Yale Collection of American Literature, Beinecke Rare Book and Manuscript Library, Yale University)

Here Babbitt is unable to express himself, to frame his complex motivations in coherent language. That he cannot do so denies him self-knowledge. By contrast, in the published version of the passage Babbitt mildly questions public opinion about the strikers: "They're not such bad people," he says, "Just foolish" (318). Missing are Babbitt's imperfect attempts at introspection and his fears that he may be losing his identity.

In a deleted passage in chapter 19, after Babbitt fires Stanley Graff for unethical behavior, Lewis showed Babbitt's inner humanity at war with his public facade:

> Presently he forgot the horrible hour when he had awakened on the sleeping-porch at four in the morning, furious[ly] admitted Graff's charges, seen himself as a failure, wondered whether it was the Wheels of Progress that he had been propelling, and suddenly blasphemed, "Oh damn all these damn phrases! Damn all this damn boost[er] stuff!! Damn the Wheels of Progress! Damn these High Endeavors!" (TS 323)

This cut was also suggested by Grace; Lewis noted at the bottom of this page, "No says G—Bab growing neurotic as Carol [Kennicott]." Grace then wrote on the page: "Hear, hear; stop at 'as a son, I had much comfort in him,'" and Lewis accordingly deleted the passage at that point in the published text (240). Grace's criticism is probably justified, but the passage shows a Babbitt who is more fully aware of himself—yet woefully inept at articulating his thoughts.

In some of these deleted passages, Lewis tried to describe Babbitt's quest for self-knowledge in prose that was often top-heavy with tropes. In chapter 27, for example, when Vergil Gunch tries to coax Babbitt into explaining why he has seemed melancholy, Lewis originally described Babbitt as "conscious that his voice wasn't hearty enough," because "Fear, looming and gray, sat beside him. For two days he did not go to the club, but ate alone at a lunch-room on Washington Avenue; and Fear, vague, inexplicable, gray, and looming, lunched with him" (TS 444). In the published text, the conversation between the two friends does not take place, and when Babbitt sees Gunch from across the street, Babbitt simply drives off (318). And in other passages not included in the published novel we see Babbitt's desire to be young warring with his realization that he is essentially a Babbitt. One such passage occurs near the end of this same chapter, when Babbitt's fears about being rejected by the "Clan of Good Fellows" increase and word begins to spread of his affair with Tanis Judique. In the published version, the chapter ends with a matter-of-fact example of

Babbitt's worries: "Could the fellows think I've gone nutty just because I'm broad-minded and liberal? Way Verg looked at me—" (319). In the typescript there follows a canceled passage in which the fairy-girl of Babbitt's dreams in chapters 1 and 7 reappears: "He forgot Tanis Judique, at the magic second when her image had almost merged with that of the fairy girl; he was restlessly and sharply awake, and in the night, behind the faintly seen elm, Fear sat silently watching" (TS 447). Here, Lewis makes concrete the suggestion that in pursuing Tanis, Babbitt is pursuing the concept of a woman, or of some form of escape, that he has been chasing for many nights of his life.

However imperfect these deleted passages are, they reveal that by the late stages of the composition of *Babbitt,* Lewis had come around to thinking of his protagonist less as the figure that Mencken called the "Booboisie" and more as a multidimensional, human character. In cutting such material, Lewis reduced Babbitt's essential humanity—as he seems also to have done by rejecting the surviving portions of the plan. This is not to say that the Babbitt of the published novel has no intelligence or understanding of himself. He seems to have more self-knowledge than Carol Kennicott does in *Main Street*—but not as much as was required for Lewis to reply satisfactorily to those reviewers of *Main Street* who had said that he could not draw character precisely or deeply enough to be considered an artist of the first rank.

Today this same critical opinion of Lewis persists. Even in a promotional pamphlet on Lewis commissioned by Harcourt, Brace and issued just after *Babbitt* was published, Stuart Pratt Sherman had to admit that the novel would have been better if Lewis had found some means (possibly through the other characters) of making Babbitt "more genuine" and "more inward," of imbuing him with some "social and personal felicity."[48] More recently, Frederick J. Hoffman concluded unsympathetically that "the crucial fact about *Babbitt* is that it is . . . two types of literary exposition poorly combined in one work": there is a "limited" presentation of "a sensitive, humane Babbitt" whose validity is canceled by "the parody Babbitt," whom Lewis was unable to humanize.[49] Throughout the planning and composition of the novel Lewis was aware of this dual focus, for he repeatedly mentioned it to others. He told Harcourt that he had tried to make Babbitt human and not a type, but at the same time he wanted the character to "completely sum up certain things in all contemporary Babbitts."[50] On another occasion he wrote Harcourt, "I want utterly to develop [Babbitt] so that he will seem not just typical but an individual."[51] He even confided to Mencken that he did not want Babbitt to be "merely burlesque . . . I've tried to make him human and individual, not a type."[52]

As both the plan and the typescript indicate, Lewis tried to create a character with more of a capacity for meaningful rebellion and change than we see in the published text, but he could not do so successfully.

Why did Lewis have such difficulty presenting Babbitt in this more sympathetic light? There are several reasons. One is that Lewis was unable to find a suitable authorial voice with which to express Babbitt's feelings. In several of these deleted typescript passages, we see Lewis trying to find a satisfactory way of signaling to the reader that he sympathized with Babbitt—as he had done successfully in *Main Street*, sparing Carol Kennicott from most of his satire. In writing *Babbitt*, Lewis attempted to fashion an authorial voice that would express understanding toward Babbitt without being clumsy or hackneyed, or without going to the opposite extreme and presenting a neurotic (as Grace observed) or overly romanticized Babbitt (as the diction in the deleted passages, with its somewhat belabored tropes, suggests). Lewis was able to create such a persona in *Main Street*, but not in *Babbitt*. Thus the only voice left to him was an ironic one—the characteristic voice of the satirist.

By the same token, Lewis was concerned that Babbitt not seem too much of a romanticized figure. In an early letter to Harcourt, Lewis wrote, "I want the novel to be the G. A. N. [great American novel] in so far as it crystallizes and makes real the Average Capable American. No one has done it . . . no one has even *touched* it except Booth Tarkington in *Turmoil* and *Magnificent Ambersons;* and he romanticizes away all bigness." Lewis may therefore have cut these typescript passages because he feared losing the satiric edge to his novel and presenting a Babbitt who embodied neither of the two qualities that Lewis tried to hold in equipoise—the human Babbitt and the clownish Babbitt—but who was merely a romantic dreamer, like Carol Kennicott, without any of the "bigness" that Lewis wanted him to have. "Babbitt is a little like Will Kennicott," Lewis told Harcourt, "but bigger, with a bigger field to work on, more sensations, more perceptions. . . . Yet, utterly unlike Carol, it never even occurs to him that he might live in Europe, might like poetry, might be a senator; he is content to live and work in the city of Zenith. . . . But he would like for once the flare of romantic love, the satisfaction of having left a mark on the city."[53]

A final reason for the lack of dimension in Babbitt may be that no one encouraged Lewis to make the character more than a satiric type. Lewis wanted the approval of certain people, and he trusted and depended on their advice. These persons were Mencken, Harcourt, and Grace, and none of them was the type of person who would have pushed Lewis to explore Babbitt more meaningfully. Certainly not Mencken: he advocated a prose literature that captured mostly the surfaces of American life. Mencken had no great regard for authors who wrote in a psychoanalytic vein or who experimented with form. In fact, he seriously undervalued several who did so, such as Hemingway and Fitzgerald. Similarly, Mencken would underrate later novels by Lewis that were essentially non-satiric, such as *Arrowsmith* and *Dodsworth,* and effusively praise those that were predominantly satiric, such as *Elmer Gantry* and *The Man Who Knew Coolidge.* (Lewis originally wrote the latter book at Mencken's behest, as a short story for the *American Mercury.*) Mencken's influence on Lewis during the composition of *Babbitt* is clear: the character of Babbitt is predominantly an example of Mencken's *boobus Americanus,* as many reviewers at the time noted. As Mencken's review of *Babbitt* indicates, he liked the novel primarily because it was "fiction only by a sort of courtesy": "All the usual fittings of the prose fable seem to be absent. There is no plot whatever, and very little of the hocus-pocus commonly called development of character. Babbitt simply grows two years older as the tale unfolds; otherwise he doesn't change at all. . . . Every customary device of the novelist is absent."[54]

Similarly, Alfred Harcourt did not push Lewis to develop Babbitt more deeply than he did. Harcourt apparently made only one major suggestion—where to place Babbitt's speech to the Zenith Real Estate Board—indicating that Harcourt thought of Lewis primarily as a satirist. Indeed, he thought that particular section was so comical that Lewis should not "give away so much of [his] point of view" at the beginning of the novel; some of the funniest bits should be saved for later chapters. Harcourt was also understandably commercial-minded, and his instincts were good: he had had an unexpected windfall with *Main Street,* so he was interested in a repeat performance with *Babbitt.*

Grace seems to have had the most significant influence on how Lewis portrayed Babbitt, judging from the comments she wrote in the margins of the typescript. Lewis trusted Grace's judgment, and she was the only person actually in Lewis's company during the creation of the novel—an important point, because Lewis needed to have a sounding board, someone on whom to try out his material as he wrote and revised. As we will see in subsequent chapters, the type of person who served Lewis in that capacity was a crucial factor in how a novel turned out.

What type of person was Grace? She was a fairly conventional woman who had been educated at a convent school. She saw herself as refined and cultured; in her memoir, she confessed her distaste for "arty, sophomoric little magazines" and the bohemian lifestyle of Greenwich Village, where Lewis was living when he met her.[55] She also commented that Lewis "was grateful always for my professional experience with manuscripts, my knowledge of printer's signs and jargon, my instinctive good literary taste."[56] In truth, however, Grace had only a little "professional experience with manuscripts," and the type of copy that she edited at *Vogue* could hardly be compared with what Lewis was writing. It is also apparent that Grace was drawn to the sentimental, escapist romances of the day. She seems not to have liked literature that attempted to lay bare motivation, experiment with point of view, or probe the subconscious mind. Grace was not the sort of person who would push Lewis to explore the psychological dimensions of his characters. The revisions that she suggested indicate that she actually discouraged him from doing so.

The judgment of these three people was for the most part sound: Lewis was at heart a satirist, and that was the type of writing that he did best. As we will see in the next chapter, however, Lewis was able to employ his mimetic abilities and write effective nonsatiric material in *Arrowsmith*—a novel that does explore character rather deeply—because he had the right sort of individual close at hand during the compositional process whom he could "absorb" and who could provide the stimulation that he needed to do that sort of writing. During the composition of *Babbitt*, Lewis had no contact with such a person.

Before Lewis left London on 13 May 1922, he attended to a number of details regarding the publication of *Babbitt*. Lewis gave Harcourt a list of "hints" for the artist commissioned to design the dust jacket, and he also asked that the binding of *Babbitt* match that of *Main Street*. He was thinking of his career over the long run, confident that he would write many more important novels: "We'll try to begin to make lines of books, all in that blue and orange, across library shelves," he said. "I know I like to have all my Conrads in the same binding."[57] On 19 May the Lewises arrived in New York on the *Aquitania*. After he delivered the manuscript to Harcourt (who seems not to have asked for any major revisions), Lewis spent some time with Grace in New York City, then bought a car and drove by himself to Sauk Centre to see his father and stepmother. Lewis spent much of that summer in the Midwest doing research for his next novel, which at the time he intended to be about a labor leader. (He was to abandon that idea and instead write *Arrowsmith*.) In late August, he rejoined his family in Hartford, Connecticut, where he proofread *Babbitt*.

During the summer Harcourt negotiated successfully with Jonathan Cape to bring out a British edition of *Babbitt*. *Main Street* had been published in England by Hodder and Stoughton, and although that novel had enjoyed fairly strong sales in Great Britain, both Harcourt and Lewis were dissatisfied with that publisher's advertising and marketing. In March 1921 Harcourt had therefore contracted for a new edition of *Main Street* with Jonathan Cape, a young publisher who was similar to Harcourt in his literary tastes and aggressive business tactics. Harcourt was pleased with Cape's promotion of *Main Street,* so he accepted Cape's proposal for a British edition of *Babbitt.* He explained to Lewis that Cape was not paying as much for *Babbitt* "as some of the older houses, but like ourselves, he doesn't let a book just drop into the hopper, and in the long run he [will] sell more . . . than anyone else."[58]

The British edition of *Babbitt* was in fact a commercial success but also something of a bibliographic curiosity. Cape had the novelist Hugh Walpole write a foreword to the book, and in the rear of the volume Cape printed a glossary listing 126 American expressions and their approximate British equivalents. Lewis agreed to both of these ideas but was not enthusiastic about either of them. He thought the idea of an introduction was fine, but he wanted it to be written by someone of higher critical repute than Walpole. He suggested H. G. Wells, John Galsworthy, May Sinclair, or Somerset Maugham instead.[59] Lewis's reservations about Walpole proved to be justified. In the introduction, Walpole hailed the novel as a masterful indictment of "modern American business life" but also imprudently suggested that the average British reader would find Lewis's "extensive detail" difficult to "penetrate." At various places in the introduction, Walpole also characterized the language of the novel as "strange," "obscure," and "complicated." (Walpole's introduction is reprinted in appendix 4.)

In addition, the glossary that Cape printed was a travesty. Someone in Cape's office (or perhaps Cape himself) butchered American slang, making any transatlantic difficulties with idioms much worse than they could possibly have been without translation. (A "hoodlum" is defined as a "crank," for example.)[60] It is unlikely that Lewis saw the British proofs, for he would surely have objected to this and other liberties that Cape took in the text by having Babbitt say "petrol" instead of "gas," "let" instead of "rent," or "two-penny car" instead of "flivver." These changes fundamentally altered the American flavor of the novel. Therefore, British readers did not get a very accurate index to Lewis's talents as an observer of the American scene. The American edition of the novel was not vetted much more carefully than the British edition; the typesetting and proofing were both done quickly—advance copies were ready by 22 July—and there were about one hundred inconsistencies and printer's errors in the text, many of which have never been corrected.[61]

On 14 September *Babbitt* was published in an enormous first printing of

80,500 copies, which quickly sold out. Sales rapidly climbed past 100,000. The reviews, both in America and in England, were favorable. Mencken was so pleased with the acid satire of the novel that he put a gaudy caricature of Lewis on the cover of the September *Smart Set*. It depicted him with a monocle in his eye and a cigarette hanging from his lips. Mencken's review in that issue, entitled "Portrait of an American Citizen," was highly complimentary, especially of Lewis's talents as a satirist. Mencken announced that he knew of no other American novel "that more accurately presents the real America" and said that Babbitt "simply drips with human juices."[62] In the *New York Times*, May Sinclair stated that in Lewis's hands, "Babbitt becomes stupendous and significant." Similarly, Burton Rascoe and Owen Johnson in separate reviews in the *New York Tribune*, John Farrar in *Bookman*, and Upton Sinclair in *Appeal to Reason* all declared that *Babbitt* was a better book than *Main Street*. English reviewers concurred. In her review of the novel for the *Statesman*, Rebecca West said of Babbitt's speech to the real estate board:

> It is a bonehead Walt Whitman speaking. Stuffed like a Christmas goose as Babbitt is, with silly films, silly newspapers, silly talk, silly oratory, there has yet struck him the majestic creativeness of his own country, its miraculous power to bear and nourish without end countless multitudes of men and women. . . . There is in these people a vitality so intense that it must eventually bolt with them and land them willy-nilly into the sphere of intelligence; and this immense commercial machine will become the instrument of their aspirations.[63]

The reviewer for the *Times Literary Supplement* was also impressed with *Babbitt*, stating that Lewis's attack on convention was not limited to America but was applicable to the lives of English readers as well.

Most of the reviews were favorable, but a great many critics pointed out that the deficiencies observable in *Main Street* persisted in *Babbitt* and that Lewis therefore had not yet developed in the manner that had been expected of him in 1920. Ludwig Lewisohn, for example, while praising *Babbitt* highly, nevertheless suggested that beneath the ironic surface of the novel Lewis failed to analyze the causes of Babbitt's desperation. In other generally favorable reviews, it was likewise noted that although *Babbitt* was a brilliant satire of the American middle class, Lewis lacked pity for his characters and offered no solutions.[64] Ernest Boyd pointed out that the "vitality" that Rebecca West had admired was either misplaced or aimless:

there were no standards in evidence, no notion of what Lewis expected of modern man.[65]

Several critics also observed that although the unappealing picture of the American small town that Lewis had painted in *Main Street* was tempered by moderate optimism and some faith in Carol Kennicott, this optimism had nearly vanished in *Babbitt*. The narrative pattern of the two novels was the same—the individual trapped in an ugly environment, desiring something more fulfilling and struggling to find it. However, where Carol at least partly succeeds, Babbitt mostly fails. Reviewers treated as a satiric norm the way that Lewis presented Carol: through her perceptions, he highlighted the unpleasant and comic aspects of Gopher Prairie. In fact, Edith Wharton (to whom Lewis dedicated *Babbitt*,) pointed out to him that in *Main Street* he had produced "a sense of unity & of depth by reflecting Main Street in the consciousness of a woman who suffered from it because she had points of comparison, & was detached enough to situate it in the universe." By contrast, Wharton said, George Babbitt was "in and of Zenith up to his chin & over, and Sinclair Lewis is obliged to do the seeing & comparing for him."[66] Thus many critics now said that Lewis's satire was too destructive. The novelist Sherwood Anderson, for example, complained that in *Babbitt* Lewis depicted only the "dreary spiritual death" of America and ignored its beauty. In the *New Republic*, Robert Littell likewise took Lewis to task for destroying society instead of offering constructive suggestions for its reform. He said that Lewis could not give a "rounded picture" of American life and could only dwell on its ugly aspects.[67] Several critics saw in Babbitt only the exemplification of Mencken's "Booboisie" and therefore lamented the fact that there was no "spiritual significance" to the novel, only grossness and vulgarity.

Whatever the aesthetic deficiencies of *Babbitt*, the novel sold in record numbers, just as *Main Street* had. By the end of 1922, sales of *Babbitt* in the United States numbered 140,997, netting Lewis $37,397.80 in royalties.[68] The word "Babbitt" quickly entered the vernacular, and the character himself soon moved into the ranks of archetypes. In 1922 a poem called "Babbitt Jamboree," by Vachel Lindsay, appeared in the periodical *Pan, Poetry, and Youth*. In 1926 a British writer, C.E.M. Joad, published a sociological study of Americans entitled *The Babbitt Warren*. And Mencken, of course, broadly appropriated the term "Babbittry" and used it frequently in his writings. Like *Main Street*, *Babbitt* became material for newspaper editorials and columns all over the country. Most of them— such as those in the *New York Times*—approved of Lewis's satire of the businessman and his milieu, but there were also a significant number of critics who denounced the book as "yellow": Edwin F. Edgett of the *Bos-*

ton Transcript, who had admired *Main Street,* thought that in *Babbitt* Lewis had maliciously ridiculed the businessman.

Babbitt remained a controversial, much-debated novel throughout the 1920s. The arguments for and against the validity of Lewis's judgments were kept alive, with much enthusiasm, in the pages of such periodicals as *Nation's Business* and *Rotarian* through 1929, and the debate also appeared in larger forums such as *Harper's, Scribner's,* and *Collier's.*[69] The book was the subject of sermons and lectures throughout the country, especially in the "service" clubs. At a meeting of the Cleveland Kiwanis Club, the subject of an after-dinner speech was "Babbitt, a Challenge to Men."

His fame as a public figure notwithstanding, Lewis knew that *Babbitt,* like *Main Street* before it, had been praised largely on social instead of artistic grounds. More than ever, he was now determined to demonstrate to his critics that he could write nonsatiric material—that he could perceive not only hollowness in modern man, but genuine integrity as well. Therefore, when he needed to choose a topic for his next novel, he looked for one that would be suitably idealistic. He told Alfred Harcourt that this next book would be "not satiric at all—rebellious as ever, perhaps, but the central character *heroic.*"

3

Arrowsmith

1922–1925

By the late summer of 1922 Lewis had established himself as a successful novelist and had ample reason to believe that he was poised on the brink of a remarkable literary career. He had secured a foothold in American literature by writing *Main Street* and *Babbitt* and had now definitely broken free of what Mencken called "the hulks" of magazine fiction. *Main Street* had almost won the Pulitzer Prize;¹ rumors were circulating about Lewis as a candidate for the Nobel Prize. Yet as he thought about his next novel, Lewis recognized that to win unanimous critical acclaim he would have to silence those reviewers who had said he was "without spiritual gifts." Similarly, he had to answer those who had asked him to write a novel in which his own standards would be sufficiently in evidence.

This breakthrough novel would be *Arrowsmith*. In 1922, however, Lewis was thinking of writing a novel about the labor movement in America featuring a Christlike central character modeled on Eugene Debs, the socialist candidate for president who had been imprisoned in 1918 for advocating pacifism. But Lewis never wrote this novel. For the next twenty-five years, in fact, Lewis talked about writing it, thought of various plots for it, and made at least seven serious attempts at planning it, but he never produced a draft. Lewis's greatest literary aspirations rode on this phantom project, and his ambitions to write the book were widely known—especially during the 1920s, when he was so visible a public figure. Any news of work on his much-touted labor novel spread quickly through the literary community. In 1952, one year after Lewis's death, the poet Ramon Guthrie claimed that the birth of the labor novel took place in 1927 (when Lewis asked him for assistance with the project); but that was actually the third time Lewis had either planned or done research for the book.[2]

There is evidence that Lewis first began planning the novel between 1920 and 1921, at the same time he was sketching out *Babbitt*. Portions of the *Babbitt* notebook indicate that the labor novel was to be part of Lewis's projected series of interrelated novels set in and around Zenith. Much of the "CHARACTERS" section of the notebook is devoted to Seneca Doane (also called Seneca Chaffee), the radical labor lawyer.[3] These and other notes on the character indicate that Lewis meant to follow up *Babbitt* with a novel about Doane, an anti-Babbitt and a member of the class of people Lewis called "great souls." He clearly had Debs in mind as his model. On one page of the notebook, Lewis identifies Doane as "a home-grown Eugene Debs" and a "Christ-like" figure. While he was writing *Babbitt*, Lewis spoke of Debs frequently, at one point instructing Harcourt to send the imprisoned Debs a copy of *Main Street* and on another occasion requesting from Harcourt copies of David Karstner's *Life of Debs* and Mary Beard's *Short History of the American Labor Movement* (both Harcourt, Brace titles).[4] Lewis would later meet Debs and interview him.

In the Babbitt notebook, Lewis planned out much of the "Doane—Labor" novel, creating many of the characters and outlining some of the plot. In the "CHARACTERS" section, Lewis marked some twenty-six names with an x in blue pencil and the notation, "imp[ortant] for Doane," and throughout the notebook there are scattered notations to "save for Doane" or "hold for Doane." Another list of names, "MEMBERS OF BOOSTERS CLUB," contains thirty-five characters, only a handful of whom appear in *Babbitt;* the notation "ALL x in Doane" appears in the upper right-hand corner of the page. The most significant of these characters are Mr. and Mrs. Putnam Dodsworth, who later became Sam and Fran Dodsworth, the protagonists of Lewis's twelfth published novel. One notation reads: "Mrs.

Putnam Dodsworth— Probably does not enter Bab much; but scene at Child Welfare Ass'n in 'Doane.' Was a popular deb." Elsewhere, Mrs. Dodsworth leads a rally supporting an unnamed organization with which Doane is connected. On two other pages Lewis worked out a separate genealogy for these characters he called "Great Souls"—"or at least good ones; scarce entering into life, and book, of Babbitt, who, when he encounters them, is puzzled; who speaks ill of them; who does not know how lively and fine a social group most of them constitute. They enter more into the life, and book, of Doane."

Lewis seems to have decided later that these characters were not appropriate for a novel about the labor movement. He probably realized that the world of labor unions was not a part of the Zenith he had created. That world was largely middle-class; union disputes and uprisings by the great unwashed were merely annoyances to the Babbitts and Howard Littlefields and Chum Frinks of this microcosmic universe. Lewis did not give up the labor project, but simply rejected the idea of setting it in Zenith and having Doane as its protagonist. He later followed through on his plan to write about an "anti-Babbitt," and this novel became *Dodsworth*.

The second incarnation of the labor novel came in August 1922, while Lewis was awaiting the fall publication of *Babbitt*. Lewis went to Chicago to do research on the labor movement and to meet Debs, whose sentence had been commuted by President Harding. Lewis was instantly fascinated with Debs. In a letter to Grace he said:

> Gene really is a Christ spirit. He is infinitely wise, kind, forgiving—yet the devil of a fighter. His face is not, like most faces, of wrinkled and drooping flesh; it is molded of bronze by the powerful hands of a great & sure sculptor. And his hands—after 50 years of leading causes—live by themselves. They draw you in, they pound home, they cajole, they threaten.[5]

Lewis sketched out for Debs his plan for a novel to be entitled "Neighbor." It was to contain "something of [Debs] himself—tho vastly different in details." Lewis had found the hero for his novel: Debs told him of his work as a railway fireman, a grocery clerk, a union secretary, and "of great adventurous days of railroad organizing when he was followed, day & night, by pug-ugly detectives; of a thousand things." Lewis was entranced by Debs, in whose description of his youth ("he was an awkward, odd boy who never could swim or dance & who read Voltaire & the encyclopedia") Lewis probably saw something of himself; he enthusiastically announced to Grace that Debs would "do anything he can to help me—anything. . . . He is so gentle, that lifetime fighter!" This was on 26 August. What happened next is baffling. Three days later Lewis had completely given up the idea of writing the "Debs—Labor" novel and was instead planning in minute detail another novel, *Arrowsmith*. Lewis had been "reading labor papers" and "hanging round" union headquarters in Chicago, gathering data just as he had done for *Babbitt*. The day after he outlined the "Neighbor" plot to Debs, Lewis visited the office of the associate editor of the *Journal of the American Medical Association*, Dr. Morris Fishbein, whom he had befriended earlier. Fishbein introduced Lewis to Dr. Paul De Kruif, a young bacteriologist who had been fired recently from the Rockefeller Institute in New York City for writing a book entitled *Our Medicine Men*. The book mocked the lofty ambitions of some Rockefeller scientists who were supposedly experimenting with a new type of serum. Lewis seems to have been as taken with De Kruif as he had been with Debs. The two men stayed up much of that night, talking about how difficult it was for a young man in America to devote himself to purely scientific research and repudiate ordinary success.

The next day, 29 August, Lewis wrote to Grace that he felt "melancholy" and "rather lost." "I shall not be able to do the Neighbor novel," he said, "that is—do it right":

> For an hour or a day I can work up a complete conformist sympathy with the union men; then the sight of a group of lolling & ignorant rough necks, addressed by an agitator who is going immediately to supplant the capitalists—& who couldn't run a fruit stand—gets my goat & I compare him with doctors, bankers, editors we know. A Debs lasts; he is pure spirit; he would walk to his crucifixion with firm & quiet joy. But there's so few Debses!

Actually Lewis could not even admire Debs without some reservations. In this same letter to Grace, Lewis commented on the surprising lack of judgment he thought Debs had shown by admitting himself to the Lindlahr sanitarium outside Chicago, where Lewis went to visit him a second time. Lewis was shocked by "the kind of credulity which permits a Debs to fall for" such a system "with its hysteric food, its chiropractic, its phony 'electronic' treatments."[6] Eventually Lewis's interest in these fraudulent medical practices led him away from labor unions and into the world of science and *Arrowsmith*. (Lewis's impressions of the Lindlahr sanitarium can be seen in the descriptions of the Rouncefield Clinic in that novel.)

In attempting this particular project, Lewis was exploring what was for him uncharted fictional territory. The world of labor unions could not be depicted in the same manner in which he had written about the midwestern village and city. What Lewis did not foresee—at this point or at any of the other times he tried to write the labor novel—was that he could not treat any subject without viewing it at least partly through the colored lens of the satirist. And, too, Lewis's creative method of immersing himself in a certain environment and recording its surface details—the method that produced *Main Street* and *Babbitt*—did not work for the labor novel because he was so unfamiliar with this particular world. If Lewis had had someone to help him understand the motivations and feelings of the people whom he observed in the labor unions, he might have been able to push forward and start the novel. But without someone to guide him through unfamiliar terrain, he was lost.

When Lewis met Paul De Kruif, he was quite literally an author in search of a character. He was looking for a heroic person on whom to base a narrative, and he found one in the young doctor. Lewis saw that Debs was the real thing, but Lewis could not understand Debs's blue-collar constituency. De Kruif was different—every bit as admirable and courageous as Debs but associated with a higher social class and a more reputable and idealistic calling, that of medical research. Lewis obviously felt more comfortable with this class of people and more confident of being able to portray them in his fiction. His mimetic talents worked perfectly in this particular environment, because Lewis felt at home in it.

At age thirty-two, Paul De Kruif was a rising star in the scientific world, having studied microbiology under the most distinguished figures in the field. After a brief service in the Army Sanitary Corps during the First World War, De Kruif was hired by the prestigious Rockefeller Institute. There, he did research with Jacques Loeb, the high priest of the mechanist doctrine in science, which held that all living things were essentially chemical machines and that behavior could therefore be determined genetically—a theory that anticipated the discovery of DNA.[7] However, De Kruif soon became disenchanted with the Rockefeller Institute as he discovered the prevalence of commercialism in modern medicine and discerned an indifference to the practical applications of experimental biology.

For some years, De Kruif had had literary ambitions: in his autobiography, *The Sweeping Wind* (1962), he mentions working intermittently on an unfinished novel in 1920 and 1921.[8] He also discusses "getting a toehold in the literary world" through the help of Mencken, George Jean Nathan, Francis Hackett, and Harold Stearns. In fact, De Kruif had anonymously contributed the chapter entitled "Medicine" to Stearns's omnibus of social criticism, *Civilization in the United States,* published in 1922. In it, De Kruif satirized the research scientists with whom he worked at the Rockefeller Institute. When, soon thereafter, the *Century Illustrated Monthly* commissioned De Kruif to write a series of four articles exposing the medical establishment, he at once accepted, again drawing liberally on his experiences at the Rockefeller Institute. These were published from January through April 1922 under the running title "Our Medicine Men / By One of Them." The editors of the *Century* had promised anonymity to De Kruif, but someone at the magazine inserted the byline "K——, M.D." at the end of the first article (De Kruif was actually a Ph.D.). De Kruif had not read the page proofs when they were sent to him, so he did not know about the existence of the byline until the first issue appeared on newsstands.

This incident reveals much about De Kruif's personality and suggests why Lewis was drawn to him. In his memoir, De Kruif suggested that he may have subconsciously desired that his authorship of the essays be revealed. He had deliberately ignored the proofs, and he hinted to his colleagues that he had been writing these articles, wondering if they would "tattle on me to the big men who were victims of my satire." De Kruif even wondered if "in a moment of bravado" he had actually "planted this news deliberately to reach the big men's ears." "It was my streak of mischief," he said.[9] The head of the Rockefeller Institute, Dr. Simon Flexner, learned that De Kruif was rumored to have written the articles. When Flexner confronted him, De Kruif admitted that he was the pseudonymous "K" and then resigned. De Kruif was very much like Lewis: flamboyant, tenacious, practically spoiling for a fight, but also hardworking and serious-minded.

When the two men met in Chicago that summer, they became friends almost instantly. Just as quickly, De Kruif agreed to assist Lewis in writing a novel about medicine. *Arrowsmith* is a morality tale about a young research scientist who seeks a means of personal and professional fulfillment without compromising his integrity. After graduating from medical school, Martin Arrowsmith practices as a country doctor and works for awhile in the office of a public health official, then secures a research position on the staff of the prestigious McGurk Institute in New York City. While there, he discovers an antitoxin for a plague that is ravaging the islands of the West Indies. When he goes to one island to test his serum, he refuses to follow the principles of scientific method and inoculates everyone who has contracted the virus. He gives up his job at the McGurk Institute and withdraws to the Vermont woods, where he sets up a makeshift laboratory with a fellow scientist. There he searches for truth, free from the constraints of society. This novel answered Lewis's critics, for it presented a hero of whom Lewis approved—an idealistic truth-seeker who transcended the environments that defeated the chief characters in *Main Street* and *Babbitt. Arrowsmith* has remained among the most praised of Lewis's novels, in large part because its satiric components—the one-dimensional characters and the indictments of twentieth-century culture that Lewis is known for—are outweighed by its sobering, pervasive idealism and its portrait of a character of some complexity and depth.

Lewis was able to make this significant shift in technique and point of view only with the help of Paul De Kruif, who was by Lewis's side at virtually every stage of the composition of the novel and most closely during a nine-week research trip that the two men took to the West Indies. Today, De Kruif's role in the making of *Arrowsmith* is virtually forgotten, although De Kruif went on to a distinguished literary career of his own as a popularizer of science history. He wrote thirteen best-sellers that dramatized the scientific detective work of such pioneers of microbiology as Ehrlich, Leeuwenhoek, and Pasteur. Those who do know that De Kruif assisted Lewis tend to think that his role was limited to providing the scientific detail for the novel—that De Kruif was merely a technical informant.[10] I believe, in contrast, that De Kruif's role was much more significant than that, and that his presence during the creative process largely accounts for Lewis's ability to write a heroic novel. The surviving notes and drafts for *Arrowsmith* (preserved at the Beinecke and at Austin) as well as De Kruif's own testimony in his autobiography and his correspondence with Grace Lewis all affirm that De Kruif was more than a research assistant for Lewis. From his various experiences De Kruif supplied many of the prototypes on whom Lewis based his characters; from De Kruif's life Lewis drew much of the plot involving Arrowsmith's career; and from De Kruif's personal philosophy Lewis extracted the basis for Arrowsmith's idealism.

In December 1922 Lewis and De Kruif met in New York at the Harcourt, Brace offices to finalize their plans.[11] A formal contract was drawn up: Lewis and De Kruif were to share top billing in a full collaboration, with 75 percent of the royalties going to Lewis and 25 percent to De Kruif. However, Harcourt decided that De Kruif's name should not go on the title page with Lewis's for fear that, as De Kruif recalled, "If the critics and the book buyers see Lewis and De Kruif on the cover, they'll say Lewis is finished. He's hiring an unknown to help write his book for him."[12] De Kruif, knowing little about the vagaries of the publishing business, acceded to Harcourt's wishes. After the novel was finished, De Kruif's friendship with Lewis cooled because of a quarrel over how De Kruif's assistance would be acknowledged.

On 6 January 1923 the two men left for an extended tour of the West Indies to gather material for the climax of the novel, the plague on St. Hubert that forces Arrowsmith to test his scientific scruples against his medical ethics and to resist inoculating the whole population with his serum in order to maintain a control group. Lewis did gather a lot of material for the novel on this trip, but he also undertook the voyage with De Kruif for personal reasons: he and Grace were having marital difficulties, and Lewis was running away from them. In fact, in *Arrowsmith* Lewis would dramatize several of his criticisms of Grace.

Schorer says that stories had begun to accumulate about the precarious state of the Lewises' marriage as early as 1920, when Lewis was finishing *Main Street*. From the start, Lewis and Grace had been an unlikely match, and at approximately the time that Lewis became a celebrity with the publication of *Main Street* Grace's pretentiousness became intolerable to him. Those qualities that Lewis had initially found desirable in her—her willingness to educate him in the social arts, for example—now were seen as methods by which she sought to control him. Virtually everyone who knew Grace commented on her snobbishness. Mencken said she led Lewis "a rough dance," exacerbating Lewis's inferiority complex by making him feel socially and sexually inadequate. In *My Life as Author and Editor*, Mencken wrote:

> After *Main Street* and *Babbitt* made her husband a celebrity, she began to put on airs, and before long had converted herself into a fake English duchess, with a broad Oxford accent and a very haughty way with poor Red. . . . He lived in wonder that so ravishing and brilliant a female had ever condescended to marry him. She was, in fact, a good-looking and well-turned-out woman, but I could never discover any evidence that she was of superior mentality. On the contrary, she was vain and shallow.[13]

Grace revealed her own pseudo-sophistication and frivolity in her memoir, saying for example that she chose a French maid because it pleased her to give orders in French in front of guests. Elsewhere, she describes a photograph of herself and Wells in formal riding dress with the comment that "riding in the Bois when the chestnuts [were] in bloom" was "a dream of years achieved."[14]

Lewis had probably been laughing at Grace's self-importance in those parts of *Main Street* where he lightly pokes fun at Carol's superior airs with the women of Gopher Prairie. Eventually, however, Lewis grew tired of Grace's artificiality, and he began to treat the subject of marriage negatively in his fiction. In *Arrowsmith*, we see Lewis's animosity toward Grace in the unflattering portraits of Madeline Fox, to whom Arrowsmith is for a time engaged to be married, and Joyce Lanyon, the society woman who becomes his second wife. Both women are spoiled, self-fashioned sophisticates whose need for attention keeps Arrowsmith from his work. Arrowsmith's courtship of Madeline Fox, for example, parallels Lewis's courtship of Grace: Arrowsmith must undergo interrogation during tea with Madeline's genteel, widowed mother, with whom she lives in a small apartment. Madeline is patronizing to people she believes to be of a lower social class than she; like Grace, she speaks with a false aristocratic accent. At one point in their courtship, she confesses to Arrowsmith: "I'm always trying to make people think I'm somebody. I'm not. I'm a bluff" (47). Lewis characterizes both Madeline and Joyce Lanyon as "Improvers," women who try "to change a person from what he is . . . into something else" (46). Both of them "bully" Arrowsmith and criticize his taste in clothes, his vocabulary and diction, and his table manners.[15]

At the end of the novel, Arrowsmith withdraws from polite society completely, setting up a laboratory in the Vermont woods where his only companion is Terry Wickett—much as Lewis withdrew by going on his voyage with De Kruif. The only other significant female character in the novel is the complete opposite of Madeline and Joyce and bears no resemblance to Grace at all: Arrowsmith's first wife, Leora, whom Lewis praises as having "an immense power of accepting people as they were" (76). Leora is selflessly devoted to her husband and leaves him alone in his work. Yet in a macabre plot twist, Leora dies as a result of an accident caused by Arrowsmith's medical experiments. In metaphoric terms, perhaps, she sacrifices herself for the sake of her husband's art.

The voyage to the West Indies fulfilled Lewis's need to get away from Grace and their domestic problems. It also enabled him to drink as much as he wanted to: Grace had become critical of his drinking, which was beginning to increase. There was a three-day alcoholic junket with Harold Stearns (a notorious drinker) to Paris in early August 1921, and Schorer tells of several similar events that took place during the summer of 1922, while Lewis was in the Midwest doing research for the labor novel. There seem to have been few other episodes until late 1922, when Lewis's difficulties with Grace had escalated. He was evidently drinking enough to cause Alfred Harcourt to be concerned about his health and even to worry that alcohol might affect his work. Harcourt asked De Kruif to try to keep

Lewis from overindulging on the trip, and De Kruif suggests in his auto-biography that Harcourt was pleased that he would be there to keep Lewis on track.[16] De Kruif evidently failed to do so, because Lewis's letters from the trip describe all manner of alcoholic revelry with various crew members and inhabitants of the islands where the ship docked. Nonetheless, at this time Lewis observed a clear division between drinking hours and working hours. Later, during the composition of *Elmer Gantry* in 1926— and the complete collapse of his marriage at that same time—Lewis's drinking would in fact interfere with his writing.

On board the steamer *Guiana*, Lewis and De Kruif worked with discipline and speed. As he had with *Babbitt*, Lewis began planning his novel by recording both factual and invented data in a looseleaf notebook. Lewis then wrote the plan, the skeletal outline of the entire narrative. By the time the trip ended and he and De Kruif arrived in England (where Lewis started writing the draft), he had compiled a plan of more than sixty thousand words—the length of a short novel itself. Lewis's capacity for generating and holding in his mind all of this material was remarkable. He seems to have needed a moderately long gestational period during which he would live with (and talk out) his story and then a relatively brief period in which to generate a draft. He clearly enjoyed planning, talking, making lists, and drawing diagrams, and he had a boyish exuberance about him that may explain the obvious delight he took in this sort of activity. He approached it as one might approach a hobby— rather like a man who enjoys model trains and builds a railroad community on a sheet of plywood in his basement. Once Lewis had thought out, planned, and constructed his world, he set it in motion, much as the train buff throws his electrical switch, and watched it go into action. With his mimetic skills, all Lewis had to do was run alongside his characters and write down what they said.

Unfortunately the plan for *Arrowsmith* does not survive, but the sixty-six pages of notes are preserved among Lewis's papers at the Beinecke.[17] These notes are divided into groups corresponding to the six main settings in the novel: the University of Winnemac, where Arrowsmith is a medical student; Wheatsylvania, his wife Leora's hometown, where he briefly practices country medicine; Nautilus, where he works in the public health department under the zealous Almus Pickerbaugh; the Rouncefield Clinic in Chicago, where he is part of a group medical practice; the McGurk Institute in New York, where he joins his medical school mentor Max Gottlieb and makes his important scientific discovery; and St. Hubert, the fictional Caribbean island where he tests his serum.

The notebook contains many maps, as detailed as those for *Babbitt*.

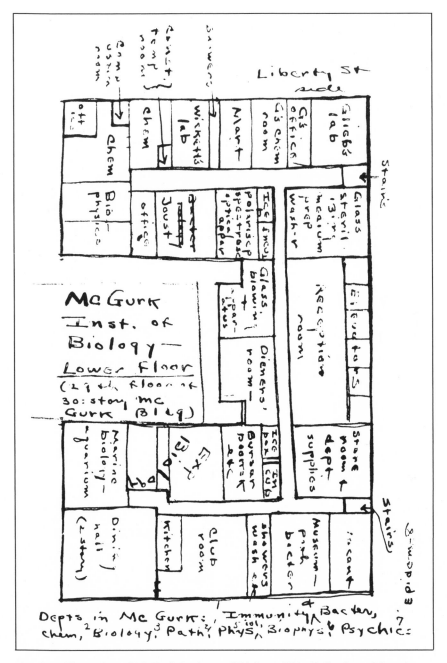

Fig. 17. Floor plan of McGurk Institute of Biology (Yale Collection of American Literature, Beinecke Rare Book and Manuscript Library, Yale University)

There is a map for the Pony River Valley, for instance, where Wheat-sylvania and "Mencken County" are located, another of each floor of the McGurk Building and the University of Winnemac Medical School, and another of the parishes of St. Hubert. For each geographic area Lewis also invented a demographic profile as he had for *Babbitt,* from its main indus-tries to such minutiae as the political affiliations of its newspapers. For many of these details in the novel, Lewis simply drew from the notebook, checking off various items after he had used them. For example, in a sec-tion entitled "Nautilus—Main Outlines," Lewis listed "Ashford Grove" as the "'best' residence section—small & smart," then, "next: Social Hill—here Mart & Leora in two-family house . . . About equal: The West Side—here Pickergill [Pickerbaugh]." There is also a page entitled "Nau-tilus data," which lists "Manufactures" as "Agricultural implements—es-pecially the Daisy Manure Spreader," "Maize Mealies," the "Cornbelt Co-operative Ins[urance] Co," and the "Tredgold Steel Windmill Co—Clay Tredgold, prest." These particular details are found in chapters 19 and 20 of *Arrowsmith,* but Lewis used this method on nearly every page of the novel.

For some parts of the book, Lewis even used his notebook as a rough draft. Compare, for example, this notebook entry for Max Gottlieb with the initial character description in chapter 12 of the first edition:

> MAX GOTTLIEB . . . German Jew. Born Germany 1850. Son of Jew-ish Banker, small Inheritance M.D. Heidelberg, Q1875. Not inter-ested in practice of medicine. Follower and admirer but not student of Helmholtz. Early researches in physics of sound. Convinced of absolute necessity of the quantitative method in medical sciences. Swept from his physical researches into biology on crest of wave of enthusiasm for Koch Pasteur et al. This between 1875–1880. An elaborately careful quantitative worker, realizing always presence of uncontrollable variables in biological problems. From 1880 worked in laboratories of Buchner, Koch, Pasteur. Interested at the same time in the early researches of Galton, biometrics.

> Max Gottlieb was a German Jew, born in Saxony in 1850. Though he took his medical degree, at Heidelberg, he was never interested in practicing medicine. He was a follower of Helmholtz, and youthful researches in the physics of sound convinced him of the need of the quantitative method in medical sciences. Then Koch's discoveries drew him into biology. Always an elaborately careful worker, a maker of long rows of figures, always realizing the pres-

ence of uncontrollable variables, always a vicious assailant of what he considered slackness or lie [*sic*] or pomposity, never too kindly to well-intentioned stupidity, he worked in the laboratories of Koch, of Pasteur, he followed the early statements of Pearson in biometrics, he drank beer and wrote vitriolic letters . . . . (123)

Here one sees the first of De Kruif's various influences on the novel. De Kruif said in his autobiography that Gottlieb was a "muddy melange" of his former professor at the University of Michigan, the microbiologist Frederick G. Novy, and Jacques Loeb. De Kruif wrote an article for *Harpers* during the fall of 1922, entitled "Jacques Loeb, the Mechanist," in which he glorified Loeb as a "god" of modern science. This worshipful attitude probably informs *Arrowsmith*'s deification of Gottlieb—particularly the famous passage at the end of chapter 17, which Lewis appended to the original ending of that chapter in typescript and which suggested to him an alternate title for the novel, "The Gods of Martin Arrowsmith," which he scribbled on the verso of that page (TS 343): "And the great god Sondelius had slain Dean Silva, as Silva had slain Gottlieb, Gottlieb had slain 'Encore' Edwards the playful chemist, Edwards had slain Doc Vickerson, and Vickerson had slain the minister's son who had a real trapeze in his barn." De Kruif later described Loeb as his "master" in the "philosophy of the mechanistic conception of life, of God a mathematician, of God a Univac, of God a superstition, of God a childish concept, of God nonexistent." These elements combined to lend to Gottlieb ("the god Loeb") the spirit of the impassioned mechanist.[18]

Eight pages of the notebook contain miscellaneous observations about the islands Lewis and De Kruif visited. Here the notes are more random but no less detailed: "In cocoa woods, piles of rotting red & yellow husks"; "Kids w[ith] nothing on but open cotton coat"; "Liquor wagon painted gaudy red w. 'His M. S. Hood'"; "pathetically pale white boys on bikes—always pale, thin hair, red-rimmed eyes, like albinos. 2 or 3 mile swarm of blacks." Another page of the notebook is entitled "Words beware in revision of M[artin] A[rrowsmith]." This is a list of adjectives, verbs, and adverbs that Lewis thought he had overused in his previous writings. Also scattered throughout the notebook are fragmentary thoughts that confirm Lewis's great expectations for the mythic proportions of the novel, such as this:

Thru-out—how Mart falls & rises, again & again in his devotion to *religion of science*—w. Silva, Sond[elius], group med[ical practice at the Rouncefield Clinic]—fable of the questing scientist . . . and

how begins a new mind in man—yet not Utopian; real vision, at
last clear & sure, of truth, and not just in genius like Voltaire or
G'lieb.

And there are endless lists of names that Lewis drew on for the major and
minor characters—some of which he developed full biographies for, while
others merited only a line or two of identification.

The remaining sections of the notebook were the result of De Kruif's
tutoring: notes on the operation of a public health office in Flint, Michigan, and the more technical "BACTERIOLOGICAL NOTES." This five-page section contains meticulous descriptions of Arrowsmith's experiments, with
step-by-step illustrations of laboratory equipment—and even drawings of
various strains of bacilli. Obviously Lewis would not have been able to
work such material into the novel without De Kruif's help. Even though
medicine was an important part of his family background (his brother was
a respected surgeon and his father a general practitioner), Lewis was igno-
rant about experimental medical research. De Kruif provided much information, and all during their voyage, Lewis found that they could "work
together perfectly. Each day I have greater respect for his totally unusual
and fine though fiery brain." His letters during that period are virtually
paeans. Lewis told Harcourt that De Kruif was "a damn clever man"; to
H. G. Wells he described De Kruif as "a man with a knife-edge mind and
an iconoclasm that really means something"; to Mencken he wrote, "Paul
was wonderful"; and to his father he reported, "It's extraordinary how
well De Kruif and I work together . . . never a row, never a disagreement—except some extremely interesting ones on an abstract theme."[19]
These disagreements were a new element in Lewis's method of research,
one that he would continue to use in writing Elmer Gantry and most of the
novels following it. Lewis would ask De Kruif a question designed to
reveal the motives of a scientist. After De Kruif gave his answer, Lewis
would cross-examine him, pressing certain points and even deriding some
of the things he had said. De Kruif would rebut Lewis's statements, and in
this way Lewis would attempt to understand the spirit of a medical researcher and test his ideals and defenses.

While it is clear that De Kruif provided the scientific ballast for Arrowsmith, it is not the "sober factuality" of the novel, to use Sheldon Grebstein's words, that distinguishes it from the rest of Lewis's oeuvre.[20] Indeed, most critics of Lewis commend Arrowsmith precisely because it is not
overladen with the detail that, it is claimed, mars the dramatic action of
Main Street and Babbitt. No one, however, has asked how much De Kruif
assisted with the nonscientific parts of the narrative. In 1931 De Kruif

(3): Gelatine Petri dish cculture. First
very precisely demonstrated by Glief, who has
virtuosity, unlike Robertshaw, elegant gestures, nor any one think substitube water for
his sulphuric acid! Petri dishes sterilized
in hot air ovens -- black tin box 24" x 12 Xx
12. Under it, roaring Bunsen flame. ▓▓From
top, thermometer, watched by students -- to
200 C. (
Fatty becomes monitor of autoclave and hot
air oven, proudly. If told exact tempetature
point, clicks right; if need brain, fail. For
this proud responsibility, Fat neglects other
duties. Bawled out by Suds, By God, by Angus,
by everybody.

Bacteria taken on platinum loop from potato.
Tube marked one; flame mouth of tube (Glief
crank on this), tube between fingers, infected
by platinum wire; tube 2 from 1, 3 from 2 and
so on. ▓▓ Tap 'em to shake. Surface and dry
colonies.......Solidify dishes beneath desk for
one day. Rem. asst who kept in incubator,
liquefying gelatine.
So colonies develope.
STUDY OF COLONY by: microscope -- 25 diam. --
Petri dish on stage of microscope.
      By hanging drop preparation.
      (Lens break cover glass, not disinfect with
      bichroride.
      Stain -- to 4.

In hanging drop tell roughly size, kind of
bacterium, whether motile. (Brownian or molec-
ular motion vs. motility.) Germans prefer --
stain, French the fresh preparation.

Fig. 18. Bacteriology notes for *Arrowsmith* (Yale Collection of American Literature, Beinecke Rare Book and Manuscript Library, Yale University)

drew up a key to *Arrowsmith* that identified the alleged real-life models for the various medical characters in the novel. He sent this list with a copy of the novel to the librarian of the New York Academy of Medicine, one Dr. Malloch, who had asked him how much he helped Lewis with the novel. The existence of this letter offers additional evidence of De Kruif's assistance—although the letter itself is actually of little use because the models were evidently just acquaintances of De Kruif's, and the published biographical information that is available about them lists only the facts of their professional careers.[21]

Other, more conclusive evidence shows that De Kruif helped Lewis extensively with the plot, the human story in the novel. At various ports of call along their route, Lewis and De Kruif would debark and explore the island, doing field research like anthropologists and scouting locations like film directors. While Lewis "kept peering from island to island for backgrounds against which to stage horrible epidemics," De Kruif's task was "to look for outlandish characters," some of whom came to life in the novel.[22] The health officer in the Barbados village of Bridgetown, for example, one "little Doctor Hutson" who showed De Kruif "that horrible epidemics were improbable on his salubrious island," seems to have been the model for Dr. R. E. Inchape Jones on St. Hubert, who says much the same thing. The Ice House in Trinidad, which De Kruif describes in his memoir with its "sinister gloom" and its "famous . . . planter's punches in cold tall glasses beaded with moisture," is echoed in the description of the Ice House in the fictional Blackwater.[23] Many of Lewis's remarks about De Kruif suggest that he assisted Lewis with the imaginative material. Lewis told Harcourt that he needed to confer with De Kruif about "not merely scientific points but the whole texture of the book for, even where I and not he have created a character, his understanding is perfect and always inspiring."[24] At about the same time, Lewis wrote Mencken to say that "all through the trip, Paul was wonderful. His greatest pleasure was to be called on for some damn hard problem, involving not only sheer scientific knowledge but also an imagination, a perception of what was dramatic."[25]

Lewis's depiction of the central character also owes a good deal to De Kruif. Many critical analyses of *Arrowsmith* have tended to emphasize the parallels between the character's career and Lewis's career. Just as Arrowsmith turns his back on marriage in favor of his work, so too did Lewis at the time shirk his responsibilities to Grace. It is also possible to read the narrative as an allegory of Lewis's own struggles as a writer. Just as Arrowsmith cannot decide whether he should use his talents to heal the sick or to devote himself to pure research (in loosely metaphoric terms, the conflict between craft and art), so too did Lewis move between writing slick magazine fiction and serious novels, especially in the early years of the 1920s. This similarity, which Lewis himself had in mind when he later entitled a mock obituary of himself "The Death of Arrowsmith," was probably what led Mark Schorer to claim that "for all the importance of Paul De Kruif's contributions to the material of *Arrowsmith*, it is interesting to note how much of Sinclair Lewis's own background" went into the novel.[26]

It is equally important to note how much of De Kruif's background informs the novel. In *The Sweeping Wind*, De Kruif says that his chief task was to "write a treatment" of Arrowsmith's career.[27] There are close parallels between the early career of De Kruif, before he met Lewis, and the fictional Arrowsmith, up to the point where he joins the McGurk Institute. A page in the notebook entitled "CHRONOLOGY OF MARTIN ARROWSMITH" divides the plot into fourteen phases of Arrowsmith's life from his birth to his resignation from the McGurk. The dates Lewis assigned to these periods are each approximately seven years earlier than the dates of similar events in De Kruif's career. (The seven-year gap in part allowed for De Kruif's military service in World War I, an event that is treated only in a minor way in the novel.)

Like Arrowsmith, De Kruif was born in the Midwest, attended a state university (Michigan), fell under the spell of a fatherly mentor, then entered medical school and became an assistant to a famous scientist. In De Kruif's case, this was Frederick G. Novy. Three years later—again like Arrowsmith—De Kruif married for the first time at the age of twenty-five. Herein lies the most interesting parallel: De Kruif's first marriage ended in divorce seven years later, in December 1922; he then married Rhea Barbarin, with whom he had been in love for some time, just before he and Lewis began work on the novel. De Kruif met Rhea while he was an intern at the university hospital; Arrowsmith meets Leora under the same circumstances. Like the fictional Arrowsmith, who must elope and keep his marriage a secret, De Kruif also married under tense circumstances. Just as De Kruif's career resembles Arrowsmith's, Rhea seems to have been something of a model for the fictional Leora. De Kruif recalled that during the planning of the novel, Lewis's "portrait of Leora—lovely in her abnegation—was growing more and more to be the image of my Rhea." (Even the names are similar.) Elsewhere, De Kruif remarks that "Leora's death kept making me see Rhea dying."[28] This similarity is significant because reviewers who had heretofore criticized Lewis for his inability to draw women characters realistically all praised the characterization of Leora. Harcourt said that Leora was "just about the best woman character in American fiction," and suggested that Lewis end the book with her death and entitle it "Leora."[29] Lewis himself publicly remarked that Leora contained most of his "capacity for loyalty to love and friendship." Yet Leora seems to have been more a part of De Kruif's experience than of Lewis's—indeed, Lewis's ideal of the undemanding wife who requires only that her husband be left alone to work and achieve fame was hardly fulfilled by Grace.[30]

Lewis seems to have deviated from the next phase of De Kruif's career, his enlistment in the army in 1916. At this point in the novel come the Wheatsylvania, Nautilus, and Chicago sections. These scenes are satiric, and the characters in them are common Lewis types—incompetents, charlatans, and opportunists. These are the only thoroughly satiric sections in the novel, probably because here Lewis was not following De Kruif's experiences as a model (though Lewis probably owes something to De Kruif's view of public health officials in the Pickerbaugh scenes).[31] According to the chronology, the last of these episodes ends in late 1917 or early 1918, when Arrowsmith joins the McGurk Institute—approximately the same time that De Kruif returned to the United States and went to work for the Rockefeller Institute. And of course, there is a clear parallel between Arrowsmith's repudiation of the McGurk and De Kruif's similar disenchantment with and resignation from the Rockefeller.

These surface connections may be simply the natural result of De Kruif's self-reflection as he thought about a hypothetical scientist. But there is a third level on which De Kruif entered the novel—the deepest and most important one. Insofar as *Arrowsmith* is a commentary on medicine and biological research, it clearly reflects De Kruif's own values and attitudes. One can see the young bacteriologist's influence on *Arrowsmith* in the *Century* essays he wrote about medicine and science, which predate his work with Lewis. In one article entitled "Are Commercialism and Science Ruining Medicine?" De Kruif mourns the loss of the "old-fashioned general practitioner" who once fulfilled the role of the patient's "comforter and friend." The "old doc," as De Kruif calls him, is being replaced by "the new god of science."[32] Here we see the two philosophies Arrowsmith struggles to reconcile—described in the very metaphor of gods and idols that Lewis weaves into the narrative. One philosophy is embodied in Arrowsmith's first "god," T.J.H. "Dad" Silva, dean of the University of Winnemac Medical School, whose description in the novel closely resembles the anonymous "T.G.H." whom De Kruif cites as his own mentor (417) and who is identified in the "key."[33] At the other end of the spectrum is Max Gottlieb, who peers through De Kruif's portrait of the "cool, disinterested, and impartial" scientist in the essay. His insistence on maintaining "untreated cases" or experimental "controls" (Gottlieb's watchword in the novel) is at cross-purposes with the ethics of the "good doctor," who believes that "*nothing should be left undone to cure the patient.*" De Kruif's essential argument, that "humanity in general is certainly not ready . . . to take the place of the laboratory guinea-pig" (424), clearly informs Arrowsmith's divided loyalties to his various "gods" and sets up the dramatic climax on St. Hubert when Arrowsmith realizes that giving the serum under test conditions means condemning thousands to die. The commercialism Arrowsmith finds in his brief employment at the Rouncefield Clinic in Chicago probably also has its basis in some of De Kruif's observations in this essay. Throughout the article, De Kruif exposes the "hypocrisy, charlatanism, loud advertisement," and "meretricious efficiency" of the medical profession, and he specifically criticizes the "coalition of specialists known as 'the group'" for doing what Arrowsmith's Rouncefield colleagues do: advising rich patients to have "operations on the flimsiest evidence of their necessity," and to undergo a battery of "very expensive" tests at the direction of the "diagnostician," who in turn refers the "sufferer" to "the appropriate surgeon of the group" (420–21; cf. *Arrowsmith*, 270–71).

The second *Century* essay, "What Is Preventive Medicine Preventing?" concerns public health movements and their relation to the study of disease. De Kruif's attack on these "shouters for public health . . . dubious Messiahs who combine the zealous fanaticism of the missionary with the Jesuitical cynicism of the politician" echoes through Lewis's descriptions of Pickerbaugh.[34] One public health doctrine that De Kruif attacks is the refusal to endorse birth control—an issue that Lewis might have had in mind in chapter 21, where Arrowsmith fights Pickerbaugh's zealous publicizing of "More Babies Week" (*Arrowsmith*, 225). Arrowsmith's public health reforms in the next chapter were also probably inspired by a series of incidents De Kruif claimed could happen when the overeager health official "causes serious embarrassment and needless economic losses" to a city. In one hypothetical scenario described in the essay, a group of plumbers are quarantined for diphtheria—over the protests of the city leaders, whose districts are being overrun by sewage problems; they eventually hound the health officer from his post (599–600). This situation is much like Arrowsmith's pyrrhic victory in quarantining an employee of Klopchuck's dairy and demolishing the unsanitary McCandless tenements in chapters 22 and 24, events that cause his resignation under fire.

These ideas surely guided Lewis as he drafted the novel. During the voyage, Lewis wrote to Harcourt that De Kruif had "not only an astonishing grasp of scientific detail" but "a philosophy behind it" and that he possessed "the imagination of the fiction writer." Lewis confided too that De Kruif's role in the creation of the novel was at least as large as his own:

> He sees, synthesizes, characters. You've sometimes said that my books are meaty; this will be much the meatiest of all—characters, places, contrasting purposes and views of life; and in all of this there's a question as to whether he won't have contributed more than I shall have. Yet he takes it for granted that he is not to sign the book with me. And he loves work . . . when I'm compiling notes into a coherent whole, De Kruif is preparing more data— clear, sound, and just the stuff for dramatic purposes.[35]

At about the same time, Lewis wrote to Mencken that De Kruif "proves to have as much synthetic fictional imagination as he has scientific knowledge, and that's one hell of a lot. . . . It's going to be my best book— though it isn't just *mine* by a long shot."[36]

All this is not to say that Paul De Kruif wrote *Arrowsmith*. Indeed, in his memoir De Kruif laid to rest the speculations of those who, when the book was published, thought that "it was not really Sinclair Lewis but De Kruif who wrote [the book]," and that De Kruif "got gypped out of the credit." "Nothing could be farther from the truth," he stated. "Sinclair Lewis wrote it." However, De Kruif added, "I helped substantially both with the science and the human story."[37] Through all of this, Lewis and De Kruif's arrangement seems to have been a marriage of true minds. Lewis needed De Kruif to help him understand the spirit of scientific research and to outline the concept of the idealistic hero—even in some ways to be a model for that figure. De Kruif benefited from watching a professional writer at work, for although De Kruif wrote in a clear, jargon-free style, he did not yet have any conception of how to draw character, how to pace a narrative, or how to create dramatic conflict. After his association with Lewis had ended and De Kruif embarked on his own writing career, he demonstrated a true talent for storytelling—and he credited Lewis with teaching him the techniques.[38]

On 6 March 1923 Lewis and De Kruif arrived in Plymouth, England, and traveled by train to London; here Lewis began to write the draft of *Arrowsmith*. Each time Lewis finished one stage of work on a novel, he almost always then moved somewhere else before beginning the next stage. By the time of *Arrowsmith,* something of a pattern had begun to emerge. Lewis seems to have divided his work on a novel into five stages: there was an initial gestational period; then came a time during which information was gathered and notes were compiled (usually this stage involved a trip); an outline was then drawn up; next, a draft was produced (at breakneck speed); then that draft was slowly revised by hand and retyped; finally, the novel was submitted to Harcourt. During the composition of *Babbitt* and *Arrowsmith,* Lewis worked on these various stages in different locations. The initial thinking for *Babbitt* was done in Washington, D.C., and for *Arrowsmith,* in New York; the research for *Babbitt* was conducted in the Midwest, that for *Arrowsmith* in the West Indies; Lewis wrote the plan for *Babbitt* in Kent and the plan for *Arrowsmith* on board the SS *Guiana;* the majority of the draft of *Babbitt* was produced in Italy, and most of the draft of *Arrowsmith* in France. Lewis revised the first drafts of both *Babbitt* and *Arrowsmith* in London, then returned to the United States.

Obviously Lewis needed the stimulus of contact with different types of people and different locales as an aid to invention and writing, but one wonders whether he perceived a connection between creativity and specific places. He was sometimes drawn back to certain houses or offices where he had worked on earlier novels. He began thinking about *Babbitt* in the same rented room in Washington, D.C., in which he had written the first draft of *Main Street.* (It was here, too, that he completed the draft of *Elmer Gantry.*) When he began writing the draft of *Arrowsmith* in London, he settled into his old rooms at 10 Bury Street, where he had worked on the draft of *Babbitt.* He may even have half-believed that a new or revisited place could refresh him creatively; at least, he sometimes suggested this idea in his fiction. At the end of *Arrowsmith,* for example, the central character flees the confines of the laboratory (and marriage) and retreats to the countryside, where untrammeled nature is his laboratory, and he feels rejuvenated. Similarly, in *Dodsworth,* which is largely autobiographical, Lewis has his middle-aged protagonist move all around Europe, hoping to rediscover the idealism he possessed in his youth.

It is also possible that this continual cycle of sampling different "worlds" and observing the different types of lives that people led in them was a way of fulfilling a lifelong need to find a world into which he fit comfortably. Since his youth in Sauk Centre, Lewis had thought of himself as an outsider; from 1915, when he embarked on his "Research Magnificent," until his death in 1951 he was almost constantly on the move. He owned permanent residences only four times during his life, and he remained in each one for only a few months before he sold it, feeling the need to travel. Edward A. Martin has noted that Lewis was always searching for a world elsewhere—"geographically, in his fiction, and in human relationships, lacerated . . . by his need for approval and affection."[39] His extraordinary mimetic abilities, his talent for blending in with a group of people in a certain setting, might have been the result of his naturally adapting himself to an environment to see if he "belonged" there.

As he did research for his novels, he was genuinely curious about the professions that he chose to write about. With Paul De Kruif he was able to see what it was like to be an intrepid medical researcher, and Lewis often remarked that he valued the scientific mind above all others. In an autobiographical essay published in 1937, Lewis stated that he had enjoyed writing more than anything "except pure research in a laboratory."[40] He was always interested in processes, and his working methods—writing from notes and detailed outlines—might even be described as scientific.[41] In composing *Elmer Gantry*, Lewis was satisfying a genuine curiosity about the ministry. He underwent a religious conversion during his year at Oberlin, which, while short-lived, was nevertheless zealous and apparently genuine.[42] And of course, Lewis had an evangelistic—one might even say self-righteous—temperament. As we will see, it found an outlet by doing research for *Elmer Gantry* in Kansas City, where in some ways he actually tried to live the life of a minister.

Once Lewis established a temporary residence in London, the first question that he took up regarding *Arrowsmith* involved the title. At sea, Lewis's working title had been "The Barbarian," or simply "Barbarian." Harcourt helped Lewis decide on a title; this was an important preliminary step for Lewis in the composition of a draft. Harcourt once said that Lewis "wrote to" a particular title.[43] An earlier choice had been "The Stumbler," but Harcourt pointed out that both titles were "tangled," and that each had "an adjectival sense." Harcourt also noted that both were satiric titles: "Is not that aspect of your work apt to be over-emphasized by critics anyway?" Harcourt asked.[44] By the end of April Lewis had finished the plan, and by 3 May he had started writing the first draft. Rhea joined De Kruif in London, and they took an apartment in Chelsea near Lewis's rooms in St. James so that De Kruif would be available when Lewis needed his assistance. Among other things, De Kruif arranged for Lewis to meet scientists and visit laboratories to watch some actual work.[45] In late June Lewis left England to meet Grace at Fontainebleau in France. Throughout the summer there Lewis pushed on with the typescript, completing it on 30 September. By Lewis's calculation, the finished product was about 245,000 words long; so during the composition of *Arrowsmith* he produced roughly three thousand to five thousand words per day. The large amount of revising done on the extant drafts indicates that his goal was simply to put on paper all the material that he had been keeping in mind during the periods of gestation, research, and planning. Later he

```
                    T I T L E S

The Stumbler ✓
The Barbarian
Barbarian ✓
Martin Arrowsmith ✓
Arrowsmith ✓
   Dr. Arrowsmith ✓
   Martin
   M.D.                        Arrowsmith, M.D. ✓


   H
   
   Civilized ✓
   The Destroyer ✓ (suggests to many)
   Test Tube ✓
   The Savage
   The Shadow of Max Gottlieb ✓
```

Objection**s** to Barbarian: Trop like Babbitt. & cf.
   novel **I** The Barb" pub. in 1923.

Objections to Martin Arrowsmith: Martin Eden,
   Chuzzlewit, but see next page. If use, look
   up in Who's Who and Medical Register. Change
   name Martin?   variants for Martin

Brian		Cyrus
Evan	Gideon	Scott
Stephen	Jason	
Titus	Luke	
Felix	Calvin	
	Conrad	

Fig. 19.   Potential titles for *Arrowsmith* (Yale Collection of American Literature,
Beinecke Rare Book and Manuscript Library, Yale University)

would cut and polish what he had written. That week, the De Kruifs joined the Lewises in France, and De Kruif read through the typescript draft.

The typescript, preserved in the Lewis Collection at Austin, numbers more than 850 pages. Lewis revised it in his usual thorough fashion, the final product being such a mess that when Lewis showed it to Arnold Bennett (who wrote his manuscripts in a neat, calligraphic hand) the latter noted in his journal, "All blue and red, with millions of alterations—a terrible sight!"[46] Through the labyrinth of revisions, however, one can find a pattern: nearly all of Lewis's large-scale cuts deleted satiric material that to some degree undercut, digressed from, or obscured the idealistic themes of the novel. Given De Kruif's role in planning the novel, one might assume that Lewis made these changes under his direction. But that was not the case. Still, Lewis did solicit De Kruif's suggestions as he wrote and revised the typescript. As Lewis typed the draft he included in it notes to De Kruif, asking him (as one would expect) to check or correct certain technical details. In Lewis's initial description of Arrowsmith's laboratory at the McGurk Institute in chapter 26, to take just one of many examples, he asked De Kruif if any details were missing, to which De Kruif responded, "Yes—a microscope and logarithm tables and hydrogen-ion charts on the walls." Lewis added these items in the revision (TS 489).

Lewis also solicited literary advice from De Kruif as well as from Grace, who also read through the manuscript. Grace corrected some minor details: in chapter 5, for example, Lewis had the students at Mohalis dancing the tango instead of the new waltz called the Boston (TS 85). More important, Grace often caught similarities in characterization or noticed that certain descriptive passages were repeated in different scenes. On typescript page 11, for example, she noted that the description of "Encore" Edwards was too much like that of Doc Vickerson, and Lewis changed it. Similarly, on typescript page 209 Grace wrote, "Trop hospital"—"Too much description of the hospital" in her odd Frenchified shorthand—and noted that the same details had been given in an earlier scene. Accordingly Lewis cut this material. Sometimes Grace and De Kruif argued in the margins about whether material should be deleted or retained. On page 216, for example, when Arrowsmith reluctantly agrees to move with Leora back to Wheatsylvania, her hometown, Grace noted, "Too much repetition of Martin's new connections and old yearnings." Below that, De Kruif wrote, "I don't agree—believe you must keep hammering at it." Lewis seems to have trusted Grace's judgment in this particular case, for he crossed out the whole page.

In general, however, De Kruif's opinions seem to have been more important to Lewis for this novel than Grace's were. Sometimes Lewis wrote notes to De Kruif in the typescript draft asking his opinion of certain details. Most of De Kruif's penciled answers are still legible on the typescript, though some have been erased or marked through, presumably meaning that Lewis rejected them. However, many of them Lewis did not reject—and in these De Kruif urged Lewis to condense or cut altogether many of the satiric scenes in the book, especially in its midsection, where Lewis evidently did not follow De Kruif's career as a model for the narrative. For example, in chapter 16, which takes place one year after Arrowsmith has settled in Wheatsylvania and is beginning to adjust to that environment, Lewis had originally written four scenes that more fully developed Arrowsmith's experience there (TS 294–313). These do not appear in the published text. In one passage, Arrowsmith wins over the antagonistic pastor of the United Brethren Church and thereby becomes a "Good Citizen," an event that almost causes him "to be taken seriously by Bert and Mr. Tozer," Leora's brother and father. In this scene, Arrowsmith is seduced by the idea of being "prosperous and Settled for Life"—a phrase that might have been spoken by George F. Babbitt, or some similar character from Lewis's storehouse of stereotypes (TS 295–96). In another scene, Lewis satirized small-town ethics and boosterism: Bert Tozer bribes a minor-league baseball star, Mike Shumway, to come to Wheatsylvania and organize a team there. The details of the town council's payoff to Shumway are clumsily covered up, and Arrowsmith refuses to sanction this underhandedness (TS 298–302). Lewis was probably trying to show Arrowsmith's successful escape from the claustrophobia of the environment, but the scene is related only tenuously to the idealism of the main character and is digressive. In the left-hand margin of one of these pages, De Kruif wrote: "cut or condense" (TS 296). Lewis evidently agreed, for he made a note in the top right-hand corner of that same page, "Go over 294–313 and cut as a whole."

In the following chapter, there is a two-section interlude in the portrayal of Arrowsmith's work in Wheatsylvania that describes a trip taken by the buffoonish Dr. Coughlin of Leopolis. In typescript, the scene is twice its length in the published novel (TS 319–30; cf. *Arrowsmith,* 175–85). The passages are humorous in their mockery of consumer culture and civic pride: Coughlin visits a physician in nearby St. Luke, and they discuss fees and the latest pharmaceutical products and office equipment. One again hears Babbittisms, set against a landscape like that of *Main Street.* Throughout such passages, Lewis queried De Kruif about the effectiveness of scenes. "Cut Coughlin's motoring [trip] a little?" Lewis asked on page 318; "maybe condense a little," De Kruif replied (TS 320). Lewis cut al-

~~it, and every one night they stayed at a hotel with the five of~~
~~th...~~ ~~...in two rooms, and a nice good bath promised...~~
~~...when they were...~~ *If your last impression...*
large ~~from~~ pennants labeld " *Lepolis* " + " *Excuse Our Dust.* "
~~...think," said Dr. Coughlin, examining his map, "that we~~

ought to go to Roundup. It says here that it has twenty-three hundred people -- didn't know it was such a big place -- and of course
it's the county seat of Rome County and -------"

"Yes, and somebody was telling me that it has a dandy
hotel. Let's go that way," said the agreeable Mrs. Coughlin.

They went to Roundup.

They found the hotel indeed excellent -- they had the best roast
beef, the best ~~string canned~~ canned string beans, and the best
lemon meringue pie they found on the whole trip, and the head waitress knew who they were -- her second cousin Matilda was the
Leopolis milliner -- and she gave them extra slices of pie and sat
down with them to tell them about the inefficiency of the Roundup
doctors, at which Dr. Coughlin did not seem displeased. After dinner they went to the movies; they saw Bill Hart in one of his best
pictures; and found an orchestra with not merely a piano but also
a violin.

~~Here's a town hardly more in half the size of Leopolis and~~
~~they got a better orchestra at the movies -- by golly somebody ought~~
~~to do something about it. I told you Pete Gorton was just running~~ *H "*
~~our movie place at home to make money out of it.~~ Wasn't that a
fine young woman, that head waitress. Interesting about Dr. Fisk
boozing too much. You certainly do learn a lot about the world when
you travel. And that's a cute stunt they got at the garage here --
that Jack so's you can get your car in without steering," said
Dr. Coughlin contentedly, as he walked back to the hotel ~~with his~~
~~...trailed by the two older Coughlin children.~~

Fig. 20.   Detail from *Arrowsmith* typescript (Harry Ransom Humanities Research
Center, University of Texas at Austin)

most all of this material and in the process reduced Wheatsylvania to a backdrop for the main focus of the novel, Arrowsmith's idealism and his work first at the McGurk, then on St. Hubert.

Lewis might have wanted to counterpoint this stage of Arrowsmith's career with the others, but the overdevelopment of this section would have amplified the contrast too obviously and become digressive. In these passages one recognizes Lewis's satiric tendencies and the typical objects of his scorn: the village hypocrite, the stupid American tourist, the con-man.

Lewis himself made many changes independently, although he often asked for De Kruif's opinion first. Many of these revisions show him restraining himself, being careful to keep the satiric elements of the novel subordinate to the theme. In chapter 22, for instance, according to a note addressed to De Kruif at the top of a typescript page, Lewis had planned for Pickerbaugh to make a bogus scientific discovery. Even at this stage of composition Lewis was still talking out his ideas: "I have retained the notes . . . at the end of [your] special material. But I'm afraid of Nautilus running too long, with all of the crucial McGurk-St. Hubert-Terry-Joyce material coming; and also it now seems to me that this Pickergill-making-discovery matter gets too far from Martin-Leora-Gottlieb who *are* the book" (TS 427). What follows instead is a scene that illustrates Arrowsmith's thorough dedication to his profession. De Kruif responded, "Good!" and "perfect" (TS 447, 449), presumably concurring with Lewis's decision. For this chapter, Lewis seems to have used the example from De Kruif's *Century* article about a diphtheria "epidemic" and its effect on the young health officer's standing in the community (*Arrowsmith*, 238–40). Two chapters later, Lewis considered extending Arrowsmith's battle with the city leaders, but noted to De Kruif that there was "no virtue to the scene . . . gets nowhere." De Kruif agreed, noting, "Vote against" (TS 475).

Later, Lewis made several similar changes in the McGurk chapters, again worrying aloud to De Kruif that they were too satiric. In chapter 26, Lewis wrote De Kruif a long note justifying his decision to discard a character, Wallace Umstead, who was to be the head of the "Dept of Psychometrics and Teleological Psych." Lewis thought this would sound "a false note" by "its making McGurk at least partly absurd that it should have such a dept. Umstead belongs in another novel with an atmosphere of cults and general idiocy, not in one of hard scientists who, with all their hardness, yet are often ineffective. Let's talk this over. What do you think?" De Kruif answered, "Yes!" (TS 506). Lewis retained the name of this character for one of Elmer Gantry's seminary classmates, who ends up working for the YMCA.

LLLLLPAUL: I'd started putting in wallace umstead, the psychical researcher, head of Dept of Psychometrics and Teleological Psych," when
it occured to me that it would probably be a false note. The problem
of McGurk is that with every desire amum (even on the part of that poor
rot Tubbs) and every facility for real science, they yet strike such
snags. The Umstead thing would be partly farce, and partly a muuuuun
weakening of the problem by its making McGurk at least partly absurd
that it should have much a dept. Umstead belongs in another novel
with an atmosphere of cults and general idiocy, not in one of hard
scientists who, with all their hardness, yet are often ineffective.
Let's talk this over. What do you think? The notes about Umstead,
and the part I wrote about him, I have preserved with what notes I
have kept -- see Plan p. 104, and Original PP of MS, 505-6......PS,
the one really valuable point we miss by omitting Umstead if Wickett's
or Joust's assertion that the totally absurd stuff of Umstead is
nevertheless better than the pseudo, partly real stuff of a Tubbs;
but I might believe this one philosophical point could be brought in
by a reference to psychic researchers in general, without having Umstead in. M Eh?)

V

Day ours.

The Rippleton Holabirds invited martin and Leora to dinner mum
a week after their coming. As Holabird's tweeds revealed Clay
Tredgold's smartness as hard and pretentious, so his dinner
made Angus Duer's affairs seem mechanical and joyless and a little
anxious. Everyone there, in the Holabirds' whom martin met at
Japanese = printed flat
on Park Avenue (Mrs. Holabird had been a Gruesling, one of the Pro-
vidence-thread Grueslings -- Holabird laughingly admitted that he
himself was a pauper) was a Somebody, though perhaps a minor
Somebody, a goodish novelist or a rising ethnologist, and all of them
had Holabirds took themselves with as much good-humored, graceful casual-
ness as did Holabird.

He was ready enough to speak of his work. The provincial Arrow-
smiths arrived on time, therefore fifteen minutes early. Before the
cocktails came in, old Venetian glass, martin
demanded, "Doctor, what problems are you getting after now in your

Finally, Lewis revised a scene that came before the satiric midpoint of the novel. With the exception of the Pickerbaugh chapters, there are few scenes in the novel as sharp as the farewell address given by Roscoe Geake in chapter 8, on "The Art and Science of Furnishing the Doctor's Office" (85–87). Geake has been called from the chair of otolaryngology at the medical school to assume the vice presidency of the New Idea Medical Instrument and Furniture Company. This scene, with its gentle satire of "the two warring schools" in office design, "the Tapestry School" and "the Aseptic School," recalls Babbitt's speech before the Zenith Real Estate Board about "Our Ideal Citizen" or Chum Frink's rhapsodic advertising jingle for the Zeeco Motor Car Company. As it reads in the published novel, the scene is Lewis at his best: a compact parody that is not heavy-handed. But Lewis again worried aloud to De Kruif that it was overly satiric. De Kruif had written in the margin, "For Christ's sake do not cut this!" Lewis, however, noted, "When all copied, read this chapter to see how much repetition in Geake" (TS 158). Lewis later eliminated some of the more outrageous passages. During the week that De Kruif worked through the draft, Lewis continued to praise his skills as an editor and adviser. On 28 September 1923 he told Harcourt, "If you could have seen how he went at *Martin* here—working night and day yet reading with such minute precision! My admiration for him is greater now than ever."[47]

As Lewis revised *Arrowsmith* during the late fall and winter of 1923–24, his energy was taxed to its limit. Alfred Harcourt had sold the first serial rights to *Arrowsmith* to the *Designer and the Woman's Magazine*. Lewis had been on holiday in Italy at the time, and Harcourt had been unable to reach him. Lewis disliked the idea of serializing his novels because he regarded it as a commercialization of his work, and since the success of *Main Street* Lewis had been careful to project an image of himself as a serious literary artist. He and Harcourt had agreed not to sell the serial rights to either *Main Street* or *Babbitt*. On the other hand, Harcourt knew that Lewis also wanted to keep attracting large audiences, and he knew that the magazines afforded him that opportunity. Harcourt was also no doubt overwhelmed by the munificent sum that the *Designer* had offered—fifty thousand dollars—part of which would come to his firm under the terms of his contract with Lewis. In the back of Harcourt's mind was probably the relative disappointment of the low sales that *Babbitt* had had in its second season—about 1,000 copies per week instead of the 1,500 that *Main Street* had sold in that period. Harcourt had also purchased the plates of Lewis's apprentice novels from Harpers and had brought them out that spring in a newly designed series. But there were still many of the old editions in the stores—"just enough to foul the market and to make the trade unwilling to stock them," he later told Lewis.[48] Harcourt therefore saw the offer from the *Designer* as a way to recoup some of his losses. Lewis, as it turned out, agreed with Harcourt: "I hate serialization but it seems foolish to lose fifty thousand."[49] Lewis thus found himself revising his not-yet-completed typescript of the novel for book publication while at the same time cutting it for separate publication as a serial. At this point, Lewis hired a secretary, Louis N. Florey, whose primary task was to type clean copies of Lewis's revised drafts.

The double revising took place in a rented house in the Kensington district of London, where Lewis had gone with Grace in November 1923. By mid-February 1924 Lewis had delivered sixty-five thousand words of the serial to the *Designer*. By the beginning of March he had finished ninety-six thousand words of it, and he delivered the remaining thirty thousand words by the end of April. The typescript that Lewis used to produce the abridged serial text is not extant; the clean typescript of *Arrowsmith* at the Beinecke is the setting copy that Lewis submitted to Harcourt for book publication. However, a complete collation of the serial and book texts was done by Lyon N. Richardson in the early 1950s. Richardson concluded that in creating the serial text Lewis eliminated "many scattered short passages which he still felt to be of value in the book but recognized as surplusage in serial form." Richardson also found that the editors of the *Designer* made minor alterations in the structure of the novel and more significant changes in certain statements of attitudes and ideas, "explosions of satire," "invective," and "uncouth expressions."[50] The first installment of the serial appeared in April 1924 and the last in April 1925, one month after the book was published.

On 19 May 1924, just a few weeks after finishing work on the serial, Lewis arrived in New York with the completed book manuscript of *Arrowsmith* and submitted it to Harcourt. Lewis rested in New York for a few days while Harcourt read the typescript. They apparently conferred about the novel, but Harcourt seems not to have requested any changes.

Once he had discussed *Arrowsmith* with Harcourt, Lewis drove to Sauk Centre to visit his family, leaving Grace and Wells to spend the summer in Nantucket. After a brief stay in Minnesota, Lewis went with his brother Claude on a hiking trip into the wilds of northern Saskatchewan. This trip lasted until late July. (Lewis would base his next novel, *Mantrap,* on this experience.) He then returned to New York to read the proofs of *Arrowsmith* and in October left once again for England with Grace.

During this period Lewis and De Kruif had broken off their friendship because of a disagreement over how De Kruif's assistance should be credited in the published book. Separating truth from legend in this incident is difficult because the surviving evidence about it is unusually sparse. As editor of Lewis's letters, Harrison Smith (then a junior partner at Harcourt, Brace) chose this point in the correspondence about *Arrowsmith* to summarize developments during late September and early October 1924, when the page proofs came through without any acknowledgment of De Kruif's work.[51] Harcourt remained conspicuously silent on the matter in his memoirs, which recounted almost everything about the Lewis–De Kruif alliance except this point.[52] However, De Kruif spoke of it at length in the information he supplied to Grace for her memoirs and in the relevant section of his own autobiography. According to De Kruif, just before Lewis left London for Fontainebleau in July 1923 he showed De Kruif a fulsome acknowledgment he had written that described his collaboration; it was to run on the "page after the title page." But when the proofs were generated in October 1924, there was merely "a little acknowledgment that left not much more for me but thanks for technical assistance." De Kruif said that he then angrily instructed the publishers to remove all mention of his assistance. Donald Brace, however, persuaded Lewis to write "a broader acknowledgment," and finally this paragraph was included in the front matter of the first edition:[53]

> To Dr. Paul H. DeKruif [*sic*] I am indebted not only for most of the bacteriological and medical material in this tale but equally for his help in the planning of the fable itself—for his realization of the characters as living people, for his philosophy as a scientist. With this acknowledgment I want to record our months of companionship while working on the book, in the United States, in the West Indies, in Panama, in London and Fontainebleau. I wish I could reproduce our talks along the way, and the laboratory afternoons, the restaurants at night, and the deck at dawn as we steamed into tropic ports.

Despite this controversy, De Kruif continued to think highly of Lewis. He remembered him as "a brilliantly imaginative man who dared to let his imagination go on paper," something De Kruif "had never dared to do" in his scientific writing. Most of all De Kruif remained grateful to Lewis for his tutelage because, as he later told Grace, "I could never have become a good writer without him."[54]

Arrowsmith stilled the voices that had criticized Lewis for lacking "spiritual gifts." Reviewers in both America and England were virtually unanimous in judging *Arrowsmith* to be Lewis's finest novel to date. Nearly all of the reviewers noted that this novel stood on firmer and deeper aesthetic ground than *Main Street* and *Babbitt* did. The *Literary Review*, for example, said that "the humanity of it outshines the science"; Joseph Wood Krutch, in the *Nation*, found it "better" than the earlier novels because it was "essentially truer." The *Atlantic Bookshelf* announced that Lewis was "no longer the composer of superlative jazz. He has shown himself an artist, sincere, powerful, restrained."[55] Although the serialization of the novel reduced advance sales somewhat (about 25 percent according to Harcourt's estimate), they nonetheless totaled more than forty-three thousand, and Harcourt ordered a first printing of 51,750 copies.[56] There was also a limited autographed edition of five hundred copies published simultaneously with the general printing on 5 March 1925. *Arrowsmith* was the best-selling novel in March, according to *Publishers' Weekly,* and by the end of the month sales had reached one hundred thousand. Although *Arrowsmith* did not outdistance *Main Street* or *Babbitt* in sales, comparatively it was quite successful given the fact that it was not a "controversial" novel and was not designed to stir up a public debate. Here and there, some physicians and scientists made known their displeasure with the caricatures in the novel, but such comments were few. In the main, *Arrowsmith* is Lewis's quietest, most controlled, and most serious-minded novel of the 1920s.

How much of this, one wonders, could Lewis have accomplished without the encouragement, advice, and assistance of someone like Paul De Kruif? The evidence for De Kruif's influence on the conception, research, planning, and editing of *Arrowsmith* is strong. That he played such a significant role is important, for the heroic theme and the idealistic nature of the protagonist seem to owe a good deal to De Kruif's presence during the creative process. Trying to guess how *Arrowsmith* would have turned out had De Kruif not assisted Lewis is difficult to do, but I believe that *Arrowsmith* would have been a much different novel without De Kruif's influence: it would have been a novel mostly of caricature, not a novel of character—a novel that debunked and satirized in the manner of *Main Street* and *Babbitt,* but that probably would have presented a less affirmative view of the idealistic in modern man.

Several facts support this assertion. For one thing, Lewis's first impulses in planning *Arrowsmith* led him to think in comic terms. De Kruif recalled that when he first told Lewis of his experiences, Lewis "roared with laughter": he thought that De Kruif's stories comprised "an epic of medical debunkology," and that they were "cynically satirical." Further, Lewis conceived of *Arrowsmith* along the lines of his earlier novels: "Medicine and medical science" seemed "like *Main Street,* and many of its greatest names turned out to be oafs like Babbitt." In *The Sweeping Wind,* De Kruif also remembered that Lewis's earliest "plots and characters" centered on "a flamboyant Swedish epidemiologist, a money-mad professor of oto-laryngology, a buffoonish missionary of public health"—that is, foils to the stark hero.[57] But as the contract for *Arrowsmith* was about to be drawn up, Lewis changed his mind about the book. He pitched the idea to his publishers not as a novel about an idealistic truth-seeker, but rather as a magazine serial for *Hearst's:* "stories with a new type of hero, a character—bacteriologist, doctor, public health detective—all in one." De Kruif pejoratively characterized it as "a kind of scientific Clarence Budington Kelland production."[58]

Moreover, Lewis was unable to draw a heroic character with complete success in any work except *Arrowsmith.* Most of his novels contain a clear pattern: a representative American idealist (in one form or another) pursues a vision, is defeated by the environment, renounces the earlier idealism, then retreats back into reality and thereby metaphorically perishes. Only *Arrowsmith* deviates from this pattern. All of Lewis's major characters before Arrowsmith have spiritual ambitions that go unfulfilled or are only partly fulfilled: Carol Kennicott and Babbitt come readily to mind, and the heroes of Lewis's apprentice fiction (such as the title character of *Our Mr. Wrenn* and Una Golden of *The Job*) all possess idealistic notions that they cannot bring to fruition. Those novels following *Arrowsmith* portray characters with either false ideals or, again, submerged ideals that cannot be realized. In *Elmer Gantry,* the next major novel after *Arrowsmith,* Lewis wrote his most vicious satire; there, he is openly contemptuous of his protagonist, a crass opportunist whose "ideals" are exploitive and ma-nipulative. When in 1943 Lewis returned to the subject of the flim-flam man, he created in the title character of *Gideon Planish* simply another version of Elmer Gantry, someone who exploits the good in society—this time through a philanthropic organization instead of a church. In *Dodsworth* we see idealism in an expatriate, but European culture does not fill the emptiness in his heart after the breakup of his marriage; his remedy is to marry again. Yet when Dodsworth reappears in Lewis's last completed novel, *World So Wide* (published posthumously in 1951), he warns its ar-chitect-hero, Hayden Chart, against the unreality of his European rootless-ness. In *Work of Art* (1934), the artist-figure is an unabashed realist who gives up his ideal of transforming a second-rate hotel into a grand one in the European tradition and settles for owning an undistinguished motel, finding that in the end he can work hard and get along just as well. With the possible exception of *Ann Vickers* (1933)—in which a social activist reforms the system yet ultimately renounces her work and then marries, thereby achieving a partial sense of fulfillment—this strain of latent idealism found full expression only in *Arrowsmith*. De Kruif's presence seems to have enabled Lewis to release it.

Following the popular success but critical skepticism attending the publication of *Babbitt,* Lewis knew that he had to create a hero, a figure whom critics and readers alike would see that he was in sympathy with. Harcourt emphasized the practical necessity for that in several letters to him, one of which argued for having the word "doctor" in the title of *Arrowsmith*. "The world pretty much knows now that your father was a small-town doctor," wrote Harcourt, "and it would readily connote to a good many thousands of people a more than glowing story with a hero of whom you approve as one of the bases of civilization."[59] Lewis had tried hard to do that with Babbitt—to be at once critical of Babbitt's view of the world, yet sympathetic to him as well. Lewis in fact longed to write a heroic novel. He tried to do so at least twice before he met De Kruif and discovered medical research as his subject. The first of these, the labor novel, he could not write because he could find no heroism among union men, despite his admiration for Eugene Debs ("But there's so few Debses!" he had told Grace). Abandoning that idea, Lewis next considered an "American abroad story" concerning "a business man, a Zenithite, but NOT a Babbitt," as he wrote to Grace, "a university man" who is "a lover of books, music."[60] This idea was the germ for *Dodsworth*. Thus Lewis's first two impulses for what would follow *Babbitt* led him in the direction of a "heroic" novel, but he seems to have lacked confidence to act on them. Yet with De Kruif's help, he successfully wrote *Arrowsmith*.

Ultimately, Lewis found in De Kruif a soulmate who was able to bring into focus the idealistic vision that seems alternately to sharpen and blur in Lewis's novels. Both men were iconoclasts who exposed hypocrisy, but their temperaments were fundamentally different. De Kruif's entire career was characterized by what he once called "smoking out pseudo-scientific sonofabitches" yet at the same time crusading to recognize and reward legitimate medical discovery. The commonplace perception of Lewis is that he attacked fraud, but his satiric stereotypes were counterbalanced too rarely by characters of integrity and his novels were based too much on destructive criticism that did not offer hope for improving human institutions. Whether or not that judgment is valid, at least *Arrowsmith* rebuts it.

4

Mantrap, Elmer Gantry, and the Pulitzer Prize

1925–1927

Lewis planned to follow *Arrowsmith* with a novel that was tentatively entitled "The Yearner." This narrative was published in 1929 as *Dodsworth*. Lewis started planning it in December 1924, and in March 1925 he told Harcourt that this novel was to be rather short—not more than one-hundred-dred thousand words—that it was not to be serialized, and that it would be ready for publication in the fall of 1926.[1] To judge from his correspondence, he made "numerous notes" for "The Yearner" during this time; but these apparently have been lost, and so we do not know exactly how he originally intended to shape this story. He was probably thinking along the same lines as he had been in August 1922, when from Chicago he wrote to Grace about his idea for an "American abroad story" featuring "a business man, a Zenithite, but NOT a Babbitt." Later, in 1927 and early 1928, Lewis would fashion this character into Sam Dodsworth and base the plot of the narrative on his own recent past: his travels around Europe with Grace, their subsequent divorce, and Lewis's courtship of and marriage to the journalist Dorothy Thompson.

Lewis could not push through with "The Yearner" so quickly after *Arrowsmith*, however. In his letters to Harcourt, he spoke of being tired and of "loafing." The double duty of revising *Arrowsmith* simultaneously for serial and book publication must have worn him out. He was probably weary in general from having done three large, heavily researched novels in five years. He therefore decided to do something that he described to Harcourt as "much shorter and more adventurous" than *Arrowsmith*, something that would allow him to keep his hand in without having to do much research.[2] During the summer of 1925 in a rented farmhouse in Katonah, New York, Lewis wrote *Mantrap*, a light adventure narrative. The exact dates of its composition cannot be determined from Lewis's correspondence, but it seems to have taken him no more than two or three months to write the novel.

Mantrap is the story of Ralph Prescott, a New York lawyer who leaves the city to experience the wilderness in the forests of northern Saskatchewan and Manitoba. Ralph is accompanied part of the way by a blustering Babbitt named E. Wesson Woodbury, his golf partner at the country club. Woodbury sees himself as a rugged outdoorsman but actually knows next to nothing about surviving in the wild. He is the embodiment of the pioneer myth that Lewis had written about in early 1921. During their trip the two men encounter a series of problems (mostly related to the lack of creature comforts), and Woodbury deserts Prescott when an Indian guide named Joe Easter appears. Easter convinces Prescott to return with him to Mantrap Landing, a fishing and hunting outpost that he manages. Prescott agrees but is soon disillusioned by this aspect of the "wilderness experience." He sneaks out of the camp at night—only to find Easter's wife, Alverna, waiting to run away with him. Prescott reluctantly allows her to join him, and they eventually become lovers. Later they are stranded by a treacherous Cree guide and nearly starve to death; but Easter suddenly appears and rescues them. In the end, all three go their separate ways—Ralph returning to his dull and safe Manhattan existence. *Mantrap* appeared serially in *Collier's* magazine from February through May 1926 and was published in book form by Harcourt in June of that year. Lewis derived some of his material for the book from the trip he took with his brother Claude during June and July 1924.[3]

After *Mantrap* was published, Lewis told Harcourt that he recalled "nothing shoddy in it, and as far as the critics who insist that I have no right to do anything but social documents, they may all go to hell."[4] Lewis was also an astute enough literary businessman to know that anything he wrote at this point would cash in on the credit he had built up with reviewers and readers for writing three such significant books as *Main Street, Babbitt,* and *Arrowsmith.* He also knew that he had talent for writing mass-market fiction; after all, he had successfully sold stories of this type to the *Saturday Evening Post* and other magazines before and just after the publication of *Main Street.* He now thought that he would like to try a narrative on this order but somewhat longer than a short story. Lewis was probably also attracted to the large fee of $42,500 that *Collier's* had offered him for the serial rights. Lewis's writing had made him comparatively wealthy, and he was not one to turn money away from the door. Lewis needed a large income to support himself and his family as they moved from place to place. He was also often living apart from his wife and son and had to maintain two temporary domiciles. This lifestyle must have been expensive.

Instead of floundering about with "The Yearner," Lewis wrote something that kept his name before the public eye and allowed him to exercise his talent for narrative. Lewis's critics seem to have understood these motives and were consequently easy on him in their reviews of the novel. They praised *Mantrap* as an adventure yarn, and many stated that Lewis should be granted the leisure of writing a change-of-pace novel. One even wrote a spirited defense of *Mantrap* as a work of art, and the British reviewers went a step further by interpreting Ralph Prescott as yet another stereotype for the American.[5] Readers today may judge *Mantrap* a weak effort, but that is only if one compares it with the novel that preceded it, *Arrowsmith.* As an adventure story, *Mantrap* is actually a rather strong performance.[6]

In November 1925 Lewis left Grace in Katonah and went alone to Bermuda, where he corrected the proofs of *Mantrap* and began again to cast about for a topic for his next major novel. The correspondence between Lewis and Harcourt during this period is scant, so we do not know what ideas he might have been considering. By early January 1926, however, Lewis had decided to write a "preacher novel." This novel would become *Elmer Gantry,* Lewis's most scathing satire of the 1920s. In *Arrowsmith,* Lewis had written approvingly of the deification of science; in *Elmer Gantry,* he set out to investigate its opposite—fundamentalist religion—and show it to be vacuous and false.

Lewis had been making scattered notes for such a novel since 1920. One item among his forty-nine pages of notes for *Elmer Gantry* at the Beinecke is a synopsis of a story in the *Baltimore Sun* of 23 October 1920 entitled "Fasting on Her." It is a report of a Kentucky minister who had starved himself for twenty-one days in an unsuccessful attempt to reform his wayward daughter. Lewis wrote: "Meantime, tho g[rea]t crowd come to his evangelistic services, his voice has sunk to whisper. Doubtless very effective tho." Lewis noted that, were a moralistic writer such as Harold Bell Wright to base a story on it, it would be a "magnificent example" of "high ethical (religious) devotion . . . and would end with her conversion." However, to Lewis it was "an unexampled story of religious tyranny."[7]

Lewis's attitude toward the ministry in his writings had always been hostile. As Sheldon Grebstein notes, several of the sketches and stories he wrote for the *Yale Courant* and *Literary Magazine* present unflattering views of the clergy, and there are derogatory references to religion throughout his apprentice fiction and his novels of the 1920s.[8] In *Main Street,* Carol Kennicott is "dismayed to find the Christian religion, in America, in the twentieth century, as abnormal as Zoroastrianism—without the splendor" (328). Babbitt finds some of the American version of religious "splendor" in his discovery that Sunday school can be managed and promoted just like a real-estate business (210). By 1925 a propitious moment to write a satire on the ministry had arrived—a moment supplied by the spectacle of the Scopes "monkey" trial in Dayton, Tennessee, and the controversy over the obscenity case against Herbert Asbury's "Hatrack," a story published in the April 1926 issue of Mencken's *American Mercury*. Lewis eagerly seized the opportunity. One might even say that he had been lying in wait: "I've planned [it] so long," he told Harcourt, "paying my compliments to the Methodist cardinals, the Lords Day Alliance . . . and all the rest—not slightly and meekly as in *M St* and *Babbitt* but at full length, and very, very lovingly."[9]

The title character of *Elmer Gantry* is another American type: the flamboyant evangelist who rose to national prominence during the 1920s. Elmer is quite a different character from Carol Kennicott, George Babbitt, or Martin Arrowsmith. He is a quintessential rogue, with none of the idealism or humanity of Lewis's other protagonists. In this novel, Lewis abandoned his familiar narrative pattern of an individual's quest for a more spiritually fulfilling existence; Elmer is an opportunist who has no self-knowledge at all—only self-deception. After graduating from college, he decides to enter a Baptist seminary and become a minister, half-believing that his personal attractiveness will make him a successful preacher despite the lack of any true religious conversion experience. The novel takes us through his consequent rise through various religious circles—first in a tiny midwestern village, then as an evangelist with the touring revival company of Sharon Falconer, next during a brief period as an exponent of New Thought, and finally through his ascent in the Methodist church.

This latter part of his career ultimately brings him to Zenith, where he achieves a large measure of fame. From his pulpit he inveighs against the evils of gambling, bootleg liquor, and prostitution, all the while indulging in these same vices. His womanizing almost brings him to public ruin, but the force of his charismatic personality and his immensely likable public image are his salvation. By the end of the novel, it appears that Elmer will rise even higher, perhaps even to a national religious post. He declares, "We shall yet make these United States a moral nation."

Elmer Gantry is Lewis's darkest and most broadly satiric novel. Its pessimism and harsh satire can be attributed to two factors. The composition of the novel was simultaneously an expansion and a compression of the method that Lewis had used for *Arrowsmith, Babbitt,* and *Main Street.* Lewis planned and wrote this new novel in only eleven months, as opposed to the year and a half to two years that he had spent on each of his previous books. With *Elmer Gantry,* Lewis combined what had earlier been the separate phases of doing research, compiling notes, and writing a plan. At the same time, he augmented his mimetic technique of immersing himself in the world of the novel by in some ways literally living out the roles of his characters: in Kansas City he actually spoke in various pulpits, and he may even have posed as a Bible salesman in rural areas.

In Kansas City, Lewis surrounded himself with a group of ministers who were largely charlatans and opportunists—a much different class of people than those like Paul De Kruif, whom Lewis had observed during the composition of *Arrowsmith.* The result was a protagonist who is essentially a buffoon. Thus Lewis gave himself no real opportunity to write a fair-minded, accurate novel about the church in America, but neither did he want to do that: he wanted to write a controversial book that satirized one particular segment of the larger spectrum of worship. Lewis was again following the lead of Mencken, as he had partly done in creating George Babbitt. Mencken, a life-long foe of "the malignant moralist" in American life, had been urging him to write such a novel.

Equally significant in the composition of *Elmer Gantry* was the turbulence in Lewis's life. Almost everything that Lewis did during the year 1926 pushed him to the edge of a nervous breakdown. He exhausted himself in Kansas City with his efforts to create as much controversy (and generate as much publicity) as he could—preaching, interviewing ministers, making public pronouncements, even refusing to accept the Pulitzer Prize when it was awarded to *Arrowsmith.* Then, when he was halfway through the draft, his father died. This event in itself was enough to distract Lewis from his writing, but it also came at just the time when Lewis realized that there was no hope for patching up his marriage to Grace; and so he began to drink quite heavily. These circumstances impaired his work on *Elmer Gantry,* and Lewis even bitterly parodied some of his troubles in the novel itself. The emotional and physical effects of these various problems partly account for the jaundiced view of humanity evident in *Elmer Gantry,* as well as for some weaknesses of plotting in the latter parts of the novel, which Lewis and Harcourt tried to repair when the book was in proof.

On 13 January 1926 Harcourt, Brace issued a press release announcing Lewis's departure for Kansas City, where he intended to gather material for what would become *Elmer Gantry.* When he arrived there in mid-January, he contacted a local minister whom Mencken had recommended: the Reverend William L. Stidger, pastor of the Linwood Boulevard Methodist Church. Lewis had in fact met Stidger earlier—in Terre Haute, Indiana, in August 1922. Stidger was then lecturing on the Chautauqua circuit; Lewis was en route to Chicago to see Eugene Debs, planning his novel about the American labor movement. *Babbitt* had just been published, and Stidger called on Lewis at his hotel to lay out his objections to the characterization of the Reverend John Jennison Drew in *Babbitt.* He suggested that Lewis come to Detroit (where he was then preaching) and learn about the clergy as they truly were. By 1926 Stidger had a new pastorate in Kansas City, at the crossroads of the Bible Belt—an even better location for Lewis's fieldwork.

Shortly after arriving in Kansas City, Lewis began interviewing Stidger and reported to Donald Brace that Stidger was a "corker," that his "book sermons" were "excellent," and that he would be of great help in writing the "preacher novel."[10] Sometime before 27 January he and Stidger took a train trip to Emporia, Kansas, ostensibly to visit the novelist William Allen White but apparently also for Lewis to reacquaint himself with the Midwest. He would set the action of *Elmer Gantry* here, after having used other settings for *Arrowsmith* and *Mantrap.* He wrote Grace, "I've had huge and delightful reglimpses of the Midwest and Babbittry and first glimpses of the church." In Emporia, Lewis toured Emporia College, which he described as "a Presbyterian school with an elegant scientific library of 72 books mostly dating from 1890." Lewis probably based parts of his description of Elmer's alma mater, Terwillinger College, on this institution (and probably also on his memories of Oberlin and its atmosphere of muscular Christianity). He also visited the University of Kansas in Lawrence. In another letter to Grace, he reported some of his impressions of the university:

Here they have private frats to live in stead of U dormotories [*sic*].
But alas they have house *mothers* to keep the boys from profanity,
vice, and naturalness. . . . The Chancellor . . . tall, slim, shock of
very fine white hair. Longing, oh so much to be a Liberal, but
scared to death of anything Rough or Destructive. . . . convocation
. . . most of the faculty, some townsfolk, all in the vast gymna-
sium, with movable chairs brung in . . . Star Spingled [*sic*] Banner,
Lord's Prayer, female sings two songs.[11]

These scattered perceptions also found their way into Lewis's descriptions
of Terwillinger College and Mizpah Theological Seminary, where Elmer
enrolls upon graduation from Terwillinger.

Shortly after concluding this trip, Lewis left Kansas City for a two-
month vacation in the Southwest, planning to return in April. He met
Grace in Tucson, Arizona, and they traveled west together, making a last-
ditch attempt to repair their marriage. This effort seems to have succeeded
temporarily; but by the time they had arrived in Kansas City their relationship was again in disrepair, and Grace returned to New York. Although his marriage was crumbling, professionally Lewis was never more
directed and driven. He was eager to start writing *Elmer Gantry*—more so,
perhaps, than he had been for any of his previous novels. Even on vacation, he was doing informal research and thinking through the plot—unlike the slow and deliberative process he usually followed. He told Harcourt on 24 February that the plan for the novel was "already formed in
my head in a rather complete way" and that producing a finished book
was only a question of "developing the details of which I have already
thought." He reported that he had been "going to a lot of churches,"
including "a fair number" in southern California.[12] One of these was the
Church of the Foursquare Gospel in Los Angeles, headquarters of the female evangelist Aimee Semple McPherson, then at the height of her fame.
(McPherson was an inspiration for the character Sharon Falconer.) Lewis
was working hard: his letters to Harcourt during this time say little about
leisure and lots about "Elmer Bloor," his initial name for the title character.[13] Lewis was also contemplating the title of the new book. He discovered that his first choice, "Sounding Brass," had already been used, and so
he decided that like *Babbitt* and *Arrowsmith* this new novel should also have
as its title the name of the central character. He tentatively settled on "Rev.
Bloor," which he decided was actually better than "Sounding Brass" because it was "distinctive" and not "metaphorical."[14]

By the time that Lewis returned to Kansas City on 4 April, he was well

```
TIMETABLE

Elmer born                              nov    1881

Grads from Terwilliger at 22                   1903

Kicked out of Mizpah, 25, spring               1906

Traveling salesman to 28                       1906 - 09 ✱

With Shaman to 30                              1909 - 11

Mrs. Riddle & New Thot to 32                   1911 - 1913

Banjo Crossing, one year                       1913 - 1914
   (900 people)

Rudd Center, one year                          1914 - 1915
   (4100)

Vulcan, 3 years                                1915 - 1918
   (47,000)
   (Nat born '16, Bunny '17)

Sparta, 2 years                                1918 - 1920
   (129,000)

Zenith, x years; in tale :—                    1920 - 1926
   (361,000 in 1920.
   (Elmer 39 in 1920.
   Probley NY in 1927
Toomis 68 in 1926.

✱ Elmer meets Shaman almost year before joins her.
```

To next page

Fig. 22. Timetable for *Elmer Gantry* (Yale Collection of American Literature, Beinecke Rare Book and Manuscript Library, Yale University)

prepared for "the field." He settled into rooms at the Hotel Ambassador and he went to work right away. He contacted Stidger again and began to accompany him as he went about his clerical duties. Stidger also began introducing Lewis to some of his fellow ministers. Within two weeks, Lewis would report to Grace that he had met "at least thirty" preachers. However, Lewis soon discovered that although Stidger was the perfect model to observe and then transform into a fictional character, he could not work with Stidger in the way that he had with Paul De Kruif. Lewis simply could not tolerate Stidger's crass, opportunistic attitude toward his work. Lewis found that he needed someone around him who was not like the people he was satirizing—someone like De Kruif, a person of integrity and high intellect.

Lewis found such a person in the Reverend Leon M. Birkhead, to whom he had been introduced by William Stidger. Lewis described Birkhead to Harrison Smith as "a Unitarian and generally disillusioned preacher who was for ten years a Methodist."[15] Birkhead, pastor of the All Souls Unitarian Church in Kansas City, was a well-known religious liberal and a leader in the Unitarian Church in America. He had attended McKendree College and the Union Theological Seminary of Columbia University. He was one of the original signers of the "Humanist Manifesto" of the church and a regular contributor of articles to the church's newsletter, the *Weekly Liberal*.[16] Lewis developed a friendship with Birkhead, and he used him as a "cyclopedia for data about church organization and the like." Birkhead became in effect Lewis's research assistant for this novel. But Lewis was quick to point out to Harrison Smith that Birkhead would be only a technical informant. Similarly, Lewis told Harcourt that Birkhead "will work with me in the matter of facts, of exact data."[17] In other words, Lewis did not try to absorb the personality and character traits of Birkhead as he had done with De Kruif. Lewis also told Smith that this time there would be no ambiguity about the authorship of his novel, as there had been with *Arrowsmith:* "He will not, however, have anything like the share taken by Paul . . . and it is distinctly understood that he is temporary assistant—in no way a collaborator."[18]

Unlike De Kruif, Birkhead seems not to have had any literary inclinations. But like the young scientist, Birkhead seems to have served Lewis as a sounding board and as a companion, both of which Lewis needed during the composition of a novel. Lewis wrote Harcourt that Birkhead was "personally most charming as well as most learned, young enough to be comradely . . . and though he doesn't even smoke, he enjoys language of the type made holy by Paul . . . and myself."[19] Lewis needed someone to talk with, to try out scenes on, to have as an audience, perhaps, for improvising bits of dialogue. De Kruif assisted Lewis with these tasks; Birkhead was by contrast simply in residence while Lewis made notes and later when he wrote the draft.

Lewis's research was as thorough as ever. In his suite at the Hotel Ambassador, he assembled a library of approximately two hundred volumes on church history and religious practices, and he made notes on his readings. Lewis was directed to nearly all of these books by Birkhead, who compiled a partial list of them in 1928 when Haldeman-Julius Publications brought out a pamphlet in its Little Blue Book series entitled *Is "Elmer Gantry" True?* Birkhead contributed three of the five essays in it: "The Writing of 'Elmer Gantry'," "Aimee Semple McPherson's Alton, Illinois, Revivalistic Orgy," and "'Elmer Gantry' and What Is Wrong with the Preachers," which he delivered as a sermon at his church on 10 April 1927. Unfortunately, none of these essays contains any information about how Lewis wrote *Elmer Gantry* (even though Birkhead and his wife were living with Lewis when he wrote the draft). However, "The Writing of 'Elmer Gantry'" does suggest the breadth and scope of Lewis's interest in the ministry, even if he probably did not consult all of the volumes listed in Birkhead's essay. According to Birkhead, these books included instructionary manuals, hymnals, sermon aids, novels, and heavy theological tomes, both modernist and pietistic. Among them were William James's *Varieties of Religious Experience*, Andrew Dickson White's *History of the Warfare of Science with Theology*, and Mary Baker Eddy's *Science and Health*. Other books had such titles as *The Pastoral Office, Principles of Preaching, Cyclopedia of Pastoral Methods, Primitive Traits in Religious Revivals*, and *The Psychology of Religious Mysticism.*[20]

Lewis also learned about the operation of the Methodist church, probably from Birkhead. In the notebook there are three pages on this topic. For example, Lewis described the "Ladies Aid Society" as follows:

General gossiping society-shop-of ch[urch] aid to pastor in raising church funds. Purchases new carpet for the pastor's study. Uusually [*sic*] serves the meals at the church, Oyster suppers, ice cream and strawberry festivals, ects., [*sic*] This sewing society makes quilts, aprons, and holds one or two bazaars each yr about Xmas and Easter time.

Commentary much like this can be found in chapter 21 of the novel, where Lewis describes Elmer's church in Banjo Crossing (294). Another notebook item is a description of the "Womens Foreign Missionary Soci-

ety," which "raises hell and money for . . . missions." There is also a page
entitled "Kinds of ME Conferences." In addition, there are two pages of
newspaper clippings about a Methodist Episcopal conference in Des
Moines, Iowa. The articles were from the church newspaper, the *Christian
Advocate,* and describe the program of events at the conference—material
that Lewis used in chapter 21, where Elmer attends the annual ME conference in Chicago and learns of his assignment to Zenith (298–302). Some
fifteen additional pages in the notebook are character lists, including
Sharon Falconer's traveling crew, Elmer's classmates at Terwillinger College and at Mizpah Seminary, the "Staff At Victory Thought-Power HQ,
San Francisco," and various "Preachers in Zenith."

These notes, however, are far less copious than those for *Babbitt* or *Arrowsmith,* and the primary method by which Lewis did research for *Elmer
Gantry* was not reading about theology or watching ministers preach. This
time he applied his mimetic abilities to a more challenging task and actually tried to live the life that his characters led, rather than just observing a
person in his or her milieu. Lewis immersed himself in the world of his
novel to the point of complete saturation. A main activity, for example,
was a weekly Thursday luncheon in his suite at the Ambassador that was
attended by some fifteen to twenty Kansas City ministers of different de-
nominations. This widely publicized gathering quickly became known as
"Sinclair Lewis's Sunday School Class," and it attracted national media
coverage.[21]

Lewis's goal in these meetings was to elicit reactions from the ministers
to a variety of theological principles, mostly fundamentalist ones. A different topic was announced for each meeting, and Lewis would arm himself
beforehand with a long list of questions that he culled from reading the
religious reference books he kept in his room. Many of the topics covered
can be found in *Elmer Gantry.* On one page of the notebook, for example,
Lewis wrote the heading "Fundaments of Fundamentalism" and listed
such issues as "verbal inspir[ation] of Bible [the inerrancy of scripture];
virgin birth; bodily resurrection; substitutionary atonement; premillenial
coming [of Christ]." In these meetings, Lewis debated such points with
members of the group in much the same way that he had argued about
certain issues in medical research with Paul De Kruif. His intentions were
to see something of the spirit of the person he was interviewing, to obtain
material for the novel, and, it would seem, to play the role of an actual
evangelist—with the missionary-like zeal of such a person but without his
religious convictions. In so doing, Lewis hoped to be able to create such a
person in the novel with verisimilitude. "What was it like to be a *real
evangelist?"* Lewis asked himself. Samuel Harkness, a Presbyterian minis-

ter who attended the sessions, wrote an account of a typical meeting for the *Christian Century:*

> Soul-shaking moments come when Lewis speaks with the passion of an Old Testament prophet, demanding, "What sacrifices do you make? What risks will you take to end these paralyzing influences which you tell me are creeping over your church? Who will give up his wife and children, house and bank account? Who will literally follow Jesus into loneliness, ridicule, and death? . . . Why don't you tell your congregations that you are agnostics? . . . The conventional Christ is sheer myth."[22]

In these meetings Lewis was also able to tune his ear to the idiom of the ministry. A page in the notebook headed "Phrases" lists the locutions that various characters utter in the novel. On pages 153 and 195 of the novel, for example, one finds the phrases "Where will you spend eternity?" "Saved by the blood of the Lamb," and "Get Right With God"; these are listed in the notebook. Some other notes are less precise, such as "Brothering each other," "Clash of voices all ascending to God in prayer at once esp on radio," and "Use of initials in all organizations." One issue that is repeatedly debated in the novel, the acceptance of Jesus' divine nature, appears several times in the notebook. On the "Phrases" page Lewis wrote: "Jesus was either the son of God or the greatest impostor the world has ever known." One sees the same sentiment expressed by the Reverend John Roach Straton (one of several models for the character of Elmer) in a clipping in the notebook that describes a debate on this topic in 1925 between Straton and Charles Francis Potter, a leading modernist. Straton is reported to have said that if Jesus was not a deity, "then He was the greatest fraud and humbug who ever walked the earth." One finds similar statements in the published novel, especially in chapters 28 and 29, where the Dayton evolution trial prompts arguments about the divinity of Jesus.

During the approximately six weeks that Lewis spent in Kansas City, he enthusiastically took advantage of every possible tangential experience that religious life there had to offer. Initially, he simply visited different churches, attending sometimes two or three services on a single Sunday. With that experience behind him, he went one step further and started speaking in various pulpits—delivering ersatz sermons in the manner of Elmer Gantry. This was yet another stage in the evolution of his mimetic method. Of one such occasion, he told Grace, "I went in and preached a fine sermon, I did, and there were five preachers in the front row, there were, and they all said I was a swell preacher, they did."[23] To Harcourt, he

Debaters on the Deity of Christ Give Outline of Their Arguments

Pastors Potter and Straton Will Meet To-Day and Arrange Details.

All arrangements for the debate of religious issues between the Rev. Charles F. Potter, pastor of the West Side Unitarian Church, and Dr. John Roach Straton, pastor of Calvary Baptist Church, will be made this morning when the two meet in the study of Dr. Straton to arrange for place and judges. The two clergymen gave The World yesterday an inkling of what form their arguments will take on the subject they will first debate—"The Deity of Christ."

Dr. Straton, Baptist fundamentalist, says:

"Undeniably, Christ did believe and did declare that He was the Son of God. If it be admitted that He was both a wise and a good man, then He was what he claimed to be—an incarnation of Deity. If not, then He was the greatest fraud and humbug who ever walked the earth. Unless He was fully God as He claimed to be, then He was a fool or a knave. We know that the author of the Sermon on the Mount was not a fool and that the unselfish Christ of Calvary was not a knave. In addition the Bible throughout recognizes Christ as God. Christ's wisdom is a proof of His Deity. His sinlessness and holiness is another attribute of God. The power of Christ, past and present, is a proof of his Deity. Our hearts respond to the glorious truth that God is our father and we know that the highest summary of the very essence of the Divine Being is given when the Bible says 'God is love.' We find in Jesus Christ the manifestation of a love so pure and holy and perfect that it proves in itself that He was God."

The Rev. Charles F. Potter, Unitarian and Modernist, says:

"The belief that Jesus of Nazareth was Almighty God incarnated in a man has come down to us from early centuries when Christian enthusiasm extended the Christian vocabulary. They called Him God because deification was the highest compliment they could pay to His unusual personality. Deifying Jesus has removed Him from men. Most Modernists are trying to rediscover the real man, Jesus. He was evidently an exceptionally good man, perhaps the best who has so far lived, but He was not a God. He was divine in the same sense that all men are, differing from them only in the degree of His divinity. He Himself frequently said 'Follow me,' but he never said 'worship me.' I find that to-day the leadership of

The Rev. CHARLES FRANCIS POTTER
© by UNDERWOOD & UNDERWOOD

The Rev. Dr. JOHN ROACH STRATON

Jesus is a much more attractive and compelling idea to modern men than the doctrine of His Deity."

Mr. Potter was for ten years a Baptist minister.

Dr. O. W. Van Osdel, Baptist pastor from Grand Rapids, Mich., was the speaker in the Fundamentalist mass meeting at Calvary Church yesterday afternoon. He expressed deep anxiety for the 500,000 Jews on the east side who are without the gospel of Christ and urged financial support of agencies working for the conversion and salvation of adherents to the Jewish faith.

When the speaker was asked, at the conclusion of his sermon, whether his anxiety for the Jews extended to the fear that, dying without belief in the fundamental Christian doctrines for which he stood, they would go to hell, he replied:

"I can't say as to hell, but they won't go to heaven."

Fig. 23. "Debaters on the Deity of Christ" clipping from *Elmer Gantry* notes (Yale Collection of American Literature, Beinecke Rare Book and Manuscript Library, Yale University) wrote, "All of this damned fool preaching in pulpits and so on which I have been doing has been largely to give me a real feeling of the church from the inside."[24]

Some of his sermons were true spectacles. Lewis seems to have wanted to be a lightning rod for controversy. One particular episode in Kansas City focused the national spotlight on him. On 18 April 1926 Lewis spoke from the pulpit of the Linwood Boulevard Christian (Campbellite) Church and gave God ten minutes to strike him dead as an infidel and thereby prove His existence. (Lewis seems to have taken his cue from George Bernard Shaw, who issued a similar challenge—although Shaw only gave the deity three minutes. "I am a very busy man," Shaw had said.) As Grace Lewis noted in her memoir, this is "the most apocryphal of the Lewis myths," and she attempted to "let the truth . . . be told"; but even her account differs from the report in the New York Times.[25]

What seems to have happened is as follows. On 11 April Luther Burbank, the experimental botanist and outspoken champion of Darwinism, had died, and fundamentalists had pointed to his death as an example of how God dealt with infidels. Lewis apparently showed his audience newspaper clippings and letters from unidentified fundamentalist groups that expressed this sentiment. (Grace said one letter was headed "Burbank Punished" and signed "A Believer in Hell.") Then, capitalizing on the macabre spectacle of William Jennings Bryan's stroke at the Scopes trial the previous summer and his death five days later, Lewis said:

> Burbank said he was an infidel and was "struck down." Bryan said he was a Fundamentalist and he became a "martyr dying in his glory." Bryan died fifteen years younger than Burbank. Why didn't God strike Burbank down at the time of his utterances and make things clear, if, as pious people say, he died only because he was an infidel? The Fundamentalist God moves slowly and by the death bed when there are no witnesses.[26]

One wonders how much of this tangential activity was actually necessary in order for Lewis to write Elmer Gantry. On the one hand, he had to be around someone for a lengthy period of time to absorb his or her personality. This explains why he spent so much time traveling to different places, meeting people, and making so many notes. But on the other hand, much of this procedure was superfluous in his composition of Elmer Gantry. Lewis already had a solid idea of the type of character he wanted to satirize, even before he went to Kansas City, and he had done sufficient preliminary research about theology and church history to write the novel.

He was also evidently writing the plan (no longer extant) at the same time that he was conducting his "Sunday school class" and making his notes. On 4 April he wrote Harcourt, "I already have the story so well organized in my mind that I hope to have the whole plan done in a month, and be into the actual writing."[27] Lewis was thus drastically streamlining the process he had used for earlier novels—even rushing through it: he told Harcourt in mid-April that the plan was "going down, fast, and all looks well." The plan itself was actually completed when he arrived in Pequot, Minnesota, and began writing the draft. As we will see, several of the ministers on whom Lewis drew in developing the character of Elmer were not part of the evangelistic community in Kansas City at all but were instead figures whose careers Lewis had been following for some years.

It might be that these other activities served Lewis instead mostly as outlets for his restless energy and as a way of generating publicity for the novel. One must also wonder whether Lewis, the perpetual outsider, was again gathering more material than he actually needed to satisfy his curiosity about a world in which he had once thought he might belong. Lewis was genuinely curious about the ministry, just as he had been curious about scientific research. Mark Schorer reported that later in life Lewis would habitually turn to the religion page of the Monday morning newspaper and read the reviews of the sermons delivered the day before.[28] In addition, as he grew in stature as a public figure, Lewis's natural showmanship became increasingly pronounced. All of these aims were well served by his sermons, although eventually this frenetic activity exhausted Lewis and nearly prevented him from finishing the novel.

Lewis's desire for publicity also led him to refuse the Pulitzer Prize for Fiction, which was awarded to *Arrowsmith* for the year 1925. As a former advertising manager for Stokes, Lewis knew the promotional value of such a gesture, and he welcomed the attention that it brought him. Schorer has shown that Lewis and Harcourt carefully laid their plans for Lewis's public rejection of the award. After being told on 23 April that he had won, Lewis drafted a letter refusing it and sent a copy to Harcourt, asking him to go over it "with the greatest care."[29] Both Harcourt and Lewis made changes in the letter, and together they deliberated about word choice, tone, and structure. The early drafts of the statement are not extant, so we cannot determine the exact changes. But from Lewis's correspondence we can see that Harcourt played an important role in shaping the announcement.

First, Harcourt told Lewis that he should wait "a day or two" after the press reported his winning the award and then issue his statement declining it. Lewis had wanted to release the statement as soon as the award was announced. Harcourt also thought that Lewis's original version of the statement was "not quite serious and dignified enough in tone." He explained to Lewis precisely what he should be objecting to: "You're taking your proper position as the champion of the artist. You are not attacking the Y.M.C.A. or the taste of suburban dinner-tables—they may really be sympathetic to your point of view."[30] Harcourt was thus able to restrain Lewis's tendencies toward flamboyance and make his refusal of the award a dignified act. Harcourt was particularly concerned about the writer's image at this time, given Lewis's antics in Kansas City. Harcourt was every bit as interested in publicity as Lewis was. He orchestrated the entire press event with the precision timing of a field commander: "a summary story released at 4:01 P.M., followed by the complete letter at 4:07."[31] But Harcourt also knew that creating publicity simply for publicity's sake could be counterproductive.

The final version of the letter (reprinted in appendix 5) is a strongly worded statement that in several ways anticipates the assessments of the American literary climate that Lewis would make in his Nobel Prize acceptance speech in 1930. The letter was headed, "SINCLAIR LEWIS REFUSES PULITZER PRIZE." In it, Lewis cogently stated his objections to the award, which he attacked as a force that was dangerous to writers, keeping them "safe, polite, obedient, and sterile." Lewis seized on the terms of the award ("for the American novel . . . which shall best present the wholesome atmosphere of American life and the highest standard of manners and manhood") to say that such conditions were hazardous to artistic freedom.

Lewis's research allowed him to develop a protagonist who resembled several real-life evangelists with whom readers of the time would have been familiar but who was not based entirely on any one individual. One obvious model for Elmer was Billy Sunday, whom Lewis had caricatured in *Babbitt* as "Mike Monday." There are in fact two episodes in *Elmer Gantry* that closely parallel real incidents in Sunday's career. Elmer steals a sermon from Robert G. Ingersoll, just as Sunday was accused of plagiarizing his address before war veterans at Beaver Falls, Pennsylvania, on 26 May 1912, from Ingersoll's Decoration Day speech given at the Academy of Music in New York on 30 May 1882.[32] The description of Sharon Falconer's crew wrecking their hotel rooms in chapter 14 also seems to be based on a similar incident in 1915 when a landlord sued Sunday for damage done to his house by Sunday's entourage.[33]

A primary model for Elmer was William Stidger. An imposing man, Stidger resembled Elmer physically. (Like Elmer, he was also apparently not very intelligent: unaware of the kind of novel that Lewis was likely to write, Stidger boasted publicly that Lewis's protagonist was to be modeled on him.) Like Elmer, Stidger was flamboyant and brash. He was well known in religious circles, though not at all respected by his fellow clerics. When Lewis met him, Stidger had written a half-dozen books on church methods, all of which described ways to attract large audiences to services. They had such titles as *That God's House May Be Filled, Building Sermons with Symphonic Themes,* and *God Is at the Organ.* One book in particular— *Standing Room Only,* published in 1922—seems to have inspired Lewis in his descriptions of how Elmer builds attendance in his various pastorates: Stidger had turned the run-down St. Mark's Methodist Episcopal Church in Detroit into the most popular church in the city, just as Elmer at the peak of his career rejuvenates a dilapidated church in a poor district of Zenith. One of Stidger's innovations was the placement of a revolving electric cross atop the church steeple, a detail that Lewis used in creating Sharon Falconer's Waters of Jordan Tabernacle. Like Elmer, Stidger had been a Baptist minister before turning to Methodism; and he too had worked up through a series of progressively more choice assignments before ending up in Kansas City, just as Elmer does before he secures his appointment to the Zenith pastorate.

A look at some of the chapters in *Standing Room Only* indicates how Stidger inspired Lewis. Elmer's "Lively Sunday Evenings" were Stidger's trademark, and in Elmer's crusade to make Christianity "a glad religion" he uses Stidger's own coinage (chapter 26). Stidger's suggestions for ministerial success were embarrassingly crass. For instance, in a chapter entitled "The Fine Art of Tripling the Loose Collections," Stidger wrote that "the first reason why a pastor . . . does progressive church work is to save souls," but that the second and third reasons were to "get a crowd and fill the church with the atmosphere of success" and to "make it pay financially" (149). On one page of this book there is even a chart showing the correlation between increased advertising expenditures and revenue from the loose collection. In one of the most candid chapters, "Selling the Church Gates to the Junkman," Stidger suggested advertising the sanctuary in the local newspapers as "cool as a cave" on hot summer days and encouraging pedestrians to "come in and rest." Stidger wrote: "Folks who were waiting for cars, tired women, women with bundles and babies, found it a blessed relief" (166–67).

Such traits went into the personality of Elmer. For other elements of his character, particularly his professional activities, Lewis drew selectively from the careers and personalities of other people. One of these was the Reverend John Roach Straton, a famous Baptist reformer whose career

Lewis followed closely. In fact, Lewis's earliest ideas for the characterization of Elmer were probably drawn from reading about and observing Straton. Lewis's notebook contains six clippings about Straton that date from 1924 and 1925, well before Lewis announced publicly that he was going to Kansas City to write a novel about the ministry. (In her memoir, Grace stated that in 1925 Lewis heard Straton preach in New York City.) If Stidger was the model for Elmer's apprenticeship and rise, then Straton must have been the inspiration for Elmer's ascent to the pastorate of the Yorkville Methodist Church in New York and the leadership of "the National Association for Purity in Art and the Press (NAPAP)." In 1918 Straton became pastor of the world-famous Calvary Baptist Church in Manhattan and upon the death of William Jennings Bryan in 1925 he became the titular leader of fundamentalist forces in America.

Straton was stern and puritanical-looking; he wore steel-rimmed pince-nez, and in photographs he looks dour and disapproving. In temperament, however, he was as flamboyant a figure as Stidger: reports in the *New York Times* during 1925 and 1926 give an outline of Straton's activities, many of which influenced Lewis's conception of Elmer. In a much-publicized sermon on "How to Save America" on 20 September 1925, for example, Straton declared that "the real sinister movements in this country" were "the motion pictures, the forces against prohibition, [the advocates of] best-sellers, race tracks, atheism and modernism and radicalism." These are Elmer's targets as well.[34] Straton was a trustee of the Anti-Saloon League and the Lord's Day Alliance, which opposed Sunday motoring—two of the several vice societies Elmer endorses in chapter 30 and throughout the Zenith sections of the novel.

Straton was perhaps most famous as a vice crusader, a mission that Elmer undertakes for its publicity value. Like Elmer, Straton declared that he could identify specific establishments of vice (chapters 23 and 26). Chapter 23 of *Elmer Gantry*, in which Elmer organizes a mudslinging campaign to discredit his fellow Zenith ministers, echoes Straton's political grandstanding. He was not content to affirm his own views, as historians of revivalism have shown; he also used his pulpit to challenge other clergymen. Finally, Straton received an honorary D.D. degree from Shurtleff College in Alton, Illinois, in 1906; there was considerable skepticism about its authenticity until the president of the college vouchsafed it. Similarly, in chapter 30 Elmer receives a suspect D.D. from Abernathy College, "an institution of Methodist learning."

According to evidence in the notebook, Lewis may have planned to use parts of Straton's career more extensively than he ultimately did. On the page entitled "TIMETABLE FOR ELMER IN ZENITH," Lewis refers to a debate that would occur during December 1925, or in roughly the final three chapters of the narrative. Although no such event appears in the novel, the debate that Lewis referred to was one that took place between Straton and Charles Francis Potter in the fall of 1925. Among the Straton clippings in the notebook are four press reports about the so-called Fundamentalist-Modernist debates, which attracted international attention. When Lewis was working on the draft of *Elmer Gantry* in July 1926, a controversial article about Straton entitled "The Fundamentalist Pope" appeared in Mencken's *American Mercury;* it doubtless kept Straton in the forefront of Lewis's thinking and planning for the novel, as did newspaper reports at about the same time concerning the twin scandals of Straton's acceptance of thirty thousand dollars in lecture fees from the Ku Klux Klan and of a revolt by Straton's congregation over his plans to build an expensive skyscraper church.[35]

Yet another partial model for Elmer was J. Frank Norris, pastor of the Calvary Church in Fort Worth, Texas. According to Schorer, Lewis made a trip to Fort Worth in February 1925 specifically to hear Norris preach. Two clippings about Norris appear among Lewis's notes. Their source and date are not identified, but next to one of them is written a Bible reference, "Luke 17: 31–36," in the hand of Paul De Kruif, indicating that at least one of these clippings dates from as early as 1922, or at the latest 1923 or 1924—well before the Kansas City trip. Norris, called "The Texas Tornado" because of his rambunctious pulpit manner, was pastor of a church that boasted eight thousand members in 1925 and claimed to be the world's largest Baptist congregation.[36] Like Straton, Norris was a vice crusader; he once preached a sermon entitled "The Ten Biggest Devils in Fort Worth, Names Given" (cf. Elmer's "Can Strangers Find Haunts of Vice in Zenith?", 315). A physically imposing man like Elmer, he too campaigned against prostitution and liquor.

Two famous stories about Norris give a good indication of his resemblance to Elmer. In 1912 Norris led a crusade to shut down the red-light district in Fort Worth and one night arrived home to find a lynching party awaiting him. He challenged them and won, but a week later his church burned down and he was charged with arson—the victim, presumably, of a plot meant to run him out of town. He also made headlines in the late summer of 1926, when Lewis was beginning to write the first draft of the novel: Norris shot and killed an unarmed man during a heated argument in the minister's study. Although he was later acquitted on the grounds of self-defense, the event earned Norris another nickname—"the pistol-toting divine."[37]

A final inspiration for Elmer may have been William H. Ridgway,

DRESSY CRUSADER OF NEW HOLY WAR IS PASTOR TO 7,000

The Rev. Dr. J. F. Norris Regards Church Liberals as Judases and Hunts 'Possums.

FORT WORTH ONCE GOT OUT A ROPE FOR HIM.

But He Met Would-Be Lynchers and They Went Home—No Church Sociables for Him.

More important than even the Crusades, and as passionate as the Reformation, is the present holy war being preached by the Fundamentalist ministers against the Modernists, according to the Rev. J. Frank Norris, D. D., of Fort Worth, Tex., one of the speakers this week at the mass meetings in Calvary Baptist Church.

The war is just beginning, and eventually there may take from within all Protestant branches two great divisions that will supersede the present diversity of sects. These will be the Fundamentalists and the Liberals.

Last Sunday at the opening of the present series of mass meetings, Dr. Norris denounced the Modernist ministers as contemporary Judases. This evening he will speak again, and this time he will discuss a subject that is in his opinion of chief importance to his cause, evolution.

Dr. Norris sat in the lobby of the Great Northern Hotel, just across the street from Calvary Church, yesterday afternoon and told about his holy war.

Dr. Norris is far from gloomy, and he rather thick. He was dressed in a well hung suit of rather light brown, a white shirt with rather wide black stripes, and a soft hat tilted slightly to one side of his head. He is smooth shaven and trim. His manner is more slick than forbidding; he would sit very comfortably in a group of traveling salesmen, but any company of prophets might look upon him with doubt.

Dr. Norris was thirty, fifteen years ago, when he became pastor at Fort Worth. There wasn't so much modernist agitation then, but there were

saloons, a red-light district and gambling. He set out to clean up the town, with the result that one night a mass meeting was called, no women or youths under twenty-one admitted. "There'll be a dead preacher in town if you've got nerve enough," said a speaker.

No Ice Cream Sociables.

"That was in nineteen and twelve," said Dr. Norris. "A friend of mine called me up and told me they were coming that-a-way with a rope. I went right downtown and met them on Peter Smith Square. 'I understand you were looking for me,' I said. Well, they didn't answer a word, just drifted off home.

"The next week my church was burned. They indicted and tried me on the charge of setting it on fire, but of course I was acquitted. And it was while the trial was going on that I converted and brought to Christ the very Judge who was trying it.

"I came out of that trouble with only 300 in the church, out of house and home, and I only weighed 129 pounds. Now we've got 7,000 in the congregation and seven big buildings and a choir of 730 voices and 22 people to assist me, and we're growing at the rate of 1,000 a year. And I weigh 179 pounds, and I'm as hard as nails; you can't tire me out."

A strange mixture of Puritan and, yes, liberal, himself is this crusader. He goes to every baseball and football game he can and he has three dogs for coon and "possum" hunting. But he deplores circus methods in running a church. "Too much pie and not enough piety," he says with a snap.

"No ice cream sociables at my church," he declares. "No church suppers. We need less ham and sham and more heaven."

Decries Fundamentalists.

On the listing vessel of his obsolete doctrines the fundamentalist stands like the boy on the burning deck, whence all but he had fled, according to Rev. Vivian T. Pomeroy, English author and divine, speaking last night at a meeting of the Unitarian Laymen's League, New York Chapters, at All Souls' Church.

Mr. Pomeroy was discussing the series of fundamentalist mass meetings at Calvary Baptist Church this week. He said such "obscurantism" in England has already dimmed to "a pathetic and dispirited protest," and predicted that fundamentalism here has long since lost its fight.

Referring to the war proclaimed by the fundamentalists on those who would not accept their creeds, Mr. Pomeroy said: "The religion which on its active side consists in attacking other people's opinions is a poor thing. It is a sense of God turned sour."

In Calvary Church last night, Rev. W. B. Riley, D. D., of Minneapolis, told another mass meeting that modernists, by machinations as skillful as any ever practiced in a political campaign, are getting control of Baptist churches and schools. There is not a school in the entire field of the Northern Baptist Convention that has a resident Baptist preacher who is not a modernist, he said.

Fig. 24. "Dressy Crusader of New Holy War" clipping from *Elmer Gantry* notes (Yale Collection of American Literature, Beinecke Rare Book and Manuscript Library, Yale University) whom Lewis had mentioned in *Babbitt*. Ridgway was an inventor and manufacturer of steam-hydraulic equipment who undertook a second career in 1907 as a writer of religious books and as a columnist for the *Sunday School Times*. He had become famous in industry for his original advertising techniques, and he carried these into his religious writing. Lewis had Babbitt read one of Ridgway's columns ("The Busy Man's Corner") for ideas about boosting church attendance: "If you have a Sunday School class without any pep and get-up-and-go in it, that is, without interest, that is uncertain in attendance, that acts like a fellow with the spring fever, let old Dr. Ridgway write you a prescription. Rx. Invite the Bunch for Supper" (210). Lewis met Ridgway in February 1926 in Los Angeles. Ridgway described the encounter in 1935 in a book entitled *"In God We Trust" (Cries the Little Red Penny) and Why Not!* According to Ridgway, Lewis claimed to be a God-fearing fundamentalist, and Ridgway believed him. Lewis added that he had been reading Ridgway's columns and that he was "an old Sunday school worker" himself. (The point of Lewis's fiction seems to have escaped Ridgway completely: he described *Babbitt* as "a story of contemporary life" and said that Lewis won the Nobel Prize "for having produced the typical American novel.")

Lewis evidently had fun misleading Ridgway. He introduced to Ridgway his secretary, Louis Florey (Ridgway calls him "Persi"), as someone who had been "brought up in a fine Christian home" but who "was sent to a New York City college, where all his mother's religion was destroyed and out of which he has come a little short of an out and out atheist." Lewis continued, in Ridgway's recollection:

> "I have talked to him a lot with no success. Last night I had him up to the Aimee McPherson tabernacle where the converted prize fighter Paul Rader is holding evangelistic meetings. I thought he might hear a message that would go to his heart and get him back to his mother's knee. But sorry to say nothing happened."

Ridgway then "witnessed" to Florey and attempted to convince him that he had contracted, "in the bad atmosphere of the classroom of the Professor of Doubts, one of the infantile anti-religious diseases." In his book, Ridgway concluded the story of the meeting by noting that it gave "an interesting view of a side of a famous author not generally known."[38]

In this encounter, Lewis was giving another mimetic performance, playing the role of a religious crusader just as he later did in some of his discussions with ministers in Kansas City. Lewis was a talented mimic; it is easy to imagine him acting his part in front of Ridgway, and one can see how effortless it was for him to translate such performances into fiction in *Elmer Gantry* (and in his other books, especially *The Man Who Knew Coolidge*). As D. Bruce Lockerbie has suggested, the meeting with Ridgway also probably gave Lewis a sample of the religious idiom of the ministry.[39]

Lewis drew Elmer Gantry as a composite portrait of various real-life ministers, but in creating the other major religious figure in the novel, Sharon Falconer, he seems not to have cast his net so widely. Falconer was based largely on the flamboyant evangelist Aimee Semple McPherson, who in the mid-1920s was reaching the peak of her fame. Like most evangelists of the time, McPherson had a trademark: she dressed completely in white except for a flowing blue cape—a modified nurse's uniform that symbolically connected her faith healing with traditional clerical garb. McPherson achieved worldwide recognition in 1923 when she dedicated her Church of the Foursquare Gospel (a version of Pentecostalism) in Echo Park near Los Angeles and named it Angelus Temple. As William Ridgway's account of his meeting with Lewis indicates, Lewis heard McPherson preach there, and the temple seems to have been the model for Sharon Falconer's Waters of Jordan Tabernacle. McPherson's church became the center of her various satellite enterprises, which were as extensive as the outreach ministries of Sharon Falconer in *Elmer Gantry*. Among McPherson's concerns were a 500-watt radio station, a monthly magazine, a twenty-four-hour telephone counseling service, a free employment bureau, and a commissary stocked with food and clothing for the needy. Her dramatized sermons, elaborate orchestral arrangements, and stage stunts brought in weekly crowds of five thousand or more. Once she rode a motorcycle through the sanctuary to illustrate a sermon entitled "The Jazz Age Is Speeding to Hell."[40]

One episode in McPherson's life was particularly bizarre. In May 1926 (after Lewis had gone to Pequot, Minnesota, where he began writing the draft) McPherson disappeared while swimming at a beach near Los Angeles. She was thought to have drowned until she appeared a month later in Mexico, claiming that she had escaped from kidnappers. But soon it became known that she had been having an affair with a married man, a former radio operator at Angelus Temple. The scandal remained news for six months, as the district attorney charged her with conspiracy to obstruct justice and subornation of perjury. The case was eventually dismissed for lack of evidence.

This real-life event has an eerie relation to the fictional narrative that Lewis was then beginning to write. According to the recollections of Leon Birkhead's widow, Agnes Birkhead, in the plan for *Elmer Gantry* Lewis originally intended Sharon to die by drowning in the river outside the temple. Mrs. Birkhead told Mark Schorer that "the idea for the character and her fate was entirely [Lewis's] own, that it derived from a dream he had of a female evangelist who drowns, and so he had planned the lady's fate in his outline."[41] According to Mrs. Birkhead, when Lewis heard of the disappearance he said that he would have to "change that whole section of the book or everyone will think that Sharon is Aimee."[42]

In sum, Lewis's research for *Elmer Gantry* demonstrates how he was able to select personality traits from several different people and blend them into a composite portrait. Lewis made Elmer and Sharon resemble their real-life counterparts just closely enough for them to seem familiar to his audience—in the same way that he had made Gopher Prairie seem to many readers an exact representation of their own village, or Babbitt seem like everyone's conception of the middle-class businessman. Herein lay Lewis's great strength in drawing characters—not as multidimensional figures whose underlying motivations and psychological complexities are explored in great detail, but as symbolic prototypes. As Alfred Kazin said in *On Native Grounds*, in his characters Lewis was attempting to "hit a certain average" in American life. Lewis's goal was to show his readers "not so much revelations of life as brilliant equivalents of it." His characters, though technically unrealistic, nevertheless "attained a fantastic representative quality":

> [In *Babbitt*,] Lewis caught the vulgarity and the perpetual salesmanship, and caught it as effortlessly as he caught the sights and sounds, the exact sound of a Ford car being cranked on a summer morning in Zenith in 1922. . . . It is doubtful . . . whether Lewis even wished to make Lowell Schmaltz credible in that long monologue, *The Man Who Knew Coolidge*. He wished only to hit him off perfectly, to make Lowell a kind of monstrous incarnate average, just as he wished to make Elmer Gantry an accumulative symbol of all the phoniness he hated in American life.[43]

Lewis was able to reproduce these sights, sounds, and personalities by being around a person or group of people for a period of time and absorbing their language, looks, habits, morals, and beliefs—and then basing characters on them. It is a testament to Lewis's powers of observation and sensation that he could do this so well.

This mimetic method explains the extremely harsh satire in *Elmer Gantry*. Elmer was based on a group of people who were variously frauds, boosters, or simply individuals of little intelligence. Lewis described them in a letter to Grace that was written sometime during his second stay in

Kansas City. He compared these ministers and their lax religious faith to his physician-brother Claude and his casual unconcern with truth in medical practice: "They're . . . like my brother; cheerfully admitting every or almost every indictment of Paul [De Kruif] against docs . . . but meantime going on removing appendixes with great cheer."[44] The people whom Lewis observed in Kansas City were quite the opposite of those he had associated with while working with De Kruif on *Arrowsmith*. Lewis was being only partly disingenuous when, asked by a reporter after the publication of *Elmer Gantry* if he thought his picture of the ministry was distorted, he said: "The book I wrote is what I saw."[45]

Elmer Gantry might have been a less vituperative novel if during his stay in Kansas City Lewis had been exposed to more clergymen of integrity like Leon Birkhead. But Lewis did not intend to write a novel about organized religion in America, in all of its aspects and at all of its levels. As his preliminary notes, the newspaper clippings, and his comments to Harcourt and Mencken make clear, he intended from the start to present a satiric picture of one segment of church activity in America: what today we call fundamentalist Christianity. This form of worship is of course the direct ancestor of "televangelism," and such figures as Jim and Tammy Faye Bakker are latter-day Elmer Gantrys and Sharon Falconers. That is why *Elmer Gantry* remains a readable and relevant novel, as indeed are *Main Street, Babbitt,* and *Arrowsmith*. Lewis addressed fundamental paradoxes or ironies in American life—usually conflicts between ideals and actuality—that will probably always be present.

A final reason for the harshness of *Elmer Gantry* may be Mencken's influence. Mencken had kept his praise of *Arrowsmith* and *Mantrap* fairly conservative. He had been disappointed in Lewis's choice of medical research as the topic for the novel following *Babbitt:* he told Lewis that that idea was "the damndest nonsense" he had ever heard, and he urged Lewis instead to write a full-length treatment of a university president.[46] The character of Arrowsmith did not interest Mencken much because, as he said in his review of that novel, "he is not typical; he is not a good American."[47] Mencken was far more interested in the buffoonish Almus Pickerbaugh, a satiric type. As for *Mantrap,* Mencken was kind enough in his review: he praised Lewis's ability to turn out such entertainments "with the left hand" but concluded, "I have presented *Mantrap* to my pastor, and return joyfully to a rereading of *Babbitt.*"

However, Mencken was ecstatic when *Elmer Gantry* was published, because in it Lewis depicted an American type that Mencken utterly detested. He had been bashing evangelists like Billy Sunday and Paul Rader for most of his career. In *Prejudices: Fifth Series,* he called this figure "the most American of all Americans, the very *Ur-Amerikaner*—to wit, the malignant moralist, the Christian turned cannibal, the snorting and preposterous Puritan."[48] Mencken had derided evangelical ministers in one way or another in at least a dozen columns, reviews, and essays he had written or that others had written and he had published in the *Smart Set* and the *American Mercury.*[49] Mencken had said of this type, "There are glimpses of him in *Babbitt,*" but he "still awaits his anatomist." Similarly, in his "Essay in Pedagogy" Mencken chastised novelists for not making fictional use of this "most salient and arresting of American types." In this essay, Mencken also deplored the practice of making the church a center for extrareligious activities, such as "the scheme of putting bowling alleys and courting cubicles into church cellars," or of "giving over the rest of every sacred edifice to debates on the Single Tax, boxing matches, [and] baby shows." In *Elmer Gantry,* Lewis satirizes these same practices. It would thus seem that Lewis took his cue at least indirectly from Mencken in choosing to write about evangelism, just as he had in deciding to write about businessmen in *Babbitt.* Lewis dedicated *Elmer Gantry* to Mencken "with profound admiration."[50]

Lewis's activities in Kansas City had exhausted him. When he left there on 15 May 1926, he needed a quiet place in which to write the draft of the novel. Therefore, with Earl Blackman, a friend of Birkhead's and one of the more liberal ministers he had met in Kansas City, Lewis drove to Pequot, Minnesota, a resort area located on Big Pelican Lake. (Grace took Wells to spend the summer with friends in St. Gilgen, Austria. The plan was that either Lewis would join her in Austria in the fall or she would return to the United States and find another house for them to live in, and they would try yet again to repair their marriage.) En route to Pequot, Lewis and Blackman stopped in Terre Haute, Indiana, and Lewis again interviewed Eugene Debs; he was still planning to write his labor novel. Lewis and Blackman arrived in Pequot on 3 June, and Blackman soon returned to Kansas City.

One week later, Lewis was joined by Leon and Agnes Birkhead and their twelve-year-old son, Kenneth. The Birkheads spent the summer with Lewis in Pequot. Lewis rented a cottage for them, and approximately one hundred yards away he had two tents set up—a large one for himself, in which he would sleep and write, and a smaller one for a hired cook. The remoteness of this place appealed to Lewis. He wrote to Hugh Walpole that it was "delightful . . . rather ragged and uncivilized woods shutting off the world on one side and a lake opening almost like an arm of the sea on the other."[51] Unfortunately for Lewis, this isolated setting did not prevent people from coming to visit him. Mrs. Birkhead remembered that people "arrived in carloads"; thus instead of settling down, Lewis was forced to resume the same frantic pace that he thought he had left behind in Kansas City. Lewis was also drinking heavily that summer, although it evidently did not impede his work on *Elmer Gantry* at this time.

Lewis's first task was to choose a title. He debated the merits of different titles with Harcourt through the mail. He asked Harcourt's opinion of three possibilities: "THE REV. DR. MELLISH—REVEREND MELLISH—THE REVEREND DOCTOR." Harcourt preferred the name "Myron Mellish" to "Elmer Bloor," Lewis's earlier choice. Harcourt took the question of the title as seriously as Lewis did, because Harcourt realized that readers formed their first impressions of a book from its title. He cautioned Lewis that the title should not be "too satirical," because he wanted "all the church people who take their preachers seriously to read the novel."[52] Lewis wrote back at once to say, "No, Myron Mellish is not right. . . . The name now is— and I hope will continue to be—ELMER GANTRY. Say it aloud. See if you don't like the sharp sound of the Gantry." Harcourt replied that "Mellish was and Mellish is a rather 'ishy' name. Gantry has a better bite."[53]

The matter of the title seems to have been the only point that Lewis had *not* already settled in his mind when he began writing. With his data brimming over in his head—and no doubt with the Birkheads as an audience on whom to test various parts of the novel—Lewis wrote the draft even more quickly than usual. From start to finish the creation of *Elmer Gantry* took no more than eleven months; *Babbitt* and *Arrowsmith,* in contrast, had consumed approximately two years each. The research for *Elmer Gantry,* the compiling of the notebook data, and the writing of the plan—which apparently totaled some twenty thousand words (forty thousand words shorter than the plan for *Arrowsmith*)—all took place at approximately the same time, between January and May 1926. The plan was finished by the time Lewis settled in Pequot and began to write the draft on 9 June. By late August he had finished approximately one-half of the draft, or almost one hundred thousand words. He wrote the remaining ninety-four thousand words of the draft and did some light revising between mid-September and mid-December in Washington, D.C. He then delivered a cleanly typed copy to Harcourt in New York. Galley proofs of the novel were generated as early as 27 December. Lewis corrected them during January and February 1927, and the novel was published on 10 March.

Lewis's rapid composition of this novel indicates that he had honed his creative method. Beginning with *Mantrap* and *Elmer Gantry,* he deliberately reduced the amount of research and planning that he did for a novel; later, he continued to streamline his technique by basing parts of his plots on his own experiences and sometimes by recycling material from earlier books.

Both the draft typescript of *Elmer Gantry* and the clean revised typescript are among Lewis's papers at the Beinecke, as are the galley proofs. The clean copy bears only a few scattered corrections and almost no substantive revisions. The same is nearly true of the draft typescript: there are deletions of redundant or superfluous sentences and much stylistic tightening and sharpening, but very few block cuts in the early chapters—and not a single large deletion from chapter 28 to the end of the book. Many pages bear no markings at all. There is little indication of the meticulous attention to detail evident in the drafts of Lewis's earlier novels.

However, one does find an unusually large number of corrections and revisions on the galley proofs, particularly in the latter portions of the novel, where Lewis made several crucial changes in the plot by canceling certain paragraphs and pasting onto the galleys half-sheets of single-spaced typewritten material. The uncharacteristically hasty and careless nature of these late changes in *Elmer Gantry* was due in part to Lewis's rapid composition of the novel and in part to his tumultuous personal life. Lewis had just finished the summer's work on the draft in late August when he learned that his father had died. Lewis had never resolved, or really even confronted, the problems that had existed between him and his father since his boyhood. They were bound up with his contempt for the narrow-mindedness of the small town. This unresolved tension was most likely what caused Lewis to go on a drinking binge that lasted through the drive to Sauk Centre with the Birkheads and the funeral and burial of his father. Since Lewis's Caribbean voyage with De Kruif in early 1923, he had increasingly sought relief from personal problems in drinking. Previously, this had not impaired his ability to work. Now it did.

After the funeral Lewis went to Washington, D.C., where Grace had rented a house for them. Here Lewis intended to finish *Elmer Gantry*. But the Lewises had hardly set up housekeeping when it became clear that any hopes for their staying together were unrealistic. Their marriage collapsed for good. Deeply depressed, Lewis began to drink uncontrollably. Until this point, he had always kept the place where he wrote—whether it was an office, bedroom, or hotel suite—an alcohol-free zone; he had observed a clear distinction between working hours and drinking hours. But according to the recollections of Mencken, Harcourt, and others who were in contact with him that autumn, Lewis was drinking heavily while he wrote the latter half of *Elmer Gantry*. (Mencken said that the final thirty thousand words of the book were produced "in a state of liquor.")[54] By the end of the year, Lewis was on the verge of a nervous breakdown. He was barely able to finish writing *Elmer Gantry;* he might have been unable to do so, in fact, had Alfred Harcourt not recognized just what terrible shape Lewis was in and put him in a sanitarium in upstate New York. There, Lewis dried out and was able to shore up some weak sections in the last few chapters.

The disintegration of his marriage, coming as it did just after the death of his father, obviously made a hellish environment for creativity. These circumstances partly explain the hurried, mechanical quality of the final third of the novel. It is testament to Lewis's strong inner drive that he was able to complete *Elmer Gantry* at all. Of course, Lewis's various difficulties with Grace and with their marriage had been building for some time, and by this time he was quite bitter toward her. It is likely that these feelings account for the misogynism in *Elmer Gantry* and perhaps also for the pessimistic view of human relationships in it.

Lewis's marriage to Grace had been unstable all along, and Lewis grew to dislike her because of her artificiality and her attempts to control him. He summarized these feelings in a candid letter that he sent to Grace sometime in September or October 1925. He wrote, "I see how completely, these last months, you have governed almost everything I have done. You have decided what clothes I would wear, what I should eat, and when, who might come to see me, whom I might go to see, what books I might buy and read."[55] Of course, for his part, Lewis had generally shirked his responsibilities as a husband and a father. He refused to put down roots and purchase a home, opting instead for a peripatetic existence that Grace could not tolerate. Grace recalled that when their son, Wells, was eight years old, he turned to her at the breakfast table one morning when Lewis was away and asked, "Mother, can't we domesticate Father?" Grace had to tell him that they could not. Lewis himself realized that he would never settle down. In another letter to Grace from this same period, he recognized her desire for "a settled life with intelligent but definitely respectable neighbors." In contrast, he wanted "an unsettled life with unrespectable neighbors."[56] In her memoir, Grace conceded that "unconsciously I must have imposed my own need upon this restless man which made him even more restless and eager to escape."[57] By 1925 the Lewises were living apart six or seven months out of the year.

Lewis's response to these problems had been to run away and live elsewhere or to drink himself into oblivion. In Washington that autumn, he drank to excess in front of dinner guests to embarrass Grace. Apparently, he also revenged himself on her through infidelities. Lewis was famous and was pursued by female admirers; naturally, he was flattered by their attentions, especially given his own unattractiveness (Carl Van Vechten said that Lewis's charm made women forget that he was ugly).[58] Grace reveals in her memoir that her attraction to Lewis was not sexual; Schorer, Mencken, and others have said more frankly that Grace was cold toward Lewis in sexual matters and that this chilly connubial situation made Lewis feel even more fully controlled by his wife.

Grace's response to their problems also had been to look elsewhere for companionship, and she had found someone receptive to her genteel behavior: a Spaniard named Telesforo Casanova, whom she had met at a party in Katonah in September 1925 (when Lewis was in Bermuda finishing *Mantrap*). Casanova belonged to a genuinely upper-class family, and he had enough money to be able to offer Grace the kind of aristocratic existence she craved. He evidently even had a hereditary right to be called "Count Casanova"; when they later married, Grace technically became a countess. Casanova fulfilled the role of the admiring and gallant gentleman that Lewis had stopped playing after his courtship, when he had appealed to her latent romanticism by casting her as a princess in the love poems that he wrote to her.

Grace's pretentious behavior, her affair with Casanova, and her eventual divorce from Lewis provided him with the basic material for *Dodsworth,* which he began to write in the fall of 1927. In that novel, Grace is the model for Fran Dodsworth, the castrating wife who eventually leaves her husband Sam to marry Kurt von Obersdorf, a German count.[59] Well before Lewis wrote *Dodsworth,* however, his troubles with Grace had found their way into his fiction. Whereas in *Main Street* Lewis had drawn a strong, mostly likable female protagonist by basing Carol on the good parts of Grace, in *Elmer Gantry* the female characters are selfish and highly unappealing.

Elmer Gantry is in fact structured around three climactic episodes in the protagonist's life; each episode involves a woman who attempts to control Elmer, and each involves some form of deception or fraud—often sexual fraud. The first climax of the novel occurs when Elmer is expelled from seminary for seducing Lulu Baines, a girl who attends the church where he is interim pastor. The second concerns his alliance with Sharon Falconer, to whom he is initially faithful, although eventually he cheats on her. The last involves his being blackmailed by Hettie Dowler, who threatens to ruin him publicly but who is ultimately blackmailed herself by Elmer. In addition to these female characters, three other women play significant roles in Elmer's life: Juanita Klauzel, a girl whom he seduces in college; Cleo Benham, his wife (he abandons both Cleo and Juanita when they deny him sex); and Beryl Gibson, a member of his church in Zenith (he makes sexual advances to Beryl but is rejected).

All of these women resemble Grace in that they try to domesticate Elmer. He reacts either by running away to another town or by pursuing other women, and always he drinks as a gesture of rebellion. Most of these women are also unwilling to accede to Elmer's sexual demands. The only exceptions are Sharon Falconer and Hettie Dowler, who are sexually aggressive women—but in surrendering to Elmer they are actually controlling him. Hettie hopes to blackmail Elmer by seducing him. Sharon, the most complex female character that Lewis ever created, is an inscrutable and volatile woman who capitulates to Elmer in a scene that is both comic and grotesque: she leads him to an altar she has had specially constructed in her Southern mansion, and here she enacts a fertility ritual in which she associates herself with various pagan deities. Once their relationship is consummated, they settle into a sedate routine, like "a long married couple, intimate and secure." She tries to control his various vices—first his drinking and smoking and then his sexual desires, causing him to seek a more lively companion in a member of their crew, Lily Anderson.[60]

In the fantastic portrait of Sharon Falconer, Lewis was probably parodying (in a sad and bitter way) his relationship with Grace. First, Elmer and Sharon are oddly suitable. They see that each has something the other needs—just as the alliance between Lewis and Grace was unlikely but pragmatic. Second, Sharon is not the person she claims to be. She portrays herself as a well-bred descendant of aristocratic Southern stock and surrounds herself with the trappings of gentility—including not just mannerisms and clothes but an allegedly genuine antebellum mansion, which, like everything else about her, turns out to be fake. Sharon is actually an ex-stenographer from Utica, New York, whose real name is Katie Jonas.[61] Even Sharon and Elmer's sexual alliance is symbolically fraudulent, because it is enacted in a fake sanctuary—the authenticity of which is further undermined by the presence of both Christian and pagan objects. The scene is a parody of spiritual and physical love (as well as of the temper of orgiastic evangelism). Elmer and Sharon eventually realize that their relationship, begun as it was for the wrong reasons, cannot last. Lewis projects his own restlessness and inability to settle down onto Elmer, who momentarily considers putting down roots but is discouraged from doing so by Sharon—whose ambitions also prevent her from having a stable, married life.

On Christmas Eve 1926, Lewis delivered the completed manuscript of *Elmer Gantry* to Harcourt in New York. He then returned to Washington. On the evening after Christmas Day he had an ugly fight with Grace that culminated in his storming out of the house drunk, taking a room for the night at a hotel, and then going to Baltimore the next morning by train, where Mencken met him and took him in for a few days. Lewis never shared living quarters with Grace again, and by the following summer they had decided to seek a divorce. From Baltimore, Lewis traveled to New York, where he went on the binge. When Lewis had recovered, he discussed *Elmer Gantry* with Harcourt, but Lewis was still in such poor shape physically and emotionally that on New Year's Eve Harcourt drove him to a sanitarium, where Lewis stayed until 8 January.

Harcourt had read the typescript of *Elmer Gantry* within forty-eight hours of receiving it. He recognized that the latter parts of the novel— composed during the previous autumn in Washington—were not of the same high caliber as Lewis's earlier work. Harcourt thought that these parts were extremely weak, in fact—so weak that for the first time in his eight-year association with Lewis, Harcourt directed him to make several significant changes in the book. But Harcourt also recognized Lewis's fragile emotional state at the time, so he made his criticisms diplomatically. On 27 December he wrote Lewis with four "general queries" regarding *Elmer Gantry.* In this letter, Harcourt told Lewis, "I think the thing as it is would just get by, but it's too bad to have a soft spot at the end."[62] This letter must not have reached Lewis, since he left for Baltimore on that date, but presumably he and Harcourt discussed Harcourt's concerns about the novel after Lewis had reached New York.

First, Harcourt suggested that Elmer's finding Sharon Falconer's charred body with a piece of the cross in her hand at the end of chapter 15 was too melodramatic, and he urged Lewis to cut that detail. Lewis did not make this change, but he did accept Harcourt's other suggestions. Harcourt next advised that Elmer be more genuinely outraged at the Ku Klux Klan's beating of Frank Shallard in chapter 29. In the original version of this scene, Elmer is unrealistically callous—even flippant—about what has happened to Frank when he meets him on the street. In the unrevised galley proof, Elmer responds to Frank's injury and public humiliation by saying, "Ha, ha, ha! Still the same old atheist, Franky! But seriously, doesn't this give you a new slant on getting right with the purposes of God?" On the galleys, Lewis canceled this and five other paragraphs and pasted below them a typewritten half-sheet. The new material, which presents Elmer in a more sympathetic but still unfavorable light, appears in the first edition (galleys 115, 116; cf. first edition, 395). The revision gives Elmer some sense of actual sorrow at what has happened, though what he says to Frank still shows him to be spineless: "This is the most outrageous thing I've ever heard of in my life, Frank! Believe me, I'm going to give the fellows that did this to you the most horrible beating they ever got, right from my pulpit!"

Harcourt also asked Lewis to "tone down" Elmer's "vulgarities" in chapter 30, as he fraternizes with other passengers on the steamship to London and Paris: "It is a little too blatant," Harcourt said, "and he must have picked up a veneer of manners from some of his parishioners by that time. It is just a little too thick." Accordingly, Lewis softened the coarseness of Elmer's remarks here, making adjustments in various bits of dialogue on galleys 115 and 116. Lastly, and most important, Harcourt questioned the plausibility of the final episode, the blackmailing of Elmer by Hettie Dowler and her accomplice, Oscar. First, Harcourt did not think that Elmer would be quite so stupid as to "be caught so completely off his guard" by Hettie. Harcourt also pointed out that such professional con artists would not target someone like Elmer in a blackmailing scheme, since Elmer is not a particularly wealthy man:

> The labor, time, rent of apartment, etc. involved [in Hettie establishing herself in Zenith] would come to more than Elmer's resources could stand. So clever a swindler would have gone after a man with a good deal more money and worked faster. While Elmer was about due to be badly caught in some of his philandering, he might also by this time be too clever and worldly wise to write [incriminating] letters.

Harcourt was quite candid with Lewis: "There are a lot of difficulties in the situation as you have done it," Harcourt wrote, "which the above observations will suggest to you. You either have to make [Hettie] a semi-innocent tool in the matter or provide more carefully for a number of contingencies":

> It occurs to us that you have Lulu ready at hand to provide the situation. She could do something foolish or hysterical. They might be caught in some piece of carelessness by the reporter who is on to him, and then have him make final use of Lulu and Floyd or Lulu alone in a made-up affidavit and statement which will clear his skirts.

Lewis agreed with Harcourt that his original scheme for having Elmer come close to ruin was not believable. He revised this episode, but in a way that was more expedient than any of those alternatives that Harcourt had suggested. Lewis changed parts of chapters 32 and 33 to reveal that

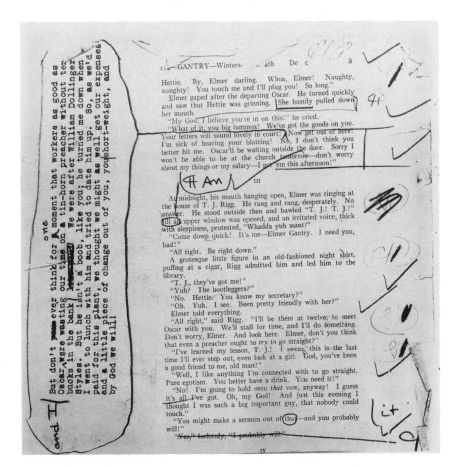

Fig. 25.   Detail from *Elmer Gantry* proofs (Yale Collection of American Literature, Beinecke Rare Book and Manuscript Library, Yale University)

Hettie and Oscar's target was not Elmer but William Dollinger Styles, a wealthy parishioner. On galley 120, Lewis appended two paragraphs to the end of section 4; these paragraphs, which appear in the first edition, describe Hettie's romantic overtures to Styles. Then, at the top of galley 124 Lewis added four sentences to the last paragraph of section 2 of chapter 32. Here, Hettie tells Elmer, "workers as good as Oscar and I were [not] wasting our time on a tin-horn preacher without ten bucks in the bank. We were after William Dollinger Styles. But he isn't a boob, like you; he turned me down when I went to lunch with him and tried to date him up" (424). Hettie explains to Elmer that when Styles rejected her advances, she and Oscar decided to blackmail Elmer instead—to "get our expenses and a little piece of change." Harcourt's suggestions for changing this last episode were more elaborate and better conceived than the revisions Lewis made. It would seem that Lewis did not want to spend the time fixing the manuscript that Harcourt's plan would have required.

Overall, Harcourt's suggestions improved the latter parts of *Elmer Gantry* considerably from Lewis's original version. This was one of the few times in which Harcourt served in a true editorial capacity for Lewis—specifically suggesting certain revisions and asking that Lewis make them before the book was published. Up to this point, Harcourt and Lewis's working relationship had functioned smoothly. Now, however, Harcourt was growing tired of Lewis's sometimes irrational behavior, particularly his antics in Kansas City during the past year. Harcourt welcomed the publicity that they generated, but he also recognized that they stemmed as much from Lewis's personal frustrations and unhappiness as from a desire for publicity for *Elmer Gantry* or from his need to gather research materials. While Harcourt continued to respect Lewis's strong drive regarding work, he also saw that these episodes were taking their toll on Lewis, and that the author was not quite as diligent and careful as he had once been—or so Harcourt indicated to Grace in a letter dated 5 January 1927. Grace had written to tell Harcourt that her marriage to Lewis was "quite thro" and that she was leaving Washington for Cromwell, Connecticut, where she planned to stay temporarily: "My last gift to [Lewis] is complete silence until the book is out and the first heated discussion dies down. For him to divorce God and wife simultaneously would be bad publicity."[63] Harcourt wrote back to tell her that Lewis had checked into a sanitarium:

> I haven't heard from him since, but he has returned some thirty galleys of *Elmer Gantry*, which he took up there with him, carefully and sharply corrected. I do hope he gets into better shape there and builds up some reserves to go on with. . . . I think the rest cure at Bill Brown's is insurance in that direction. I do really hope that you can achieve serenity in the course of time. Of course I hope Hal can also, but those hopes are much more faint.[64]

During the next year and a half, Harcourt would become less willing to look after Lewis's interests. He eventually came to think of Lewis as troublesome and querulous, and when in early 1931 Lewis wanted to sever their business relationship, Harcourt did not try to dissuade him from doing so.

Lewis finished correcting the galleys of *Elmer Gantry* during January

1927. Harcourt had sent the typescript to the printers as soon as he received it from Lewis, and the printers had been typesetting the novel and supplying galleys in batches. Knowing that sales would more than compensate for any last-minute production costs, Harcourt had told Lewis that changes could be done in proof. After the galleys were corrected, Lewis was still unwell, and he had to enter another sanitarium for three days near the end of January. He then left the country for an indefinite stay abroad, going on walking excursions in southern England and later in France to restore his health. He was accompanied on this trip by Earl Blackman, the Kansas City minister who had driven him to Pequot the previous summer. Lewis also thought it best that he not be in the United States when *Elmer Gantry* was published. With the controversy it was sure to incite, and with rumors circulating about a forthcoming divorce, he knew he would be hounded by the press and thus unable to regain his emotional equilibrium.

While Lewis was out of the country, Alfred Harcourt orchestrated the publicity for *Elmer Gantry*. He was able to pique interest in the novel and create a demand for it well in advance of its publication on 10 March. First, the Book-of-the-Month Club named it as its March selection. Harcourt then began drawing up various news releases about Lewis and his activities in Kansas City and sending them to the wire services, along with copies of the book, so that reporters could "work up their own sensational stuff in their own way." Harcourt ordered an enormous first printing of 138,000 copies (the Book-of-the-Month Club took between thirty-five and forty thousand of those copies). He also sent out press statements about how his firm was preparing to meet the expected demand for the novel. One of these was entitled "What It Means to Manufacture the First Edition of *Elmer Gantry*." It provided statistics on such materials as binding, paper, and ink and emphasized that it was the largest first printing of any novel in American publishing history.

Nearly all of the one hundred thousand copies of *Elmer Gantry* available in its first printing were sold on publication day. Harcourt cabled Lewis: "News stories everywhere. Kansas [City] Star five columns. Reviews violent either way. Clergy hot. Reorders already. Letter and clippings mailed. Everything lovely."[65] Within six weeks *Elmer Gantry* sold slightly more than 175,000 copies; and at the end of ten weeks two hundred thousand copies had been sold. *Elmer Gantry* was the number-one-selling fiction title for March 1927 and remained so through July. It proved to be the most controversial novel that Lewis had written; it sold more copies, incited more debate, and in general influenced more readers than either *Main*

Street or *Babbitt*. Soon after its publication, it was banned in Kansas City, Boston, and Camden, New Jersey. News stories developed from people reading the novel; Harcourt tracked such reports and used them in advertising. Someone in Virginia invited Lewis to his own lynching party. In Boston he was called "one of the greatest egoists in the world." A cleric in New Hampshire suggested that Lewis be imprisoned for a minimum of five years; another reader even suggested that he be sent to the electric chair, "ahead of Judd Gray."[66] Harcourt came across the following article from an Ohio newspaper and printed it as a press release:

> Trouble in the home of Leo Roberts, general manager of the Roberts Coal and Supply Company, began when his wife brought home a copy of *Elmer Gantry* and he burned it as undesirable reading matter, according to Mrs. Roberts at a hearing Wednesday before Judge Bostwick of Probate Court, when Roberts was ordered to a private sanitarium for a short rest, after his wife . . . charged him with lunacy.[67]

On 31 March, Harcourt wrote Lewis: "The publicity on *Elmer Gantry* is amazing, and it still keeps pouring in. We keep a daily bulletin of sales here, and it is very amusing to watch it catch on in one territory after the other. We are advertising it, of course, in every conceivable way from here to the Pacific Ocean."[68]

As one might expect, the clergy vilified Lewis and derided the idea that the novel had any basis in fact. Billy Sunday said that if he had been God, he "would have soaked Mr. Lewis so hard that there would have been nothing left for the devil to levy on." John Roach Straton called Elmer a "gross caricature" and stated that the novel was the product of a "disordered imagination." He also claimed that "there never has been an Elmer Gantry or a Sharon Falconer."[69] One minister called the novel "a huge exaggeration . . . an impossibility . . . a gross caricature."[70] Another said that Elmer was a "monstrosity" who was only partly credible.[71] In a long essay in a religious journal, one reader painstakingly "disproved" the credibility of most of the events in the novel and concluded that "there never was an Elmer Gantry in the Baptist or any other ministry."[72] In Sauk Centre, the Reverend Sparks, pastor of the Congregational Church, deplored the book and said that the town was ashamed of its famous son. The pulpit fury raged on for at least a year.

The number of readers who thought that Lewis had accurately depicted evangelism was almost as large as the number of those who did not. In response to John Roach Straton's denunciation of *Elmer Gantry* as unrealis-

ST. PAUL REFORMED CHURCH
WAYNESBORO, PA.
CLEMENT W. DeCHANT, PASTOR

April
Fifth –

Mr. Sinclair Lewis,
Harcourt, Brace *and* Company
New York.

Dear Sir:

I have read many reviews of "Elmer Gantry." I have Read much superior opinion expressed. I have read it!

You have given me a huge jolt. Elmer Gantry, sadly, is too true and I see so much of him in me. In forcing him upon myself, in right keen suffering. I try severely to ungantry Gantry.

Thanks!

Clement W. De Chant.

Fig. 26. Letter from a reader of *Elmer Gantry* (Yale Collection of American Literature, Beinecke Rare Book and Manuscript Library, Yale University)

tic, Paxton Hibbard printed in the New Masses a list of well-known debaucheries by various clergymen in America, beginning with Henry Ward Beecher. And if Lewis received a large amount of hate mail for deriding preachers, he also received a fair amount of correspondence from readers congratulating him on his exposé of evangelism. Many ministers wrote Lewis to say that his novel was a useful tonic; one from Chehalis, Washington, applauded Lewis for striking a note "which is timely and to the point." Most interesting was a letter from a pastor in Waynesboro, Pennsylvania, who—in a fit of contrition apparently induced by reading Elmer Gantry—wrote Lewis to confess: "You have given me a huge jolt. Elmer Gantry, sadly, is too true and I see so much of him in me. Unloosing him upon myself, in right keen suffering, I try severely to ungantry Gantry." Many readers wrote to Lewis to tell him of an Elmer in their midst. An insurance agent in Muskogee, Oklahoma, for example, sent Lewis a clipping about a Texas preacher who absconded with the collection from his tent meetings. A man in Charlotte, North Carolina, sent a news story about a local Methodist pastor who had an affair with a young church worker and was deposed.[73]

The critical reception of the novel was unusual. Like the clergy and lay readers, the reviewers were also sharply divided—not on the artistic merits of the book, as one might expect, but on the accuracy of its reportage. Those who reviewed the novel unfavorably did so because they believed that Lewis was condemning not Elmer, but the whole Christian church. These critics included W. E. Woodward, Carl Van Doren, Joseph Wood Krutch, and Leon Whipple. Conversely, those who admired the novel thought that Lewis had not attacked all clergy but rather had simply exposed hypocrisy in one sector of the ministry, that of evangelism. Among these critics were Rebecca West, Robert Littell, and Heywood Broun. The only reviewer who did not address this question was Mencken, who was (predictably) wholly enthusiastic about the novel. Mencken thought Elmer Gantry to be the best of Lewis's works thus far. In his review in the American Mercury, he assumed the believability of the main character and said that Lewis had avoided the pitfall of making the novel "a mere lampoon"; he compared Lewis's skill to that of Voltaire.[74]

Because of the controversy that the novel created, there was virtually no actual critical analysis in the reviews, and today Elmer Gantry remains the most neglected of Lewis's novels from this period. Several reviewers did observe that the strain of idealism that had appeared in Main Street, faded in Babbitt, then reappeared in full force in Arrowsmith had now vanished entirely, but that was the only such comment on the artistry of the novel or on its cultural relevance. Ultimately, the images of evangelism that

Lewis projected in *Elmer Gantry*—like the images of medical research in *Arrowsmith*, business in *Babbitt*, and the village in *Main Street*—had a powerful effect on the consciousness of both America and Europe: in a widely syndicated newspaper article published later in the year, "The New American People," H. G. Wells based his observations of American culture on the novels of Sinclair Lewis, singling out *Elmer Gantry* as an especially perceptive social document. Today, Lewis's novel remains a relevant account of the evangelical strain in the American character.

5

The Man Who Knew
Coolidge and Dodsworth

1927–1929

The hurried composition and revision of *Elmer Gantry,* Lewis's frenetic activities during 1926, and the emotional turmoil caused by the death of his father and the collapse of his marriage had left Lewis exhausted. From Paris in February 1927, Lewis wrote Harcourt to say that he "felt very well": "I *am* still tired; it'll take a couple of months more for me to get that fundamental tiredness out of my system; and I'm living as quietly as possible."[1] He and Earl Blackman, his minister friend, stayed in Paris for some time and then visited Venice and Florence. When Blackman had to return to the United States, a new friend, the poet Ramon Guthrie, joined Lewis in Italy; they went on various walking trips through Europe, staying in Corfu, Athens, Dresden, and Munich. These excursions had been prescribed for Lewis by his physicians, and they succeeded in restoring his health. He reported to Harcourt in March that he was feeling well but was still tired: "I'm going to write very little—as you can imagine, I've had

enough of writing for a while!" Later that year, he would say that he had
not "for years felt so serene" and "secure."[2] He was certainly not the rambunctious and combative Lewis of the previous year.

. His creative energies, as they slowly reawakened, were thus directed
toward two projects that were quite unlike *Elmer Gantry*. He was again
thinking about the labor novel and about "The Yearner," the narrative that
would become *Dodsworth*. Lewis was now calling the latter novel "Evening," and he reported to Harcourt that its planning was proceeding "tran-
quilly."[3] That is all that Lewis said about "Evening" in his uncharacteristically brief letters to Harcourt at this time. He seems to have
continued to work on this novel through the spring: on 25 April he wrote
to Harrison Smith that he was "planning the new novel."[4] However, according to the recollections of Ramon Guthrie, this was not "Evening"
but a new version of the labor novel, which Lewis had been discussing
with Guthrie during a three-week walking tour through Alsace. It is likely
that Lewis was testing Guthrie's reactions to both of these ideas.

According to Guthrie, during this time Lewis was truly a changed man.
Instead of being energetic and garrulous, Lewis withdrew into himself. He
became somewhat ascetic: he carried with him only a rucksack containing
a shaving kit, a popular novel, a copy of *The Imitation of Christ,* and the
Bible.[5] This change in Lewis's behavior affected his plans for the labor
novel: Guthrie recalled that this third incarnation of the narrative was
rather esoteric in nature. Lewis planned to build the novel around the
theme, "Blessed are they which are persecuted for righteousness' sake."
Guthrie also said that Lewis may have been influenced by the highly publicized Sacco-Vanzetti case, which Lewis had commented on and which
pointed to some of the very conflicts he intended to treat in the labor
novel. Lewis probably saw Sacco and Vanzetti's situation as analogous to
that of Eugene Debs: martyrs persecuted by a reactionary society.

As the "new" labor novel began to take shape, its title changed from
"Neighbor" to the more philosophical "The Man Who Sought God."
There was another significant shift as well: Lewis decided not to model the
central character on Debs or set the novel in the Midwest; instead he concentrated on the political philosophy that would underlie the book. The
hero became a cynical worker who awakens to political awareness and
struggles with a messiah complex that eventually destroys his humility
and integrity. Unfortunately, we know little more about the book at this
stage because no notes for this version seem to survive. When their trip
ended, Lewis confidently told Guthrie that the labor novel was going to be
better than anything he had yet written—"even better than *Arrowsmith,*"
Lewis said, a claim he was to make many times.

Lewis continued to talk with Guthrie about "The Man Who Sought God" through the end of the summer, and his interest in writing a novel about labor was further stimulated in Berlin in early July when he met Dorothy Thompson, the woman who would soon become his second wife. Lewis had drifted to Berlin in late June; on 9 July he was invited by a friend to a dinner party Thompson was giving that evening in her flat to celebrate her thirty-third birthday. By all accounts, when Lewis met her that evening he fell in love right away. For the next several months he pursued her ardently, proposing marriage many times until she finally accepted. They were married in London on 14 May 1928, just a few weeks after Lewis's divorce from Grace became final.

Dorothy Thompson was the best-known female journalist in Europe at the time. Her star was rising rapidly, and within a few years she would be among the half-dozen or so most admired women in America, familiar to heads of state and an informal adviser to Franklin D. Roosevelt. When Lewis met her, she was the Berlin correspondent for the *Philadelphia Public Ledger* and *New York Evening Post* and chief of the Central European Service in Berlin. She and Lewis were very much alike. Dorothy had also come from a small town; she had been born in upstate New York, the daughter of a Methodist minister. After graduating from Syracuse University, she had taken a job as a spokesperson for the Woman's Suffrage Party at its headquarters in Buffalo. Then she moved on to New York City, where she worked for awhile writing publicity. She eventually became a foreign correspondent for the *Evening Post* and was assigned first to Vienna, then four years later to Berlin. She shared many of Lewis's attitudes: she was contemptuous of fraud and shallowness, and she delivered her opinions with implacable self-confidence. Her friend Dale Warren said that Dorothy could not tolerate "cant, hypocrisy, sloth, shiftlessness, willful stupidity, resignation, and whatsoever is cheap, shoddy, and meretricious."[6] Most important, Dorothy and Lewis had both experienced unhappy first marriages. Only a day or two before they met, Dorothy had received from Budapest her divorce decree from a young Hungarian poet and intellectual, Josef Bard, whom she had been supporting financially.

Dorothy would play as significant a role in Lewis's career as Grace had, although Dorothy's influence on Lewis's writing would not be felt fully until 1931, when he began composing *Ann Vickers*. The title character of that novel is in many ways based on Dorothy, and its quasi-feminist themes are probably also the result of Dorothy's influence.[7] She also assisted Lewis with *Dodsworth;* as Grace had done before her, she read Lewis's drafts and commented on them in the margins. Dorothy was a good critic, and her suggestions for *Dodsworth* improved the novel—especially in the characterization of the protagonist, Sam. Lewis described his admiration and love for Dorothy in the flattering portrait of Edith Cortright in the novel; Sam goes to live with Edith after separating from Fran. When Lewis began courting Dorothy, however, he seems not to have been thinking about *Dodsworth*. Rather, he was most interested in writing the labor novel. On 18 July, in fact, he went with Dorothy to Vienna, where workers' riots had broken out. Lewis wrote two articles about the riots for the *Public Ledger* syndicate. On 7 August Lewis and Dorothy went with Ramon Guthrie and his wife on a four-week walking trip in England, and during this period there was more talk about the labor novel. This was followed by a shorter excursion that Lewis and Guthrie took through the Rhineland after Dorothy had to return to Berlin. But Lewis evidently still did not feel ready to write the labor novel (or so Guthrie claimed); and he wanted to write one more novel first. Lewis therefore turned away from the project to write *Dodsworth*, just as he had twice earlier put it aside, first for *Arrowsmith* and then for *Elmer Gantry*.

Lewis and Guthrie returned to Berlin in early September, and Lewis intended to start work on *Dodsworth* (the novel was variously called "Evening," "Sunset," "A Man Alone," "The Yearner," "Blind Giant," and "Exile"). By 30 September Lewis had found an apartment near Dorothy's, and from there he wrote Harcourt of his decision to put aside the labor novel and start work on *Dodsworth*. He already had a schedule of work planned out: he said that the novel would not exceed 110,000 words, that it would be finished in the spring of 1928, and that it might even be ready for publication the next fall.[8] But Lewis did not follow through with this plan. (The novel was actually completed in the fall of 1928 and published in the spring of 1929.) He seems to have been unfocused and perhaps not quite certain that he was ready to undertake another mammoth project. Instead of beginning *Dodsworth*, Lewis wrote a story of about fifteen to sixteen thousand words for Mencken's *American Mercury*. Mencken had been asking Lewis to contribute something to the magazine for a long time, and Lewis had had to put him off while he worked first on *Arrowsmith* and then *Elmer Gantry*. The story, which Lewis was able to dash off quickly, took the form of a monologue spoken by an empty-headed Babbitt giving vent to his views of American life. It was entitled "The Man Who Knew Coolidge."[9] In writing the story, Lewis was also limbering up before starting on a new novel. It had been some time since he had put himself through the drill of writing a first-rate book like *Arrowsmith* or · *Babbitt*.

After completing his story for the *American Mercury* in early November,

Lewis felt ready to start on *Dodsworth*—but again he did not push through with it. He wrote fifty thousand words of a draft during November—approximately the first ten to twelve chapters—but he must not have been satisfied with it, because three months later he completely rewrote this material. After finishing these fifty thousand words, Lewis abruptly stopped work on the novel and undertook a different project: expanding "The Man Who Knew Coolidge" into a book-length work. He seems to have been losing his ability to work on large projects for long stretches of time. He was also growing tired of going through his elaborate preparatory routine. He had begun writing *Dodsworth* without an outline and with virtually no notes. At the Beinecke there are eight pages of character biographies for *Dodsworth* and one page containing a timetable for the Dodsworths' travels in Europe, but that is all.[10] Plainly, he wanted to produce something that was less complex and involved than the researched novels he had been writing.

In a letter dated 25 October 1927, Lewis described to Harcourt his idea for expanding "The Man Who Knew Coolidge": "It's the account by a Babbitt, entirely in his own words without any comment by the author, as to how he called on Coolidge in the White House—and not till the last page do we find that he never really saw Coolidge. Of course I love this sort of drool—and it'll be my swan-song to Babbittism."[11] Harcourt, however, was not receptive to this idea. Both he and Donald Brace had read the *Mercury* story and had found it hilarious, but neither one thought that fifty or sixty thousand words of such material would be very funny. It appears that Harcourt avoided responding to Lewis's letter, because Lewis mentioned his plan again in a letter of 12 November in which he updated Harcourt on his work on *Dodsworth*. Harcourt replied to this letter, but still he did not respond to Lewis's proposal about "The Man Who Knew Coolidge"; instead, Harcourt wrote, "Your recent letters sound as if you are hard at work on the new novel [i.e., *Dodsworth*]. . . . Good luck to you and to it!"[12] Finally, on 9 December Harcourt told Lewis that the *Mercury* sketch was "perfectly splendid" but that he did not think it a good idea for Lewis to expand it or "combine it with anything else." Harcourt offered to publish the original story in the spring of 1928 "as a little book at $1.00."[13]

Lewis, however, was determined to turn his story into a book. When he returned from a trip to Moscow with Dorothy on 11 December, he sent this urgent cable to Harcourt:

> If you publish Coolidge skit alone twill be merely timely pamphlet also being serialized Mercury have smaller sale. Can and wish unite

it with three similar pieces be called something like Soul of Lowell Schmaltz as complete novel to have enduring sale. Probably never be desirable for me do more than one such stunt and shame waste it with this quarter finished effort. . . . Can write this stuff incredible speed.[14]

Harcourt replied: "While could get more dollars this spring from Schmaltz volume you describe we feel most readers may know all they want to of him from this piece."[15] But Lewis insisted on a fifty-thousand-word book, despite Harcourt's later warning that he shouldn't "force the new material to 50,000 words if it doesn't come naturally." "It's much better," Harcourt advised, "to have too little than too much of such highly humorous, satirical material."[16] Harcourt was correct, and Lewis's scheme was ill advised. When Lewis sent Harcourt the completed manuscript at the end of December, he told him to be prepared for the "possibility" of "another 200,000 sale" like that of *Elmer Gantry;* but sales were far more modest when the book appeared early the following April.[17]

The Man Who Knew Coolidge: Being the Soul of Lowell Schmaltz, Constructive and Nordic Citizen consists of six monologues spoken by the title character, but it is essentially a one-joke book. Schmaltz is a typical Lewis caricature: he represents the mindless yet also arrogant and assertive citizen of the Boom Years. Schmaltz spews forth all the platitudes of his time, which are largely advertising slogans and jingoistic expressions that sound good but say nothing significant: "The United States is the greatest nation in the world, with more autos and radios and furnaces and suits of clothes and miles of cement pavements and sky-scrapers than the rest of the world put together!" (176). This sounds like part of Babbitt's speech to the Zenith Real Estate Board, exaggerated to an absurd degree. A sampling:

In Chicago I usually do the bulk, you might say, of my business with Starbright, Horner, and Dodd; and Billy Dodd himself looks after me, and say, there's a man that it's a pleasure to do business with, a square-shooter if ever there was one, and always got a good story and a two-bit cigar for you, and acts like he was glad to see you, and he isn't one of those fellows to throw seven kind of catfits if maybe a fellow is temporarily a little short and wants an extension of a couple of days or a month or so. Yes sir, and many's the good lunch I've had with Billy in the old Palmer House before they tore it down, and though of course this new Palmer House is you might say a regular palace, still, there was kind of an atmosphere about the old place, and say, they certainly did know how to cook steak and fried onions to a turn. Um! And oyster stew. (55)

Lewis's talents as a mimic are at their best in these sketches.

The basic flaw of the book is that such monologues are interesting for only a few pages. After awhile, the sheer intensity of such a performance wearies the person reading it. The book is merely one of Lewis's cocktail-party performances—an extended improvisation. A remedy might have been for Lewis to have used multiple narrators: begin with the voice from the original *Mercury* piece, then have someone else deliver the next monologue—perhaps a friend of Schmaltz's in the community—then adopt another voice, and so forth, rather like Edgar Lee Masters's technique in *Spoon River Anthology*. Lewis might even have brought back some of the characters from *Babbitt,* such as Chum Frink or Howard Littlefield. Together, these sketches might have composed a collective picture of the fictional Zenith. Lewis did not hit on this idea, however. The absence of any controlling themes or dramatic conflicts may have prevented Lewis from seeing that he was writing burlesque, not satire.

The reception of *The Man Who Knew Coolidge* was lukewarm. This time only Henry Seidel Canby offered praise, perhaps out of allegiance to Lewis; the *New York Times Book Review* gave the volume a page-one spread, but the review was an open plea to the author not to write another one like it. Other reviewers were not so kind: Heywood Broun said that it was "the dullest writing ever to come from a first-class writing man." Franklin P. Adams, in his *Diary of Our Own Mr. Pepys,* reflected that the entire book could have been packaged in six sketches of two thousand words each.[18]

Alfred Harcourt's commercial instincts proved to be sound: he was correct in predicting that the book would neither sell well nor be favorably received. Why didn't Lewis listen to Harcourt? After all, he had trusted his judgment in the past. One reason may be that in expanding the original sketch into a book Lewis was heeding the advice of H. L. Mencken, at whose behest he had written the original story. Mencken persuaded Lewis to develop the sketch into a book; he even told Lewis that if Harcourt wouldn't publish the book, he would print it in a special issue of the *American Mercury.* Mencken liked the story so much because it was pure burlesque, and to him, Lowell Schmaltz was an even better creation than Babbitt. Schmaltz was a complete boob, without any of Babbitt's humanity. Thus Mencken again pushed Lewis to let his instinctive comic-satiric tendencies guide him—just as he had influenced how Lewis wrote *Babbitt* and *Elmer Gantry.*[19]

Mencken's urgings were probably only a secondary factor, however. Lewis thought of *The Man Who Knew Coolidge* as he had of *Mantrap:* as a jeu d'esprit that he could write with "incredible speed." He also saw that he could recycle material from earlier novels such as *Babbitt,* and that he could cash in on a talent he had honed perfectly: rendering the idiom of a character such as Lowell Schmaltz. He realized that the intensive work of the past seven years had left its mark on him: it had cost him his marriage and turned him into a problem drinker.

Alfred Harcourt probably understood that Lewis was losing some of his drive, but he was nonetheless growing annoyed with his star author. The two men had worked together smoothly for most of the previous eight years because Lewis was producing first-rate literature that was timely and controversial—and that sold in record numbers. Harcourt's attempts to dissuade Lewis from expanding the *Mercury* story into a book indicate that he was no longer willing to accept uncritically whatever Lewis wrote. Harcourt probably also viewed *The Man Who Knew Coolidge* as another example of Lewis's antics, which were becoming tiresome to him. Eventually, these various factors would cause Harcourt to let Lewis break his contract with the firm and seek another publisher.

Lewis's increasing tendencies to write books "out of his head," to stream-line his time-consuming composing methods, and to recycle material from previous books fundamentally affected the creation of *Dodsworth.* This work is quite different from Lewis's earlier novels. It is largely nonsatiric, and it is not a debunking of a particular segment of American society. The novel instead tells the story of Sam Dodsworth, a pioneer in the automotive industry. As the novel opens, Sam has just sold his Revelation Motor Car Company to a large corporation and now has the time and money to do the things in life that he feels he has missed out on and that his wife, Fran, desires. They close their house in Zenith and go abroad for an indefinite stay during which Sam attempts to learn the value of history, art, and philosophy. Fran, however, turns into a snob. She flirts with American expatriates and European noblemen and makes Sam feel clumsy, confused, and inadequate. Eventually, Fran leaves Sam to marry a German count, but she is rejected by the aristocratic society to which she thinks she belongs.

In the meantime Sam has fallen in love with Edith Cortright, a widowed American living in Italy who accepts Sam at face value and does not try to control him or mold him into something that he is not. When Fran asks Sam to forgive her, however, he gives in and they are reunited until, en route home to America, Sam recognizes that his wife has not fundamentally changed. He returns to Italy to live with Edith. The plot thus roughly parallels Lewis's recent past with Grace and Dorothy Thompson. Ultimately, however, Lewis is ambivalent about whether Sam has permanently learned the lesson of self-worth and has grown capable of seeing the transparency of Fran. At the end of the novel, Sam is "so confidently happy that he completely forgot Fran and did not again yearn over her, for almost two days."[20]

Although there are some excellent passages of nonsatiric writing in *Dodsworth,* the novel is not entirely successful as a treatment of love and marriage. Lewis used his practiced themes of rebellion, freedom, and the quest for identity, but in this novel these ideas are somewhat flat. Or, as Bridget Puzon says, Lewis "did not complete" his familiar narrative pattern of escape and return, nor did he "consistently maintain the satiric tone" he established in the early parts of the narrative.[21] Another problem with the novel is Lewis's contradictory treatment of Sam—a fact noted by many reviewers when the book was published. Sam is shown to be both intelligent and foolish, an anti-Babbitt and a Babbitt. Glen A. Love notes that as the novel progresses, Lewis "reveals a troublesome lessening of intensity" toward the depiction of Sam as a serious-minded quest figure and "an inability or unwillingness" to follow him through to the completion of his quest.[22] The blurred characterization of Sam resulted from Lewis shifting his intentions for the book. The prepublication materials for *Dodsworth* indicate that Lewis did not initially envision the novel as a loosely autobiographical chronicle of his travels with Grace in Europe, their subsequent breakup, and his relationship with Dorothy Thompson. Nor did Lewis initially think of *Dodsworth* as a study of love and marriage. He thought of it first as a novel about a Zenithite, a "captain of industry," and his search for self-fulfillment. Lewis intended to treat this figure in his usual satiric manner. According to Ramon Guthrie, when Lewis discussed the novel with him in the spring of 1927 he intended for Sam to be a "counter-balance" to George F. Babbitt, but Guthrie felt that Lewis did not really believe in the character "overmuch." "The Samuel Dodsworth that finally emerged in the novel is somewhat of an unwitting composite of John D. Rockefeller, Jr., whom Red didn't know, and Sinclair Lewis, whom he scarcely knew either,"[23] Guthrie reported. His recollections indicate that Lewis was moving forward with his original idea for this novel from 1921, when he made sporadic notes about the characters called the Dodsworths in the *Babbitt* notebook. This was evidently the basic conception of the novel that he kept in mind over the ensuing seven years—the "American abroad story" about "a business man, a Zenithite, but NOT a Babbitt" that he had mentioned to Grace in 1922.

Further, Lewis planned to back the narrative with research on Sam's profession and to immerse himself in that world, as he had done for his earlier novels. Guthrie recalled that Lewis hired a secretary to gather information on the automobile industry (specifically, on the shape and design of early engines) but fired the secretary some time later. Lewis decided instead to base the novel on his own marital difficulties and make that his dramatic conflict. In his desire to streamline his composing method, Lewis may even have thought to himself that this period with Grace in effect had been a time of research and study—or self-study—that was as rich in its own way as the fieldwork he had done for *Elmer Gantry, Arrowsmith, Babbitt,* or *Main Street.* He probably also thought that in *Dodsworth* he could explore the same themes that he had in *Main Street:* Sam and Fran may be seen as middle-aged versions of Will and Carol Kennicott. Of course, the central conflict in *Dodsworth* is the reverse of that in *Main Street.* This time, Lewis wrote about marriage from the husband's point of view, and the main object of his satire shifted dramatically from the midwestern citizen, the husband Sam, to the snooty wife who looks down on her provincial surroundings. Lewis had at hand a model for Fran in Grace, whom he could also avenge himself on in writing the book. Thus in *Dodsworth* Lewis transformed Carol Kennicott, who was patterned on the "good part" of Grace, into Fran Dodsworth, who became all the bad parts of Grace.

As Lewis began to draw on his own experiences for material, he naturally began to identify with Sam, and Sam's story increasingly became Lewis's story—specifically, his version of the breakup of his marriage. As Lewis pushed ahead with the draft, however, he did not jettison his earlier satiric point of view toward Sam; instead he seems to have tried to counterbalance the satiric material with nonsatiric passages that showed Sam to be perceptive and intelligent. Dorothy Thompson, who read through the draft and commented on it in the margins, pointed out some of these contradictory passages to Lewis. He seems to have agreed with her judgments, for he cut much of the satiric element from the book. Lewis had performed a similar type of editorial surgery on the typescript of *Main Street,* where he deleted passages that portrayed Carol as too foolish to be a sympathetic figure. But in revising *Dodsworth,* Lewis was not able (or not willing) to cut all such material—perhaps he did not want to, given his knowledge of what his readers would expect of him as a satirist. Lewis also tried to introduce passages of genuine introspection; but what he wrote was mawkish and clumsy, and he ended up cutting many of these as well. Ultimately, the aesthetic obstacle that Lewis could not overcome in writing *Dodsworth* was his inability to see himself impartially and portray himself fictionally. Lewis could not adapt his mimetic method of absorbing other people and their milieus and apply it to himself.

The shift in Lewis's intentions for *Dodsworth* can be seen in the earliest stages of its composition, in two crucial prepublication drafts of the first chapter that are today preserved at the Beinecke. These ur-chapters were written by Lewis in November 1927 and January 1928, respectively. (The November 1927 chapter was part of the fifty thousand words of the narrative that Lewis completed in that month before breaking off to expand "The Man Who Knew Coolidge" into a book.) Both chapters bear the title "EXILE / A Novel by / Sinclair Lewis." The first document, dated 3 November 1927, is twenty-two pages long. The second, dated 20 January 1928, totals fifteen pages. Both chapters are revised lightly, and they bear only a family resemblance to the published chapter 1. The ur-chapters describe Sam's senior year as a student at Yale, his friendship with Tub Pearson, and his desire to do meaningful work and at the same time keep a humane and artistically enhanced perspective on life. The chapters also describe at length Sam's courtship of Fran. In the published text, Lewis telescoped this material and instead described Sam's first job (at the Zenith Automotive Works) and his progress through the ranks at the Revelation Motor Car Company. He especially shortened the courtship scenes, which in the published text occupy only two pages.

The two openings are quite different from each other, as well. In the November 1927 chapter (hereafter chapter A), Lewis focuses on Sam as a student at Yale, and his theme is Sam's questing after his most idealistic side; in the January 1928 chapter (hereafter chapter B), the focus is Sam's courtship of Fran and her iciness toward him, even in her youth. In both chapter A and chapter B, Lewis's attitude toward Sam is satiric. Fran, however, is portrayed differently in the two openings. In chapter A, she is a fairly bland character without much edge to her personality. She is rather like Leora Arrowsmith in that she seems devoted to her man. In chapter B, Fran more closely resembles her character in the published novel: aloof and haughty.

According to chapter A, Lewis intended to begin the novel with a kaleidoscopic view of Sam's last semester at Yale, when at age twenty-one he begins to question the nature of his existence and think about his future. In other words, Lewis had planned to show the origins of Sam's "rebellion" and his subsequent questing rather than simply having him leave his job and start his travels, as he does in the published text. In chapter A, Lewis employed the ironic metaphor of Sam as an explorer—in much the same way that Lewis had satirized Babbitt by chronicling his drive to the office in mock-heroic fashion and invoking the image of a pirate ship to describe his motorcar. In this rejected opening chapter of *Dodsworth,* Sam thinks of himself in the romantic image of a Richard Harding Davis hero—as in the following passage, for example, which does not appear in the published text:

> He would do very romantic and lucrative things against a background of palms, volcanoes, Spanish balconies, and gold lace. He would found and control a whole settlement, with railroads, warehouses, docks. . . . His engineering projects would be admired by all the titled English magnates who came to look at them. He would splendidly "do something with life." (chap. A, p. 4)

Lewis also wrote several passages in which Sam wonders "what he was going to do [with] this product of having for four years played at work and most earnestly worked at play. He felt puzzled and a little annoyed" (chap. A, p. 2).

In chapter B, this material was streamlined greatly: Lewis reduced it by about 50 percent and deleted altogether the ironic commentary on Sam's self-reflections. In the published text all of this material is omitted, except for two sentences on page 13. In practical terms, Lewis eliminated the theme of Sam's search for identity, and he replaced this material with scenes describing Sam's courtship of Fran. The identity theme in chapter A thus gradually gave way to the marriage theme in chapter B and more or less disappeared completely from the beginning of the published text.

Lewis also fundamentally changed the characterization of Fran between chapter A and chapter B. In the former, Fran is not the "angel of ice" that she is in chapter B and in the published text. She is somewhat assertive, but she is not arrogant or shrewish. Some of the differences between Fran's personality in chapter A and chapter B are startling. For instance, compare the two versions of this passage, in which Lewis contrasts Sam's enthusiasm for building automobiles with Fran's cosmopolitan airs.

> [*Chapter A:*]
> [Sam:] "I've been working on my mechanical drawing a lot on the side lately and I've got some ideas ——— I think we ought to get entirely away from imitating carriages. Make a, you might call it, a new kind of beauty for autos. . . . The boss of the new company thinks I'm crazy. . . . What do you think? Or do you think I'm crazy, too?"
> "I think it's splendid. As if you cared what I think!" . . .

He groaned, "Oh Lord you're so —— You've got a lot more sense than I have. Too!"

"I have not! If you knew how I've admired your planet from my small skipping star! Some day you'll go to Europe, too, and you'll learn more in three months than I did in a year!"

"Perhaps we'll see it together!"

She was silent. He touched her hand. For an instant she did not withdraw hers. "Let me drive you home in my auto," he said.

"No, Mama is coming for me."

"You've got to let me take you for a drive!"

"Perhaps. Perhaps next Sunday. . . . We must go back."

They returned to [the] dance in a silence of intimacy. He said only, "I'm sorry I tried to bully you. Forgive me?" and only a soft "Yes" did she answer, and so he felt more pleasantly bullying and protective than ever; he agreed within [himself] that she was right in believing that he could master Europe far faster than she—so yielding, so delicate. (17–19)

[*Chapter B:*]

[Sam:] "I suppose you'll be bored in Zenith."

She laughed in a small competent way. "I know so much about Europe—I'm no Cook's tripper! . . . What are you doing now, by the way?"

"I'm second assistant supe at the Locomotive Works. Guess I might possibly have a chance to be president of the Works some day, but I'm going to take a big gamble and —— Ever ride in an automobile?"

"Oh, yes, several times, in Paris and New York, and I saw Herr Benz exhibiting a new auto in Berlin . . ."

"Well, I'm crazy about 'em. . . . I've been working on my mechanical drawing a lot lately, and I've got the idea that autos ought to get away from imitating carriages. . . . What do you think?"

"Oh, splendid!"

"And I've bought me an automobile of my own."

"Oh, *really?*"

"Let me drive you home tonight."

"No, sorry; Mama is coming for me."

"You've got to let me take you for a ride. Soon!"

"Perhaps next Sunday. . . . We must get back to the clubhouse, don't you think?"

He sprang up, meekly. As he lifted her to her feet, as he felt her

Herkules Haus,
Berlin,
November 3, 1927.

E X I L E

A Novel by

Sinclair Lewis

CHAPTER I

As the most popular man in his class, as the best football
tackle Yale had known for years, ~~Lincoln~~ *Samuel* Dodsworth was not allowed
to waste time in thinking. To read enough books (to) pass examinations was considered decent, ~~though regrettable~~, since otherwise he
would have flunked, but most of his days and evenings he was be-
sieged by the duties of being a ~~man of importance, being~~ a good
fellow, and "doing something for old Yale," which meant getting the
name of ~~the university~~ *the* university into the sports pages. | He was
busy with track athletics, baseball politics, sports items for the
college paper, the Prom; he had to be solemn at meetings of the
sacred ~~schoolboy society~~ *boys' club* known as Skull and Bones, which bored
him, meetings of the Y.M.C.A., which irritated ~~gdm~~ him, calls upon
girls, who did not abnormally interest him; it was the proper thing
to do a good deal of tussling and book-heaving in dormitory rooms;
and particularly he had to do the respectable amount of loafing.

Figs. 27–29.   First pages of the "EXILE" fragments and the *Dodsworth* typescript
(Yale Collection of American Literature, Beinecke Rare Book and Manuscript
Library, Yale University)

New Chapters at
beginning: started
Berlin, Jan. 20th,
1928.

Arbor

E X I L E

A Novel by

Sinclair Lewis

CHAPTER I

Ever since Tap Day, Sam Dodsworth had felt out of it. He
was as unimportant now as though he were a janitor or a professor
of mathematics, yet a wee k ago he had been one of the four or five
Great Men of his generation in Yale: All America football tackle,
last man tapped for Bones , and in his day on the Prom committee.
Now the Juniors had ~~sophomores~~ swept in, and even such magnificent
Seniors as Dodsworth could only disappear meekly into a bored
world outside.

Thus demoted, he became so desperately anti-social as to
sit alone and think!

For four years, as the most popular man in his class, he had
never been allowed to waste time in thinking. He had to "do something for good old Yale." It had been permissible to study enough
for the passing of examinations: it was proper to do a ~~decent~~ ~~sum~~
good deal of tussling in dormitory-rooms, and even to loaf on the

Fig. 28

DODSWORTH

never an August evening more moon-washed & spacious, & proper for respectable romance.

~~A Novel by~~
Sinclair Lewis

CHAPTER ~~I~~ **1**

The aristocracy of ~~the city of~~ Zenith were dancing at the Kenne-
peose Canoe Club, ~~this spacious moon-washed evening of August,~~ They
two-stepped on the wide porch, with its pillars of ~~unpeeled~~ pine
trunks, its bobbing Japanese ~~funk~~ lanterns; and ~~m~~ never were there
~~xixxxxxxxxxxxx~~ dance-frocks with wider sleeves, or hair more sen-
suously piled on little smiling heads; ^

Three *guests* ~~motors~~ had come in these new-fangled automobiles, for it
was now 1903, ~~practically~~ the climax of ~~the ages,~~ *civilization.* A fourth was
approaching, driven by Samuel Dodsworth.

~~In~~ The ~~whole~~ scene was ~~like~~ a sentimental chrome -- ~~moonlit~~
crisping lake, ~~and her maidens~~ lovers in canoes singing "Nelly Was a A
Lady," *all* very lugubrious and happy -- ~~yet~~ Sam Dodsworth enjoyed it, ~~for~~ *and*
~~he was sentimental himself, though he looked like a granite boulder.~~
He was a ~~very~~ large and formidable young man, ~~tall and beamy,~~ with
a healthy brown mustache and a ~~tangle of~~ *chaos* ~~of~~ brown hair on a massive
head. He was, ~~now, at the age of~~ *at* twenty-eight, assistant superintendent
of that most noisy and unsentimental institution, the Zenith Locomotive Works, and in Yale (class of 1896) he had played better than

two slim hands, he murmured, "Europe! Golly, I'd like to see it, some day. Maybe I might run into you over there, and you might show me some of it."

"I'd love to."

Ah, if she loved Europe, he would master it for her, and give it to her on a platter of polished gold! (11–12)

In both of these passages, Lewis is clearly making fun of Sam and his delusion that he has charmed Fran completely. But more important are the changes Lewis made in Fran. In chapter A, she virtually gushes with admiration for Sam, telling him, "I've admired your planet from my small skipping star." Sam thinks of her as "yielding" and "delicate"; by contrast, in chapter B she is cool and self-assured, laughing "in a small competent way" at Sam's desire to work his way up through the ranks of the automotive plant. She smoothly parries his awkward verbal advances.

Other substantial changes in Fran's personality from chapter A to chapter B can be seen in the passage where Sam and Fran kiss for the first time and Sam proposes marriage. In the first version, Fran yields to Sam's caresses: "she smiled foggily at him again . . . he kissed her again, and she was more responsive" (chap. A, p. 21). In chapter B, Sam's offer is received this way:

She slipped from the shelter of his raincoat and, arms akimbo, said impishly, "Oh, really? Is that a new law."

"It is, by God!"

"Oh, the great Yale athlete speaks! The great automobile magnate!"

Very gravely: "No, Fran. Was I ever a great athlete? I don't know. Now I'm just a scared lump of meat, telling you I *worship* you!"

Still she stared at him, there among the autumn-bedraggled weeds on the high river bank, stared at him impudently. (13–14)

In this passage, which Lewis carried over into the published chapter 1 with only minor stylistic revisions, Fran is playfully haughty but also patronizing and self-interested. Lewis describes her as "impish" and "impudent," and he continues to satirize Sam by having him exult over his "conquest" of Fran: "That just *shows* she isn't one of these flirts that are always letting boys paw 'em. And if I'm awfully tender and careful and patient with her, she'll be—wow!—a regular furnace."

A final example of Lewis making Fran unsympathetic and amplifying the idea that she will control Sam can be seen at the end of each document. Chapter A reads: "And never, these twenty years, did he come nearer to South American jungles than Wall Street; never nearer to the tinkling roofs of China than the Crow Wing [Revelation] warehouse on Railroad Avenue, Kansas City" (22). The following paragraph was added to the preceding sentence in chapter B, and it remains in the published text: "But he was too busy to be discontented; and now and then he managed to believe that Fran was not merely his wife but that she really loved him" (15).

These early chapters indicate that Lewis probably did not start thinking of the main characters as being based on him and Grace until January 1928, when he wrote chapter B. At that point, he also shifted his concerns from Sam's loss of identity and his "yearning" after what he has missed in life to the incompatibility of Fran and Sam, her frigidity, and the disintegration of their marriage.

By late January or early February 1928 Lewis was therefore writing a different story than the one he had begun the previous autumn. After producing chapter B, Lewis rewrote this first chapter a third time and then continued on with the draft, reworking the remaining fifty thousand words he had produced in November and pushing forward with the rest of the narrative. By 19 March Lewis had completed 105,000 words and had tentatively changed the title of the book to *Dodsworth*.[24] On 14 May 1928 Lewis and Dorothy Thompson were married in London, and one week later they set out on their honeymoon, a caravan trip through the English countryside (their every stop attracting a crowd of reporters). Lewis worked on the book steadily throughout this trip, and by 13 July the draft was completed.[25]

Before Lewis and Dorothy returned to the United States on 28 August, Lewis gave the draft to Ramon Guthrie and asked him and his wife to check it for factual inaccuracies and make "any criticisms and suggestions" they thought appropriate. Guthrie and his wife did so—evidently rather quickly, for Guthrie said that there was so little time before Lewis and Dorothy sailed that it was "a day-and-night job" to read the draft. The Guthries then typed up "several pages" of comments and suggestions. No such notes seem to survive; Guthrie said that they "were relatively unimportant" and that "if they occasioned any of the changes that [Lewis] eventually made in the manuscript, they were slight ones."[26]

Lewis revised the draft typescript at Twin Farms, a country estate that he and Dorothy bought upon their return to the United States. The domicile consisted of two farmhouses on adjoining plots of land between the villages of Barnard and Pomfret, Vermont. (Ironically, Dorothy got from

Lewis what Grace had always wanted: a permanent home.) The larger of the two farmhouses, called the "Big House" or "Dorothy's House," was extensively remodeled. Here Dorothy slept and worked, and the Lewises did their entertaining. The smaller of the two buildings became known as "Red's House." Here, Lewis revised *Dodsworth* during October, November, and early December 1928; printer's copy was ready for Harcourt on 15 December.[27]

In revising the draft (now at the Beinecke), Lewis cut or toned down many passages that satirized Sam. Lewis wanted to give Sam more intelligence and make him more sympathetic than he had done initially. For example, Lewis had often depicted Sam in stereotypical terms as a bumbling American abroad. In revising, Lewis cut many of these passages. At the beginning of chapter 8, for instance, when Sam sits down to his first English breakfast, Lewis deleted a silly comment that Sam makes about the taste of British coffee: "Half a dozen times he tried to be cultured and original; half a dozen times he tried to avoid the inevitable phrase; but at the end he said emphatically: 'Coffee that tastes like dish-water!'" (TS 100). Another example may be found in chapter 15, as Sam thinks about Fran's easy friendliness with the hollow Madame de Penable and her circle of sycophants. Lewis wanted Sam to show good judgment in seeing through the falseness of such people, but he ended up making him sound like someone from Gopher Prairie who is awestruck when shown a veneer of sophistication: "Fran is getting so she can parlez-vous with 'em splendid. Great girl!" Dorothy helped Lewis to see that he was often satirizing Sam instead of presenting him sympathetically. In several places like these, Dorothy pointed out to Lewis (through marginal notes) that Sam appeared foolish. Beside this particular passage, Dorothy wrote, "Absolutely Babbitt!" (TS 234). Elsewhere she noted, "He's not a consistent character. He couldn't like Mencken and believe all labor agitators were paid by Russia" (TS 226). Lewis saw that her judgment was accurate and redid this scene.

A similar type of change was made in the beginning of chapter 13. This chapter is crucial to our understanding of Sam because in it Lewis attempts to establish that Sam possesses the most desirable elements of the national character but at the same time is receptive to the humane values of European culture. In this scene, Sam sits alone in the lobby bar of his Paris hotel and reflects on his "Americanness." He assesses what he has seen of Europe so far and admits to himself that Europeans place a higher value on the fine arts than Americans do. Sam thinks of himself as a typical American—too busy building industrial strength ("pioneering") to foster the development of art.

In typescript, this passage was approximately three hundred words

the American~~s~~ presented their ~~American~~ heroes ~~as loud-mouthed~~ Yankee

~~b~~arbarians who were proven superior t~~umanihmEumumsams~~ because they

coul~~d~~ out-tip and out-shout any of the degenerate post-~~war~~ Europeans.

One of them chronicled a ~~farstmahsam~~ thick-necked fifty-year-old washing-machine manufacturer

who was to be regarded as ~~an~~ ~~enikasnenfikysoninpnhemurngerhmtmxmxm~~ ~~whn~~

exemplar of American citizenship because he was stronger than a

poor little wimp of a fifth-rate Greenwich Village playwright,

because he did not become sea-sick during a storm, because he

shouted songs in the smoking-room of the steamer, because he won the

favor of African jewel-vendors by paying whatever they asked, ~~and~~

because he showed himself to be a noble fellow and a good husband

by buying that African jewelry for his unspeakable shrew of a wife

whenever she lost her temper ~~a~~ for no reason whatever, and because

he (most improbably) had the chance to make love to a really civilized

woman and refused it on behalf of his ~~mah~~ statedly insane ~~had~~ hag of

a wife. Another showed an American family timid before the demands

~~adixammuarpmakmbhammhh~~ of their unspeakable child who demanded tp

see the more jolly and obscene objects in the Parisian museums. A

third demonstrated that any ~~mh~~ American oil millionaire will, if

he rent a castle and buy the acquaintanceship of ~~shahhpmgmtmshm~~

the decayed noblesse, get drunk and show his independence by acting

the fool.

"Damn it," said ~~Sammah~~ Samuel Dodsworth, "the kind of Amer-

icans I know may like their liquor, but they don't try to show their

superiority to Europeans by getting drunker and shouting louder.

I guess it would cramp ~~thehxmahyhampxhmhmxhmmhxhidxhihmmnhmmmtmxhmhhm~~

~~thmmmfhmhimmmunithmmm~~ the style of all these American fiction-

writers that show what husky and obnoxious rough-necks we are

~~abroad, and I'd dead sure it would~~ spoil ~~the Eu~~

you look like a cross between Sir Lancelot and Jack Dempsey."

But Mr. Atkins had not yet heard of cocktails. And Mr. Atkins
held forth. He had been everywhere, and he could make everywhere sound
uninteresting. ~~he had met every one, and he described every one as~~
~~so genteel and literate that they seemed terrifying.~~ He would look at
you earnestly and demand to know whether you had made a pilgrimage
to Viterbo to see the Etruscan remains, and he made it sound so
nagging a duty that ~~Dodsworth~~ ^{Sam} vowed that he would never
let himself be caught near Viterbo; ~~and~~ ^{he} ~~Fran ever made him~~ go
~~there,~~
~~he would ... flee ... music entirely away~~
~~from all sight of Etruscan remains. Atkins~~ was so severe
about American music that he made Sam long for jazz; ~~he was so stern~~
~~about ...~~
~~about the lack of artistic appreciation among Rotarians that Sam want~~ed
~~to join the Rotarians.~~

Toward the seven deadly arts ~~Sam~~ Sam had ~~always~~ had the ~~shy~~ ^{inarticulate}
reverence which ~~a~~ ^{an} Irish policeman might have toward ~~the~~ ^a shrine of
~~the~~ Virgin on his beat. They were to him escape, romance, ~~a joyous~~
~~...~~ ^{and he} ~~He~~ was ~~...~~ ^{irritated} ~~bewildered~~ when they were presented to him
as a ~~...~~ preacher presents the ~~...~~ virtues of sobriety and
~~...~~ chastity. ~~...~~ ^{He hadn't the training to lose himself}
~~in~~ ^{Bach or Goethe; but} ~~in~~ ^{Chesterton,}
~~let his weary soul escape into that spacious serenity; he would forget~~
~~in Schubert, in a Corot, he had been~~
~~...together,~~
~~as he sat ... in the gay insanity of "Able's Irish Rose" Thursday~~ or
~~able, Smith, to forget motors~~
~~Alec Kynance.~~ But with rising stubbornness he asserted
that if he had to take ~~the seven arts~~ ^{the arts} as something in which he must
pass an examination, he would chuck them altogether and be content
with poker.

longer than it is in the published text. Lewis originally had Sam continue to pursue this topic—but not with the reasoned, mature judgment evident in the published passage. Originally, Sam's thinking ran thus:

> I'm not like some of those expatriate lads there in London. We've got the future. One thing: an old hardboiled Yank like me can come here and appreciate it, while the Europeans come only to lecture and to gather as many dollars as they can by lecturing about what dollar cashers we are! God knows Fran and I aren't here to pick up a few francs by telling the Frogs that no decent high brow ought to pick up francs! (TS 198)

In this speech, which Lewis deleted, Sam sounds a lot like George Babbitt, stuck in his own muddled thinking and self-defeating language. In a later scene in this chapter, Lewis had made a similar error in character analysis. In Sam's conversation with Matthieu, his room-waiter at the hotel, he had said in typically provincial fashion of the French "modernistic films" that he would "hate to be a fairy-lad whimpering about [the] pictures," but that if he had to "choose between that and one of these Rotarians that these authors represent as the ideal American citizen" he would choose the former (TS 203–4). Here, Dorothy pointed out that Sam was being presented in a contradictory fashion: that he was not exactly a Babbitt, but neither was he of a "higher order" than the Babbittry, as Lewis wanted him to be. "Well how about the Rotarians he liked so well[?]" she asked, referring to the foregoing scenes where Sam approves of the behavior of "solid citizens." (Earlier, she had noted that Sam sounded "like someone in New Rochelle" [TS 119].) In revising, Lewis made Sam reasonable and mature; the chapter thus presents Sam in a favorable light.

There are other examples in the typescript of Lewis balancing the twin poles of Sam's character. In many places in the published text, the image of Sam as a chauvinistic American comes to the fore because, in addition to treating the theme of marriage, Lewis was also analyzing the differences between American and European society. Thus besides driving the plot, the characters in the novel have the additional burden of delivering Lewis's opinions on the two cultures. In reading through the typescript Dorothy singled out such sections for comment, and she urged Lewis to tone down the vulgarities of Sam's jingoistic Americanisms. Lewis again seems to have taken her advice.

In one passage, he did some rather drastic editing that changed Sam from a vulgar provincial into something approaching his first conception of the character in 1921—a "Great Soul," sensitive to humanistic values.

This scene takes place in chapter 23, where Sam and Professor Braut discuss how Americans and Europeans view each other's cultures. In the original version of this scene, Sam argues ineffectively that the true excellence of a culture should be determined not by the number of great men it produces (Braut's contention) but rather by the American aim of average achievement for the many. Lewis carefully changed Sam's statements so that in the published text he admits the validity of Braut's test and reasonably grants to Braut that, although they represent different cultures, they essentially agree on several points. Lewis also revised two paragraphs in which Sam rebuts the image that he thinks Europeans have of Americans as either ruthless capitalists or gangland gunmen (252). Dorothy placed brackets around this passage; and although she did not write a note about it, she did comment on the pages preceding and following it: "Too long" (TS 391) and "Too long—compress" (TS 390).

Up to this point, we have seen the extent to which Dorothy's criticisms helped Lewis iron out inconsistencies in the characterization of Sam. Lewis himself recognized many of these discrepancies, and he made many such changes on his own initiative. Yet many such passages remain in the published text. Thus Lewis appears to be ambivalent about whether Sam is admirable or silly. A useful comparison might be drawn here between Lewis's revisions in the draft of *Dodsworth* and those in the draft of *Babbitt*. In writing the latter, Lewis started out to make the protagonist sympathetic and to explore his inner life. But by cutting many passages of introspection, Lewis ended up mostly satirizing Babbitt and portraying him as a figure similar to Mencken's "Booboisie." In writing *Dodsworth,* the opposite occurred: Lewis started out to satirize his protagonist, but as he made Sam's story more and more like his own story, he cut many satiric passages and tried to make Sam a sympathetic character. In both novels, there is a dual focus. Neither character is completely realized as either an object of satire or a sympathetic figure. Lewis could not very successfully blend these elements in drawing character.

In chapter 2, we saw why he could not achieve this delicate balance with the character of Babbitt—the lack of anyone to encourage him to do so, his own ambivalence about writing as a satirist versus writing as a "novelist," and his desire not to romanticize the protagonist and thus lose the satiric edge of the novel. Some of these same factors also seem to explain why Sam Dodsworth is not a fully realized character, and there are additional reasons as well.

With his mimetic talents, Lewis could observe a world and a particular person and then represent them fictionally—as he had done with Paul De Kruif or William Stidger, for example—but he could not do so with himself and his own world. He had tried to do this twice in *Main Street* and had seen that it did not work: first in the ur-protagonist he envisioned in 1905, the figure of the bitter young lawyer, then in Guy Pollock in the rejected chapter 36 of the typescript. Lewis was not a good self-analyst. James Lundquist has suggested that one of the reasons Lewis traveled so much was that it kept him from "looking inward"; when he did examine his life, "he seemed to be both repelled and bored by what he saw, apparently more interested in the motives of others than in his own."[28] Moreover, in his earlier work Lewis had investigated a particular world with the help of someone whom he could draw on for the controlling intelligence of his novel. In creating *Main Street,* for example, he had observed Grace in Sauk Centre and asked himself, "What would it be like to be this type of woman living in this type of town?" Similarly, in doing research for *Babbitt* he had mingled with the types of people who embodied Babbittry, and his method was to observe how these people behaved. For *Arrowsmith* he had listened to Paul De Kruif tell of his experiences and asked, "What was it like to be a scientist?" In Kansas City in 1926, he had answered the question, "What was it like to be a minister?" by actually speaking in pulpits himself and engaging in other activities that enabled him to live out the roles of his characters. By contrast, as he wrote *Dodsworth* he did not have a person to talk to; he tried instead to observe himself. The question he thus ended up asking was, "What was it like to be Sinclair Lewis?" He of course could not answer that question satisfactorily—few people truly understand their own behavior or can fathom their own motivations.

Most writers are rather self-conscious and are given to exploring their thoughts and feelings in diaries, journals, and memoirs, sometimes ad absurdum. Lewis did not write any memoirs. He kept a diary only twice in his life—as a youth from 1900 to 1908, and from 1942 to 1946 when he was living in Duluth, Minnesota—but there is little in either of these journals about himself.[29] They are filled mostly with information about his activities and surface impressions of what he observed around him. He wrote several short reminiscences of his days as a newspaper reporter and a publishing representative as well as two autobiographical sketches (one of them in August 1927, just before he started *Dodsworth*), but these also reveal only superficial details. Just as he was not particularly good at reading character in other people, he was not inclined to do so to himself, either. This is not to say that Lewis had no self-knowledge; he was simply not skilled at being a novelist of the subjective life.

What Lewis was good at was absorbing the emotions and behavior of others. The best parts of *Dodsworth* are his depictions of Grace as she appears in the character of Fran. Lewis could "do" Grace perfectly—in such scenes as where Fran publicly chastises Sam for being a "dirty drunk" (320), in her feigned "thoughtfulness about economy" while living lavishly (221), in her haughty manner with servants and people whom she considers to be socially inferior to her, and in her many flirtations and general snobbishness. He even reproduces Grace's exact mannerisms: the fake English accent, the pronunciation of "schedule" as "shedule," and the Continental habit of crossing the number "7" so that it looks like an "F."[30] In Grace, Lewis had the best possible model for his character because he had observed her for the past thirteen years. Lewis had practiced his skills at parodying Grace in creating Carol Kennicott, Madeline Fox, Joyce Lanyon, and Sharon Falconer. But those portraits were trial sketches; in the picture of Fran Dodsworth, Lewis filled in all the details.

Lewis's descriptions of Grace in the novel are sometimes cruel, and he tells a one-sided story, omitting his role in their failed marriage. (He also transferred to Fran, as he had to Sharon Falconer, his own restlessness and rootlessness.) On balance, however, Fran is more than merely a fictionalized version of Grace. As Dorothy Thompson remarked in her diary after reading the draft of the novel, Lewis treats Fran both with scorn and with insight; she is the perfect bitch, and she is at times rather charming.[31] She has more dimensions to her character than Carol Kennicott, and at times we even feel sorry for Fran, in a more complex emotional way than we do for Carol. Fran Dodsworth is a precursor to a type of female character who has since become commonplace in American fiction—the self-centered, castrating female. She anticipates such later, better-known characters of this type as Hemingway's Margot Macomber, Fitzgerald's Baby Warren in *Tender Is the Night,* and Edward Albee's Martha in *Who's Afraid of Virginia Woolf?*

Another explanation for why *Dodsworth* does not rise to the level of Lewis's previous work may be that in composing his other novels, Lewis worked from detailed outlines and notes. But there were apparently no such materials for *Dodsworth;* and without the certainty of direction guaranteed him by these reliable tools of composition, Lewis did not have a clear thesis or focus for his novel. Lewis needed to go through these preparatory stages to write out, to his satisfaction, a cogent statement of his themes and purpose in a novel—as he had done with *Main Street, Babbitt,* and *Arrowsmith.* Lewis also needed the material generated by doing research and immersing himself in a particular milieu. Unlike Fitzgerald or Faulkner, Lewis did not have the kind of powerful imagination that allowed him to write meaningful fiction out of stored experience and his personal life. When he wrote "out of his head," he generated two kinds of material. One kind was burlesque, such as *The Man Who Knew Coolidge,* which was largely an improvisational performance in which Lewis exhibited his gifts for monologue and mimicry. The other kind was escapist fiction, such as *Mantrap*. In that novel, he took his personal experiences in the wilds of northern Saskatchewan and made them comically melodramatic: Ralph Prescott is a self-mocking sendup of Sinclair Lewis on a camping trip. Both *The Man Who Knew Coolidge* and *Mantrap* were undertaken by Lewis as jeux d'esprit. In contrast, *Dodsworth* was conceived as a serious fictional treatment of modern marriage.

Finally, Lewis could not achieve the balance between satire and sympathy in the characterization of Sam because Lewis was instinctively a satirist. The altered or deleted passages in the typescript of *Dodsworth* suggest how deeply this genre had become embedded in Lewis's imagination. He did not want to satirize Sam completely; he could have created other outlets in the novel for his satiric talents, as he had done in *Babbitt*. In that novel Lewis does not focus exclusively on his character's quest for self-knowledge; he also casts his satiric eye across a wide range of targets—businessmen's conventions, dinner parties, Sunday school. But Lewis did not put such additional dimensions into *Dodsworth,* and so he had to place the animus of the novel in Sam, whom he half-regarded satirically and half-idealized as a portrait of himself. Thus Lewis's imagination was once again divided between satire and idealism. We have seen how many times these tendencies were at war with each other and how in such cases the satiric strain always absorbed the idealistic one. The only exception was *Arrowsmith,* and that was because Lewis was guided by Paul De Kruif in drawing his protagonist.

The typescript of *Dodsworth* indicates that as Lewis wrote the novel, he worked in the natural manner of the satirist—the manner in which he had been writing throughout the 1920s. In revising the draft he was usually working against the grain, trying to alter the original satiric tone of the manuscript and mute its humor. Lewis was at his best when he was creating evenhanded satire; he was not as gifted at writing nonsatiric material. In treating Sam, he was often trying to be serious about material that probably should have been satirized. Perhaps Lewis could not see this clearly because much of the time he was writing about his own thoughts and emotions.

Lewis delivered the completed manuscript of *Dodsworth* to Alfred Harcourt in late December, and Harcourt accepted the novel for publication right away, apparently without asking for any major revisions. When *Dodsworth* was published on 14 March 1929, it was greeted with none of

the rambunctious enthusiasm Lewis had earlier attracted with *Main Street,*
Babbitt, or *Elmer Gantry,* probably because it was not a satiric send-up of
American society. Many reviewers thought *Dodsworth* augured a maturity
in Lewis's development as a writer, but an equal number had mixed or
lukewarm reactions. In addition to noting the blurred characterization of
Sam, many critics also commented on the lack of satire and sociohistorical
detail in the novel. The reviewers uniformly praised the portrait of Fran,
saying that it showed Lewis's satire at its sharpest.

In *Commonweal,* Ernest Brennecke thought that the novel was unsuccessful in its treatment of both the marriage theme and the international
theme but that it was partly redeemed by Lewis's acidic descriptions of
Fran. The *Saturday Review* complained that *Dodsworth* was "a little too
long," but it too praised the characterization of Fran. Dorothy Parker's
review in the *New Yorker* was mixed. In the *New York Times,* Louis Kro-
nenberger praised Lewis—but his assessment was based mostly on Lewis's
earlier achievements.[32] T. S. Matthews, the reviewer for the *New Republic,*
was puzzled over the lack of realistic detail in the novel. Matthews was
accustomed to the sociological character of Lewis's earlier work; he
thought that the few examples in *Dodsworth* of Lewis's "journalistic facul-
ties" rescued the book from complete failure.[33] Several British reviewers
were also perplexed by the lack of documentation in the novel. For example, while praising *Dodsworth* highly, E. M. Forster commented that it
lacked the "camera eye" quality of his best work:

> What has happened? What has changed the Greek Confectionary
> Parlour at Gopher Prairie, where every decaying banana matters, to
> this spiritless general catalogue? The explanation is all too plain:
> photography is a pursuit for the young. So long as a writer has the
> freshness of youth on him he can work the snapshot method, but
> when it passes he has nothing to fall back upon.[34]

Other British notices, such as those in the *Outlook and Independent, Specta-*
tor, Nation and Athenaeum, Bookman, and *London Saturday Review,* were
lukewarm.[35]

H. L. Mencken's review in the *American Mercury* placed *Dodsworth* in the
context of Lewis's earlier novels. Mencken was disappointed that Lewis
was again forsaking satire, as he had in *Arrowsmith.* As Mencken said in
one of his autobiographical volumes, he urged Lewis repeatedly "to stick
to the broad national types that he knew so well how to depict, but . . .
from *Dodsworth* onward the people he dealt with became less and less interesting." This type of thinking is suggested by Mencken's review of

Dodsworth. He complained that the portrait of Sam was not consistent, identifying the very problem Lewis had encountered in composing the narrative: "Lewis first shows that [Sam] is intelligent, and then pictures him playing the complete fool." Mencken concluded that this was the natural result of a satiric writer like Lewis putting "such folks" into his book and thus getting into "dangerous waters." Mencken then praised what he considered to be the merits of the book. According to Mencken, those "passages which show Lewis at his best" were the ones in which he was "unctuous, ingenious, penetrating, and devastating." Mencken applauded the satiric or simply comic episodes in the novel—"the ante-nuptial dinner at the grandiose, Norddeutscher-Lloyd home of old Herman Voelker; the encounter between Sam and Alec Kynance"; "the grand drunk with Tub Pearson in Paris"; and of course the scenes involving Fran. Mencken likened them to other typical Lewis portraits: "Babbitt shaving, Dr. Kennicott operating, Gantry drunk."[36]

By this point, Lewis's reputation was so firmly established that his novels, no matter how they might be reviewed, were bound to be strong sellers. Within six months, *Dodsworth* had surpassed the one hundred thousand mark. Lewis was in high spirits. In his letters from this period, he spoke of new beginnings and new directions. Lewis would in fact be honored in 1930 by becoming the first American to win the Nobel Prize for Literature; but his career after 1930, although largely a success in commercial terms, would not be as significant in artistic terms as it was during the 1920s. By the time of *Dodsworth*, Lewis was simply running out of material. When he began to cast about for a new project, he came up empty.

6

The Labor Novel
and the
Nobel Prize

1929–1930

After completing *Dodsworth,* Lewis was again unfocused and uncertain as to what the subject of his next novel should be. Since *Arrowsmith,* he had had difficulty moving easily from one project to the next. In the past he had been able to push through fairly quickly and begin a new book; this time, however, he was blocked. To keep his hand in, he wrote a series of thirteen stories for *Cosmopolitan* magazine that appeared in 1929 and 1930, but he would not publish a new novel for four years—until 1933, when *Ann Vickers* was issued.

Various factors seem to have come into play. Although Lewis felt that he had overcome the emotional turmoil caused by the death of his father and his divorce, he had never fully recovered from these events. This was also the first time that Lewis had led a sedentary life since setting off from Long Island with Grace in 1915 on their "Research Magnificent." The enforced domesticity created by establishing a household on a Vermont farm instead of traveling from place to place was not good for Lewis's creativity. Also, he rarely saw or talked to other people during this time; he needed this type of interaction to produce creative work. Lewis's letters from this period are full of invitations to his friends to visit him in Vermont—but the farm was difficult to get to, and few seem to have wanted to make the trip. Lewis wanted to travel, thinking that by doing so he could regain both his emotional equilibrium and his creative energy, but Dorothy was pregnant with their first child, and he was tied down by the responsibilities of overseeing the renovation of Twin Farms (which was also eating up much of his income). Perhaps because of these last two circumstances, Lewis's relationship with Dorothy was turning sour rather quickly, and he had begun to drink heavily.

Lewis's inability to get moving on a new project during 1929 made him despondent. According to Vincent Sheean, a journalist friend of Dorothy's who lived with the Lewises at Twin Farms for awhile, Lewis was so unfocused that he was an object of pity:

> It can be said of most writers . . . that work is their one salvation, but never have I seen anybody of whom it was more true than it was of poor Red. He could work like a regiment of engineers, cold sober, implacable in his resolution; but when he did not have work to do (which, in his mind, meant a very big novel, nothing less) he lost his power altogether and became a weak, tremulous thing.[1]

Lewis enjoyed the act of writing, and he needed to write. It served as an outlet for his restlessness, and traveling, doing his research, and making his notes and outlines provided an iron framework of discipline that stabilized him emotionally and offset his inclination to drink.

Without a new novel to work on, Lewis grew querulous. He vented some of his frustration by complaining to Alfred Harcourt about Harcourt's management of his books. Up to this point, Lewis had only occasionally questioned Harcourt's business decisions; but rather suddenly Lewis started taking issue with much of what Harcourt was doing. For example, he was angry at Harcourt for allowing Grosset and Dunlap, a cheap reprint house, to market "*Main St* etc. just as they do Zane Grey" and thereby issue his books "on a lowbrow basis" when in fact he thought there were a large number of "would-be highbrow buyers." Harcourt explained to Lewis that his books were "popular enough to profit by the wider distribution" in inexpensive editions.[2] But Lewis complained that both the new Modern Library series of books published by Random House and the similar series published by Doubleday, Doran were better advertised than the Grosset and Dunlap line, and so he angled for contracts with those houses. He eventually made a deal with the Modern Library, but he and Harcourt had another disagreement when Lewis wanted the popular artist Peggy Bacon to illustrate the Modern Library edition of *Babbitt*. Harcourt insisted on a different artist. Although Lewis seems not to have realized it, Harcourt was probably correct in rejecting Bacon because, as he told Lewis, her work "lean[ed] too much on the side of caricature to suit *Babbitt*."[3] Lewis, however, seems to have resented Harcourt's interference.

Perhaps the greatest point of contention between the two men was Lewis's effort to persuade his publisher to issue a collected edition of his works. Initially, Lewis was thinking of a set priced reasonably at $1.75 a volume. But soon he was talking about a "library set," and at Dorothy's urging he had come up with a list of people to write introductions to each novel and thus make the set "a really fine edition" at "$3.00 or $3.50 a volume, or even more." Harcourt disliked this scheme, mainly because (as he repeatedly told Lewis) publishing had been "generally flat" since the stock market crash in October 1929.[4] Harcourt's friendship with Lewis was being tested again, as it had been at the end of Lewis's work on *Elmer Gantry* and during the composition of *The Man Who Knew Coolidge*.

Finally, near the end of the year, Lewis put aside his quarrels with Harcourt and focused his energies on writing a new novel. This revitalized him briefly and kept him occupied through the fall of 1930—when it was announced that he had won the Nobel Prize, and his other plans were temporarily put on hold. Unfortunately, the project that Lewis chose to undertake in late 1929 was the labor novel, and eventually this also frustrated him and stifled his creativity. It would take some time for Lewis to realize that he simply could not write such a book.

Lewis persisted because he came to believe that this novel would be the crowning achievement of his career; at one point, he remarked to the journalist William L. Shirer that the book was to be "nothing less than a history of America."[5] Lewis's intentions to write a labor novel were so well known that many of his colleagues began to press Lewis to do the book. Upton Sinclair was perhaps the most persistent, sending Lewis information on current labor disputes and even putting him in touch with a celebrated political prisoner in San Quentin, J. B. McNamara, whom Lewis later visited. But Lewis continued to brush off Sinclair's attempts to prod him into action—saying at one point, "The time has not yet come" for the novel, another time refusing Sinclair's help on the grounds that "two novelists discussing it would see it in too literary a way."[6] Yet Lewis seemed to want to write the book more than ever. According to Lincoln Steffens,

Lewis "pumped" him for information; and in the same manner in which he had worked out the dramatic scenes for *Arrowsmith* with Paul De Kruif, Lewis urged Steffens to challenge his views, declaring, "I can't do a novel unless I can get in a rage."[7]

Lewis made two attempts to get started on this phantom novel in the late summer and early fall of 1929—just before the October stock market crash, a darkly ironic moment for Lewis to begin. He had just returned from Marion, North Carolina, where he had reported on a textile workers' strike for the Scripps-Howard newspapers. Moving away from the philosophical orientation of the "Man Who Sought God" plan, Lewis reverted to his tested method of doing research and immersing himself in the world of the novel. First, he returned to his earlier title, "Neighbor." Then—apparently seeking stimulation by talking with all the authorities on labor problems he could find—Lewis literally convened a board of consultants to be in residence at Twin Farms. Night after night for about two weeks, he listened to them discuss the issues—hoping, it seems, that by sheer exposure to the ideas he would be able to write about them. This method was not unlike what he had done in Kansas City during the "Sunday school class" he had conducted with ministers for *Elmer Gantry*.

But his practiced method did not work this time. These meetings turned out to be ill-conceived because Lewis himself, according to one of those "experts" present (Benjamin Stolberg, a young labor journalist), "seemed baffled" by the discussion. Lewis had invited a diverse group of people, each with his own opinion of how the labor movement should be organized and what its goals should be. While the visitors worked out the plot of the novel, Lewis would "take naps" or "read detective stories."[8] Everybody but the author was writing the novel. In the end, Lewis's "godseeker" was ruled out by his friends as too idealistic. If Lewis wanted to write the book, they said, he must acquaint himself more deeply with Marx, Bakunin, Liebknecht, and other political theorists. Lewis eventually gave up, probably because he did not want to write a novel according to the specifications of others. He may also have lacked the energy to tackle such a massive project.

Shortly thereafter, in early October 1929, Lewis again tried to immerse himself in the world of labor. He attended the annual convention of the American Federation of Labor in Toronto, and there he met Carl Haessler, a reporter for the *Federated Press,* a labor newspaper. Lewis was quickly impressed by Haessler's knowledge of the issues. After meeting with him twice in one day, Lewis decided on the spot that he had "met exactly the right man for the De Kruif–Birkhead of [his] novel"; he typed out a formal contract naming Haessler as his collaborator and giving him a percentage of the royalties. This agreement was approved by Harcourt, to whom Lewis once again expressed his enthusiasm: "I'm keener about this novel than anything since *Arrowsmith*," he wrote.[9]

Lewis was returning to his tested methods of invention and composition, but they failed him once more. Lewis and Haessler embarked on a five-week research trip through the industrial towns of the Merrimack Valley in Massachusetts, then moved on to the Pittsburgh area. By 11 January of the new year, however, Lewis had decided (as he told Haessler) that the novel would simply be "thin, sketchy, journalistic." He half-seriously added, "I must take perhaps a year of fasting and prayer before I can ever begin." Behind Lewis's self-deprecating humor was the realization that everyone was expecting him to write the novel; he worried to Haessler about the "cost of derision because I haven't carried out my plans."[10] That same month he confided to John D. Chase, the publicity director for Harcourt, Brace, that inasmuch as the labor novel looked "enormous and the task so vast as to be discouraging" he might never finish it; he therefore asked Chase to "not say anything about it" in publicity materials.[11]

When on 5 November 1930 it was announced that Lewis had won the Nobel Prize, he naturally put aside the labor project. After the excitement abated, he eventually got started on *Ann Vickers,* published in 1933. Other scattershot attempts at the labor novel followed in the early 1930s, but they failed—until the success of the dystopian *It Can't Happen Here,* published in 1935, encouraged him once again to tackle the project. This seventh and final serious attempt at the book and its effect on Lewis's career are important. His struggles reveal much about the peculiar talents, and the shortcomings, that made him successful in the 1920s. That he repeatedly tried to write this novel and could not do so also might supply reasons for Lewis's inability to produce much work after 1930 that equaled the caliber of his 1920s novels.

Some of Lewis's notes for this seventh attempt are preserved at the Baker Memorial Library of Dartmouth College. Ramon Guthrie was teaching there when Lewis enlisted his aid a second time in June 1936. Lewis gathered fresh material with Guthrie by traveling across the Naugatuck and Connecticut Valleys, interviewing factory owners and workers and taking copious notes. The twenty-three pages of notes from this phase of the project that are extant indicate that the novel was to have had the same type of protagonist and philosophical premise that Lewis had in mind nine years earlier: an intellectually unformed worker comes to embrace radicalism and is martyred for his beliefs. This time the book was to be entitled "Unconquerable," and it was to tell the story of Roy Blodgett, "an artist among mechanics" who comes of age in Grimstead, Connecti-

ROY BLODGETT, central character; an
artist among mechanics. Born in
Grimstead, Conn., 1911 -- 18 in 1929
when depression comes; 25 at end of
book. Grimstead High School, where
he is capn of basket ball team and
sprinter on track team and in glee
club; year in Berkshire Christian College; works in Plandamon Electric
Supply Co. factory in Grimstead; in
Lilywhite & Dove typewriter & arms
corporation, Sladesbury, Mass. Looks
like H.M.Knickerbocker -- pale, thin,
quick, almost orange thick hair.
LESTER BLODGETT, his father; born
Grimstead 1873, son of a horse-trader-
horse-doctor-farmer. Furniture store
& undertaker; insurance agent when loses
business after depression. In Gt. War,
in quartermaster corps, and invested all
he had in North States Furniture Camp
Furniture Co., which made field desks,
cots, etc....38 when Roy born; 44m when
entered army; 56 at depression, 1929;
63, and dies, in 1936. (#32 when Sheldon b.)

MINNIE, Roy's mother (christened Mary);
daughter of small-town store-keeper,
school teacher as a girl.

SHELDON BLODGETT, Roy's brother, born
born 1905 -- 6 yrs older -- handsome,
popular, athletic, industrious, enter-
prising, grand manners, noble voice,
gracious handshake, and a liar and
crook when found out. Bl hair, brown
eyes, almost suede-dark complexion vs
which almost too perfect teeth.

Fig. 32. Notes on characters for "Unconquerable" (Baker Memorial Library,
Dartmouth College)

cut, during the Depression.[12] A "home-grown Gene Debs," Roy goes through a series of crises that eventually bring him a false sense of self-knowledge as Lewis shows him "groping for a god." He has a dangerous affair with Zoe Plandamon, the daughter of Darwin Plandamon, a wealthy industrialist who disapproves of Roy but employs him and his brother Sheldon at Zoe's request. Sheldon steals from Plandamon and is arrested; Zoe, antagonized by her father, leaves Grimstead with Roy. The other main character is Lester Blodgett, Roy's father, who is depicted as a man of strong character but naive intellect; after his death early in the novel, Roy's break with his past is complete.

Roy enrolls in an undistinguished college, "takes [a] course in Industrial Democracy," and "gets ideas (pretty vague and discoordinated)" about "Govt, labor industry; Marx." He becomes determined to attend the Massachusetts Institute of Technology (his "New Jerusalem") but never does, leaving college "without too much regret" because it "has come to seem theoretical and pointless." He continues to read widely but has no direction. He comes to depend on Zoe for that, but she has become absorbed in her own political causes and eventually realizes that she is intellectually superior to him. Roy tries his hand at radicalism but neither understands it nor is able to embrace it with conviction. He demonstrates during the 1936 presidential election, going through the strike-beleaguered decade "like Stendahl's hero in battle, pretending at socialism but knowing of it nothing but newspaper headlines and a few amiable pickets."

Eventually Lewis intended to have Roy develop a "Messiah complex" that would destroy him. Lewis did not say what climactic event in the character's life would change his destiny, but the other scenes described in the notes indicate that Roy was to have run afoul of society and be imprisoned, just as Debs was. In one "surrealistic" sequence, Roy undergoes a shock of vision as he sits brooding in his jail cell. He "suddenly sees himself as [a] self-dramatizing charlatan, reveling in his martyrdom," and he contemplates suicide. Lewis also evidently planned to have the later parts of the novel focus on Roy's trial. In one scene a fictionalized Clarence Darrow defends the hero in court but tries to persuade him that his cause is hopeless and that the wisest course of action would be simply to plead guilty. Finally, Lewis created another character, called "the international waiter," who is mentioned only once in the notes but is described as a "sardonic, picaresque, wise expert on life" who would slip into the story "as a foil to the innocence and idealism of the hero."

This is the most intriguing of all the scenarios Lewis invented for the labor novel, although there were several more, altogether different attempts in the 1940s. In the summer of 1945, while in Minnesota to do research on race relations for *Kingsblood Royal,* Lewis told the journalist Betty Stevens that he intended to seek out officials in the Farmer-Labor Party of Minnesota to obtain information for a labor novel.[13] And in 1946, just five years before his death, Lewis's mind again turned to the project, and he visited the factory town of Waterbury, Connecticut, for still more research.

Indeed, the data Lewis gathered could have filled several volumes on the topic of labor, but none of it led to the composition of a novel. Why was Lewis never able to complete this project? Louis Adamic, one of the young Marxist writers with whom Lewis discussed his ideas for the book, suggested that Lewis was afraid to write a controversial novel that might not sell as well as his earlier books.[14] That is an obvious misreading of Lewis's character: not only was he the enfant terrible of American letters, but his flamboyancy had also made him quite wealthy. Refusing the Pulitzer Prize for *Arrowsmith* brought him more attention than he would have received had he accepted the award. Defying God to strike him dead in Kansas City was one reason *Elmer Gantry* sold more than 175,000 copies in six weeks. If Lewis's career proves anything, it is that he was often spoiling for a fight.

More sympathetically, Sheldon Grebstein concluded that labor in America was "in such a state of flux" and was "so gigantic and far-reaching a topic" that it defied the "definitive treatment Lewis wanted to give it."[15] This explanation seems to come closest to pinpointing why Lewis could not write the novel, because it suggests that he could only write about the universal and the general (the small town, the businessman, the scientist)—not about something so specific as the labor movement in America.

My own belief is that Lewis's talents as a satirist prevented him from applying his imagination to this subject. With his particular skill at detecting pretension and fraud, Lewis certainly could have found plenty to satirize in the labor movement (as his letters to Grace during his Chicago research trip in 1922 suggest). But labor was a sacrosanct topic at this time—at least to the leftist critics whom Lewis seems to have been trying to please by writing this novel. Visible, important authors were under tremendous pressure to write proletarian novels. Hemingway, for example, wrote *To Have and Have Not* and *For Whom the Bell Tolls* in response to this same type of pressure. Probably something similar was wanted from Lewis, or so reviewers' comments at this time indicate. But Lewis could not deliver, in large part because he had difficulty treating any subject in a nonsatiric manner.

Lewis perhaps could have extended his analyses of American culture to such a specific historical moment as the rise of labor unions (he attempted to do this—without much success—in a late novel, *The God-Seeker*), but he could not have written about the figures involved in the labor movement with the same degree of uncanny accuracy that informed the characters in his 1920s novels. Lewis essentially wrote novels of character, as he himself pointed out to Haessler in explaining his decision to abort the project: he claimed that he could write the novel only if he did it more as a "novel of character and less one of ideas and propaganda."[16] Further, Lewis's novels anatomized the American middle class; Lewis understood this part of society in ways that few novelists have since.[17] A novel about union laborers would have been outside Lewis's experience, and even with an assistant like Guthrie or Haessler to guide him through unfamiliar territory he would have had difficulty creating such a world in the natural manner in which he had created Gopher Prairie or Zenith.

Moreover, Lewis's writing gift was largely mimetic. One of his most impressive skills was his ability to reproduce the idiom and slang of American speech. Heywood Broun commented in his review of *Main Street* that Lewis was "so unerringly right in reproducing talk" that his written dialogue possessed "deeper than phonographic exactness."[18] In one of the letters he wrote to Grace from Chicago in 1922, Lewis complained that the labor people he had met had "no special speech which I can *hear*."[19] In the 1920s union workers came from many classes, regions, and nationalities, and the rhythms and nuances of their speech must have sounded alien to Lewis. Despite Guthrie's assertion that in the Naugatuck Valley the workers "talked naturally and easily with him," Lewis himself was probably uncomfortable in their midst.

Lewis's mimetic talents were crucial to his ability to draw character. William Rose Benet, in an article on "the essential Lewis," recalled dining with Lewis one evening when a stranger, a traveling salesman, engaged them in conversation. Benet found the man boring; Lewis found him fascinating. Lewis drew the man out and put him so much at ease that he "revealed more about himself than he probably realized." After the stranger left, Benet asked Lewis if he genuinely liked that sort of person. Lewis replied, "That's the trouble with you, Bill. You regard him as *hoi polloi*, he doesn't even represent the cause of labor or anything dramatic— but I understand that man—by God, I love him."[20] All the research that Lewis compiled during the twenty-odd years he tried to complete the labor project could not help him as long as he was unable to identify with ·union men in the same way that he did with Carol Kennicott, George Babbitt, and Martin Arrowsmith. Even though there was much about the Babbitt "type," for example, that Lewis disliked, he understood that man—and to some degree sympathized with him. In a *Nation* article entitled "Mr. Lorimer and Me," Lewis declared his fondness for the middle-class world, despising its hypocrisy but admiring its industry and pragmatism (two qualities that Lewis himself possessed). "I like the Babbitts, the Dr. Pickerbaughs, the Will Kennicotts, and even the Elmer Gantrys rather better than any one else on earth," Lewis wrote. "They are good fellows. They laugh—really laugh."[21] Giving a voice to the American middle class was among Lewis's most significant contributions to American literature. It is unlikely that he could have absorbed the world of labor unions as easily as he had absorbed other segments of American society.

Lewis himself seems to have realized the limits of his sociological imagination. In a letter to Grace written after Lewis's death, Dorothy Thompson recalled that Lewis had once explained to her his inability to write the labor novel:

> Hal's real trouble with the labor novel was not the fault of his advisers. He simply could not write about a world of which he had no first hand experience. When he decided to drop the project, he explained to me that it was because "I know it will be phoney. The only class I understand is the one to which I belong—the middle class." He added, as nearly as I can recall his words, "And I suspect that 'Labor' is just Babbitt in overalls." You know as well as I do that when Hal ventured into places where his instincts and *unconscious* observations failed to serve him, he became a terrible sentimentalist.[22]

That Lewis did not write the novel, and particularly that his most concentrated efforts to do so came after winning the Nobel Prize, may partly account for the loss of power in many of his later works and the subsequent decline in his reputation. Lewis's literary career after 1930 was characterized by conservatism, sentimentality, and indecision. After 1930, between the sporadic false starts on the labor novel, Lewis produced relatively weak books that were essentially reprocessed versions of his 1920s novels. The title character of *Gideon Planish* (1943) is a flim-flam man much like Elmer Gantry; *Cass Timberlane* (1945) treats marriage in the same ways and in much the same setting as *Main Street* does; *World So Wide*, published posthumously in 1951, is a portrait of the American abroad, drawn earlier in *Dodsworth*. Other late novels were nostalgic, sometimes inconsistent treatments of earlier subjects, such as *The Prodigal Parents* (1938)—the book Lewis wrote after abandoning "Unconquerable" in 1936: a sympathetic portrait of a small-town Babbitt named Fred Cornplow who steadfastly supports his worthless children, one of whom is a phony radical.

The widespread fame Lewis achieved during the 1920s made him come to feel that he had to write the labor novel—perhaps even that it was incumbent upon him to do so as a Nobel laureate. Once, for example, when it was rumored that Lewis was at work on the labor novel, Laurence Todd, a labor reporter, wrote him: "[Do not] forget that your labor audience is waiting for the publication of your best book."[23] At another point, Mencken sent Lewis a large number of "subjects for your future researches," among them "the crooked (or, more usually, idiotic) labor leader," and then dramatically stated, "This, I believe, is your job . . . there are plenty of writers of love stories and Freudian documents . . . but there is only one real anatomist of the American Kultur. . . . It deserves to be done as *you* alone can do it."[24]

That Lewis himself actively publicized his plans to write the novel only fueled the expectations of critics in the 1930s, expectations that Lewis couldn't meet. In an unfavorable review of *Ann Vickers* (1933), for example, Bernard de Voto took Lewis to task for having "chucked the labor manifesto about which rumors once circulated."[25] V. F. Calverton, disappointed in Lewis's work after the Nobel Prize, thought it a "hopeful sign" that his next novel was "to deal with Eugene Debs and the life of a more energy-giving class."[26] Lewis was not able to deliver on such a novel, probably because he saw too much in leftish labor movements that he could not really accept. As late as 1949 the critic John Woodburn lamented the absence in the historical novel *The God-Seeker* of any "social consciousness" about organized labor beyond the paper-thin character of Lanark, an honorary member of a worker's guild.[27] Although unwritten, the labor novel became by public decree Lewis's "best book."

Among Lewis's papers at the Beinecke is a manuscript that may represent the only substantive result of all his research on labor. It is the script for a play that was never produced, entitled "Responsible." He completed it in 1947, just three years before his death, and with characteristic enthusiasm he spoke hopefully of it to several friends. The play concerns one Willard Hardhack, president of a machine tool company, who battles the attempts of a crooked CIO official to organize the shop.[28] The play perhaps symbolically presents the worst of Lewis's style. The characters are wooden, their speech is mechanical, and the unidentified locale is neither a Main Street nor a factory town. The play is certainly not, to use Benet's phrase, "the essential Lewis." In attempting to write the labor novel, Lewis tried to transcend his essential talent; and while one cannot claim that this single project stifled all of his creative energies, clearly it was an important goal for him. And one might well argue that Sinclair Lewis spent much of the rest of his life trying to write something that was artistically impossible for him to write.

The high point of Lewis's career came on 5 November 1930, when it was announced that he had become the first American to win the Nobel Prize for Literature. When the news broke, Lewis went to the Harcourt offices and held a press conference at which he formally accepted the honor.[29] The announcement made headlines across the world. On 29 November Lewis and Dorothy sailed for Sweden, arriving in Stockholm on 9 December. Then followed a three-day period of festivities, culminating in the awards ceremony on 12 December. In his acceptance speech, Lewis challenged the old picture of America popularized by writers in the genteel tradition and pointed to the many current social issues that made America a ripe field for meaningful, provocative literature. He cited the accomplishments of some of his colleagues—among them Theodore Dreiser, Sherwood Anderson, and Willa Cather—and he spoke approvingly of the nascent generation of writers, naming Hemingway, Faulkner, and Thomas Wolfe. Lewis called his speech "The American Fear of Literature," and it was widely reprinted in the press. The *New York Times*, in fact, carried it on page one ("Sinclair Lewis hits old school writers, champions new"). Some controversy was generated by the choice of Lewis for the award—several writers and academic critics thought his work was "an insult to America"—but by and large columnists and editorial writers, as well as many of Lewis's peers, felt that he deserved it.[30]

The choice of Lewis was not surprising, given the fact that he began angling for the award as early as January 1921 when he asked Harcourt to make connections with Scandinavian critics and "see if there may not be one chance in 50,000 that we'd get the Nobel prize on *M St* or a later novel." In March 1925 Lewis again asked Harcourt if he could pull any strings and get the Nobel judges to read *Arrowsmith*.[31] Moreover, no other American writer at the time was as well known as Lewis. Everywhere he went he attracted attention; the press routinely sought his comments on national and international events. He and Harcourt had also carefully arranged for his books to be promoted in Europe, and especially in Scandinavia. By 1930 eleven of Lewis's thirteen books had been translated into Russian, German, and Polish; seven into Hungarian, Danish, Norwegian, and Czech; six into French; four into Dutch; two into Spanish; and one, *Babbitt,* into Italian and Hebrew.[32] Most of Lewis's books had also been translated into Swedish, and all had been highly praised by reviewers there—some of whom, in fact, were members of the Nobel committee for 1930.[33]

Receiving the Nobel Prize was undeniably the peak of Lewis's career. He should have shared his sense of achievement with Alfred Harcourt and at least partly credited him with engineering the award: all along, the two men had seen their respective enterprises as a partnership of sorts, and Harcourt had worked hard at promoting Lewis's novels. As it turned out, however, Lewis's receiving the Nobel Prize was what finally broke apart his relationship with Harcourt.

Before he arrived in Stockholm on 9 December, Lewis had cabled Harcourt to tell him to get into print an accurate text of his acceptance speech as soon as possible after the ceremony, along with the remarks made by his sponsor on the Nobel committee, Erik Axel Karlfeldt. Unfortunately, Harcourt used the *New York Times* version of Lewis's speech, which had been relayed by transatlantic cable and was therefore somewhat garbled. Outraged, Lewis demanded that Harcourt destroy the undistributed two thousand copies of the five thousand that had been printed. Lewis performed a series of minute revisions on his speech (all of them stylistic) and even corrected in a footnote Karlfeldt's mangled statement in the *Times* text that American streets stank because there were no sewers in America.[34] Harcourt then brought out a new edition of the speech. But he could not have been happy about Lewis's behavior toward him and the trouble of having to issue a second edition of the pamphlet.

Lewis seems to have used this incident as an excuse to end his business relationship with Harcourt. On 21 January 1931 Lewis wrote to Harcourt "about matters which have been bothering me for a long time."[35] Lewis implied that publishing the garbled acceptance speech was merely the latest in a long series of incidents demonstrating that Harcourt was no longer interested in his career. Lewis's main grievance, he told Harcourt, was that the firm had not promoted his books in ways that would take full advantage of the Nobel Prize—namely, by publishing a collected edition of his works, which Lewis had been pressing Harcourt to do for some time. However, in mid-August Harcourt had agreed to bring out an inexpensive but still uniform edition priced at $1.25 per volume, but without the introductions to each novel that Lewis had wanted. It was published as the Nobel Prize Edition of the Works of Sinclair Lewis, exactly one week after Lewis's letter.

His other charge against Harcourt was that he had not given enough attention to marketing and promoting his novels. This complaint is also difficult to understand. Harcourt had put many of the resources of his firm into publicizing Lewis's novels. *Publishers' Weekly,* in fact, once said that no other house in recent times had done so effective a job at promoting books as Harcourt, Brace had with the Lewis novels. Nonetheless, Lewis told Harcourt he was quite dissatisfied and wanted to switch to a different publisher. "It comes down to this," Lewis wrote: "I have the impression, and the impression is backed up by too many facts to be merely fanciful, that the firm of Harcourt, Brace, and Co., and you personally, feel that they have just about done their duty by Sinclair Lewis. And I feel that I have just about done my duty by Harcourt, Brace and Co." Lewis added that he might have discussed these and other matters sometime earlier if he "hadn't felt so tied to the firm, by the fact that we all began our careers together." He nonetheless asked to be released from his contract for the next novel, as yet unnamed, as well as for "Neighbor," so that he could seek another publisher.

Helen B. Petrullo has suggested that Dorothy Thompson may have been responsible for Lewis's dissatisfaction with Harcourt. Since early 1929, Lewis's letters to his publisher had grown redundant with complaints about Harcourt's handling of reprint and foreign rights and about the relatively small royalty income Lewis received. On 26 October 1929, for example, he questioned the accuracy of his royalty statement for the first half of 1929. Lewis had misread the report, and he dropped the complaint on seeing his mistake; but in late April or early May 1930 Dorothy read over his statement for the second half of 1929, and she thought that Harcourt's receiving one-third of all royalties on foreign editions was "scandalous." She also thought it unnecessary for Lewis then to have to pay an additional 10 percent commission to his British agent, Curtis Brown, and 10 percent more to "a foreign agent." "I don't see where Harcourt on these deals is contributing anything at all," she wrote Lewis.[36] Dorothy's attitude was understandable under the circumstances: she was his second wife, there was a first wife to whom alimony and child support had to be paid, she was expecting a child herself, and the remodeling of Twin Farms was turning into a very expensive project. Dorothy was probably unaware of the extent of Lewis's experiences with Harcourt— both professional and personal—and of the generous and flexible business arrangements they had made in the past. Lewis's royalty percentages had often been reduced by mutual consent to cover his share of advertising costs for a particular book; this may explain the size of Harcourt's cut on these particular books. In his memoirs, Harcourt also noted that Lewis was extremely generous in their financial dealings. According to Harcourt, Lewis insisted that the publisher "take a larger share of some of the rights [to his books] than I had proposed."[37] Lewis had also maintained his business interest in the firm and had apparently invested a considerable amount in it. In 1930 he received a one-thousand-dollar dividend from the company. Harcourt's "share" of the royalties might have been invested in the firm on Lewis's behalf.

Dorothy's complaints about royalty income probably contributed to Lewis's growing dissatisfaction with Harcourt, but most likely Lewis simply felt that he had outgrown his publisher. After finishing *Dodsworth*, Lewis had reached a turning point in his career: a certain phase in his work was completed, and he had been honored with the Nobel Prize. He felt that he was now (like Sam Dodsworth) on the threshold of a new stage in life, and he was ready to move in a new direction. He probably also associated this just-completed part of his life with a number of unpleasant memories—namely, his divorce and his drinking problems. It would have been natural for him to want to make a clean break with his past.

Harcourt was typically good-natured in his reply to Lewis's letter. He did not try to hold Lewis to his contract, nor did he implore Lewis to reconsider his decision. Harcourt had probably seen this break coming, and he too realized that a natural ending point had been reached. He told Lewis, "I know you have some idea of how sorry I am that events have taken this turn. You and we have been so closely associated in our youth and growth that I wish we might have gone the rest of the way together. If I've lost an author, you haven't lost either a friend or a devoted reader."[38]

For his part, Lewis seems not to have considered Harcourt's contributions to his career very carefully. Harcourt's work on Lewis's behalf was a significant factor in Lewis's success. Harcourt devoted much of his attention to publicizing Lewis's novels and to keeping them advertised after they had had their initial run. He also worked to have Lewis recognized by the critical establishment, first with the committee in charge of awarding the Pulitzer Prize and later with the Nobel committee. Harcourt's business acumen aided Lewis in numerous ways, and Harcourt was a much-needed source of stability and reasoned judgment. He frequently kept Lewis focused on his work-in-progress: more than once, he dissuaded Lewis from undertaking frivolous projects. He often restrained his impetuous author, too, when Lewis's publicity stunts threatened to damage his public image.

Perhaps most important, Lewis needed the friendship that Harcourt provided. Lewis had an almost morbid fear of loneliness, and to produce good work he needed an interested and sympathetic person to whom he could talk of his plans for a novel or his difficulties in getting a particular passage or characterization just right. Many of the hundreds of letters that Lewis wrote to Harcourt during this ten-year period were Lewis's way of asking Harcourt to confirm that he was on the right track, that his next novel would be even better than the previous one; Harcourt did this faithfully and cheerfully. Lewis might not have been as productive as he was without Harcourt's constant encouragement. And he never received the kind of personal attention from the publishers of his later novels that he had from Alfred Harcourt. Although several of Lewis's later works (published first with Doubleday, Doran and then with Random House) were best-sellers, the period of Lewis's greatest sustained success was exactly coequal with his association with Harcourt.

Harcourt and Lewis remained friendly for the rest of their lives. According to Harcourt, as late as 1949 they had "long and intimate visits" at the publisher's home in Santa Barbara, California.[39] In his memoirs, Harcourt praised Lewis as a devoted professional and a generous and helpful friend. He particularly valued Lewis for urging him to start his own publishing house, saying that he probably would not have done so were it not for Lewis's encouragement.[40]

At the end of the 1920s Lewis was in a position similar to the one he had occupied at the beginning of the decade: he was a successful, savvy professional writer, but without the right material and without much inspiration. After 1930 Lewis often returned to familiar territory and themes from his most successful books. His best novels from this period were those in which he responded to a current issue in American life, as he had done in *Main Street* and *Babbitt*. In particular, *It Can't Happen Here,* which concerned the rise of fascism in America, and *Kingsblood Royal,* which concerned race relations, are noteworthy. *Ann Vickers,* his first novel after winning the Nobel Prize, is also interesting in that it treats topics that Lewis characteristically did not write about—women's suffrage, penology, abortion, and lesbianism—and is written in a terse style quite unlike the satiric tone of his 1920s novels.

By 1930 Lewis had grown tired, and he had mined a particular vein of material that, by the time of *Dodsworth,* was beginning to run out. He still liked to write, and he still worked from notes and outlines based on his research into different fields—social work in *Ann Vickers,* hotels in *Work of Art,* the theater in *Bethel Merriday*. But these immersions into different milieus were briefer and less elaborate than his automobile trips through the Midwest with Grace, his fascinating Caribbean sojourns with Paul De Kruif, his interviews with Eugene Debs, and his pulpit appearances in Kansas City. He had come to understand what it required (and what it took out of him) to write a major novel such as *Babbitt* or *Arrowsmith*. By the end of the 1920s he was probably beginning to realize that he simply did not have many more such novels in him. Still he persisted, especially with the labor novel, and it took him many years to admit that he could not write that book.

Lewis's reputation today rests primarily on his achievement between 1920 and 1930. His career during that decade was by any standard phenomenal. He had a remarkable ten-year run during which he attained that enviable and often elusive position that all writers strive for: simultaneous critical and popular success. He was highly regarded by the literati and was an important public figure. He was also honored with two of the preeminent awards in the literary world, the Pulitzer Prize and the Nobel Prize. Lewis's industriousness and diligence are admirable: he produced seven books in ten years, and (except for *Mantrap* and *The Man Who Knew Coolidge)* each of them sold more than one hundred thousand copies. Four of these books—*Main Street, Babbitt, Arrowsmith,* and *Elmer Gantry*—remain relevant treatments of American life, and Lewis's thoroughness in investigating and then bringing to life the particular milieus of those novels has rarely been surpassed.

Perhaps most important, Lewis was very much a novelist of the people. His analyses of American culture found a large and receptive audience because he was perfectly attuned to the American character and to the important issues and developments of his time. The majority of Americans in the 1920s lived as Sinclair Lewis's characters did: they were conventional, mostly middle-class citizens who were inclined to react against the new moralities of the postwar age. They quested after a less prosaic and more meaningful existence but did not know how to attain it. This point was underscored particularly well by Grace Lewis in her memoir; she wrote, "Were the 1920s really the Jazz Age except for a few? . . . There was more substance to life than Fitzgerald's glossy version."[41] Of course, Lewis did not have the aesthetic sensitivity and understanding of human values that Fitzgerald had—but he was read by far more people than Fitzgerald was at the time. Similarly, Dorothy Thompson wrote that although Lewis was not one of those "few stupendous novelists" who revealed the human condition "for all places and all times," he would always be "an ineradicable part of American cultural history in the twenties. . . . No one seeking to recapture and record the habits, frames of mind, social movements, speech, aspirations, admirations, radicalisms, reactions, crusades, and Gargantuan absurdities of the American *demos* during those . . . years will be able to do without him."[42]

Lewis's most lasting contributions lay in his creating archetypes, characters and situations that enabled American literature to come into its own in the first half of the twentieth century; in his influencing public thinking by reaching large audiences through satiric and controversial novels; and in his giving Europeans a new way of looking at Americans, and Americans a new way of looking at themselves.

Appendix 1:
Deleted Chapter 36
from *Main Street*

Chapter XXXVI

She found Guy Pollock standing on Main Street, looking up at the new lamp-posts of the White Way and cynically rubbing his chin.

"We're grand, aren't we?" he reflected.

"Very. I have no doubt that before long we'll be having stock yards, and soft coal smoke, and all the charms of a real city. Have you become patriotic?"

"No. I'm rather unpopular because I'm not a good booster. But perhaps I'm wrong. Perhaps I lack energy. Perhaps —— Oh, well! Where have you been keeping yourself, Carol? I've scarcely seen you, this summer."

"You've endured it rather well!"

"Not at all," with extreme gallantry. "I have lost at least five hours of sleep a night, thinking of you."

"Is that why you haven't been strong enough to totter as far as our porch?" Suddenly she was impatient at this tossing of cheaply colored balls, this jiggling + grimacing of small talk, this humorless humor of

Source: Main Street typescript, Harry Ransom Humanities Research Center, University of Texas at Austin. The rejected chapter is rendered here in diplomatic transcription: Lewis's punctuation and orthography have been preserved, except in a small number of places where an unusual spelling would be unclear; these instances have been silently corrected.

badinage, this itch to appear clever, which poisons most conversation. She flung:

"Oh, stop it! We're neither of us good fencers. My dear, we're the only civilized people on this desert island. We're surrounded by savages in war paint, ululating their barbarous cry of 'Pep, red-blooded pep and punch,' And then we try to fence when we ought to be making bullets. I think I shall go to your office and call on you and talk about 'The Rock of Gold.'"

It took him a moment to get the petty sophistication out of his eyes, but he said, "Lets!" with blessed simplicity.

She was rested by the brown slovenliness of his bachelor office. He said vigorously, "The thing that infuriates me about men like Blausser is their attitude of 'Thank God I *am* a publican. Thank God I don't read poetry and I'm not fussy about shaving. I'm an honest-to-God reg'lar fellow.'

Blausser slaps me on the back and says, 'My boy, before I get through with this town, you'll have some decent legal business to do. Dunno but what maybe I'll bring the county seat here.' Probably he will, too. Really, I admire him—except when you bring your confounded soft inquiring eyes around, and start me questioning."

Two nights after, he "dropped in," as they said, and talked to Carol and Kennicott for an hour.

She meditated, "Guy and I ought to have a close dear friendship the rest of our lives. He is halfway between Erik and Will; he has Erik's fineness yet he has Will's solidity. He is my solution. He's a quiet place to which to retire from Blausserizing. . . . How fine and shapely his chin is."

Guy had important legal business at the county seat, Wakamin, which took him away for a day or two every week, but for the rest of the time Carol seemed to encounter him at least once a day. And she seemed to arouse him. There was an undoubted change. He spoke more joyously. He looked at her more interestedly.

When he returned from the county seat one summer afternoon he came straight to the house. He cried:

"Carol, I've found a way to beat the Village Virus."

"What is it?"

"I'm going to do something ——"

"Not going away?"

"No, it's much less obvious than that. In fact it's rather hard for me to explain. I've been such a loafer that you'll laugh at me if I say that I'm really going to relate myself to the town—I'm going to make use of the knowledge of human nature that a lawyer can't keep getting to some extent, and ——"

"I know! You're going to write a book about the town!"

"Well, sort of."

"I'm so glad. Write an honest one. Be fair to the generous people, but don't lie—don't assert that whatever is ours must therefore be perfect."

"No, I won't lie. I'll —— Oh, you don't want to hear about it."

"I do! You must bring it to me."

"I will. When I write it I'll bring it to you first of all because you're the one who will be sure to understand it."

She rejoiced, when he had gone, "I'm so glad of his book. He *is* fond of me. And I am of him. He gives color to the town. But there mustn't be anything but friendship. I mustn't encourage him too much. There's really no one in the world but Will or an imaginary Erik that I've created! . . . Why do I lie to myself? It's Erik I'm faithful to, and I always will be. But I'm proud that Guy likes me."

The benediction which she gave to the thought of his book, her hope that it would sing and march, that it would have something of nobility, that it would discover the beauty of reality, was a prayer of thanksgiving and loyalty.

Guys legal affairs took him to Mpls [Minneapolis] for a week, and he sent her a card with the message, "Like idea of the book; you'll see some manuscript before long."

Three days later, when the afternoon train had come in, she answered the bell, and he bounced into the hall chuckling, "Carol! I've brought you the beginning of the book!"

But he had no manuscript in his hand.

"Where is it, Guy?"

"Left it out on the porch—to surprise you. You're to be the first in town to see it." He opened the door, and shouted, "Come on! She doesn't suspect a thing!"

A girl appeared, a slight inconspicuous girl of twenty. Guy said with elaborate intonation, "Mrs. Carol, allow me to present my *wife!*"

Carol could not speak. There was nothing in this girl to which to speak. The child was anemic, meekly sulky; there was no light in her face, no distinction in her raw new frock with its fussiness of ribbons and buttons and braid and beads; she was the small-town bachfisch in clumsy perfection. She had the prettiness and healthy youth of a calf.

"I said I'd bring her to you first of all. I'm going to bowl the town over. Nobody ever thought the old bach would marry," said Guy—no, not the familiar Guy, but a fatuous bridegroom.

Carol was kissing her as ardently as she could and crooning, "You must be so tired, dear, after your trip."

The child submitted stupidly to the caress, and mumbled, "Yes. It was hot. I liked Minneapolis. We had a room with a bath."

"And I showed her the flour-mills. But it made the little head ache, didn't it, chickabiddy!" gloated Guy.

The child looked vacuous.

"What did you like best in Minneapolis?" asked Carol, feeling old, so old and mothering.

"We saw a show. There was an awfully handsome fellow in it."

Carol helped him put the living room behind his office in order for the few days before he should move to the bungalow which he had recently bought, ostensibly as an investment. Carol reflected, "She can't be as stupid as she seems. There's been too much moon love, with Guy starved so long —— Oh it's sordid, beastly. Sacred marriage love! Sanctified seduction! —— with some fat wife of a thin preacher beaming on the outrage! She's an amiable mammal."

Guy gurgled, "Well, I've fooled the whole town. Bettikins lived in Wakamin, and I told everybody I went there for legal business. Now how do you like the 'book I was writing'? This beats any silly book for readjustment to life, eh? I tell you, Carol—oughtn't to spoil her by saying it in the little bride's presence—but this girlie has the finest sweetest evenest nature I've ever seen, to say nothing of being a beauty. Say, she and I certainly did have to laugh about the 'book.'"

"Yes, it was a good joke on me." Carol had the heroism to say.

While they tried by dusting and good will to make bachelor chamber anything but the brown den it was, Bettikins—whose name was Elizabeth—sat and looked helpless.

"Would it be a good idea for me to run out and buy some scrim curtains? Do you like them?" demanded Carol, as determined of well-doing as Vida Sherwin

"I don't know. Curtains would be nice," the child said listlessly.

"I bet she has adenoids—I hope she has 'em—he deserves just that," thought Carol. But she chanted, "I'm sure Mr. Pollock will make the bungalow charming."

"He says I can have the biggest Victrola in town, and lots of dance records. I just love to dance." Elizabeth's face was, for that first time, not quite vacant of expression.

By sweeping + being violently agreeable Carol so worked the chagrin out of herself that afterward she had but a few moments of cynical bitterness.

"Why—why—why?" How could Guy marry her? Why couldn't he be decent and manly enough to realize what he really wanted? Why couldn't he run off with her, and desert her, leave her to the freedom of suicide, instead of betraying her into marriage, into years of being puzzled and hurt by his whimsicality?

"The Erik thing hurt. I was raw. But my aspiration for his 'book,' is his thing, leaves me a fool. Bettikins will make it a good dinner story. I had nothing, a few weeks ago, a decent bare nothing. Now I have less than nothing. It's not death and hunger that are tragic—it's standing before the world a presumptuous fool.

"Oh, nonsense! I'm not worthy the distinction of being one of God's Fools.

"She *has* adenoids, I know she has."

#2

For a week Carol sought to believe that hidden by shyness in Elizabeth Pollock were delicate graces. She craftily tried the child on fifty topics. She discovered that manners, art, and business affairs, were equally unrevealed to Elizabeth. Her mind was completely virginal. It was as pure as salt. She had absolutely escaped the pollution of knowledge. She must, in her 20 years, have encountered one or 2 facts but she was mentally deaf + psychically blind. She hadn't even the gaiety of youth. Her ethics were comprised in a confidential, "I don't think a lady ought to flirt with men after she's married," and her ambition betrayed by, "Guy says he hasn't touched any land-deals, but I tell him, my! he's so bright he ought to have the biggest house in town. So he's going to buy some farms." She wasn't even a housekeeper. She c[oul]d cook nothing more complicated than plain steak, which she burned, and sweeping "gave her such a headache."

Carol gave it up. "I suppose she fits Guy's shoulder and likes to cuddle, so she fulfills her function. She'll have five children and misrear three of them and let the other two die, so this admirable human race will be carried on to produce other Elizabeths who will produce other Elizabeths designed to produce other Elizabeths. . . . Dear God I am so lonely."

One thing Guy had found in marriage —— the chance to serve. The gratification of egotism [unreadable] in seeming necessary to some one. Elizabeth permitted him to find her slippers, to prepare her breakfasts, to tell her his suddenly conceived plans to become rich. She demanded that he learn to dance, that he take her motoring. He bought a second-hand roadster and proudly though apprehensively drove through town.

#3

Carol helped her to furnish the bungalow, to make new frocks. Carol tried to keep her from buying red stockings + lithographs of sunsets over the old mills. Carol introduced her to the town at an afternoon coffee. Elizabeth was consistently shy and stupid at the affair + at the parties given by Juanita Haydock, Maud Dyer, Rita Gould, and Ella Stowbody. Nor did she seem grateful, she placidly accepted anything in life.

Yet within two weeks Carol saw that she was welcomed by the town as she herself never had been. Elizabeth did not hint criticisms. She assumed that Gopher Prairie and her own adjacent Wakamin made up the focus of the universe, and that the ways of Juanita or Ella were in no wise to be improved upon. For that righteousness and understanding she was forgiven all things. Juanita did murmur, "Guy goes and waits fifty years and then picks out a squab that doesn't know a dish-pan from a royal flush." But Juanita invited her to join the Jolly Seventeen.

"I've always been unjust to the town in one thing," Carol concluded. "They do welcome strangers—if they're guaranteed never to be showy."

At the great Sunday party of all the cottagers down at the lake, in early September, Carol saw that Elizabeth Pollock, tho' she was as spiritless as ever, quite naturally took her part in passing out sandwiches, she had in six weeks become more definitely a part of the town life than Carol had in six years.

Behind the cottages Carol found Guy sitting alone on a tree trunk.

His eyes seemed tired, his face was abnormally flushed, his cheeks beginning to look baggy, as tho he had been tippling.

"Guy aren't you working too hard? Do go easy. You don't need to hurry so to get the bungalow furnished."

"It isn't that. I'm trying to put through some land speculation. Like your husband and these other practical fellows. I've been neglecting my opportunities; pretending that I was superior to dollar-hunting when I was merely lazy." Challengingly: "A man ought to make a stake for his family, first thing he does and —— Carol: I wonder if you couldn't get Bettikins to read some poetry with you? She has an awfully fine mind. Really! But you see her family didn't care much for those things. Could you? Oh. If you do, start in something—you know—not too complex—say Longfellow."

They all danced in the living-room of the Haydock cottage. As Guy tried to guide Elizabeth, he smiled, nodded to the music, even shouted at Dave, "I'm getting to be a great little dancer." The room was crowded. Guy and Elizabeth danced out through the door, they circled along the porch and passed thru the lite from the window, Carol saw that Guy's face, over his wife's shoulder, was twitching and very old,

The Pollocks drove home with the Kennicotts, Carol and Elizabeth on the back seat. Guy was lively again; a dozen times he volunteered that he had had "a bully time." He turned and cried:

"Chickabiddy! Look over the top of the woods at that star. The big one there. It's the green one I told you about. Do you know what that is? It's the lover's star."

He waited, twisted round in his seat beside the stodgily driving Kennicott. Elizabeth thought about it for a time, and answered:

"I can't see as it's so very green. I don't like that necktie you got on. I thought Mr. Dyer's necktie was real pretty. Why don't you get a necktie like Mr. Dyer's?"

#4

It was some time afterward, at the Jolly Seventeen, when Honest Jim Blausser took a fancy to Elizabeth Pollock, and pawed her, and in his hearty fashion threatened to kiss her. She giggled and blushed.

Carol knew that Guy Pollock detested Blausser. But the strange thing was that far from luring his wife away from the man, Guy was cordial to him, and disappeared from the room, leaving them together.

[The following section was omitted from typescript chapter 39.]

#2

A few weeks after the Haydocks' visit Kennicott wrote that Guy Pollock was sick, "quite sick." Of what he did not say, nor did he mention Guy's young wife, but he did add, "I have a hunch that Pollock is in debt + I guess he is the kind that doesn't like to be in debt."

There was so much of the wistful small boy in Guy: he would go down the dark way like Olaf Bjornstam, alone and hurt and not quite understanding. Thinking of him Carol held Hugh tight, and somehow identified Her Boy Hugh with Her unhappy child Hugh & Her unhappy child Guy.

A week later Kennicott wrote briefly that Guy was dead; and two months after that Elizabeth Pollock had suddenly married a boy, a year her junior, a ratty handsome boy who loafed in the pool-room, that they had sold Guy's bungalow, all his books, and were going out to Dakota to try to keep store.

Appendix 2:
"The Pioneer Myth"

The Pioneer Myth
By Sinclair Lewis
Author of "Main Street"

Of course Orin Clark never will be a writer. He is at present a flour salesman travelling out of Minneapolis, and he is looking rather seriously into the market for middlings and bran. But there was a time in his junior year at the University of Minnesota when he decided "to write"—not to write anything in particular, perhaps, but at least to receive checks and to have his picture in the literary columns. He was creeping toward a less peddleresque attitude, under the influence of West, Nichols, and Beach, when he confessed the ambition to his father, Sam Clark of Gopher Prairie.

To Sam it was as absurd as all these wild impractical notions of Carol Kennicott—"Cultured Carrie," as Mrs. Bogart cleverly called her. But still, Sam reflected, you couldn't most always sometimes tell; there were a lot of these fellows that got next to the movies and pulled out maybe 50,000 plunks a year! If Orin could cash in on his expensive education that way, it'd put it all over the hardware business! So, "All right, hop to it. Why don't you try and shoot a good snappy love story into one of the popular magazines?" Sam considered.

"Not on your life!" Orin protested. "I'm going to be a highbrow. I'd like to write for the *Atlantic* and *Century* and *Harper's* and all them."

Source: New York Evening Post Literary Review, 5 Feb. 1921, sec. 3, pp. 1, 2.

"Highbrow! Rats! Who the devil wants to wade through a lot of sex and psychology and all that junk! When I get through the day's work I want to read something amusing—like a good detective story, or a nice auto yarn." "B-but—but in Europe—but in Europe they—everybody likes to read stuff that you got to think about!"

"That's all right for Europe, but here—I tell you, my boy, we're pioneers. That's what we Americans are—we're pioneers—we're empire builders. We're too busy clearing the fields, and building factories and railroads and homes, to have time for all this leisure. Maybe that's all right in Europe, where there's a lot of Willy boys that haven't got a darn thing to do but live on Papa's money; but we're pioneers, and doing real honest-to-God work. That's what all these fellows that criticise American towns because they don't look like a bunch of Greek temples can't seem to get through their noddles. You can't expect a nation that's fighting the wilderness to stop and hitch up its galluses and fuss over a lot of poetry!"

Orin's answer is not recorded, but it is believed that Sam turned him from his ludicrous ambition, for Sam was a kind parent and well loved. Certainly it is surmised from the energy with which Sam continued this thesis at Del Snafflin's barber shop, next afternoon, that he was in earnest. Indeed, as he walked along Main Street he was, without knowing that he was doing it, making believe that he wore hairy pants, that he carried a carbine and rode a bronc, and that he was in danger of slaughter by innumerable and treacherous Sioux. He believed it, as 90,000,000 of his fellow Americans believed it. Yet the only Indians Sam had seen in his fifty-two years were nine mangy Piutes in a Wild West show, and three Chippewas on the reservation near which he went duck hunting. (These three were discussing the ignition of their tractor.) Sam, the forest clearer, had never in his life cut down a tree, never ridden any steed save Sally the plough horse on an Ohio farm, never seen mountains or bears or rattlesnakes or hairy pants except from a Pullman or the motor bus in Yellowstone Park.

Sam illustrates all the Americans who justify—who for a hundred years have justified—by the pioneer myth their unwillingness to ponder anything but bookkeeping and amours.

Of that dread of thinking our pioneer is one of half a dozen causes, and so far Sam is right. But it is the first rule of ethics that a cause is not an excuse. We have pioneered, yes, and do; we build railroads in Alaska and find oil in Texas; and along the road from Miles City to Billings nail-studded leather chaps may still be seen. But a nation with enough surplus of wealth to buy billions of dollars' worth of motor cars, ice cream, chewing gum, is no longer starving in log cabins. It is somehow inconsistent to boast, as almost every city in the country does boast, that it has one motor for every five or six inhabitants, and to sigh unctuously that we cannot yet take the time for economics or belles-lettres. We can afford everything *but* leisure!

The executive controlling 5,000 men asserts that (being a clearer of forests) he knows nothing about syndicalism, say, or ethnology, that he hasn't any time to waste on all these fads; and with equal placidity he looks out on his daughter as, in a suit one month later than Paris, in a $5,000 roadster, she goes off to the country club to play auction and golf, and to poke at pastry prepared by the former second chef of Grand Duke Alexis. His workers discuss syndicalism and, as they belong to twenty-seven variant races, they regard ethnology as a matter not altogether preposterous, but they are recent imports—they haven't been here long enough to know that any American, whether born in Back Bay, in Boston, or on the Charleston Battery, is *ex officio* an active pioneer, a combination of lumberjack, scout, Andrew Carnegie, Dan'l Boone, and Bill Nye.

And all the while it is doubtful whether America is doing or ever has done more pioneering than Europe!

To state this is as seditious as to question whether boys who have "earned their way through college" are invariably braver and honester than boys who did not earn their way; almost as sacrilegious as to assail the Salvation Army or the Boy Scouts or the banking system.

We have pioneered, widely, stoutly. But has our thrusting of the frontier from Philadelphia to Nome and Manila been a greater labor or more burning adventure than England's expropriations in Africa, India, Australia, Canada, and a thousand islands; Holland's domination round the world; France's invasion of the Near East and Siam; Spain's settlement of Southern America? Remembering how for hundreds of years the young men of Europe have poured out on ventures as dangerous and absorbing as our Indian wars and the gold rush of '49, it is as amazing as the theory of the divine right of brewery barons to assume that America alone among great nations has used up its spiritual energy in pioneering.

Even at home Europe has not precisely sat in libraries while we were clearing fields. And not all of America is so new as it pleases us to believe.

New York was probably first visited by Europeans, by the expedition of Giovanni Verrazzano, in 1524; the first European houses were built in 1613; in 1623 began the first permanent colony. Very recent is this compared with immemorial London or Paris. But consider Petrograd. The foundations of the present Russian city were not laid until 1703—eighty years after the first trading colony on Manhattan Island! And Berlin. As a fishing village, Berlin existed in 1100, yet at the end of the Thirty Years War, in 1648—twenty-five years after the colonization of New York—Berlin had only 6,000 inhabitants. In 1910 it had 2,000,000. The Berliners had done a bit of building, of pioneering at home! Or Liverpool. Liverpool was known in 1350—as a flourishing Main Street town of 800 people!—but in 1700 it was still under 6,000 population, which same magic 6,000 was also the population of Manchester in 1650. It may be assumed that since that time the English of Manchester have erected a few factories and cleared a few fields themselves. It is even doubtful whether in 1650 Manchester had completed its railroad sidings or its telephone system or its motor deliveries or all its power-looms.

Add to the (comparative) antiquity of New York the foundation of St. Augustine in 1565, of Santa Fe in 1605, Hartford in 1635, Philadelphia in 1683, and a heretic might conclude that, far from being the infant among the nations, a good deal of the United States is of an age not very different from that of Northern Europe. Of the Europeans' slow accretion of civilization since Neolithic man, we are equal sharers. It is as much America's past as it is Europe's past. We have not, as we rather assume, developed a language, a custom, an industrial life all our own since 1492. The first settlers brought with them as much of science and art as Europe itself had. To present them as complete innovators, lacking all the traditions of a European past, is comparable to a South Seas colony of younger sons of English Bishops taking to cannibalism because their island has been settled so recently that they must needs be primitive folk.

If a man in one of the new districts of London which a hundred years ago was far out in the open fields were to assert that he really couldn't be expected to have heard of Shakespeare because his part of the world had been so recently settled that his ancestors hadn't had time to glance at books, he would seem, to a judicious mind, a philosopher of no very high quality. Yet we differ from him only in degree, not at all in kind. The Atlantic is not and never has been, even in the days of the most perilous seafaring, a barrier to European books, recipes, frocks, and lecturers. We naively assume that our Emersons, our Poes, our Jonathan Edwardses were aboriginal, untouched by European currents. An investigation of their works fails to confirm this, Dr. Kenelm Digby tells us.

Yet the theory of our being cultural sucklings does persist, appears ever as a rebuke to such malign critics of our institutions as desire us to be something more than frontier storekeepers. The myth is purveyed by politicians, editors, and particularly by our rich fund of movies and Western fiction. In 1921 quite as much as in 1881 we rejoice annually in at least a hundred novels in which all decent American males are presented as inhabiting ranches, lumber camps, mining camps, or New York cabarets of a sort more brutal and incomparably more naive than any ranch. And most of us accept this agreeable thesis, unconsciously if not consciously. It appears in the cheery tones of every jobber, doctor, manicure girl, aviator, or statistician who says proudly, "I'm so busy I don't get any time for reading." Time for the movies, auction bridge, motoring, golf, two-hour luncheons, and exacting perusal of the funnies in the evening paper they do have but, being pioneers, they cannot be expected to observe such inconsequential phenomena as "Ethan Frome," "McTeague," and "The Titan," such petty events as "Men and Steel," "The Dark Mother," "Poor White," and "Miss Lulu Bett."

And our pioneer writers themselves, they cannot be expected to master the tedious motives of real human beings when they are fearlessly riding the range with their fellow cowpunchers of Concord, Mass.; Brooklyn, and Hollywood.

It's a great myth!

Let there be a proviso. These notes are not meant as part of that sudden attack on everything American which has recently absorbed a number of young journalists. To them everything American is not only utterly, but permanently, bad. They croon that never has America treated native literature with anything but vicious neglect, and that never will Americans create beauty unless they move to Birmingham, Paris, or Nizhni Novgorod. Occasionally these gentlemen Cassandras must, with brief annoyance, dispose of some fragment of American literature which seems to disprove their gallant theory, but after a vexed moment spent in discouraging the heretic by comparing him with James Joyce or the Neo-Hellenists, they go on joyously wailing that our vile race discourages heretics.

Such 100 per cent. Un-Americanism, like Palmerism and the propaganda of the Lord's Day Alliance and all other forms of Hundredpercentism, irritates testy, normal people because of its egotistical humility. Of such masochism these notes are distinctly not a part. They rise from a love of Main Street, from a belief in Main Street's inherent power, a belief so strong that the writer is not willing, like the Wild West fictioneers, to insult America by believing that we are all so commonplace that we can find romance only by making believe that we are frontier homicides.

So long as Sam Clark sees himself as a contemporary of Kit Carson he will be a contemporary of Kit Carson—minus only the courage and the hardihood!

Appendix 3:
Unpublished Introduction to *Babbitt*

THIS IS THE STORY OF THE RULER OF AMERICA.

The story of the Tired Business Man, the man with toothbrush mustache and harsh voice who talks about motors and prohibition in the smoking compartment of the Pullman car, the man who plays third-rate golf and first-rate poker at a second-rate country club near an energetic American city.

Our conqueror, dictator over our commerce, education, labor, art, politics, morals, and lack of conversation.

There are thirty millions of him, male and female, and his autocracy is unparalleled. No czar controlled the neckware and dice-throwing of his serfs; no general in the most perilous climax of war has codified his soldiers' humor or demanded that while they engaged the enemy they admire narratives about cowpunchers and optimistic little girls. But this completeness our ruler has attained.

Though English morals and French politics and German industry have been determined by the Sound Middle-Class, the Bourgeoisie, the Pumphreysie, have never dared also to announce standards in sculpture and table-manners. For in those lands there are outcasts and aristocrats who smile at the impertinence of the unimaginative. But in America we

Source: "Babbitt Notebook," Yale Collection of American Literature, Beinecke Rare Book and Manuscript Library, Yale University. The introduction is rendered here in diplomatic transcription.

have created the superman complete, and the mellifluous name of the archangelic monster is Pumphrey, good old G. T. Pumphrey, the plain citizen and omnipotent power.

Note: Above too much hints of another Main St. Most of this and all of "pos. part of Intro." cd be used, say, as Chapter [word unreadable] in Part III or IV.

Though this is the individual romance of one G. T. Pumphrey and not the breviary of his community, that community enters his every moment, for it is himself, created in his varnished image. Monarch City is every "progressive, go-ahead, forward-looking, live, up-to-date" city of more than eighty thousand in the United States and Western Canada, with 8 or 10 venerable exceptions.

These exceptional cities Pumphrey visits with frequency, and stirs their theaters, hotels, books, and wholesalers to emulate the perfection of Monarch City, that even we who faint may win at the last to purity, efficiency, and ice water.

Distinctly, however, Pumphrey is not a satiric figure, nor a Type.

He is too tragic a tyrant for the puerilities of deliberate satire. And he is individual, very eager and well-intentioned, credulous of pioneering myths, doubtful in his secret hours, affectionate toward his rebellious daughter and those lunch-mates who pass for friends—a god self-slain on his modern improved altar—the most grievous victim of his own militant dullness—crying in restless dreams for the arms of Phryne, the shirt of Jurgen and the twilight sea that knows not purity nor efficiency nor 34 × 4 casings.

As a PART OF INTRODUCTION, or in the story, or just implied in the story, or in an appendix on Main Street vs. the Boulevard vs. Fifth Ave.

———

They are complex phenomena, these American cities of from 80,000 to 1,000,000. They are industrially magnificent. They supply half the world with motor cars, machine tools, flour, locomotives, rails, electric equipment—with necessities miraculous and admirable. They are provided with houses more elaborate than any palaces, with hotels and office buildings as vast as and more usable than any cathedral. Their citizens are not unaccustomed to Fifth Avenue, to Piccadilly, to the Champs Elysees. Hither comes Galsworthy to lecture, Caruso to sing, Kreisler to play (even though they do beg him always to play the Humoresque), and here, in a Little Theater, a Schnitzler play may have a hearing as soon as Vienna, long before London. Yet they are villages, these titanic huddles. They import Kreisler as they import silks—not because they passionately love music or silks, but because those obvious symbols of prosperity give social prestige. To attend a concert is almost as valuable a certificate of wealth as to be seen riding in a Pierce-Arrow car. It is not an elegant and decorous listening to a great violinist which attests musical understanding; it is a passionate playing of one's own music—though the playing may be very bad indeed; may be nothing but the agitated scratching of four old cellists in a beery cellar. Since there is—as yet—no instrument which measures ergs of spiritual energy, the matter cannot be neatly and, statistically proven, but one suspects that there is not one of these cities with a million, or half a million, people which has one tenth of the joyous mental activity of little Weimar, with its 35,000—among whom once moved no Cracka-jack Salesmen, perhaps, but only Goethe and Schiller.

And those glorious Little Theaters—those radiant and eager Little Thea-ters—indeed they do revel in Glaspell and Eugene O'Neill and Ervine—for one season or two; and then the players who have gone into this new sport for social prestige grow weary; the professional producer grows yet wearier of begging for funds, and of seeing newspapers which give a col-umn to a road-company in a musical comedy, and two columns to a wed-ding between patent medicines and steel, present a brilliant performance of Shaw in two paragraphs with four solecisms; he goes his ways, and the Little Theater is not.

Villages—overgrown towns—three-quarters of a million people still dressing, eating, building houses, attending church, to make an impres-sion on their neighbors, quite as they did back on Main Street, in villages of two thousand. And yet not villages at all, the observer uneasily sees, as he beholds factories with ten thousand workmen, with machines more miraculous than the loaves and fishes, with twice the power and ten times the skill of a romantic grand duchy. They are transitional metropolises—but that transition will take a few hundred years, if the custom persists of making it a heresy punishable by hanging or even by ostracism to venture to say that Cleveland or Minneapolis or Baltimore or Buffalo is not the wisest, gayest, kindliest, usefullest city in all the world. So long as every teacher and journalist and workman admits that John J. Jones, the hustling sales-manager for the pickle factory is the standard in beauty and courtesy and justice—well, so long will they be sore-stricken with a pest of J. J. Joneses.

It is not quite a new thought to submit that though admittedly Mr. Jones somewhat lacks in the luxuries of artistic taste and agreeable man-ners, yet he is so solid a worker, so true a friend, and so near to genius in the development of this astounding and adventurously new industrial sys-tem, that he is worthier, he is really more beautiful, than any Anatole France or [word omitted]. Are his pickle machines with their power and ingenuity a new art, comparable to vers libre, and is there not in his noisiest advertising, his billboards smeared across tranquil fields, a passion for achievement which is, to the unprejudiced discernment, a religious fervor, an esthetic passion, a genius such as inspired the crusader and explorer and poet? Is not his assailant a blind and reactionary fellow who demands in this rough glorious pioneer outworn standards and beauties dead and dry?

Only it happens that these generous inquirers who seek to make themselves comfortable by justifying their inescapable neighbor, Mr. Jones, give him somewhat too much credit. Mr. Jones, the sales manager, Mr. Brown, the general manager, Mr. Robinson, the president—all the persons in the pickle hierarchy most to be accredited with passion and daring and new beauties—are nothing in the world but salesmen, commercial demagogues, industrial charlatans, creators of a demand which they wistfully desire to supply. Those miraculous, those admittedly noble machines—they were planned and built and improved and run by very common workmen, who get no credit whatever for pioneering. Those astounding pickle formulae, they were made by chemists, unknown and unglorified. Even those far-flung billboards, the banners of Mr. Jones's gallant crusade—their text was written by forty-a-week copy-writers, their pictures—their very terrible pictures—painted by patient hacks, and the basic idea, of having billboards, came not from the passionate brain of Mr. Jones but was cautiously worked out, on quite routine and unromantic lines, by hesitating persons in an advertising agency.

And it is these workmen, chemists, hacks, who are likely to be eager about beauty, courageous in politics—Moon-Calves—children of the new world. Mr. Jones himself—ah, that rare and daring and shining-new creator of industrial poetry, he votes the Republican ticket straight, he hates all labor unionism, he belongs to the Masons and the Presbyterian church, his favorite author is Zane Grey, and in other particulars noted in this story, his private life seems scarce to mark him as the rough, ready, aspiring, iconoclastic, creative, courageous innovator his admirers paint him. He is a bagman. He is a pedlar. He is a shopkeeper. He is a camp-follower. He is a bag of aggressive wind.

America has taken to itself the credit of being the one pioneering nation of the world; it has thereby (these three hundred years now) excused all flabbiness of culture and harshness of manner and frantic oppression of critics. And, strangely, Europe has granted that assertion. Never an English author descends upon these palpitating and grateful shores without informing us that from our literature one expects only the burly power and clumsiness of ditch-diggers. We listen to him, and are made proud of the clumsiness and burliness—without quite going so far as to add also the power.

It is a national myth.

England has, in India, Africa, Canada, Australia, had quite as many new frontiers, done quite as much pioneering—and done it as bravely and as cruelly and as unscrupulously—as have we in pushing the western border from the Alleghenies to Honolulu. Thus France in Africa, Holland in the West Indies, Germany all over the world. And England has quite as many Rough Fellows as America. Lord Fisher criticizing the British navy in the tones of a tobacco-chewing trapper—is he so much less of a Rough Fellow and Pioneer and Innovator than the Harvard instructor reading Austin Dobson by candle-light? The silk salesman, crossing the Arizona desert—in a Pullman—is he so much bolder a ditch-digger than Ole Bill, the English Tommy?

A myth! America is no longer an isolated race of gallant Indian-slayers. It is a part of the world. Like every other nation, it is made up of both daring innovators and crusted crabs. Its literature and its J. J. Joneses are subject to the same rules as the literature and the bustling innumerous J. J. Joneses of England or Spain or Norway. Mr. Henry van Dyke is no newer or more pioneering than Mr. H. G. Wells—and subject to no more lenient rules or more provincial judgments.

Of this contradiction between pioneering myth and actual slackness, these Monarchs, these cities of 300,000 or so, are the best examples. Unfortunately American literature has discerned as types of communities only the larger or older cities—as New York, San Francisco, Richmond—and the villages, with nothing between. Yet there is a sort of community in between, an enormously important type—the city of a few hundred thousand, the metropolis that yet is a village, the world-center that yet is ruled by cautious villagers. Only Booth Tarkington, with his novels flavored by Indianapolis, and a few local celebrities eager to present the opulence of their several Monarchs, have dealt with these cities which, more than any New York, produce our wares and elect our presidents—and buy our books. Yet they are important enough to quarrel over—they are great enough to deserve the compliment of being told one's perception of the truth about them.

Just use "city man & country girl" How dif from N.Y.

To say that they are subject to the same rules as Munich or Florence does not at all mean that they are like Munich or Florence. They have grown so rapidly, they have been so innocent and so Republican and so Presbyterian and so altogether boosting and innocent, that they have produced a type of existence a little different from any other in the world. It may not continue to be so different—it sometime may be subject also to fine tradition and the vision of quiet and honest work as against noisy selling of needless things—but this fineness it will not attain without self-study, and an admission that twenty story buildings are not necessarily nobler than Notre Dame, and that the production of 19,000 motor cars a day does not of itself prove those cars to be better built than cars produced at one a day.

This foreshadowing of a future adoption of richer traditions does not, of course, mean at all that in the future these Monarchs are to be spiritually or physically like Munich or Florence. It is a paradox of psychology that it is precisely the richest philosophies, with the largest common fund of wisdom from all ages, which produce the most diverse and lovely products while it is the thinner and hastier philosophies which produce the most standardized and boresomely similar products.

German Munich and Italian Florence are vastly and entertainingly different in all that counts—in passions, wines, aspirations, and furniture—for the reason that they have both digested and held and brilliantly changed a common wisdom of Plato and Shakespeare and Karl Marx. But German Milwaukee and Italian Hartford are uncomfortably alike because they have cast off all the hard-earned longings of mankind and joined in a common aspiration to be rich, notorious, and One Hundred Per Cent American.

It is this fact which is the second great feature of the American cities of 300,000—and as important as their other feature of unconquerable village-ness. It is this fact which makes a novel that chanced to be local and concrete and true regarding twenty other cities. Naturally, they are not all precisely alike. There is a difference resulting from situation—from a background of hills or plain, of river or seacoast; a difference from the products of the back-country—iron, wheat, cotton; a distinct difference from the various ages—the difference between Seattle and Charleston.

But these differences have for a long time now tended to decrease, so powerful is our faith in standardization. When a new hotel, factory, house, garage, motion-picture theater, row of shops, church, or synagogue is erected in gray Charleston, rambling New Orleans, or San Francisco of the '49ers, that structure is precisely, to the last column of reinforced concrete and the last decorative tile, the same as a parallel structure in the new cities of Portland or Kansas City. And the soul of those structures—the hospitality of the hotels, the mechanical methods in the garages, the minutest wording of the sermons in the churches—are increasingly as standardized as the shells.

It would not be possible to write a novel which would in every line be equally true to Munich and Florence. Despite the fundamental hungers equally true to all human beings, despite the similarity of manners and conversation in the layer of society which contentedly travels all over the world, despite the like interest of kissing at Fiesole and at Gansedorf, so vastly and subtly are the differences in every outward aspect, every detail of artistic aspiration and national pride and hope, that the two cities seem to belong to two different planets.

But Hartford and Milwaukee—the citizens of those two distant cities go to the same offices, speak the same patois on the same telephones, go to the same lunch and the same athletic clubs, etc., etc., etc.

Novel unlike M. St. cf Carol [Kennicott] on standardized life in U.S.

The test of the sameness is in the people. If you were by magic taken instantly to any city of over 80,000 in the United States and set down in the business center, in a block, say, with a new hotel, a new motion-picture theater, and a line of newish shops, not three hours of the intensest study of the passing people—men on business errands, messenger boys, women shopping, pool-room idlers—would indicate in what city, indeed in what part of the country, you were. Only by traveling to the outskirts and discovering mountains or ocean or wheat fields, and perhaps Negro shanties, Mexican adobes, or German breweries, would you begin to get a clue—and these diverse clues lessen each year. They know it not but all these bright women and pompous men are in uniforms, under the discipline of a belligerent service, as firmly as any soldier in khaki. For those that like it—that is what they like; but there are those of us who hesitated about being drafted into the army of complacency.

Appendix 4:
Hugh Walpole's Introduction
to the
British Edition of *Babbitt*

The English Edition of *Babbitt*

Jonathan Cape has just published Sinclair Lewis's *Babbitt* and the English edition has been appearing occasionally over here. Critics have been having great sport with the glossary which defines "*dumbbell* as silent tool; *flivver* as cheap motor-car of delicate build; *ice-cream soda* as ice-cream in soda-water with fruit flavoring, a ghastly hot-weather temperance drink; *hoodlum* as crank" etc. The introduction to the book by Hugh Walpole continues a discussion, started by Sinclair Lewis himself, of whether American books are read in England; it estimates *Babbitt* especially for English readers and as it has not been much noticed over here, it is of great interest. We quote it complete below:

Introduction

Quite recently there has been a lively correspondence in the Press as to whether American books are read in England, and if not why not? Mr.

Source: Publishers Weekly, 2 Dec. 1922, p. 1995.

Sinclair Lewis himself was the first to stir the dust by his vigorous denunciation of our English patronage and indifference.

We are, I think, in England indifferent to the Arts. We are, at any rate, quite sure that Life is of more importance than Art, and what we demand of Art is that it should be an assistance to our enjoyment of Life rather than a beautiful thing in itself.

It follows from this that we are not, in the main, interested in the Art of other countries, and when an atmosphere seems to us ugly and alien from our own atmosphere we do not wish to hear about it. Now I do think that it has been the fault of some of the newer American writers that, clever tho they are, they have presented modern American life to us in so ugly a fashion—ugly in speech, in background, in thought. Joseph Hergesheimer, James Cabell, and Willa Cather alone of the newer American novelists have not done this.

Main Street, the book with which Mr. Lewis won fame in the United States, seemed to many English readers an ugly book dealing with ugly people. Personally I think that they were wrong and that both the heroine of that book and her husband were beautiful characters most tenderly revealed.

But I do agree that very much of Mr. Lewis's detail was difficult for an English reader to penetrate, and that it did to some extent obscure the reader's view of the book's essentials.

At first sight it might seem as tho *Babbitt* is guilty of the same crime. Let us admit at once that the English reader will find the first fifty pages difficult, the dialogue strange, the American business atmosphere obscure and complicated.

Let him persevere. Soon he is sitting with Babbitt himself in his office, finding in his soul a strange and affectionate comradeship with this stout middle-aged man and (if he is she) an urgent maternal desire to comfort him and straighten his perplexities.

For it is Mr. Lewis's triumph in this book that he has made his Babbitt own brother to our Mr. Polly, Uncle Ponderovo, Denry of the Five Towns, the Forsyte family, and even Mr. George Moore. He has brought him on to the very hearth of our own familiar friends and has introduced him there because, without extenuating one of his follies, his sentimentalities, his snobbishness, his lies, and his meannesses, he has made him of common clay with ourselves.

Babbitt is a triumph, and behind him the indictment of modern American business life is a triumph also.

We over here in England cannot say whether or not it is a true indictment, but because we believe in Babbitt we believe also in his life and the life of the town behind him. We see Babbitt in relation to the Whole Duty of Man—Business, Domestic, Religious, Stomachic, Sensual, Civic, Communal, Spiritual. Mr. Lewis has omitted nothing, and always the central figure is true to himself. Simply Mr. Lewis turns the figure round and allows us to view it from every possible angle.

English readers will be making a very serious mistake if they miss this book. As a work of art it is fine, true, complete, and understanding. As a piece of life it is yet finer, revealing to ourselves not only Babbitt but also—some one much nearer home. "There but for the grace of God goes ——."

And so when the book is closed we are wiser not only about Babbitt and his companions but about ourselves and our own hypocrisies. But not only is Babbitt a warning, he is also a friend.

And, thru him, the country of which he is a citizen.

Hugh Walpole
August 25, 1922

Appendix 5:
Letter Refusing the
Pulitzer Prize for *Arrowsmith*

SINCLAIR LEWIS REFUSES PULITZER PRIZE
(For Release Thursday, May 6th, 1926)

The Hotel Ambassador,
Kansas City, Mo.

To the Pulitzer Prize Committee,
Courtesy of Mr. Frank D. Fackenthal, Secretary,
Columbia University
New York City,

Sirs:—

I wish to acknowledge your choice of my novel "Arrowsmith" for the Pulitzer Prize. That prize I must refuse, and my refusal would be meaningless unless I explained the reasons.

All prizes, like all titles, are dangerous. The seekers for prizes tend to labor not for inherent excellence but for alien rewards: they tend to write this, or timorously to avoid writing that, in order to tickle the prejudices of a haphazard committee. And the Pulitzer Prize for novels is peculiarly objectionable because the terms of it have been constantly and grievously misrepresented.

Source: Yale Collection of American Literature, Beinecke Rare Book and Manuscript Library, Yale University.

Those terms are that the prize shall be given "for the American novel published during the year which shall best present the wholesome atmosphere of American life and the highest standard of American manners and manhood." This phrase, if it means anything whatever, would appear to mean that the appraisal of the novels shall be made not according to their actual literary merit but in obedience to whatever code of Good Form may chance to be popular at the moment.

That there is such a limitation of the award is little understood. Because of the condensed manner in which the announcement is usually reported, and because certain publishers have trumpeted that any novel which has received the Pulitzer Prize has thus been established without qualification as *the best* novel, the public has come to believe that the prize is the highest honor which an American novelist can receive.

The Pulitzer Prize for Novels signifies, already, much more than a convenient thousand dollars to be accepted even by such writers as smile secretly at the actual wording of the terms. It is tending to become a sanctified tradition. There is a general belief that the administrators of the prize are a pontifical body with the discernment and power to grant the prize as the ultimate proof of merit. It is believed that they are always guided by a committee of responsible critics, though in the case both of this and other Pulitzer Prizes, the administrators can, and sometimes do, quite arbitrarily reject the recommendations of their supposed advisers.

If already the Pulitzer Prize is so important, it is not absurd to suggest that in another generation it may, with the actual terms of the award ignored become the one thing for which any ambitious novelist will strive; and the administrators of the prize may become a supreme court, a college of cardinals, so rooted and sacred that to challenge them will be to commit blasphemy. Such is the French Academy, and we have had the spectacle of even an Anatole France intriguing for election.

Only by regularly refusing the Pulitzer Prize can novelists keep such a power from being permanently set up over them.

Between the Pulitzer Prizes, the American Academy of Arts and Letters and its training-school, the National Institute of Arts and Letters, amateur boards of censorship, and the inquisition of earnest literary ladies, every compulsion is put upon writers to become safe, polite, obedient, and sterile. In protest, I declined election to the National Institute of Arts and Letters some years ago, and now I must decline the Pulitzer Prize.

I invite other writers to consider the fact that by accepting the prizes and approval of these vague institutions we are admitting their authority, publicly confirming them as the final judges of literary excellence, and I inquire whether any prize is worth that subservience.

I am, sirs,

Yours sincerely,
[signed] Sinclair Lewis

Appendix 6:
Speech Accepting the Nobel Prize for Literature

The American Fear of Literature

An Address by Sinclair Lewis, December 12,
1930, on Receiving the Nobel Prize
In Literature.

Members of the Swedish Academy; Ladies and Gentlemen: Were I to express my feeling of honor and pleasure in having been awarded the Nobel Prize in Literature, I should be fulsome and perhaps tedious, and I present my gratitude with a plain "Thank you."

I wish, in this address, to consider certain trends, certain dangers, and certain high and exciting promises in present day American literature. To discuss this with complete and unguarded frankness—and I should not insult you by being otherwise than completely honest, however indiscreet—it will be necessary for me to be a little impolite regarding certain institutions and persons of my own greatly beloved land.

But I beg of you to believe that I am in no case gratifying a grudge. Fortune has dealt with me rather too well. I have known little struggle, not much poverty, many generosities. Now and then I have, for my books or myself, been somewhat warmly denounced—there was one

Source: Typescript of speech text as delivered, corrected by Lewis, in Dorothy Thompson Papers, George Arents Research Library, Syracuse University.

good pastor in California who upon reading my "Elmer Gantry" desired to lead a mob and lynch me while another holy man in the State of Maine wondered if there was no respectable and righteous way of putting me in jail. And, much harder to endure than any raging condemnation, a certain number of old acquaintances among journalists, what in the galloping American slang we call the "I Knew Him When Club," have scribbled that since they know me personally, therefore I must be a rather low sort of fellow and certainly no writer. But if I have now and then received such cheering brickbats, still I, who have heaved a good many bricks myself, would be fatuous not to expect a fair number in return.

No, I have for myself no conceivable complaint to make, and yet for American literature in general, and its standing in a country where industrialism and finance and science flourish and the only arts that are vital and respected are architecture and the film, I have a considerable complaint.

I can illustrate by an incident which chances to concern the Swedish Academy and myself and which happened a few days ago, just before I took a ship at New York for Sweden. There is in America a learned and most amiable old gentleman who has been a pastor, a university professor, and a diplomat. He is a member of the American Academy of Arts and Letters and no few universities have honored him with degrees. As a writer he is chiefly known for his pleasant little essays on the joy of fishing. I do not suppose that professional fishermen, whose lives depend on the run of cod or herring, find it altogether an amusing occupation, but from these essays I learned, as a boy, that there is something very important and spiritual about catching fish, if you have no need of doing so.

This scholar stated, and publicly, that in awarding the Nobel Prize to a person who has scoffed at American institutions so much as I have, the Nobel Committee and the Swedish Academy had insulted America. I don't know whether, as an ex-diplomat, he intends to have an international incident made of it, and perhaps demand of the American Government that they land Marines in Stockholm to protect American literary rights, but I hope not.

I should have supposed that to a man so learned as to have been made a Doctor of Divinity, a Doctor of Letters, and I do not know how many other imposing magnificences, the matter would have seemed different; I should have supposed that he would have reasoned, "Although personally I dislike this man's books, nevertheless, the Swedish Academy has in choosing him honored America by assuming that the Americans are no longer a puerile backwoods clan, so inferior that they are afraid of criticism, but instead a nation come of age and able to consider calmly and maturely any dissection of their land, however scoffing."

I should even have supposed that so international a scholar would have believed that Scandinavia, accustomed to the works of Strindberg, Ibsen, and Pontoppidan, would not have been peculiarly shocked by a writer whose most anarchistic assertion has been that America with all her wealth and power has not yet produced a civilization good enough to satisfy the deepest wants of human creatures.

I believe that Strindberg rarely sang the "Star Spangled Banner" or addressed Rotary Clubs, yet Sweden seems to have survived him.

I have at such length discussed this criticism of the learned fisherman not because it has any conceivable importance in itself, but because it does illustrate the fact that in America most of us—not readers alone but even writers—are still afraid of any literature which is not a glorification of everything American, a glorification of our faults as well as our virtues. To be not only a best-seller in America but to be really beloved, a novelist must assert that all American men are tall, handsome, rich, honest, and powerful at golf, that all country towns are filled with neighbors who do nothing from day to day save go about being kind to one another; that although American girls may be wild, they change always into perfect wives and mothers; and that geographically, America is composed solely of New York, which is inhabited entirely by millionaires; of the West, which keeps unchanged all the boisterous heroism of 1870, and of the South, where every one lives on a plantation perpetually glossy with moonlight and scented with magnolias.

It is not to-day vastly more true than it was twenty years ago that such novelists of ours as you have read in Sweden, novelists like Dreiser and Willa Cather, are authentically popular and influential in America. As it was revealed by the venerable fishing Academician whom I have quoted, we still most revere the writers for the popular magazines who in a hearty and edifying chorus chant that the America of a hundred and twenty million population is still as simple, as pastoral, as it was when it had but forty million; that in an industrial plant with ten thousand employees, the relationship between the worker and the manager is still as neighborly and uncomplex as in a factory of 1840, with five employees; that the relationships between father and son, between husband and wife, are precisely the same in an apartment in a thirty-story palace to-day, with three motor cars awaiting the family below and five books on the library shelves and a divorce imminent in the family next week, as were those relationships in a rose-veiled five-room cottage in 1880; that, in fine, America has gone through the revolutionary change from rustic colony to world-empire, without having in the least altered the bucolic and Puritanic simplicity of Uncle Sam.

I am, actually, extremely grateful to the fishing Academician for having somewhat condemned me. For since he is a leading member of the American Academy of Arts and Letters, he has released me, has given me the right to speak as frankly of that Academy as he has spoken of me. And in any honest study of American intellectualism to-day, that curious institution must be considered.

Before I consider the Academy, however, let me sketch a fantasy which has pleased me the last few days in the unavoidable idleness of a rough trip on the Atlantic. I am sure that you know, by now, that the award to me of the Nobel Prize has by no means been altogether popular in America. Doubtless the experience is not new to you. I fancy that when you gave the award even to Thomas Mann, whose "Zauberberg" seems to me to contain the whole of intellectual Europe, even when you gave it to Kipling, whose social significance is so profound that it has been rather authoritatively said that he created the British Empire, even when you gave it to Bernard Shaw, there were countrymen of those authors who complained because you did not choose another.

And I imagined what would have been said had you chosen some American other than myself. Suppose you had taken Theodore Dreiser.

Now to me, as to many other American writers, Dreiser more than any other man, marching alone, usually unappreciated, often hated, has cleared the trail from Victorian and Howellsian timidity and gentility in American fiction to honesty and boldness and passion of life. Without his pioneering, I doubt if any of us could, unless we liked to be sent to jail, seek to express life and beauty and terror.

My great colleague Sherwood Anderson has proclaimed this leadership of Dreiser. I am delighted to join him. Dreiser's great first novel, "Sister Carrie," which he dared to publish thirty long years ago and which I read twenty-five years ago, came to housebound and airless America like a great free Western wind, and to our stuffy domesticity gave us our first fresh air since Mark Twain and Whitman.

Yet had you given the Prize to Mr. Dreiser, you would have heard groans from America; you would have heard that his style—I am not exactly sure what this mystic quality "style" may be, but I find the word so often in the writings of minor critics that I suppose it must exist—you would have heard that his style is cumbersome, that his choice of words is insensitive, that his books are interminable. And certainly respectable scholars would complain that in Mr. Dreiser's world, men and women are often sinful and tragic and despairing, instead of being forever sunny and full of song and virtue, as befits authentic Americans.

And had you chosen Mr. Eugene O'Neill, who has done nothing much in American drama save to transform it utterly, in ten or twelve years, from a false world of neat and competent trickery to a world of splendor and fear and greatness, you would have been reminded that he has done something far worse than scoffing—he has seen life as not to be neatly arranged in the study of a scholar but as a terrifying, magnificent and often quite horrible thing akin to the tornado, the earthquake, the devastating fire.

And had you given Mr. James Branch Cabell the prize, you would have been told that he is too fantastically malicious. So would you have been told that Miss Willa Cather, for all the homely virtue of her novels concerning the peasants of Nebraska, has in her novel, "The Lost Lady," been so untrue to America's patent and perpetual and possibly tedious virtuousness as to picture an abandoned woman who remains, nevertheless, uncannily charming even to the virtuous, in a story without any moral; that Mr. Henry Mencken is the worst of all scoffers; that Mr. Sherwood Anderson viciously errs in esteeming sex as so important a force in life as fishing; that Mr. Upton Sinclair, being a Socialist, sins against the perfectness of American capitalistic mass-production; that Mr. Joseph Hergesheimer is Unamerican in considering graciousness of manner and beauty of surface as of some importance in the endurance of daily life; and that Mr. Ernest Hemingway is not only too young but, far worse, uses language which should be unknown to gentlemen, that he acknowledges drunkenness as one of man's eternal ways to happiness, and asserts that a soldier may find love more significant than the hearty slaughter of men in battle.

Yes, they are wicked, these colleagues of mine; you would have done almost as evilly to have chosen them as to have chosen me; and as a Chauvinistic American—only, mind you, as an American of 1930 and not of 1880—I rejoice that they are my countrymen and countrywomen, and that I may speak of them with pride even in the Europe of Thomas Mann, H. G. Wells, Galsworthy, Knute Hansum, Arnold Bennett, Feuchtwanger, Selma Lagerlof, Sigrid Undset, Verner von Heidenstam, D'Annunzio, Romain Rolland.

It is my fate in this paper to swing constantly from optimism to pessimism and back, but so is it the fate of any one who writes or speaks of anything in America—the most contradictory, the most depressing, the most stirring, of any land in the world to-day.

Thus, having with no muted pride called the roll of what seem to me to be great men and women in American literary life to-day, and having indeed omitted a dozen other names of which I should like to boast were there time, I must turn again and assert that in our contemporary American literature, indeed in all American arts save architecture and the film, we—yes, we who have such pregnant and vigorous standards in commerce and science—have no standards, no healing communication, no heroes to be followed nor villains to be condemned, no certain ways to be pursued and no dangerous paths to be avoided.

The American novelist or poet or dramatist or sculptor or painter must work alone, in confusion, unassisted save by his own integrity.

That, of course, has always been the lot of the artist. The vagabond and criminal Francois Villon had certainly no smug and comfortable refuge in which elegant ladies would hold his hand and comfort his starveling soul and more starved body. He, veritably a great man, destined to outlive in history all the dukes and puissant cardinals whose robes he was esteemed unworthy to touch, had for his lot the gutter and the hardened crust.

Such poverty is not for the artist in America. They pay us, indeed, only too well; that writer is a failure who cannot have his butler and motor and his villa at Palm Beach, where he is permitted to mingle almost in equality with the barons of banking. But he is oppressed ever by something worse than poverty—by the feeling that what he creates does not matter, that he is expected by his readers to be only a decorator or a clown, or that he is good-naturedly accepted as a scoffer whose bark probably is worse than his bite and who probably is a good fellow at heart, who in any case certainly does not count in a land that produces eighty-story buildings, motors by the million, and wheat by the billions of bushels. And he has no institution, no group, to which he can turn for inspiration, whose criticism he can accept and whose praise will be precious to him.

What institutions have we?

The American Academy of Arts and Letters does contain, along with several excellent painters and architects and statesmen, such a really distinguished university-president as Nicholas Murray Butler, so admirable and courageous a scholar as Wilbur Cross, and several first-rate writers: the poets Edward Arlington Robinson and Robert Frost, the free-minded publicist James Truslow Adams, and the novelists Edith Wharton, Hamlin Garland, Owen Wister, Brand Whitlock and Booth Tarkington.

But it does not include Theodore Dreiser, Henry Mencken, our most vivid critic, George Jean Nathan, who, though still young, is certainly the dean of our dramatic critics, Eugene O'Neill, incomparably our best dramatist, the really original and vital poets, Edna St. Vincent Millay and Carl Sandburg, Robinson Jeffers and Vachel Lindsay and Edgar Lee Masters, whose "Spoon River Anthology" was so utterly different from any other poetry ever published, so fresh, so authoritative, so free from any gropings and timidities that it came like a revelation, and created a new school of native American poetry. It does not include the novelists and short-story writers, Willa Cather, Joseph Hergesheimer, Sherwood Anderson, Ring Lardner, Ernest Hemingway, Louis Bromfield, Wilbur Daniel Steel, Fannie Hurst, Mary Austin, James Branch Cabell, nor Upton Sinclair, of whom you must say, whether you admire or detest his aggressive socialism, that he is internationally better known than any other American artist whosoever, be he novelist, poet, painter, sculptor, musician, architect.

I should not expect any Academy to be so fortunate as to contain all these writers, but one which fails to contain any of them, which thus cuts itself off from so much of what is living and vigorous and original in American letters, can have no relationship whatever to our life and aspirations. It does not represent literary America of to-day—it represents only Henry Wadsworth Longfellow.

It might be answered that, after all, the Academy is limited to fifty members; that, naturally, it can not include every one of merit. But the fact is that while most of our few giants are excluded, the Academy does have room to include three extraordinarily bad poets, two very melodramatic and insignificant playwrights, two gentlemen who are known only because they are university presidents, a man who was thirty years ago known as a rather clever humorous draughtsman, and several gentlemen of whom—I sadly confess my ignorance—I have never heard.

Let me again emphasize the fact—for it is a fact—that I am not attacking the American Academy. It is a hospitable and generous and decidedly dignified institution. And it is not altogether the Academy's fault that it does not contain many of the men who have significance in our letters. Sometimes it is the fault of those writers themselves. I cannot imagine that grizzly-bear Theodore Dreiser being comfortable at the serenely Athenian dinners of the Academy, and were they to invite Mencken, he would infuriate them with his boisterous jeering. No, I am not attacking—I am reluctantly considering the Academy because it is so perfect an example of the divorce in America of intellectual life from all authentic standards of importance and reality.

Our universities and colleges, or gymnasia, most of them, exhibit the same unfortunate divorce. I can think of four of them, Rollins College in Florida, Middlebury College in Vermont, the University of Michigan, and the University of Chicago—which has had on its roll so excellent a novelist as Robert Herrick, so courageous a critic as Robert Morss Lovett—which have shown an authentic interest in contemporary creative literature. Four of them. But universities and colleges and musical emporiums and schools for the teaching of theology and plumbing and sign-painting are as thick in America as the motor traffic. Whenever you see a public building with Gothic fenestration on a sturdy backing of Indiana concrete, you may be certain that it is another university, with anywhere from two hundred to twenty thousand students equally ardent about avoiding the disadvantage of becoming learned and about gaining the social prestige contained in the possession of a B.A. degree.

Oh, socially our universities are close to the mass of our citizens, and so are they in matter of athletics. A great college football game is passionately witnessed by eighty thousand people, who have paid five dollars apiece and motored anywhere from ten to a thousand miles for the ecstasy of watching twenty-two men chase one another up and down a curiously marked field. During the football season, a capable player ranks very nearly with our greatest and most admired heroes—even with Henry Ford, President Hoover, and Colonel Lindbergh.

And in one branch of learning, the sciences, the lords of business who rule us are willing to do homage to the devotees of learning. However bleakly one of our trader aristocrats may frown upon poetry or the visions of a painter, he is graciously pleased to endure a Millikan, a Michaelson, a Banting, a Theobald Smith.

But the paradox is that in the arts, our universities are as cloistered, as far from reality and living creation, as socially and athletically and scientifically they are close to us. To a true-blue professor of literature in an American university, literature is not something that a plain human being, living to-day, painfully sits down to produce. No; it is something dead; it is something magically produced by superhuman beings who must, if they are to be regarded as artists at all, have died at least one hundred years before the diabolical invention of the typewriter. To any authentic don, there is something slightly repulsive in the thought that literature could be created by any ordinary human being, still to be seen walking the streets, wearing quite commonplace trousers and coat, and looking not so unlike a chauffeur or a farmer. Our American professors like their literature clear and cold and pure and very dead.

I do not suppose that American universities are alone in this. I am aware that to the dons of Oxford and Cambridge, it would seem rather indecent to suggest that Wells and Bennett and Galsworthy and George Moore may, while they commit the impropriety of continuing to live, be compared to any one so beautifully and safely dead as Samuel Johnson. I suppose that in the Universities of Sweden and France and Germany there exist plenty of professors who prefer dissection to understanding. But in the new and vital and experimental land of America, one would expect the teachers of literature to be less monastic, more human, than in the traditional shadows of old Europe.

They are not.

There has recently appeared in America, out of the universities, an astonishing circus called "The New Humanism." Now of course "humanism" means so many things that it means nothing. It may infer anything from a belief that Greek and Latin are more inspiring than the dialect of contemporary peasants to a belief that any living peasant is more interesting than a dead Greek. But it is a delicate bit of justice that this nebulous word should have been chosen to label this nebulous cult.

Insofar as I have been able to comprehend them—for naturally in a world so exciting and promising as this today a life brilliant with Zeppelins and Chinese revolutions and the Bolshevik industrialization of farming, and ships, and the Grand Canyon and young children and terrifying hunger, and the lonely quest of scientists after God, no creative writer would have the time to follow all the chilly enthusiasms of the New Humanists—this newest of sects reasserts the dualism of man's nature. It would confine literature to the fight between man's soul and God or man's soul and evil.

But, curiously, neither God nor the devil may wear modern dress, but must retain Grecian vestments. Oedipus is a tragic figure for the New Humanists; man, trying to maintain himself as the image of God under the pressure of dynamos, in a world of high pressure salesmanship, is not. And the poor comfort which they offer is that the object of life is to develop self-discipline—whether or not one ever accomplishes anything with this self-discipline. So this the whole movement results in the not particularly novel doctrine that both art and life must be resigned and negative. It is a doctrine of the blackest reaction introduced into a stirringly revolutionary world.

Strangely enough, this doctrine of death, this escape from the complexities and danger of living into the secure blankness of the monastery, has become widely popular among professors in a land where one would have expected only boldness and intellectual adventure, and it has more than ever shut creative writers off from any benign influence which might conceivably have come from universities.

But it has always been so. America has never had a Brandes, a Taine, a Goethe, a Crocce.

With a wealth of creative talent in America, our criticism has most of it been a chill and insignificant activity pursued by jealous spinsters, ex-baseball-reporters, and acid professors. Our Erasmuses have been village schoolmistresses. How should there be any standards when there has been no one capable of setting them up?

The great Cambridge-Concord circle of the middle of the Nineteenth

Century—Emerson, Longfellow, Lowell, Holmes, the Alcotts—were sentimental reflections of Europe, and they left no school, no influence. Whitman and Thoreau and Poe and, in some degree, Hawthorne, were outcasts, men alone and despised, berated by the New Humanists of their generation. It was with the emergence of William Dean Howells that we first began to have something like a standard, and a very bad standard it was.

Mr. Howells was one of the gentlest, sweetest, and most honest of men, and he had the code of a pious old maid whose greatest delight was to have tea at the vicarage. He abhorred not only profanity and obscenity but all of what H. G. Wells has called "the jolly coarsenesses of life." In his fantastic vision of life, which he innocently conceived to be realistic, farmers and seamen and factory-hands might exist, but the farmer must never be covered with muck, the seaman must never roll out bawdy chanties, the factory-hand must be thankful to his good kind employer, and all of them must long for the opportunity to visit Florence and smile gently at the quaintness of beggars.

So strongly did Howells feel this genteel, this New Humanistic philosophy that he was able vastly to influence his contemporaries, down even to 1914 and the turmoil of the Great War.

He was actually able to tame Mark Twain, perhaps the greatest of our writers, and to put that fiery old savage into an intellectual frock coat and top hat. His influence is not altogether gone to-day. He is still worshipped by Hamlin Garland, an author who should in every way have been greater than Howells but who under Howells' influence was changed from a harsh and magnificent realist into a genial and insignificant lecturer. Mr. Garland is, so far as we have one, the dean of American letters to-day, and as our dean, he is alarmed by all of the younger writers who are so lacking in taste as to suggest that men and women do not always love in accordance with the prayer-book, and that common people sometimes use language which would be inappropriate at a women's literary club on Main Street. Yet this same Hamlin Garland, as a young man, before he had gone to Boston and become cultured and Howellsised, wrote two most valiant and revelatory works of realism, "Main-Travelled Roads" and "Rose of Dutcher's Coolie."

I read them as a boy in a prairie village in Minnesota—just such an environment as was described in Mr. Garland's tales. They were vastly exciting to me. I had realized in reading Balzac and Dickens that it was possible to describe French and English common people as one actually saw them. But it had never occurred to me that one might without indecency write of the people of Sauk Centre, Minnesota, as one felt about them. Our fictional tradition, you see, was that all of us in Midwestern

villages were altogether noble and happy; that not one of us would ex-
change the neighborly bliss of living on Main Street for the heathen gaudi-
ness of New York or Paris or Stockholm. But in Mr. Garland's "Main-
Travelled Roads" I discovered that there was one man who believed that
Midwestern peasants were sometimes bewildered and hungry and vile—
and heroic. And, given this vision, I was released; I could write of life as
living life.

I am afraid that Mr. Garland would be not pleased but acutely annoyed
to know that he made it possible for me to write of America as I see it,
and not as Mr. William Dean Howells so sunnily saw it. And it is his
tragedy, it is a completely revelatory American tragedy, that in our land of
freedom, men like Garland, who first blast the roads to freedom, become
themselves the most bound.

But, all this time, while men like Howells were so effusively seeking to
guide America into becoming a pale edition of an English cathedral town,
there were surly and authentic fellows—Whitman and Melville, then Dreiser and James Huneker and Mencken—who insisted that our land had
something more than tea-table gentility.

And so, without standards, we have survived. And for the strong
young men, it has perhaps been well that we should have no standards.
For, after seeming to be pessimistic about my own and much beloved
land, I want to close this dirge with a very lively sound of optimism.

I have, for the future of American literature, every hope and every eager
belief. We are coming out, I believe, of the stuffiness of safe, sane, and
incredibly dull provincialism. There are young Americans to-day who are
doing such passionate and authentic work that it makes me sick to see that
I am a little too old to be one of them.

There is Ernest Hemingway, a bitter youth, educated by the most in-
tense experience, disciplined by his own high standards, an authentic artist
whose home is the whole of life; there is Thomas Wolfe, a child of, I
believe, thirty or younger, whose one and only novel, "Look Homeward,
Angel," is worthy to be compared with the best in our literary production, a gargantuan creature with great gusto of life; there is Thornton Wil-
der, who in an age of realism dreams the old and lovely dreams of the
eternal romantics; there is John Dos Passos, with his hatred of the safe and
sane standards of Babbitt and his splendor of revolution; there is Stephen
Benet who, to American drabness, has restored the epic poem with his
glorious memory of old John Brown; and there are a dozen other young
poets and fictioneers, most of them living now in Paris, most of them a
little insane in the tradition of James Joyce, who, however insane they may
be, have refused to be genteel and traditional and dull.

I salute them, with a joy in being not yet too far removed from their determination to give to the America that has mountains and endless prairies, enormous cities and lost far cabins, billions of money and tons of faith, to an America that is as strange as Russia and as complex as China, a literature worthy of her vastness.

Notes

Citations of Sinclair Lewis's novels are to the first editions.

Our Mr. Wrenn: The Romantic Adventures of a Gentle Man (Harper, 1914)
The Trail of the Hawk: A Comedy of the Seriousness of Life (1915)
The Job: An American Novel (1917)
The Innocents: A Story for Lovers (1917)
Free Air (Harcourt, Brace, 1919)
Main Street: The Story of Carol Kennicott (1920)
Babbitt (1922)
Arrowsmith (1925)
Mantrap (1926)
Elmer Gantry (1927)
The Man Who Knew Coolidge: Being the Soul of Lowell Schmaltz, Constructive and Nordic Citizen (1928)
Dodsworth (1929)
Ann Vickers (Doubleday, Doran, 1933)
Work of Art (1934)
It Can't Happen Here (1935)
The Prodigal Parents (1938)
Bethel Merriday (1940)
Gideon Planish (Random House, 1943)
Cass Timberlane: A Novel of Husbands and Wives (1945)
Kingsblood Royal (1947)
The God-Seeker (1949)
World So Wide (1951)

Introduction

1. "Sinclair Lewis Revisited," *Gazette of the Grolier Club*, n.s., no. 37 (1985): 15–16.
2. "Sinclair Lewis and the Nobel Prize," *MidAmerica* 8 (1981): 21.

3. This situation seems to be changing: the centennial of Lewis's birth in 1985 prompted the publication of a number of articles about him in periodicals and scholarly journals, and three collections of reprinted critical writings on Lewis have been published since that time: Harold Bloom, ed., *Sinclair Lewis: Modern Critical Interpretations* (New York: Chelsea House, 1987); Harold Bloom, ed., *Sinclair Lewis's Arrowsmith: Modern Critical Interpretations* (New York: Chelsea House, 1988); and Martin Bucco, ed., *Critical Essays on Sinclair Lewis* (Boston: G. K. Hall, 1986). There have also been volumes on *Main Street* and *Babbitt* in Twayne's Masterwork Studies series (by Martin Bucco and Glen A. Love, respectively, both in 1993); *The Job, Free Air,* and *Ann Vickers* have been reprinted by the University of Nebraska Press in its Bison Books series; and a full-scale biography of Lewis, to be brought out by Random House, is now being written by Richard Lingeman.

4. *Sinclair Lewis: An American Life* (New York: McGraw-Hill, 1961), 813 (hereafter cited as *American Life*).

5. "The World of Sinclair Lewis," *New Republic* 128 (6 April 1953): 18–20; "The Monstrous Self-Deception of Elmer Gantry," *New Republic* 133 (31 October 1955): 13–15 (expanded into "Sinclair Lewis and the Method of Half-Truths," in *Society and Self in the Novel: English Institute Essays, 1955,* ed. Mark Schorer [New York: Columbia University Press, 1956], 117–44); afterword to *Arrowsmith,* Signet Classic ed. (New York: New American Library, 1961), 431–38; afterword to *Babbitt,* Signet Classic ed. (New York: New American Library, 1961), 320–27; afterword to *Dodsworth,* Signet Classic ed. (New York: New American Library, 1972), 355–63; afterword to *Elmer Gantry,* Signet Classic ed. (New York: New American Library, 1967), 419–30; afterword to *Main Street,* Signet Classic ed. (New York: New American Library, 1961), 433–39; introduction to *It Can't Happen Here* (New York: Dell, 1961), 5–17; introduction to *Lewis at Zenith: A Three-Novel Omnibus* (New York: Harcourt, Brace and World, 1961), vii–xii; "My Life and Nine-Year Captivity with Sinclair Lewis," *New York Times Book Review* (20 August 1961), 7, 26; "Main Street," *American Heritage* 12 (October 1961): 28–31, 74–77; "Sinclair Lewis and the Nobel Prize," *Atlantic Monthly* 208 (October 1961): 83–88; "Sinclair Lewis as a Young Publisher," *Publishers Weekly* 180 (24 July 1961): 36–39; *Sinclair Lewis: A Collection of Critical Essays,* (Englewood Cliffs, N.J.: Prentice-Hall, 1962); "The Burdens of Biography," *Michigan Quarterly Review* 1 (autumn 1962): 249–58; introduction to *I'm a Stranger Here Myself and Other Stories by Sinclair Lewis* (New York: Dell, 1962), 7–16; *Sinclair Lewis,* University of Minnesota Pamphlets on American Writers, no. 27 (Minneapolis: University of Minnesota Press, 1963); "Sinclair Lewis: *Babbitt,*" in *Landmarks of American Writing,* ed. Hennig Cohen (New York: Basic Books, 1969), 315–27; preface to Richard O'Connor, *Sinclair Lewis* (New York: McGraw-Hill, 1971); "Sinclair Lewis," in *American Writers: A Collection of Literary Biographies,* vol. 2 (New York: Charles Scribner's Sons, 1974), 439–60.

6. "The Last Flight from Main Street," in Bucco, *Critical Essays,* 145–46.

Chapter 1   *Main Street, 1905–1920*

1. Schorer, *American Life,* 18.

2. "Introduction to *Main Street,*" in *The Man from Main Street: A Sinclair Lewis Reader,* ed. Harry E. Maule and Melville Cane (New York: Random House, 1953), 214 (hereafter cited as *Man from Main Street*).

3. Quoted in Schorer, *American Life,* 101.

4. "Introduction to *Main Street,*" 214.

5. I am excluding *The Man Who Knew Coolidge* (1928), which is not a novel but a set of six monologues spoken by a fictional character, Lowell Schmaltz.

6. Lewis had done this in several of his apprentice novels. Ruth Winslow in *The Trail of the Hawk* (1915) and Una Golden in *The Job* (1917) are idealized half-portraits of Grace.

7. Grace Hegger Lewis, *With Love from Gracie: Sinclair Lewis, 1912–1925* (New York: Harcourt, Brace, 1955), 25.

8. Ibid., 89–90. See also Grace Hegger Lewis, "When Lewis Walked Down Main Street," *New York Times Magazine* (3 July 1960), 10, 28–29.

9. Grace Lewis, *With Love from Gracie*, 106. Cf. *Half a Loaf* (New York: Liveright, 1931), 124.

10. Grace Lewis, *With Love from Gracie*, 95.

11. Reprinted in James J. Napier, "Letters of Sinclair Lewis to Joseph Hergesheimer, 1915–1922," *American Literature* 38 (May 1966): 235–46.

12. SL to Hergesheimer, 9 December 1918, quoted in Napier, "Letters," 242. Napier misdates this letter as "1919"; the original is in the Lewis Collection, Austin.

13. As early as February 1916, in fact, he had told Harcourt that if his editor at Harpers, Elizabeth Jordan, were to leave the firm, then he would move to Holt in order to work with him. See SL to AH, quoted in Schorer, *American Life*, 231–32.

14. H. L. Mencken, *My Life as Author and Editor*, ed. Jonathan Yardley (New York: Knopf, 1993), p. 338.

15. Alfred Harcourt, *Some Experiences* (Riverside, Conn.: privately printed, 1951), 27.

16. Ibid., 30–31.

17. Ibid., 35–36.

18. Harcourt had been joined in the venture by two other people. Donald C. Brace was a former classmate from Columbia and head of the manufacturing department at Holt who was also uncomfortable with Henry Holt's .politics. Will D. Howe had been head of the English Department at Indiana University and coauthor of the original grammar text now known as the *Harbrace College Handbook*. Howe was placed in charge of the textbook department; he would leave after six months to accept a more lucrative position with Scribner's. The firm opened offices in an old Georgian house located at 1 West 47th Street.

19. Grace Lewis, *With Love from Gracie*, 126.

20. In *Half a Loaf*, the fictional Susan Hale cites this as the reason for her author-husband Timothy's restlessness.

21. See SL to Cabell, "Early in 1920," quoted in Schorer, *American Life*, 259.

22. Cabell, "The Way of Wizardry," in *Straws and Prayer-Books* (New York: McBride, 1924), 46–47.

23. Quoted in ibid., 51.

24. See "Sinclair Lewis and Sherwood Anderson: A Study of Two Moralists," *Century* 110 (July 1925): 362–69.

25. Grace Lewis, *With Love from Gracie*, 118.

26. Ibid., 191,118.

27. Dorothy Thompson, "The Boy and Man from Sauk Centre," *Atlantic Monthly* 206 (November 1960): 39–48; reprinted as an appendix to Vincent Sheean, *Dorothy and Red* (Boston: Houghton Mifflin, 1963), 331–52 (this passage is on 344).

28. Grace Lewis, *With Love from Gracie*, 145.

29. Cf. *Half a Loaf*: "He would bring back ten pages of the novel at a time . . . she read and made notes on the margins, and ringed words which were repetitious, uninspiring, inexact" (156).

30. Grace Lewis, *With Love from Gracie*, 145.

31. SL to AH, 15 December 1919, in Sinclair Lewis, *From Main Street to Stockholm: Letters of Sinclair Lewis, 1919–1930*, ed. Harrison Smith (New York: Harcourt, Brace, 1952), 20 (hereafter cited as *Letters*).

32. Grace Lewis, *With Love from Gracie*, 146.

33. In *Half a Loaf,* the final draft of Timothy Hale's manuscript is typed by a "public stenographer" (178).

34. The typescript is contained in six folders. Following is the collation of the extant pages; the beginnings of chapters are indicated in brackets. The largest gaps in sequence are between ff. 187 and 269 and ff. 362 and 401. Folder one: [I] 1; 3– [II: 17] 28; 40; 46– [IV: 48] 58; [V] 81. Folder two: 84–86; 97–98; 115– [VII: 127] 128; 131–32; 135–37; 186–87; 269–74; 301– [XV: 306] 307; 311; 330–31; 353–58. Folder three: 360–62; 401–3; 406–7; 416; 423; 425; 430; 435–36; 439; 445–47; 455; 457; 465; 468–69; 470–71; 483; [XXIV] 488–93. Folder four: 494–96; 498–501; 510–11; 513–16; 523–34; 539; 560–61; 565–66; [XXIX] 567; 582–85. Folder five: 588–89; 595–99; 605–7; 612–15; 622–25; 628–29; 635–36; 638; 647; 649–50; 654–56; [XXXIV] 666–68; 674–75. Folder six: [XXXVI] 684–95; 704– [XXXVIII] 707; 714; 718–19; 720–21; 723–31; [XL] 744–45; 747; 754–55.

35. Grace Lewis, *With Love from Gracie,* 191.

36. See Martin Bucco, *Main Street: The Revolt of Carol Kennicott* (New York: Twayne, 1993), esp. chap. 7.

37. Quoted in Schorer, *American Life,* 346.

38. Harcourt, *Some Experiences,* 55–56.

39. *Letters,* 34. Harcourt did mention the incident again, in a letter to Lewis of 27 February 1922, in which he said that he would not make any suggestions about *Babbitt* until he had read the whole manuscript: "If I have suggestions to make, I'll make them, as I did about the episode you left out of *Main Street*" (ibid., 101).

40. See SL to AH, 11 August 1920, *Letters,* 34–35.

41. AH to SL, *Letters,* 35–36. A similar episode took place after the publication of *Babbitt.* Lewis told Harcourt to "get a nice blurb" about the novel from the British author Hugh Walpole. Harcourt replied that he did not think it wise to "just blow in or write Hugh Walpole for something we can quote." Harcourt noted that Walpole was "apt to do so incidentally in an interview or article soon, and then we can quote him that way." See AH to SL, 29 September 1922, *Letters,* 112.

42. AH to SL, 14 August 1920, *Letters,* 36.

43. See especially SL to AH, 24 December 1919, *Letters,* 21.

44. SL to AH, 8 February 1920, *Letters,* 25.

45. Harcourt, *Some Experiences,* 56–57.

46. Ibid., p. 57.

47. See "Best Sellers in Fiction during the First Quarter of the Twentieth Century," *Publishers' Weekly* 107 (14 February 1925): 525–27; and "The Most Popular Authors of Fiction between 1900 and 1925," *Publishers' Weekly* 107 (21 February 1925): 619–22.

48. These various letters are in the Lewis Collection, Beinecke.

49. Schorer, *American Life,* 270.

50. Edward A. Martin, *H. L. Mencken and the Debunkers* (Athens: University of Georgia Press, 1984), 117.

51. Letters of Grace Sprague to SL, 30 December [1920?]; F. M. Holly, 31 December 1920; Ellis W. Potter, 17 January 1921; and Arthur T. Vance, 14 December 1920, all in the Lewis Collection, Beinecke.

52. Letter of Percy A. Beach to SL, 17 November 1920, Lewis Collection, Beinecke.

53. Hackett, "God's Country," *New Republic* 25 (1 December 1920): 20–21; Lewisohn, "The Epic of Dulness [*sic*]," *Nation* 111 (10 November 1920): 536–37.

Chapter 2   *Babbitt, 1920–1922*

1. SL to AH, 30 Nov. 1920, *Letters,* 52.

2. SL to AH, 28 Dec. 1920, *Letters,* 59.

3. SL to AH, 27 October 1920; AH to SL, 4 November 1920; and SL to AH, 11 November 1920 and 20 November 1920, *Letters*, 39, 41–42, 47. The name "Pumphrey" was retained in the published text for Professor Joseph K. Pumphrey, owner of the Riteway Business College. Other possibilities listed in the notebook were Bassett, Hornby, Witherbee, Bundy, and Bates.

Choosing a name for a character was an important part of Lewis's creative method. The novelist John Hersey, who was Lewis's secretary during the summer and fall of 1937, remarked that Lewis believed that "people *became* their names." When Lewis had to name a new character, "he would make a list of a dozen possibilities and leave the list on the piano in the living room; day after day he would pick up the list and cross off a name or two, until he had made his final choice by elimination. I would sometimes hear him at his desk calling out names, as if summoning lost souls" ("Sinclair Lewis," in *Life Sketches* [New York: Knopf, 1989], 25).

Lewis at one point compiled an alphabetical listing of all the names he had used in his novels and kept an ongoing list of possible names to use in future work. These lists are at the Beinecke (boxes 407 and 408) and include such categories as "Cornish Names," "Oriental Rugs," and "Flower Names," as well as names from "Jewish Cemetery January 1940, New Orleans," "U.S. Pensioners as Listed in 1813," and "MIT grads 1936."

4. The "Babbitt notebook," which is not paginated, is in box 155, Lewis Collection, Beinecke.

5. Lewis was reading and studying Balzac as early as 1909: a copy of *Illusions Perdues*, Calmann-Levy edition, belonging to Lewis and inscribed with his address at this time, is at the Beinecke (box 345). On the fly-leaf there are manuscript notes "for a novelette in 7 chaps." entitled "The Fathers." The plot as outlined, however, does not resemble any of Lewis's 1920s novels.

6. He was possibly thinking of more. On the verso of page 468 of the typescript there is a list of seven "fields," with a notation to think of "3 more?" ranging from "Mining & metal industries" to "Lumber & building" to various "Professions[,] Arts[,] Sciences." These are subdivided into "medicine, law, ministry, arts," and "govt." Below this is a rough, hand-drawn map of the United States divided into ten numbered categories. Above it, Lewis has written: "10 categories—1 from each section."

7. Monthly statement, Harcourt, Brace, dated 25 April 1923, box 5, series 3, folder 8, Dorothy Thompson Papers, Syracuse. See SL to AH, 5 September 1921, *Letters*, 83. Harcourt had proposed a similar arrangement for *Free Air;* see AH to SL, 20 October 1919, *Letters*, 16.

8. SL to AH, 17 December 1920, *Letters*, 57. Other possibilities were "Population, 300,000," "Good Business," "Sound Business," "A Good Practical Man," "A He-Man," "The Booster," "A Solid Citizen," and "Zenith" (SL to AH, 12 July 1921, *Letters*, 77). Stephen Tanner speculates that in choosing the name "Babbitt," Lewis may have been lampooning the academic critic Irving F. Babbitt, the titular leader of the New Humanism, which Lewis opposed; see "Sinclair Lewis and the New Humanism," *Modern Age* 33 (1990): 33–41.

9. *Man from Main Street*, 21.

10. Quoted in Schorer, *American Life*, 284. Lewis had published a short story in the *Smart Set* in 1916 entitled "I'm a Stranger Here Myself." The story contained the same types of characters and themes that appear in *Main Street:* in the tale, a middle-aged couple from the Midwest go on a tour of Florida and the East Coast and are unhappy when they encounter anything or anyone different from what they are accustomed to. They trust and make friends with only those storekeepers and fellow tourists who are themselves midwesterners.

11. "Consolation" [review of *Main Street*], *Smart Set* 64 (January 1921): 138.

12. SL to Mencken, quoted in Schorer, *American Life*, 290–91.

13. See, for example, William Manchester, *Disturber of the Peace: The Life of H. L. Mencken* (New York: Harpers, 1951), 134–36, 158; Martin, *Mencken and the Debunkers*, 121–23; and Stephen A. Young, "The Mencken-Lewis Connection," *Menckeniana: A Quarterly Review* 94 (summer 1985): 10–16.

14. Quoted in Schorer, *American Life*, 291.

15. Mencken to SL, 6 February 1922, in *Letters of H. L. Mencken*, ed. Guy Forgue (New York: Knopf, 1961), 233.

16. In reading *Main Street*, for example, Mencken thought that Carol was completely foolish and that Lewis had meant to show that her "superior culture is, after all, chiefly bogus."

17. Mencken himself misleadingly bragged about his role in Lewis's career some years later, when he remarked to his wife, Sara Haardt, that he was at least the "midwife" of *Arrowsmith*, if not its "grandpa" (letter of 11 April 1925, in *Mencken and Sara: A Life in Letters*, ed. Marion Elizabeth Rogers [New York: McGraw-Hill, 1987], 205).

18. SL to AH, 16 February 1921, *Letters*, 63.

19. Lewis's mimetic inclinations explain his later fascination with writing for the theater. He also performed in his own plays.

20. Hersey, *Life Sketches*, 17.

21. Schorer, *American Life*, 455.

22. Ibid., 458.

23. Harcourt, *Some Experiences*, 83.

24. "Afterword," in *Babbitt* (New York: New American Library, 1961), 320–21.

25. SL to AH, 15 June 1921, *Letters*, 72.

26. SL to AH, 15 June 1921 and 12 July 1921, *Letters*, 72, 77. The "Plan" is in box 32, Lewis Collection, Beinecke.

27. One assumes that Lewis wrote a complete scenario for the novel and that only the seven and a half pages discussed here have survived.

28. See AH to SL, 20 January 1922, and SL to AH, 20 January 1922, *Letters*, 94, 95. Later, on 12 February 1922, Lewis added: "Any sophisticated reader, would, even without the Introduction, know pretty much all of Babbitt's ideation before the end of Chapter II" (*Letters*, 97).

29. The last page of this fragment (p. 32), designated to be placed chronologically in "Jan. 1921" of the novel, shows another change in focus and offers additional evidence that Lewis was thinking of a series of linked novels: he intended to have Will and Carol Kennicott enter the novel. Will was to have been Babbitt's second cousin, visiting Zenith from Gopher Prairie. Lewis's notes read, "Ken's boasts re G.P. Contrast Bab and Ken," indicating that he would have used this material to examine further the evolution of the midwestern city; he intended to show ironically the two men "boosting" their hometowns—Babbitt having been conditioned to do so and Kennicott just becoming accustomed to such behavior.

30. Harcourt may have been partly responsible for changing Lewis's thinking: after reading the first fifty-seven pages of the typescript, Harcourt suggested that Lewis "keep the whole book as the story of a man, and let it show what it will about big towns, small towns, or civilization, or any other damn thing" (AH to SL, 13 February 1922, *Letters*, 99). Lewis, however, was worried that critics were expecting *Babbitt* to be another study of a particular place, as *Main Street* was. He therefore wrote Harcourt about "the need for sending out a note" to the press "about the new novel not being *Zenith* but *Babbitt*" (SL to AH, 12 February 1922, *Letters*, 97).

31. Sheldon Grebstein, *Sinclair Lewis* (New York: Twayne, 1962), 85.

32. H. L. Mencken, "Portrait of an American Citizen," *Smart Set* 69 (October 1922): 139.

33. SL to AH, 10 September 1921, *Letters*, 84.

34. SL to AH, 21 June 1921, *Letters*, 75.

35. SL to AH, 18 November 1921, *Letters*, 88–89.

36. SL to AH, 4 February 1922, *Letters*, 96. See also Mencken, *My Life*, 368–72.

37. Quoted in Schorer, 309.

38. Ibid., 310.

39. Ibid.

40. Grace Hegger Lewis to Ellen Eayres (Harcourt's secretary), 20 July 1921, *Letters*, 78; SL to Eayres, 27 July 1921, *Letters*, 80.

41. Grace Hegger Lewis to Harcourt, 20 July 1921, *Letters*, 78–79.

42. These drawings have been reprinted in Helen Batchelor, "A Sinclair Lewis Portfolio of Maps: Zenith to Winnemac," *Modern Language Quarterly* 32 (1971): 401–7. Lewis evidently carried these maps with him in his various travels while he wrote *Arrowsmith*, *Mantrap*, *Elmer Gantry*, *The Man Who Knew Coolidge*, and *Dodsworth*.

43. SL to AH, 3 August 1921, *Letters*, 81. On the title page of the typescript, which bears the heading "BABBITT / The Story of A [Solid] Standardized Citizen," Lewis wrote: "Bearsted, Kent / August 20, 1921 (planning begun / Cornwall / July 5)."

44. SL to AH, 18 October 1921, *Letters*, 85.

45. SL to AH, 26 October 1921, *Letters*, 85.

46. SL to AH, 5 November 1921, *Letters*, 87.

47. In a few of these block cuts Lewis dropped some of his most comical scenes. In the original version of this passage, Chum Frink offered as entertainment "one of his higher-grade poems," one not "run-in in the form of prose for use by the newspaper syndicate" but rather "for use by the agricultural and household magazines." The verse, which is set to music, is a parody of the sentimental ballads about mothers that were popular at the time. The song, entitled "She's Kind of a Saint to Me," resonates with saccharine sentiments about "little old mother": she is one of "The saints in the olden churches . . . As they stand among lillies or birches / With a shining sword in their hand":

> Processionals come from the chantry
> All lauding their saints' high praise—
> But my saint stands in the pantry
> Or the kitchen, all her days.   (TS 182)

48. Stuart Pratt Sherman, *The Significance of Sinclair Lewis* (New York: Harcourt, Brace, 1922), 20.

49. Frederick J. Hoffman, *The Twenties: American Writing in the Postwar Decade* (New York: Viking, 1955), 369.

50. SL to AH and Donald Brace, 20 January 1922, *Letters*, 95.

51. SL to AH, 28 December 1920, *Letters*, 59.

52. SL to Mencken, "August 1921," quoted in Schorer, *American Life*, 291.

53. SL to AH, 28 December 1920, *Letters*, 59.

54. Mencken, "Portrait of an American Citizen," 140.

55. Grace Lewis, *With Love from Gracie*, 32–33.

56. Ibid., 145.

57. SL to AH, 18 November 1921, *Letters*, 88.

58. AH to SL, 4 February 1922, *Letters*, 96.

59. See SL to Brace, 22 July 1922, *Letters*, 105.

60. See Matthew J. Bruccoli, "Some Transatlantic Texts: West to East," in *Bibliography and Textual Criticism*, ed. O. M. Brack Jr. and Warner Barnes (Chicago: University of Chicago Press, 1969), 249–50. A complete list was printed in the *Chicago Daily News* on 1 November 1922 under the title "Translating Babbitt into the English Language." Lewis attempted to have the glossary removed from later editions, but it appeared in all reprints at least up through the Nobel Prize edition issued by Jonathan Cape in 1931; see Carl Van Doren and Harvey Taylor, *Sinclair Lewis: A Biographical Sketch* (Garden City, N.Y.: Doubleday, Doran, 1933), 103.

61. See Matthew J. Bruccoli, "Textual Variants in Sinclair Lewis's *Babbitt*," *Studies in Bibliography* 11 (1958): 263–68. After the novel was published, a man named Louis N. Fiepel, who made a hobby of proofreading published books, found the errors and sent them to Lewis. He in turn told Harcourt, "You ought to hire him [Fiepel] to go over page proofs." Presumably Lewis was suggesting that this be done not just for future novels but also for subsequent printings of *Babbitt*; however, there is no evidence that any corrections were

made until the fourth printing. Fredson Bowers discusses some of these in *Textual and Literary Criticism* (Cambridge: Cambridge University Press, 1959), 18–20; 26–27. See *Letters*, 113–14.

62. Mencken, "Portrait of an American Citizen," 139.

63. May Sinclair, "The Man from Main Street," *New York Times Book Review*, 24 September 1922, 1, 11; Johnson, "Mr. Sinclair Lewis as a Polemicist," *New York Herald Tribune*, 17 September 1922, 7:1; West, "Notes on Novels: *Babbitt*," *New Statesman* 23 (21 October 1922): 78, 80. For other favorable reviews, see Burton Rascoe, "A Mirror of Mediocrity," *New York Tribune*, 17 September 1922, 5:8; L[udwig] L[ewisohn], *Nation* 115 (20 September 1922): 284–85; and Upton Sinclair, "Standardized America," *Appeal to Reason* [later called *Haldeman-Julius Weekly*], no. 1399 (23 September 1922): 1.

64. J[ohn] F[arrar], "Hail Rotarians!" *Bookman* 56 (October 1922): 216; anon., "Briefer Mention," *Dial* 73 (October 1922): 456; anon., "A Reviewer's Notebook," *Freeman* 6 (18 October 1922): 142–43; anon., *North American Review* 216 (November 1922): 716–17; H.M.T., "The World of Books," *Nation and Athenaeum* 32 (21 October 1922): 121; and R. D. Townsend, "Among the New Books," *Outlook* 132 (11 October 1922): 253.

65. Boyd, "Sinclair Lewis," in *Portraits: Real and Imaginary* (New York: Doran, 1924), 183–88.

66. Wharton to SL, 27 August 1922, in *The Letters of Edith Wharton*, ed. R.W.B. Lewis and Nancy Lewis (New York: Scribner's, 1988), 455.

67. Sherwood Anderson, "Four American Impressions: Gertrude Stein, Paul Rosenfeld, Ring Lardner, Sinclair Lewis," *New Republic* 32 (11 October 1922): 171–73; Robert Littell, "Babbitt," *New Republic* 32 (4 October 1922): 152.

68. Lewis was quite wealthy by this point: on the back of his monthly royalty statement dated 25 April 1923, he calculated his net assets and expected earnings for 1924 and predicted that by the beginning of 1925 he would have $7,000 cash on hand and $97,000 "solidly invested." Special editions of *Main Street* had brought in $3,685, the first serial rights to *Babbitt* earned him $1,000, and the movie rights to *Babbitt* were sold to Warner Brothers for $39,000 (Lewis Legal and Financial Papers, box 5, series 3, folder 8, Dorothy Thompson Papers, Syracuse).

69. See Thomas S. Hines Jr., "Echoes from 'Zenith': Reactions of American Businessmen to *Babbitt*," *Business History Review* 41 (1967): 123–40.

Chapter 3   *Arrowsmith, 1922–1925*

1. See Fritz H. Oehlschlaeger, "Hamlin Garland and the Pulitzer Prize Controversy of 1921," *American Literature* 51 (1979): 409–14.

2. "The 'Labor Novel' That Sinclair Lewis Never Wrote," *New York Herald Tribune Book Review* 28 (10 February 1952): 1, 6. See also Sheldon Grebstein, "Sinclair Lewis's Unwritten Novel," *Philological Quarterly* 37 (1958): 400–409.

3. Schorer suggested that the name "Doane" was similar to that of Charles T. Dorion, the attorney who Lewis befriended in Sauk Centre in 1905. Schorer thought that Lewis had Dorion in mind when he created the character of Doane.

4. SL to AH, 12 February 1922, *Letters*, 98.

5. SL to Grace Hegger Lewis, 26 August 1922, in Grace Lewis, *With Love from Gracie*, 210–11.

6. SL to Grace Hegger Lewis, 29 August 1922, in ibid., 212–13.

7. There is no full-scale biography of Loeb, but the accounts in the *Dictionary of Scientific Biography*, 3:445–47, and the memorial sketch by W.J.V. Osterhout in *Journal of General Physiology* 8 (1928): ix–lix, are useful. An interesting recent discussion of Loeb's similarity to Gottlieb and of his general importance to the American intelligentsia in the 1920s is provided by Mary G. Land, "Three Max Gottliebs: Lewis's, Dreiser's, and Walker Percy's View of the Mechanist-Vitalist Controversy," *Studies in the Novel* 15 (1983): 314–31.

8. Paul De Kruif, *The Sweeping Wind* (New York: Harcourt, Brace, 1962), 35.

9. Ibid., 51.

10. For example, see Grebstein, *Sinclair Lewis*, 86: "De Kruif was to help Lewis by providing and authenticating the novel's scientific detail"; or D. J. Dooley, *The Art of Sinclair Lewis* (Lincoln: University of Nebraska Press, 1967), 99: "[Lewis] found the ideal scientific informant in de Kruif."

11. One wonders whether Harcourt approved of the idea of Lewis writing a nonsatiric novel. In a letter dated 13 September 1922, Harcourt did not respond to Lewis's initial report on the plan for *Arrowsmith* but instead told Lewis that there was "no really good serious novel of Washington national and international life for the forty years since [Henry Adams's] *Democracy* was published." He urged Lewis to cast his eye "that way for a theme" for a possible novel (*Letters*, 109). Harcourt may have thought that in undertaking *Arrowsmith*, Lewis was straying from his talents for writing satire.

12. De Kruif, *Sweeping Wind*, 85.

13. Mencken, *My Life as Editor and Author*, 329–30.

14. Grace Lewis, *With Love from Gracie*, 85.

15. Grace found Joyce Lanyon to be "quite improbable." In her memoir, she commented: "The 'society' scenes [in *Arrowsmith*] are exact in the tedium of the talk . . . but [Lewis] is obviously impatient with this background and can only scoff" (*With Love from Gracie*, 257–58).

16. Harcourt was worried that Lewis had become unfocused since the completion of *Babbitt*. In the fall, before the plans for *Arrowsmith* were solidified, Harcourt had had to gently dissuade him from rewriting one of his apprentice novels, *The Job*. Harcourt convinced him that the amount of time required to rewrite it would have been about the same as that needed to write a new novel (see *Letters*, 114–15).

17. *Arrowsmith* notes (unpaginated), box 155, Lewis Collection, Beinecke. The *Arrowsmith* plan was probably destroyed. In various notes to De Kruif in the typescript pages, Lewis refers to "what notes" or "what pages I have kept"—so presumably after he had written a section of the typescript, he discarded the corresponding pages of the plan.

18. Lewis used the term "god seeker" many times in his writings. A later version of the labor novel was to have been called "The Man Who Sought God." The title of a late novel is *The God-Seeker*; it is one of his worst.

19. The first two comments are found in *Letters*, 121 and 122; the following three are quoted in Schorer, *American Life*, 365, 372, and 367.

20. Grebstein, *Sinclair Lewis*, 91.

21. De Kruif stipulated that the letter be sealed for thirty years. It reads: "None of the prototypes correspond in any physical way to the fictive characters. Nor do their careers correspond to Lewis's creations. It is rather the *spirit* of these various people that Lewis tried to portray, at the same time building round that spirit flesh and blood people who have no resemblance whatever to their originals." The model for Arrowsmith De Kruif lists as one "R. G. Hussey, Now Professor of Pathology at Yale." What information I have been able to find on Hussey's career, however, does not suggest any parallels with that of the fictional Arrowsmith. The rest of the letter follows (De Kruif to Malloch, 16 April 1931, quoted in Schorer, *American Life*, 418–19):

Doc Vickerson	created by Lewis	no prototype
Max Gottlieb	F. G. Novy / Jacques Loeb	
Fatty Pfaff	Theodore Adams	medical student at U. of Michigan circa 1916; now obstetrician
John A. Robertshaw	Warren P. Lombard	
Angus Duer	Henry J. Vanden Berg	now prominent surgeon at Grand Rapids, Michigan
T.J.H. Silva	T. G. Huizinga	formerly practitioner at Zeeland, Michigan
Roscoe Geake	R. Bishop Canfield	
A. DeWitt Tubbs	Simon Flexner	
Sondelius	by Lewis	no prototype
Almus Pickerbaugh	Wm. de Kleine	Medical Director of Red Cross
Rippleton Holabird	Peyton Rous / Rufus Cole	
Terry Wickett	T. J. LeBlanc / J. H. Northrop	

22. De Kruif, *Sweeping Wind*, 97.

23. Ibid., 98; cf. *Arrowsmith*, 342–43, 345. See also De Kruif's introduction to the first installment of *Arrowsmith* in the *Designer*, "An Intimate Glimpse of a Great American Novel in the Making," *Designer and the Woman's Magazine* 60 (June 1924): 64.

24. SL to AH, 1 March 1923, *Letters*, 126–27.

25. Quoted in Schorer, *American Life*, 372–73. Mencken evidently understood Lewis to mean that De Kruif *was* more than a research assistant. In an 11 April 1925 letter to his future wife, Sara Haardt, he said that "large parts" of *Arrowsmith* "were done by De Kruif—some of the best parts" (*Mencken and Sara: A Life in Letters*, ed. Marion Elizabeth Rogers [New York: McGraw-Hill, 1987], 205).

26. Schorer, "Afterword," in *Arrowsmith* (New York: New American Library, 1961), 433. "The Death of Arrowsmith" appeared in *Coronet* magazine in July 1941 and is reprinted in *Man from Main Street*, 103–7.

27. De Kruif, *Sweeping Wind*, 94.

28. Ibid., 99.

29. AH to SL, 11 March 1925, *Letters*, 179. The remark about ending the novel with Leora's death De Kruif attributes to Harcourt (*Sweeping Wind*, 109).

30. Lewis, "Self-Portrait (Berlin, August 1927)," in *Man from Main Street*, 46. Lewis's second wife, Dorothy Thompson, had a favorable initial impression of Leora when she read the novel during their courtship in 1927. In a diary entry dated 9 September 1927, she wrote, "Leora . . . represents the sexual ideal of the truly dynamic and creative male. . . . her life fulfills the longing of the real woman. One is willing to be swallowed up by a man" (quoted in Sheean, *Dorothy and Red*, 33).

31. The notebook indicates that Lewis initially intended to develop the Nautilus chapters much more than he did. Under "NAMES IN NAUTILUS," Lewis had worked out a series of social classes like those in the notebook for *Babbitt* ("smart set," "aldermen," etc.).

32. "Are Commercialism and Science Ruining Medicine?" *Century Illustrated Monthly* 104 (1922): 416 (hereafter cited parenthetically).

33. This is probably T. G. Huizinga, a general practitioner in Zeeland, Michigan, De Kruif's hometown, who is mentioned frequently in *The Sweeping Wind*.

34. "What is Preventive Medicine Preventing?" *Century Illustrated Monthly* 104 (1922): 594 (hereafter cited parenthetically).

35. SL to AH, 13 February 1923, *Letters*, 125.

36. Quoted in Schorer, *American Life*, 366.

37. De Kruif, *Sweeping Wind*, 108; De Kruif quoted in Grace Lewis, *With Love from Gracie*, 284.

38. De Kruif's first book was *Microbe Hunters*, which Harcourt brought out in 1926. It was published early in the year and was a steady seller. By September the book had reached the number-nine spot on the *Publishers' Weekly* list of monthly best-sellers. In November it dropped to the number-ten position and then did not appear on the list again. Lewis recommended publication of the book to Harcourt, and he was so enthusiastic about it that he even offered to back the financial obligation of the advance that he thought Harcourt should give De Kruif (see *Letters*, 135).

39. Martin, *Mencken and the Debunkers*, 120.

40. "Breaking into Print," in *Man from Main Street*, 74.

41. In *Half a Loaf*, the physician who delivers Susan's baby tells her that her husband should have been a research scientist: "Got the scientific mind, he has, and asks darn intelligent questions for a layman" (130).

42. Like Elmer Gantry in chap. 7 of that novel, Lewis taught Sunday school at a nearby town during his time at Oberlin, traveling to church by pumping a railroad handcar in bitter winter weather.

43. AH to SL, 23 April 1923, *Letters*, 131.

44. Besides "Arrowsmith" and "Martin Arrowsmith" (the latter was its British title), other possibilities were "Courage," "White Tile" (suggested by Grace), "Horizon," "Civilized," "The Merry Death," "The Savage," "Strange Islands," "Test Tube," and "The Destroyer."

45. See SL to AH, 25 April 1923, *Letters*, 131.

46. Entry for 4 January 1924, *The Journal of Arnold Bennett* (New York: Viking Press, 1933), 3:34.

47. SL to AH, 28 September 1923, *Letters*, 141.

48. AH to SL, 18 July 1923, *Letters*, 136.

49. SL to AH, 6 November 1923, *Letters*, 144.

50. See Lyon F. Richardson, "*Arrowsmith*: Genesis, Development, Versions," *American Literature* 27 (1955): 225–44. The title is misleading: Richardson does not discuss the sources, planning, or first draft of the novel.

51. See *Letters*, 164.

52. Harcourt, *Some Experiences*, 79–81.

53. De Kruif, *Sweeping Wind*, 108. For some years, the Signet paperback has been the only edition of *Arrowsmith* in print. It does not carry the acknowledgment note. Because there is no complete descriptive bibliography of Lewis, it is not possible to tell when it was dropped from earlier editions.

54. Ibid., 110; De Kruif, quoted in Grace Lewis, *With Love from Gracie*, 284.

55. For representative reviews, see Stuart Pratt Sherman, "A Way Out: Sinclair Lewis Discovers a Hero," *New York Herald Tribune Books*, 8 Mar. 1925, 1–2; Robert Morss Lovett, "An Interpreter of American Life," *Dial* 78 (June 1925): 515–18; Grant Overton, "The Salvation of Sinclair Lewis," *Bookman* 61 (April 1925): 179–85. The *Atlantic Bookshelf* comment is on page 1 of the April 1925 issue.

56. See *Letters*, 177.

57. De Kruif, *Sweeping Wind*, 65, 79.

58. Ibid., 76. Clarence Budington Kelland was a popular novelist whose works, such as *Conflict* (1920) and *Rhoda Fair* (1925), dealt with current fads and manners.

59. AH to SL, 1 October 1923, *Letters*, 142; see also 12 December 1923, 148.

60. Lewis to Grace Hegger Lewis, 29 August 1922, Grace Lewis, *With Love from Gracie*, 212–13.

Chapter 4   *Mantrap, Elmer Gantry,* and
the Pulitzer Prize, 1925–1927

1. See SL to AH and Donald Brace, 11 December 1924, and SL to AH, 26 March 1925, *Letters,* 167, 180.

2. SL to AH, 3 December 1923, *Letters,* 147.

3. See Donald Greene and George Knox, eds., *Treaty Trip: An Abridgment of Dr. Claude Lewis's Journal of an Expedition Made by Himself and His Brother, Sinclair Lewis, to Northern Saskatchewan and Manitoba in 1924* (Minneapolis: University of Minnesota Press, 1959); and Greene, "With Sinclair Lewis in Darkest Saskatchewan," *Saskatchewan History* 6 (1953): 47–52.

In box 127 of the Lewis Collection at the Beinecke there are eight pages of holograph notes and two pages of typed notes for *Mantrap:* "Miscellaneous Observations" (2 pp.); "Characters—Ralph <Nickerson> Prescott" (1 p.; TS); hand-drawn maps of Saskatchewan (5 pp.); and notes about the title (2 pp.). Alternate titles were "Mantrap River," "Lake Midnight," "Ghost Squaw River," "Horizon," "Young Squaw," and "Ghost Rapids."

4. SL to AH, 10 November 1925, *Letters,* 188.

5. A representative British view is in *Spectator* 137 (17 July 1926): 105. The "defense" of *Mantrap* was by Ernest Sutherland Bates, "Lewis as Romantic," *Saturday Review of Literature* 2 (26 June 1926): 887. There have been two recent critical essays written in the same vein. In "Ambivalences and Anxieties: Character Reversals in Sinclair Lewis's *Mantrap,*" *Studies in American Fiction* 16 (1988): 229–36, Sanford E. Marovitz contends that *Mantrap* is as much a satire as Lewis's other novels; it attacks "the hypocrisy and folly of society by focusing on a handful of characters within it." Robert E. Fleming suggests that *Mantrap* may be a parody of "the formulaic characters, melodramatic situations, simplistic values, and false assumptions inherent in the western romances" of Lewis's time, in particular those of Zane Grey ("Sinclair Lewis vs. Zane Grey: *Mantrap* as Satirical Western," *MidAmerica* 9 [1982]: 124–38).

6. *Mantrap* sold comparatively well. Advance orders were between twenty-five thousand and thirty thousand (*Letters,* 218); according to Harcourt, it had a "steady sale but [was] no walk-away" (*Letters,* 220). By 5 November 1930, 84,952 copies had been sold in all editions (Carl Van Doren and Harvey Taylor, *Sinclair Lewis: A Biographical Sketch* [Garden City, N.Y.: Doubleday, Doran, 1933], 110). Upon publication of *Mantrap,* the movie rights were sold for fifty thousand dollars. The film, which came out in 1926, starred Ernest Torrence and Clara Bow.

7. *Elmer Gantry* notes (unpaginated), box 155, Lewis Collection, Beinecke. See SL's comments about the idea in his letter to AH, 27 December 1923, *Letters,* 150.

8. Grebstein, *Sinclair Lewis,* 99.

9. SL to AH, 27 December 1923, *Letters,* 150.

10. SL to Donald Brace, 23 January 1926, *Letters,* 193.

11. SL to Grace, 27 January 1926, in Speer Morgan and William Holtz, "Fragments from a Marriage: Letters of Sinclair Lewis to Grace Hegger Lewis," *Missouri Review* 11 (1988): 71–98.

12. SL to AH, 24 February 1926, *Letters,* 197.

13. Stephen Tanner speculates that the name "Elmer" may have been a swipe at Paul Elmer More, the coleader (with Irving F. Babbitt) of the New Humanism; see Tanner, "New Humanism," 35. A page in Lewis's notebook entitled "Names for Gantry" lists some other choices: Tunket, Smeesby, Trospor, and Tillish.

14. SL to AH, 29 March 1926, *Letters,* 201.

15. SL to Smith, 4 April 1926, *Letters,* 202.

16. I have been unable to locate any published biographical information on Birkhead except for a brief entry in *Who's Who in America.* For much of the information in this paragraph I am indebted to James Gill, archivist at All Souls' Unitarian Church, Kansas City.

17. SL to AH, 4 April 1926, *Letters*, 204.

18. SL to Smith, 4 April 1926, *Letters*, 202.

19. SL to AH, 2 May 1926, *Letters*, 211.

20. L. M. Birkhead, *Is Elmer Gantry True?* (Girard, Kan: Haldeman-Julius, 1928), 13–16.

21. For example, see *New York Times*, 18 May 1926, 1.

22. Samuel Harkness, "Sinclair Lewis's Sunday School Class," *Christian Century* 43 (29 July 1926): 938–39.

23. SL to Grace, 27 January 1926, in Morgan and Holtz, "Fragments from a Marriage," 80.

24. SL to AH, 21 April 1926, *Letters*, 207.

25. See Grace Lewis, *With Love from Gracie*, 301.

26. "Lewis Dares Deity to Strike Him Dead," *New York Times*, 20 April 1926, 2.

27. *Letters*, 204.

28. Schorer, *American Life*, 653.

29. SL to AH, 26 April 1926, *Letters*, 209.

30. See AH to SL, 29 April 1926, *Letters*, 210–11.

31. See AH to SL, 5 May 1926, *Letters*, 214–15.

32. See Grover C. Loud, *Evangelized America* (New York: Dial, 1928), 316–17. Sunday's denial of the charge was carried in the *New York Times* on 30 January 1915.

33. See the entry on Sunday in *DAB* supp. 1, 679. There is no authoritative biography of Sunday.

34. "Stick to Fighting Sin, Dr. Straton Advises," *New York Times*, 21 September 1925, 22. See also James Benedict Moore, "The Sources of 'Elmer Gantry,'" *New Republic* 143 (8 August 1960): 17–18.

35. "Calvary Quarrel Is Again in Court," *New York Times*, 6 September 1925, 14; "Dr. Straton Quits Supreme Kingdom, but Defends It," *New York Times*, 20 January 1927, 1. Lewis also drew on Straton in creating Dr. Howard Bancock Binch, a minor character who appears in chapter 14. Binch, "the great Baptist defender of the literal interpretation of the Bible, president of the True Gospel Training School for Religious Workers, editor of *The Keeper of the Vineyard*, and author of 'Fool Errors of So-Called Science,'" meets Elmer and Sharon Falconer in Joliet, Illinois, on his way to receive "his sixth D.D. degree (from Abner College)" (206).

36. For these details on Norris's career I have relied on the sketch of him in *DAB*, supp. 5, 516–17.

37. Ibid., 516.

38. Ridgway, *"In God We Trust"* (Boston: W. A. Wilde, 1935), 60–61, 65.

39. D. Bruce Lockerbie, "Sinclair Lewis and William Ridgway," *American Literature* 36 (1964): 68–72.

40. For the information in this paragraph I have relied on William G. McLoughlin's essay in *Notable American Women*, first series, 477–80, and "Aimee Semple McPherson: 'Your Sister in the King's Glad Service,'" *Journal of Popular Culture* (winter 1967): 193–217. A full-dress biography of McPherson has recently been published: Daniel Mark Epstein, *Sister Aimee* (New York: Harcourt, Brace, Jovanovich, 1993).

41. On the draft typescript Lewis canceled a longer version of the disclaimer, "No character in this book is [a] the portrait of any actual person." Originally, Lewis had written:

> [For example,] the woman evangelist here depicted was not suggested by a [certain renowned] woman evangelist familiar to all newspaper readers and other good Christians, but was [definitely] planned several years before the actual lady rose to [such] fame. Here, as in all other portions of this manual, it is [cheerfully] reverently asserted that the ways of God and his representatives are at least mysterious. SL

In many other places in the typescript Lewis removed references to the foregoing models for Elmer: for instance, J. Frank Norris (TS 252; cf. first edition, 168) and William Jennings Bryan (TS 254; cf. first edition, 169).

42. Quoted in Schorer, *American Life*, 461.

43. Alfred Kazin, *On Native Grounds* (New York: Harcourt, Brace, 1942; reprint, New York: Doubleday, 1956), 174, 176, 178.

44. SL to Grace, 27 January 1926, in Morgan and Holtz, "Fragments from a Marriage," 83. The *New York Times* reported that upon leaving Kansas City, Lewis told his "Sunday school class," "You're a fine bunch. You get up and preach things that neither you nor your congregations believe. Why don't you be honest in your pulpits?" (18 May 1926, 1).

45. Schorer, *American Life*, 481.

46. Quoted in ibid., 362.

47. Review of *Arrowsmith*, *American Mercury* 4 (April 1925): 507–9.

48. H. L. Mencken, *Prejudices: Fifth Series* (New York: Knopf, 1926), 221, 228.

49. Charles Angoff, Mencken's assistant on the latter periodical, wrote that Mencken was so keen on finding things to ridicule about Protestantism that he subscribed to and regularly read church publications, looking for items to run in the "Americana" section of his magazine.

50. Lewis had been promising Mencken that he would write some sort of "pious essay" for the *American Mercury* since November 1923, but he never did. The two men also had planned jointly to cover the 1925 political conventions for the *Chicago Tribune*, but Lewis had begged off at the last minute, saying that he had too much work to do on *Arrowsmith* (see Schorer, *American Life*, 387).

Mencken printed several satirical articles on Protestantism; one of the better ones was written by James M. Cain. Entitled "The Pastor," it appeared in the May 1925 issue of the *American Mercury*.

51. Quoted in Schorer, *American Life*, 459.

52. AH to SL, 14 April 1926, *Letters*, 207.

53. SL to AH, 12 June 1926, and AH to SL, 15 June 1926, *Letters*, 220.

54. Quoted in Schorer, *American Life*, 741.

55. SL to Grace, [September 1925], in Morgan and Holtz, "Fragments from a Marriage," 76.

56. SL to Grace, [September or October 1925], quoted in Grace Lewis, *With Love from Gracie*, 327.

57. Grace Lewis, *With Love from Gracie*, 242.

58. Schorer, *American Life*, 322.

59. In a letter Lewis wrote to Grace in the fall of 1925, he describes her in the precise terms in which he would describe Fran Dodsworth (SL to Grace, in Morgan and Holtz, "Fragments from a Marriage," 75):

> You more than any one I have ever known resent the coming of middle-age; and you have never found quite what you wanted in life—and with me you never could or would. Naturally, that Something you Want is indefinite, but in part it's the thing you represented to yourself as a kid when you used to dream of yourself as the wife of an ambassador—people glittering yet intelligent . . . surrounded by the smoke and aroma of Great Affairs. And the successes of an author prove to be rather dreary matters of sweat and carbon paper.

60. In her memoir, Grace made an interesting remark about sexuality in *Elmer Gantry*. She said that "in the first draft of this book, considerably subdued later, the bigness of the theme, the vast research, the devastating satire, were blanketed by a lechery which caused one to read with nasty curiosity rather than with literary appreciation" (*With Love from Gracie*, 325). It is likely that she recognized Lewis's anger at her in his negative portrayal of women in the book. (Cf. Susan Hale's comments in *Half a Loaf* on the "sexually restless" men in her husband's novel [345].) Grace's remark suggests that she read the draft of *Elmer Gantry*, presumably in Washington, D.C., in the autumn of 1926, but there are no markings of hers on that document; neither is there any evidence to suggest that Lewis subdued any sexually suggestive passages.

61. In the notebook, Lewis originally called Sharon "Shaman," but he later substituted

"Sharon." Perhaps he thought that the symbolism inherent in this name was heavy-handed: it literally means "witch doctor" and suggests "sham" or fraud.

62. AH to SL, 27 December 1926, *Letters*, 229.

63. Grace to AH, 4 January 1927, *Letters*, 231.

64. AH to Grace, 5 January 1927, *Letters*, 231.

65. AH to SL, 11 March 1927, *Letters*, 235.

66. The sensational Judd Gray–Ruth Snyder murder case dominated the newspapers in 1927. Gray was a corset salesman who conspired with Snyder to murder her husband. The lovers then turned on each other after their arrest. The incident was the basis for James M. Cain's novel *The Postman Always Rings Twice* (1934).

67. Quoted in Schorer, *American Life*, 474.

68. AH to SL, 31 March 1927, *Letters*, 237.

69. For the comments by Sunday and Straton, see "The Storm over Elmer Gantry," *Literary Digest* 93 (16 April 1927): 28–29.

70. *New York Times*, 4 April 1927, 26.

71. *New York Times*, 11 April 1927, 24.

72. Edward Shillito, "'Elmer Gantry' and the Church in America," *The Nineteenth Century and After* 101 (May 1927): 740.

73. These various letters are in the Lewis Collection, Beinecke.

74. Woodward, "'Elmer Gantry' Is Truth as a Study of Hypocrisy," New York *Evening Post Literary Review* 7 (12 March 1927): 1, 10; Van Doren, "St. George and the Parson," *Saturday Review of Literature* 3 (12 March 1927): 639; Krutch, "Mr. Babbitt's Spiritual Guide," *Nation* 124 (16 March 1927): 291–92; Whipple, "'Red' Lewis in a Red Rage," *Survey* 58 (1 May 1927): 168, 170; West, "Sinclair Lewis Introduces Elmer Gantry," *New York Herald Tribune Books*, 13 March 1927, 1; Littell, "The Preacher Fried in Oil," *New Republic* 50 (16 March 1927): 108–9; Mencken, "Man of God: American Style," *American Mercury* 10 (April 1927): 506–8.

Chapter 5   *The Man Who Knew Coolidge* and *Dodsworth*, 1927–1929

1. SL to AH, 24 February 1927 and 23 March 1927, *Letters*, 234, 236.

2. SL to AH, 25 October 1927, *Letters*, 255.

3. SL to AH, 24 February 1927, *Letters*, 234.

4. *Letters*, 241.

5. This account of the labor novel is taken from Ramon Guthrie, "The 'Labor Novel' That Sinclair Lewis Never Wrote," *New York Herald Tribune Book Review* 28 (10 February 1952): 1. *The Imitation of Christ* (ca. 1427) is a devotional work by the German monk Thomas à Kempis (1379 or 80–1471). It encourages a distrust of the human intellect and a liberation from worldly inclinations.

6. Quoted in Schorer, *American Life*, 487.

7. See Sally E. Parry, "The Changing Fictional Faces of Sinclair Lewis's Wives," *Studies in American Fiction* 17 (1989): 65–79.

8. SL to AH, 30 September 1927, *Letters*, 251.

9. Mencken had heard Lewis give a performance of this monologue at a party, and he urged him to turn it into a story. Mencken recalled that he gave the story its title (*My Life as Author and Editor*, 330–31).

10. Box 127, Lewis Collection, Beinecke.

11. *Letters*, 255.

12. AH to SL, 29 November 1927, *Letters*, 259.

13. *Letters*, 259.

14. Ibid., 260.

15. AH to SL, 12 December 1927, *Letters*, 260–61.

16. AH to SL, 14 December 1927, *Letters*, 261.

17. SL to AH, 23 December 1927, *Letters*, 263. According to Van Doran and Taylor's bibliography, of the first printing of thirty thousand only twenty thousand were sold at regular price; the rest were remaindered (*Biographical Sketch*, 113). In "Revision in Sinclair Lewis's *The Man Who Knew Coolidge*," *American Literature* 25 (1953): 326–33, Lyon N. Richardson shows that for the book text of the title sketch Lewis made substantial additions to and alterations in the phraseology or idiom of the *Mercury* version.

18. Canby, "Schmaltz, Babbitt & Co.," *Saturday Review of Literature* 4 (24 March 1928): 697–98; for comments by Broun and F.P.A., see Schorer, *American Life*, 500.

19. One wonders whether Lewis thought that Mencken had given him bad advice: Lewis inscribed Mencken's copy of the book with the words, "To H. L. Mencken, who is entirely to blame for my having written this book."

20. According to Ramon Guthrie, who read the novel in typescript, Lewis initially intended that at the end of the book, Sam would return to America with Fran and remain married to her. See Guthrie, "The Birth of a Myth, or How We Wrote 'Dodsworth,'" *Dartmouth College Library Bulletin*, n.s., 3 (April–October 1960): 50–54.

21. Bridget Puzon, "From Quest to Cure: The Transformation of *Dodsworth*," *Modern Fiction Studies* 31 (1985): 574.

22. Glen A. Love, *Babbitt: An American Life* (New York: Twayne, 1993), 82.

23. Guthrie, "Birth of a Myth," 52.

24. *Letters*, 264–65.

25. SL to AH, 13 July 1928, *Letters*, 267.

26. Guthrie, "Birth of a Myth," 53–54.

27. Evidently there was little correspondence between Lewis and Harcourt, Brace, during this time, and thus there is no detailed record of his progress on the manuscript. According to another note on the typescript, he had revised through page 508 (chapter 33) by 25 September.

28. James Lundquist, *Sinclair Lewis* (New York: Frederick Ungar, 1973), 25.

29. "Diary," boxes 315, 316; and "Minnesota Diary," box 520, Lewis Collection, Beinecke.

30. Grace was so similar to the character of Fran that when Sidney Howard dramatized the novel in 1934, Lewis would call Fay Bainter, the actress who played the role of Fran, "Grace." Once, during a rehearsal, he reportedly called out to Bainter, "Come on, Gracie, you can be much bitchier than that!" (Schorer, *American Life*, 596).

31. Diary entry of 3 May 1928, quoted in Sheean, *Dorothy and Red*, 94.

32. Brennecke, "A Man Between Worlds," *Commonweal* 9 (17 April 1929): 691–92; Henry Seidel Canby, "Sex War," *Saturday Review of Literature* 5 (30 March 1929): 821–22; "Constant Reader" [Dorothy Parker], "Reading and Writing: And Again, Mr. Sinclair Lewis," *New Yorker* 5 (16 March 1929): 106–7; "Sinclair Lewis Parts Company with Mr. Babbitt," *New York Times Book Review*, 17 March 1929, 2.

33. T. S. Matthews, "Spleen," *New Republic* 58 (10 April 1929): 232.

34. "Our Photography: Sinclair Lewis," *New York Herald Tribune Books*, 28 April 1929, 1, 6; reprinted as "A Camera Man," *Life and Letters* 2 (May 1929): 336–43.

35. See Ford Madox Ford, *Bookman* 69 (April 1929): 191–92; L. P. Hartley, *Saturday Review* (London) 147 (6 April 1929): 482; Raymond Mortimer, *Nation and Athenaeum* 44 (30 March 1929): 915; and Rachel Annand Taylor, *Spectator* 142 (23 March 1929): 485–86.

36. Mencken, "Escape and Return," *American Mercury* 16 (April 1929): 506–8.

Chapter 6   The Labor Novel and the Nobel Prize, 1929–1930

1. Sheean, *Dorothy and Red*, 171–72.
2. See AH to SL, 10 July 1929, and SL to AH, 16 July 1929, *Letters*, 275, 277.
3. AH to SL, 29 May 1929, *Letters*, 273.
4. SL to AH, 16 July 1929 and 6 August 1930; AH to SL, 29 May 1929, *Letters*, 276, 291, 278.
5. Quoted in Schorer, *American Life*, 657.
6. SL to Upton Sinclair, 14 March 1930, Sinclair Papers, Lilly Library, Indiana University.
7. Quoted in Schorer, *American Life*, 532.
8. Quoted in Guthrie, "'The Labor Novel' That Lewis Never Wrote," 1; see also Benjamin Stolberg, "Sinclair Lewis," *American Mercury* 53 (1941): 455–56.
9. SL to AH, 26 October 1929, *Letters*, 283.
10. Quoted in Schorer, *American Life*, 528.
11. 15 October 1929, *Letters*, 281.
12. Ramon Guthrie Papers, Baker Memorial Library, Dartmouth College.
13. See Betty Stevens, "A Village Radical Goes Home," *Venture* 2 (summer 1956): 17–26.
14. Lewis Adamic, "'Red' Lewis," in *My America* (New York: Harper and Brothers, 1938), 103.
15. Sheldon Grebstein, "Sinclair Lewis's Unwritten Novel," *Philological Quarterly* 37 (1958): 409.
16. Quoted in Schorer, *American Life*, 548.
17. One notable exception to this is John Updike, who has acknowledged his indebtedness to Lewis in the *Rabbit* novels—once saying in an interview that he had "worked up" *Babbitt* before beginning *Rabbit, Run*. The third novel in the series, *Rabbit Is Rich*, has as its epigraph an excerpt from Babbitt's speech to the Zenith Real Estate Board about "Our Ideal Citizen." For an excellent analysis of the ways in which the emergent middle class was treated in fiction, see Christopher P. Wilson, *White Collar Fictions: Class and Social Representation in American Literature, 1885–1925* (Athens: University of Georgia Press, 1992).
18. Quoted in Schorer, *American Life*, 285.
19. SL to Grace, 29 August 1922, in Grace Lewis, *With Love from Gracie*, 215.
20. "The Earlier Lewis," *Saturday Review of Literature* 10 (20 January 1934): 422.
21. "Mr. Lorimer and Me," *Nation*, 25 July 1928, 18.
22. Quoted in Grace Lewis, *With Love from Gracie*, 215.
23. Quoted in Schorer, *American Life*, 548.
24. Quoted in ibid., 741.
25. "Sinclair Lewis," *Saturday Review of Literature* 9 (28 January 1933): 398.
26. "Sinclair Lewis: An American Phenomenon," *New Review* (Paris) 1 (January–February 1931): 52.
27. "Lament for a Novelist," *New Republic* 120 (16 May 1949): 16.
28. "Responsible," unpublished typescript, box 426, Lewis Collection, Beinecke.
29. In his statement, Lewis addressed the question of why he was accepting the Nobel Prize when earlier he had refused the Pulitzer Prize for *Arrowsmith*. Lewis noted that unlike the Pulitzer, the Nobel Prize was awarded "on the basis of excellence of work" with "no strings tied"; the Pulitzer Prize was given to a particular book because it presented "the wholesome atmosphere of American life." Additionally, Lewis pointed out that the Nobel Prize was given on the basis of a writer's entire body of work, not just one book; thus, he again justified his decision to reject the earlier award, which one year could go to a book chosen from "four or five first-rate novels" and the next "four or five third-rate novels." See *Letters*, 296–97.

30. See Sheldon Grebstein, "Sinclair Lewis and the Nobel Prize," *Western Humanities Review* 13 (1959): 163–71; and David D. Anderson, "Sinclair Lewis and the Nobel Prize," *MidAmerica* 8 (1981): 9–21.

31. See *Letters,* 61, 180.

32. Grebstein, "Lewis and the Nobel," 164. See also "The Nobel Prize for Literature," *Publishers' Weekly* 118 (8 November 1930): 2197. These figures are taken from an unpublished M.A. thesis by D. W. Woolery, "A Bibliography of the Translations of Sinclair Lewis's Novels with Foreign Book Reviews and Critical Articles" (University of Minnesota, 1949), a copy of which is in box 459, Lewis Collection, Beinecke.

33. See Carl L. Anderson, *The Swedish Acceptance of American Literature* (University Park: Pennsylvania State University Press, 1957), chaps. 3 and 5.

34. Lewis's corrected version of the first impression is in the Hersholt Collection, Rare Book and Special Collections Division, Library of Congress.

35. *Letters,* 299.

36. See Helen B. Petrullo, "Dorothy Thompson's Role in Sinclair Lewis's Break with Harcourt, Brace," *Courier* 8 (April 1971): 50–58.

37. Harcourt, *Some Experiences,* 84.

38. 3 February 1931, *Letters,* 302. The contract for "Neighbor," dated 24 January 1929, is in the Dorothy Thompson Papers at Syracuse (series 3, box 5, folder 8). Harcourt returned it to Lewis on 3 February 1931: on the outside leaf is written, "cancelled by mutual / consent February 3, 1931. / Harcourt, Brace, & Co., Inc. / A Harcourt / Pres."

39. Harcourt, *Some Experiences,* 83.

40. Ibid., 35–36.

41. Grace Lewis, *With Love from Gracie,* 187.

42. "The Boy and Man from Sauk Centre," in Sheean, *Dorothy and Red,* 352.

Selected Bibliography

Important articles, book-length studies, and other sources cited in the endnotes are listed below, as are some other significant works on Lewis that the reader may consult for further study. Reviews of Lewis's works are not cited here, but they are listed in the standard secondary bibliography of Lewis by Robert E. Fleming, *Sinclair Lewis: A Reference Guide* (Boston: G. K. Hall, 1980). Fleming has updated his guide twice: "A Sinclair Lewis Checklist: 1976–1985," in *Sinclair Lewis at 100: Papers Presented at a Centennial Conference,* ed. Michael E. Connaughton (St. Cloud, Minn.: St. Cloud State University, 1985), 267–70; and "Recent Research on Sinclair Lewis," *Modern Fiction Studies* 31 (autumn 1985): 609–16.

There is no complete primary bibliography of Lewis. A partial descriptive inventory of his publications through 1930 is available in Carl Van Doren and Harvey Taylor, *Sinclair Lewis: A Biographical Sketch* (Garden City, N.Y.: Doubleday, Doran, 1933). A complete but unannotated listing entitled "A Sinclair Lewis Checklist" is included in Mark Schorer, *Sinclair Lewis: An American Life* (New York: McGraw-Hill, 1961), 815–26.

There are six collections of reprinted criticism on Lewis: Harold Bloom, ed., *Sinclair Lewis's Arrowsmith: Modern Critical Interpretations* (New York: Chelsea House, 1988); Harold Bloom, ed., *Sinclair Lewis: Modern Critical Interpretations* (New York: Chelsea House, 1987); Martin Bucco, ed., *Critical Essays on Sinclair Lewis* (Boston: G. K. Hall, 1986); Martin Light, ed., *The Merrill Studies in Babbitt* (Columbus, Ohio: Charles E. Merrill, 1971); Robert J. Griffin, ed., *Twentieth-Century Interpretations of Arrowsmith* (Englewood Cliffs, N.J.: Prentice-Hall, 1968); and Mark Schorer, ed., *Sinclair Lewis: A Collection of Critical Essays* (Englewood Cliffs, N.J.: Prentice-Hall, 1962). Many of the articles cited herein are reprinted in one or more of these collections.

Two other collections of reviews and criticism have been published, although they are not widely available: Michael E. Connaughton, ed., *Sinclair Lewis at 100: Papers Presented at a Centennial Conference* (not copyrighted; St. Cloud, Minn.: St. Cloud State University, 1985); and *The New York Times Book Review Critiques of Sinclair Lewis's Works* (1969), a limited edition folio of twenty-four of its reviews and articles, a copy of which is in the Lewis Collection at the Beinecke.

Adamic, Louis. "'Red' Lewis." In *My America*. New York: Harper and Brothers, 1938.

Anderson, Carl L. *The Swedish Acceptance of American Literature*. University Park: Pennsylvania State University Press, 1957.

Anderson, David D. "Sinclair Lewis and the Nobel Prize." *MidAmerica* 8 (1981): 9–21.

Anderson, Hilton. "A Whartonian Woman in *Dodsworth*." *Sinclair Lewis Newsletter* 1 (1969): 5–6.

Anderson, Sherwood. "Four American Impressions: Gertrude Stein, Paul Rosenfeld, Ring Lardner, Sinclair Lewis." *New Republic* 32 (11 October 1922): 171–73. Reprinted in Schorer, *Critical Essays*.

Batchelor, Helen. "A Sinclair Lewis Portfolio of Maps: Zenith to Winnemac." *Modern Language Quarterly* 32 (1971): 401–8.

Belgion, Montgomery. "How Sinclair Lewis Works," *Bookman* 65 (January 1924): 195–96.

Benet, William Rose. "The Earlier Lewis." *Saturday Review* (20 January 1934): 421–22.

Birkhead, L. M. *Is "Elmer Gantry" True?* Girard, Kans.: Haldeman-Julius, 1928.

Bruccoli, Matthew J. "Some Transatlantic Texts: West to East." In *Bibliography and Textual Criticism*. Ed. O. M. Brack Jr. and Warner Barnes. Chicago: University of Chicago Press, 1969.

———. "Textual Variants in Sinclair Lewis's *Babbitt*." *Studies in Bibliography* 11 (1958): 263–68.

Bucco, Martin. *Main Street: The Revolt of Carol Kennicott*. New York: Twayne, 1993.

———. "The Serialized Novels of Sinclair Lewis." *Western American Literature* 4 (1969): 29–37. Reprinted in Bloom, *Modern Critical Interpretations,* and Bucco, *Critical Essays*.

Cabell, James Branch. "The Way of Wizardry." In *Straws and Prayer-Books*. New York: Robert M. McBride, 1924.

Coard, Robert L. "Edith Wharton's Influence on Sinclair Lewis." *Modern Fiction Studies* 31 (1985): 511–27.

———. "Names in the Fiction of Sinclair Lewis." *Georgia Review* 16 (1962): 318–29.

Conroy, Stephen S. "Sinclair Lewis's Sociological Imagination." *American Literature* 42 (1970): 348–62. Reprinted in Bloom, *Modern Critical Interpretations*.

Davis, Jack L. "Mark Schorer's *Sinclair Lewis*." *Sinclair Lewis Newsletter* 3 (1971): 3–9.

De Kruif, Paul. "An Intimate Glimpse of a Great American Novel in the Making." *Designer and the Woman's Magazine* 60 (June 1924): 64.

———. *The Sweeping Wind*. New York: Harcourt, Brace and World, 1962.

Dooley, D. J. *The Art of Sinclair Lewis*. Lincoln: University of Nebraska Press, 1967.

Dupree, Ellen Phillips. "Wharton, Lewis, and the Nobel Prize Address." *American Literature* 56 (1984): 262–70.

Eby, Clare Virginia. "*Babbitt* as Veblenian Critique of Manliness." *American Studies* 34 (1993): 5–23.

Fleming, Robert E. "Sinclair Lewis vs. Zane Grey: *Mantrap* as Satirical Western." *MidAmerica* 9 (1982): 124–38.

Foster, Ruel E. "Lewis's Irony—A Paralysis of the Heart." *West Virginia University Philological Papers* 33 (1987): 31–39.

Grebstein, Sheldon. *Sinclair Lewis*. New York: Twayne, 1962.

————. "Sinclair Lewis and the Nobel Prize." *Western Humanities Review* 13 (1959): 163–71.

————. "Sinclair Lewis's Unwritten Novel." *Philological Quarterly* 37 (1958): 400–409. Reprinted in Bucco, *Critical Essays.*

Greene, Donald. "With Sinclair Lewis in Darkest Saskatchewan." *Saskatchewan History* 6 (1953): 47–52.

Greene, Donald, and George Knox, eds. *Treaty Trip: An Abridgment of Dr. Claude Lewis's Journal of an Expedition Made by Himself and His Brother, Sinclair Lewis, to North Saskatchewan and Manitoba in 1924.* Minneapolis: University of Minnesota Press, 1959.

Guthrie, Ramon. "The Birth of a Myth, or How We Wrote 'Dodsworth.'" *Dartmouth College Library Bulletin,* n.s., 3 (April–October 1960): 50–54.

————. "The 'Labor Novel' That Sinclair Lewis Never Wrote." *New York Herald Tribune Book Review* 28 (10 February 1952): 1, 6.

————. "Sinclair Lewis and the 'Labor Novel.'" *Proceedings of the American Academy of Arts and Letters and the National Institute of Arts and Letters* (1952): 68–82.

Harcourt, Alfred. *Some Experiences.* Riverside, Conn.: privately printed, 1951.

Harkness, Samuel. "Sinclair Lewis's Sunday School Class." *Christian Century* 43 (29 July 1926): 938–39.

Haworth, Jane L. "Revisions of *Main Street;* or, From 'Blood, Sweat, and Tears' to the Loss of a 'Literary Curiosity.'" *Sinclair Lewis Newsletter* 5–6 (1973–74): 8–12.

Hersey, John. "First Job." *Yale Review* 76 (winter 1987): 184–97. Reprinted in *Life Sketches.* New York: Knopf, 1989.

Hilfer, Anthony C. *The Revolt from the Village.* Chapel Hill: University of North Carolina Press, 1969. Reprinted in Light, *Merrill Studies in Babbitt.*

Hines, Thomas S., Jr. "Echoes from 'Zenith': Reactions of American Businessmen to *Babbitt.*" *Business History Review* 41 (1967): 123–40.

Hoffman, Frederick J. *The Twenties: American Writing in the Postwar Decade.* New York: Viking, 1955. Reprinted in Light, *Merrill Studies in Babbitt.*

Hutchisson, James M. "Edith Wharton and Grace Lewis." *Sinclair Lewis Newsletter,* n.s., 3 (fall 1994): 5.

Kazin, Alfred. "The New Realism: Sherwood Anderson and Sinclair Lewis." In *On Native Grounds.* New York: Harcourt, Brace, 1942. Reprint, New York: Doubleday, 1956. Reprinted in Schorer, *Critical Essays.*

————. "Sinclair Lewis Revisited." *Gazette of the Grolier Club,* n.s., no. 37 (1985): 6–20.

Koblas, John J., and Dave Page, eds. *Selected Letters of Sinclair Lewis.* Madison, Wis.: Main Street Press, 1985.

————. *Sinclair Lewis: Final Voyage.* Madison, Wis.: Main Street Press, 1985.

————. *Sinclair Lewis and Mantrap: The Saskatchewan Trip.* Madison, Wis.: Main Street Press, 1985.

Land, Mary G. "Three Max Gottliebs: Lewis's, Dreiser's, and Walker Percy's View of the Mechanist-Vitalist Controversy." *Studies in the Novel* 15 (1983): 314–31. Reprinted in Bloom, *Sinclair Lewis's Arrowsmith.*

Lewis, Grace Hegger. *Half a Loaf.* New York: Liveright, 1931.

————. "When Lewis Walked Down Main Street." *New York Times Magazine,* 3 July 1960, 3, 28–29.

————. *With Love from Gracie: Sinclair Lewis, 1912–1925.* New York: Harcourt, Brace, 1955.

Lewis, Sinclair. *From Main Street to Stockholm: Letters of Sinclair Lewis, 1919–1930.* Ed. Harrison Smith. New York: Harcourt, Brace, 1952.

———. *The Man from Main Street: A Sinclair Lewis Reader.* Ed. Harry E. Maule and Melville Cane. New York: Random House, 1953.

Light, Martin. *The Quixotic Vision of Sinclair Lewis.* West Lafayette, Ind.: Purdue University Press, 1975.

Lockerbie, D. Bruce. "Sinclair Lewis and William Ridgway." *American Literature* 36 (1964): 68–72.

Love, Glen A. *Babbitt: An American Life.* NY: Twayne, 1993.

———. "New Pioneering on the Prairies: Nature, Progress, and the Individual in the Novels of Sinclair Lewis." *American Quarterly* 25 (1973): 558–77.

Lunden, Rolf. "Theodore Dreiser and the Nobel Prize." *American Literature* 50 (1978): 216–29.

Lundquist, James. *Sinclair Lewis.* New York: Frederick Ungar, 1973.

Marovitz, Sanford E. "Ambivalences and Anxieties: Character Reversals in Sinclair Lewis's *Mantrap.*" *Studies in American Fiction* 16 (1988): 229–36.

Martin, Edward A. "Sinclair Lewis: The Mimic as Artist." In *H. L. Mencken and the Debunkers.* Athens: University of Georgia Press, 1984.

Mencken, H. L. *Letters of H. L. Mencken.* Ed. Guy Forgue. New York: Knopf, 1961.

———. *Mencken and Sara: A Life in Letters.* Ed. Marion Elizabeth Rogers. New York: McGraw-Hill, 1987.

———. *My Life as Author and Editor.* Ed. Jonathan Yardley. New York: Knopf, 1993.

Moore, James Benedict. "The Sources of 'Elmer Gantry.'" *New Republic* 143 (8 Aug. 1960): 17–18.

Morgan, Speer, and William Holtz. "Fragments from a Marriage: Letters of Sinclair Lewis to Grace Hegger Lewis." *Missouri Review* 11 (1988): 71–98.

Napier, James J. "Letters of Sinclair Lewis to Joseph Hergesheimer, 1915–1922." *American Literature* 38 (1966): 236–46.

Oehlschlaeger, Fritz H. "Hamlin Garland and the Pulitzer Prize Controversy of 1921." *American Literature* 51 (1979): 409–14.

———. "Sinclair Lewis, Stuart Pratt Sherman, and the Writing of *Arrowsmith.*" *Resources for American Literary Study* 9 (1979): 24–30.

Orwoll, Mark. "A Battle in Bohemia: The Sinclair Lewis–Harold Stearns Feud." *Lost Generation Journal* 9 (fall/winter 1989): 2–5.

Parrington, Vernon L. *Sinclair Lewis: Our Own Diogenes.* University of Washington Chapbooks, no. 5. Seattle: University of Washington Bookstores, 1927. Reprinted in Schorer, *Critical Essays.*

Parry, Sally E. "The Changing Fictional Faces of Sinclair Lewis's Wives." *Studies in American Fiction* 17 (1989): 65–79.

Petrullo, Helen B. "Dorothy Thompson's Role in Sinclair Lewis's Break with Harcourt, Brace." *Courier* 8 (April 1971): 50–58.

Puzon, Bridget. "From Quest to Cure: The Transformation of *Dodsworth.*" *Modern Fiction Studies* 31 (1985): 573–80.

Reitinger, D. W. "A Source for Tanis Judique in Sinclair Lewis's *Babbitt.*" *Notes on Contemporary Literature* 23 (November 1993): 3–4.

Richardson, Lyon F. "*Arrowsmith:* Genesis, Development, Versions." *American Literature* 27 (1955): 225–44. Reprinted in Bloom, *Modern Critical Interpretations*; Bloom, *Sinclair Lewis's Arrowsmith*; and Griffin, *Twentieth-Century Interpretations.*

———. "Revision in Sinclair Lewis's *The Man Who Knew Coolidge.*" *American Literature* 25 (1953): 326–33.

Rosenberg, Charles E. "Martin Arrowsmith: The Scientist as Hero." *American Quarterly* 15 (1963): 447–58. Reprinted in Bloom, *Modern Critical Interpretations*; Bloom, *Sinclair Lewis's Arrowsmith*; and Griffin, *Twentieth-Century Interpretations.*

Schorer, Mark. *Sinclair Lewis: An American Life.* New York: McGraw-Hill, 1961.

———. "Sinclair Lewis and the Method of Half-Truths." In *Sinclair Lewis: A Collection of Critical Essays.* Englewood Cliffs, N.J.: Prentice-Hall, 1966. Reprinted in Bloom, *Modern Critical Interpretations.*

Sheean, Vincent. *Dorothy and Red.* Boston: Houghton Mifflin, 1963.

Sherman, Stuart Pratt. *The Significance of Sinclair Lewis.* New York: Harcourt, Brace, 1922.

Shillito, Edward. "'Elmer Gantry' and the Church in America." *Nineteenth Century and After* 101 (1927): 739–48.

Sinclair Lewis Newsletter. St. Cloud, Minn.: St. Cloud State College, 1969–1975; n.s., Normal, Ill.: Illinois State University, 1992– .

Stevens, Betty. "A Village Radical Goes Home." *Venture* 2 (summer 1956): 17–26.

Stolberg, Benjamin. "Sinclair Lewis." *American Mercury* 53 (1941): 450–60.

"The Storm over Elmer Gantry." *Literary Digest* 93 (16 April 1927): 28–29.

Tanner, Stephen L. "Sinclair Lewis and Fascism." *Studies in the Novel* 22 (1990): 57–66.

———. "Sinclair Lewis and the New Humanism." *Modern Age* 33 (1990): 33–41.

Thompson, Dorothy. "The Boy and Man from Sauk Centre." *Atlantic* 206 (November 1960): 39–48. Reprinted in Sheean, *Dorothy and Red.*

Town, Caren J. "A Dream More Romantic: *Babbitt* and Narrative Discontinuity." *West Virginia University Philological Papers* 33 (1987): 41–49.

Updike, John. "Exile on Main Street." *New Yorker,* 17 May 1993, 91–97.

Van Doren, Carl. Introduction to *Main Street.* Cleveland: World Publishing, 1946, 7–9.

———. "Revolt from the Village: 1920." *Nation* 113 (12 Oct. 1921): 407–12. Reprinted in Griffin, *Twentieth-Century Interpretations*; Light, *Merrill Studies in Babbitt*; and Schorer, *Critical Essays.*

Vidal, Gore. "The Romance of Sinclair Lewis." *New York Review of Books* 39 (8 October 1992): 14, 16–20.

Wagenaar, Dick. "The Knight and the Pioneer: Europe and America in the Fiction of Sinclair Lewis." *American Literature* 50 (1978): 230–49.

Wharton, Edith. *The Letters of Edith Wharton.* Ed. R.W.B. Lewis and Nancy Lewis. New York: Scribner's, 1988.

Wilson, Christopher P. "Sinclair Lewis and the Passing of Capitalism." *American Studies* 24 (1983): 95–108.

Young, Stephen A. "The Mencken-Lewis Connection." *Menckeniana: A Quarterly Review* 94 (summer 1985): 10–16.

Index